THE
WARRIOR
DIPLOMATS

Guardians of the National Security
and Modernization of Turkey

Metin Tamkoç

UNIVERSITY OF UTAH PRESS, SALT LAKE CITY

To My Teachers

CONTENTS

ILLUSTRATIONS

FOREWORD

There is relatively little scholarly literature available on modern Turkey, particularly in the English language. There is virtually nothing on the "interplay between domestic and external variables that influence the formulation of foreign and domestic policies" — the area Dr. Tamkoç has chosen to emphasize.

Consequently, Dr. Tamkoç had a fairly unique problem in at least two dimensions. First, he could not simply take for granted a widespread knowledge among his readers of the principal Turkish leaders, even of the presidents of Turkey. Second, he could not utilize abundant, easily accessible archives for the later period of his study because those materials are either only partially available or partially informative. He deals, after all, with what, from first to last, has been an authoritarian society. For this reason, even the abundant secondary materials Americans take for granted in filling out the details of an analysis of United States policy are by-and-large scarce or nonexistent.

The very complicated interplay between the domestic and external environments, in which contexts the Turkish leaders made their decisions, is very ably described and documented in this study. In form, Dr. Tamkoç after describing the elite group of Young Turks who, overthrowing the sultan, then quarreled and competed for power, turns to the primacy otherwise of foreign over domestic problems. He explains the process by which Turkey was modernized — as time permitted. The heart of his study, however, is a detailed analysis of the warrior diplomats and their approaches to Turkish foreign relations. In Part Three, he proceeds chronologically and systematically from Atatürk, through İnönü, Bayar, Gürsel, Sunay and Korutürk. As he examines the background of these presidents, and then adds biographical material on the prime ministers and the foreign ministers, the reader becomes aware of the heavily military background of the Turkish elite throughout (only one president was not a general or admiral), and the extreme compactness of that elite: Besides the six presidents there were another fifteen prime ministers and sixteen ministers of foreign affairs.

What emerges from Dr. Tamkoç's careful study is a picture of modern Turkey under the tutelage of a small group of determined men who embarked upon radical changes for the most conservative of reasons: To keep Turkey alive as a nation amidst foreign dangers and functioning as a people amidst the aftermath of war and prolonged misrule.

It is this sense of priorities which accounts for the nature of the "Turkish Revolution." In its fundamental meaning, as the author brings out, the "revolutionary" phase was only relevant for the early period, the War of Independence. That is to say, radical changes continued beyond that period but they did not redistribute property or involve eliminating an elite class, other than the family of the sultan and a handful of ardent supporters of the traditional political institutions. Changes introduced modern methods, but these changes came from the top. Turkey remained throughout an authoritarian, traditionalist, and elitist society, with political power always emanating from the head of state. The fact that the head of state also had Turkey's foreign policy directly under his hand made coordination possible.

Dr. Tamkoç's study brings out the tendency since the 1960s for the foreign and domestic politics of Turkey to reflect more and more the corporate needs, established traditions, and the attitudes of the military and civilian institutions which have grown up over the decades. Where these initially were created to carry out presidential wishes they have acquired some significance in their own right.

One of the most refreshing aspects of the approach in this study is that it is divorced from the heavily legal and abstract flavor of much of what is written about Turkish institutions. Throughout the book, Dr. Tamkoç attempts to look dispassionately and without preconceptions at what he sees.

The meticulous scholarship of the author has succeeded in filling a great gap in the literature concerning the foreign policy elite of Turkey. It is a pleasure for me to introduce it with these words to its readers.

Frederick H. Hartmann
Alfred Thayer Mahan Professor of
Maritime Strategy
Naval War College
Newport, Rhode Island

PREFACE

This book describes and analyzes the ways in which the twin objectives of national security and modernization of Turkey have been realized by the presidents of the Republic and their principal advisers who are identified as "warrior diplomats." It is not a lengthy treatment of the formulation and implementation of Turkey's foreign and domestic policies. Instead, it focuses attention on the foreign policy elite of Turkey and their handling of those major and highly significant problems of foreign policy which have had direct bearing on the issues of national security and modernization.

Unfortunately, the scholarship in the foreign relations of Turkey has been limited to works which, in the main, give only cursory accounts of the actual roles of personalities directly involved in the formulation and execution of foreign policy decisions. The few available studies do not deal with the interplay between the domestic and external variables that influence the formulation of foreign and domestic policies. The paucity of scholarly works in this field may be due to its complexity and to the difficulty in bringing the necessary data to light.

In order to present an accurate description and analysis of the fundamental objectives of Turkey, I had to probe beneath the surface appearance to uncover the highly significant roles played by the foreign policy elite. It was indeed difficult to proceed along the narrow, and often secret, alleys of an authoritarian society, to penetrate the security of the governmental agencies in Turkey. I was able to gather a considerable amount of primary source material for the period from 1918 to 1930 in the United States National Archives and in the Public Records Office of the British Foreign Office. But it was astonishing to discover that very few memoirs of Turkish statesmen and politicians contain substantive information concerning how important foreign policy decisions were made or how the Turkish diplomats conducted negotiations with their foreign counterparts. I was left, therefore, with no other choice than to rely on secondary sources, including the daily newspapers that served as the organs of the parties and governments in power. Admittedly, a number of my observations and generalizations in this study are based on my intuitions and impressionistic evidence. I therefore wish to take full responsibility for any errors of judgment or misinterpretations that might have arisen from my treatment of the available material.

If not otherwise specified, the translations of works and documents are mine. Turkish sources are translated freely so that they reflect events, views, and thoughts accurately. Throughout the text and footnotes, Turkish names, titles, and titles of books and articles have been spelled as they originally appear in Turkish, with the exception of *Paşa* which is given as *Pasha*.

This study could not have been undertaken without a NATO Research Fellowship from 1967 to 1969. I wish to acknowledge with many thanks the assistance and support rendered by Mr. John Vernon, cultural relations director of NATO. I am also grateful to the Committee on International Exchange of Persons of the Conference Board of Associated Research Council, Washington, D.C., for its special research grant during the summer of 1966. I am indebted to Professors Lynwood M. Holland and Jack W. Hopkins, chairmen of the Department of Political Science, for reducing my academic load so that I might complete the manuscript.

My deepest obligation of gratitude is to the late Dr. Tevfik Rüştü Aras, who helped me to crystalize my thinking on many aspects of the foreign relations of Turkey and who provided me with immense inspiration and courage to go ahead with the difficult task. I would like to express my deep appreciation to Ü Halûk Bayülken, the former Minister of Foreign Affairs, for his close interest in my work, for his complimentary remarks on the original manuscript, and for his personal support of the publication of this study.

The late Hamid Aral unselfishly shared with me his hard-earned data on the biographies of the foreign service officers of Turkey. I recall my working with him with special fondness. I wish to acknowledge with many thanks the help rendered by my old friends Ambassadors Ö. Faruk Şahinbaş and H. Kaya Pırnar in obtaining documents and publications on Turkey's foreign relations. These two distinguished diplomats unselfishly shared with me their deep insight into the foreign policy and the conduct of foreign relations of Turkey. My former students Erhan Yiğitbaşoğlu and others now serving as foreign service officers also deserve special thanks for their invaluable assistance.

Among many of my friends to whom I owe debts of gratitude, Professor Tarık G. Somer, the president of the Middle East Technical University, and Lt. Col. (Ret.) Mehmet Kabasakaloğlu deserve special recognition. I am thankful to them for their never failing encouragement and assistance.

I gratefully acknowledge my indebtedness to Mrs. Norma B. Mikkelsen, the director of the University of Utah Press, and to Suzanne Shetler, Rodger Reynolds, and the other members of the editorial staff for their suggestions on substance, organization, and style of my manuscript and for their meticulous care and attention in editing this work.

The arduous task of typing the final manuscript has been cheerfully undertaken by Connie Schreiber, the secretary of the Department of Political Science. I am sincerely grateful to her.

I could not conclude my acknowledgments without mentioning my wife's efforts on behalf of this work. For the countless readings of the manuscript and the comments, criticisms, and encouragement she has rendered, words are inadequate.

Metin Tamkoç
Texas Tech University

PROLOGUE

The Ottoman principality consisted of a band of Turkish professional warriors who conducted frequent military expeditions against neighboring peoples, states, and empires. The Ottoman polity, as described aptly by a historian, was a ghazi state.[1] Led by ghazi rulers — veterans of wars — the Ottomans ultimately seized the whole of Anatolia, the Balkans, and much of the Middle East and North Africa. During the rise of the Ottoman ghazi state, its rulers made a successful transition of the polity from a frontier society into an empire with a unique arrangement of military, political, economic, administrative, and legal institutions. The Ottoman rulers, who assumed the title of sultan, and later sultan-caliph, gained extraordinary experience and skill in diplomatic affairs.

As Ottoman drive for conquest began to wane and until it finally ceased in 1918, the skillful diplomacy of the Ottoman warrior statesmen helped to prolong the life of the empire in the face of continuous onslaught by the European powers. At the time of the final collapse of the empire, there appeared a group of young Turkish warriors of superior military record who, endowed with the ghazi spirit of their ancestors, were determined to save their nation from the danger of extinction. To this end they called upon their compatriots to take up arms against the invasion forces of the Allied

---

[1] For a brief review of the nature of ghazi society and the movements of the Turkish ghazi states in Anatolia see Sydney N. Fisher, *The Middle East: A History* (New York: Alfred A. Knopf, 1960), pp. 168–70.

Powers. For they were convinced that in order to ensure Turkey's right to independence and equal treatment it was absolutely essential to rely on military force. These warriors where equally convinced, however, that no territory ought to be claimed by the Turks beyond that which military force could reasonably hold.

In addition to their military campaigns in the Turkish War of Independence, this small band of warriors conducted diplomatic and political campaigns on all existing fronts. Their diplomatic feats were no less successful than their military victories; each reinforced the other. The defeat of the Ottoman Empire in the First World War was ultimately turned into a solid victory which guaranteed the right of the Turks to sovereign independent existence. The Republic of Turkey was fathered by a handful of ghazis and was born in the revolutionary War of Independence.[2]

The next and equally difficult task of these ghazis was to assure the progressive development and modernization of Turkish society and to guarantee national security. They viewed the modernization of society as a matter of paramount importance for the maintenance of national security as well as a good end in itself. Thus, the two were set as inseparable goals of the Republican regime.

However, throughout the period of the War of Independence and during the first few years of the Republican era there were wide differences of opinion within the ranks of the leading warriors, sometimes over fundamental principles concerning the politico-socio-economic organization of the polity, and at other times over the adoption and exception of domestic and foreign policies. These differences, which stemmed essentially from the personal traits, the political beliefs, and the aspirations for political power of these young nationalists, inevitably led to a great power struggle for the ultimate leadership of the Nationalist Movement and the Republican regime. In this struggle Mustafa Kemal Pasha, who had led Turkish nationalist armies to victory, emerged as an unchallengeable leader.[3] In

---

[2] "Ghazi," or *gazi* in Turkish, is an honorary title given to those who have participated in wars. It is used in Turkey even today. The veterans of the War of Independence and the Korean War are commonly referred to as "ghazis."

[3] *Pasha* was a title placed after the name borne by civilian and military officials of high rank. In the military establishment it was equivalent to the rank of general. In November 1934 a law was passed abolishing all titles and hereditary positions. But even today a general in the armed forces is commonly referred to as *pasha*.

order to raise Turkey to the level of contemporary Western civilization and to protect and promote national security, Mustafa Kemal
Pasha instituted an authoritarian political system similar to that of
the Ottoman Empire.

Authoritarianism, a necessary manifestation of the ghazi spirit,
is woven into the fabric of traditional Turkish society. And in this
authoritarian society, the personal characteristics and aspirations of
the Ottoman heads of state made the difference between the development and decay, rise and fall of the empire. In the authoritarian,
traditionalist, and elitist Turkish society, political power has always
been concentrated in the center and has emanated from the person
of the head of state. Although the Ottoman Empire was a thing of
the past, its traditional culture in general and political beliefs in
particular — as imbedded in the minds of both the elite and the
masses — could not be abolished during the Republican era. The
leaders of the regime themselves were products of the traditional
culture and, as such, subscribed to the old political beliefs. They
simply could not disown their cultural heritage.

Mustafa Kemal Pasha and his successors, who were graduates
of the school of the bitter experiences of the War of Independence,
and who came to reside in the presidential palace in Ankara after
their victories in the preceding clashes of wills, determined foreign
and domestic policies in accordance with their own perceptions and
their own definitions of the situation at hand. They proceeded to
draw the traditional society step by step toward modernity — by
authoritarian methods. But once the political system had been
liberalized during the latter part of the 1940s, the political scene
became a battlefield of personalities, principally of the War of
Independence vintage. The decades which followed were marked
by further power struggles within and between opposing elite groups
and their leadership, due to the convergence of the authoritarian and
democratic practices in politics and the absence of a charismatic
and decisive leader — a Mustafa Kemal — who could restore stability and assure the further development of the Turkish polity.

The leaders of Turkey believed that the realization of the
twin goals of national security and modernization was contingent
upon the existence of order and tranquility in the country and the
existence of peace in the external world. Mustafa Kemal had proclaimed, and his successors repeatedly declared, "We want peace
at home and peace in the world." Nevertheless, they felt that they

had to act as warriors in both arenas because they were firmly convinced that "he who desires peace should be prepared for war." Indeed, Mustafa Kemal and his successors at the head of state may have sheathed their swords, but they never completely beat them into plowshares. They saw themselves as guardians of the national good, whether by naked force or by skillful persuasion — whichever method was more effective. Their behavior in both domestic and international affairs reveals that they were committed to Karl von Clausewitz's proposition that "war" and "politics" are nothing but "clashes of wills" carried on by a mixture of violent and nonviolent means.

It might therefore be said that their successes in the War of Independence, in guarding national security and in achieving steady progress in the modernization of Turkey have won the heads of state and their principal advisers the title "warrior diplomats."

I

The Warriors and Their Power Struggle

"The horse is his that rides it, and the sword is his that carries it."

TURKISH PROVERB

Chapter One
INTRODUCTION

The Turkish Nationalist Movement in Anatolia was conceived and organized in 1919, and the ensuing National Struggle *(Milli Müca-dele)* or the Turkish War of Independence of 1919 to 1923 was brought to its successful conclusion by a handful of warriors of exceptional military record. The principal warrior nationalists were Gazi Mustafa Kemal (Atatürk) Pasha,[1] former naval Captain Hüseyin Rauf (Orbay), former Lieutenant Colonel Ali Fethi (Okyar), Ali Fuat (Cebesoy) Pasha, Kazım Karabekir Pasha, Colonel Refet (Bele), Fevzi (Çakmak) Pasha, and Colonel İsmet (İnönü).[2]

Fevzi Pasha and Colonel İsmet had joined the ranks of the nationalists in Ankara in 1920. They were followed by Ali Fethi who, upon his release from confinement on the island of Malta by the British authorities, rejoined his friends in Ankara in 1921. As the Nationalist Movement gained further momentum and as

---

[1] In 1919 Mustafa Kemal was a general ("Pasha" or in Turkish *Paşa*). The title Gazi was bestowed on him by the Grand National Assembly of Turkey on September 19, 1921, upon his victory at the battle of Sakarya. At the same time he was promoted to the rank of marshal. Until 1934 he preferred to use the name Gazi Mustafa Kemal. On November 26, 1934, the Grand National Assembly bestowed on him the family name *Atatürk* (Father of the Turks). The family names of the other nationalist leaders, adopted since 1934, are given in parenthesis. Hereinafter they will be referred to by their first names, followed by "Bey" (meaning Mister or esquire) or by the military title Pasha.

[2] For biographical sketches of these leaders and of all the foreign policy elite, see the Appendix.

the National Struggle began to achieve unqualified military and diplomatic successes, other members of the Ottoman military and civilian elite associated themselves with the eight principal nationalist leaders and their cohorts in Ankara, which was made the seat of the new government of the Grand National Assembly of Turkey.[3]

Indeed, without the total commitment of the Anatolian Turks — men, women, and children — to the national cause, without their personal sacrifices and their heroic fighting spirit, the National Struggle would probably have had disastrous consequences for the leaders of the Nationalist Movement.

It must be noted that as the Nationalist Movement was launched by Mustafa Kemal Pasha and his close friends and associates, it was almost destroyed from within by internal strife. Interpersonal power struggle among the eight warriors for reaching the pinnacle of political power did not come to an end in 1923 but was carried over into the Republican era. Following the death of Atatürk, political power struggles surfaced once again in the 1940s; they ultimately culminated in the first coup d'état of the Republican

---

[3] In addition to the eight nationalist leaders mentioned above, the prominent personalities of the War of Independence period who had assumed ministerial posts in the Ankara government included the following: Celalettin Arif Bey, Bekir Sami (Kunduk) Bey, Hamdullah Suphi (Tanrıöver) Bey, Mustafa Fehmi Efendi, Hakkı Behiç Bey, Nazım Bey, Ata Bey, Yusuf Kemal (Tengirşenk) Bey, Hafiz Mehmet Bey, İsmail Fazıl Pasha, Ömer Lutfi Bey, Dr. A. Adnan (Adıvar) Bey, Mahmut Celal (Bayar) Bey, Ferit Bey, Kazım (Özalp) Pasha, Rıza Nur Bey, Refik Şevket Bey, Hasan (Saka) Bey, Hasan Fehmi Bey, Vehbi Bey, Dr. Refik (Saydam) Bey, Sırrı Bey, Abdullah Azmi Efendi, Mehmet Vehbi Bey, İsmail Safa Bey, Rifat Bey, Mahmut Esat (Bozkurt) Bey, Reşat Bey, Fuat Bey, Musa Kazım Efendi, Seyit Bey, Fevzi Bey, Necati Bey. For the composition of the Council of Ministers of this period see Kazım Öztürk, *Türkiye Cumhuriyeti Hükümetleri ve Programları* (Istanbul: Baha Matbaası, 1968), pp. 1–55.

Among the other old friends and/or close associates of Gazi Mustafa Kemal Atatürk during 1919–1938, the following may be mentioned: Nuri Conker, Salih Bozok, Saffet Arıkan, Dr. Tevfik Rüştü Aras, Seyfi Fuat Düzgoren, Falih Rıfkı Atay, Cevat Abbas Gürer, Şükrü Kaya, Kılıç Ali, Ruşen Eşref Ünaydın, Yunus Nadi Abalıoğlu, Recep Peker, Hikmet Bayur, Hilmi Uran, Dr. Reşit Galip, Ali Çetin Kaya, Ali Rana Tarhan, Şükrü Saracoğlu, Şakir Kesebir, Fuat Agralı, M. Abdülhalik Renda, Muhlis Erkmen. See Walter F. Weiker, "Associates of Kemal Atatürk, 1932–1938," *Belleten* 34 (1970): 633–52.

A woman of excellent education and sophisticated outlook, Halide Edib (Adıvar), the wife of Dr. A. Adnan (Adıvar), also took an active part in the National Struggle and achieved fame as the leading female nationalist.

regime in 1960. The following years were marked by further power struggles within and between political and military elite groups.

The political power struggle within the ranks of the elite deserves close scrutiny. It is the most significant and enduring feature of the history of the Republican regime.

Chapter Two

THE CLASHES OF WILLS AMONG
THE EIGHT NATIONALIST LEADERS
AND THE RISE OF MUSTAFA KEMAL

The eight principal nationalist leaders who spearheaded the Nationalist Movement in 1919 were young but experienced military officers. All were educated in the War College and later graduated from the Staff Academy in Istanbul. In 1919 their average age was a little over thirty-eight. Four of them, Mustafa Kemal, Ali Fuat, Kazım Karabekir, and Fevzi, had attained the rank of general; Hüseyin Rauf had retired from the navy as captain; Refet and İsmet were commissioned as colonel; and Ali Fethi had retired from the army as lieutenant colonel. In addition, Hüseyin Rauf, Ali Fethi, and Fevzi had assumed important ministerial posts in the Ottoman government prior to their involvement in the Nationalist Movement.

Of these eight leaders, five were born of highly cultured and sophisticated families in the cosmopolitan atmosphere of the capital of the empire. Mustafa Kemal, Ali Fethi, and İsmet were born in small towns. Among the last three, only Mustafa Kemal's family was poor. Only he experienced the agonies and frustrations of being a son in an impoverished family lacking a father's presence. However, Mustafa Kemal was determined to surpass all his comrades of upper-class families in status and prestige. His brilliant mind, his resilience and energy, and above all his indomitable will to succeed in his aspiration for power predestined him to a great future.

He was an ardent advocate of drastic changes in the society in general and in the superstructure of the polity in particular. In contrast, those of his friends and classmates with higher social status and more comfortable childhoods were imbued with the traditional social, religious, and political ideas of their conservative environment. They represented the conservatism which Mustafa Kemal was determined to do away with. Hüseyin Rauf Bey, Ali Fuat Pasha, Kazım Karabekir Pasha, and Colonel Refet differed fundamentally with Mustafa Kemal in mentality and spirit, if not in outlook.

All were young patriotic officers willing to sacrifice themselves in the cause of saving the motherland from foreign occupation and domination. Initially, however, they disagreed among themselves over the territorial limits of their country. With the exception of Mustafa Kemal Pasha and possibly of Colonel İsmet, they favored the maintenance of the empire around the seat of the sultanate-caliphate. They could not reconcile themselves to the fact that the Ottoman Empire and its ruling institutions were things of the past.

But when these young men witnessed the actual occupation of Istanbul and various parts of Anatolia by the Allied forces, and when they began to realize that the Allied Powers were determined to dismember the Ottoman Empire, they sided at once with Mustafa Kemal Pasha, who was advocating the idea of concentrating all efforts toward saving Anatolia from enemy control. They were also in agreement with Mustafa Kemal on the fundamental issues of foreign policy. They all agreed that to overcome the onslaught of the Western European powers it was necessary to establish friendly relations and cooperative ventures with the Bolshevik rulers of Russia, Turkey's traditional enemy.

But on the major issues of domestic policy Hüseyin Rauf Bey, Ali Fuat Pasha, Kazım Karabekir Pasha, Colonel Refet, and Mustafa Kemal Pasha were irrevocably divided. However, each one of these men aspired to assume the leadership of the Nationalist Movement and then to reorganize the superstructure of the society in accordance with his own political ideas and beliefs.

No sooner had they spearheaded the Nationalist Movement, the conflicting aspirations of the principal warriors brought about bitter interpersonal rivalry, encouraging factionalism within the ranks of the nationalists gathered in Ankara. The leading personalities of the Nationalist Movement actually represented a wide variety of political philosophies — ecclesiasticism, secularism, conservatism, radicalism, monarchism, republicanism, Ottomanism, Turkism, etc. However, when the Grand National Assembly convened for the first time in April 1920, these divergent and often conflicting ideologies were soon crystallized into "Westernism" and "Easternism."[1]

A brief account of Westernism and Easternism may help to place this power struggle in its proper perspective. H. Rauf Bey,[2] Kazım Karabekir Pasha, Ali Fuat Pasha, and Colonel Refet, together with Dr. Abdulhak Adnan (Adıvar) and his wife, Halide Edib,[3]

---

[1] For an excellent study of these opposing ideologies see Niyazi Berkes, *The Development of Secularism in Turkey* (Montreal: McGill University Press, 1964), pp. 431–60; see Samet Ağaoğlu, *Kuvayi Milliye Ruhu* (Istanbul: Nebioğlu Yayınevi, 1945), pp. 31–32.

[2] At this time Hüseyin Rauf Bey, who was better known as Rauf Bey, was not in Ankara. He was one of the deputies of the Ottoman Parliament deported to Malta by the British occupational authorities, following their raid on the parliament. S. I. Aralov, the first Soviet ambassador accredited to the government of the Grand National Assembly, asserts that "Rauf Bey was hoping to reinstate the reactionary administration of Sultanate with the help to foreign powers and to declare himself dictator." *Bir Sovyet Diplomatının Türkiye Hatıraları*. Translated by Hasan Ali Ediz (Istanbul: Burçak Yayınevi, 1967), p. 184.

[3] Abdulhak Adnan Adıvar was born in Gelibolu in 1882; he received an M.D. degree from Istanbul Medical School and Berlin Medical School; he served as assistant of Internal Medicine at the Istanbul Medical School during 1905–1909; he was later appointed professor of Medicine and served as the director of the School of Medicine; he participated in the Tripoli War; he served during World War I as major, medical officer; he was elected deputy from Istanbul and entered the Ottoman Parliament, 1919–1920; he joined the Grand National Assembly in Ankara as deputy, 1920–1926; he was elected Minister of Health on May 3, 1920, and served until May 1922; he was appointed the representative of the Grand National Assembly in Istanbul in 1922 and served until 1924; he joined the opposition Progressive Republican Party in 1924; he was self-exiled in France and England between 1926 and 1939. In 1926 he was appointed professor of Turkish in the School of Oriental Languages, University of Paris, and served until 1934; he then became editor-in-chief of the Encyclopedia of Islam, Istanbul, 1939–1944; he was elected deputy on the Democratic Party ticket in 1950 and served until the next election in 1954. He retired from political life in 1954 and died in 1955 in Istanbul. He spoke fluent German, French, and English.

Halide Edib Adıvar was born in Istanbul in 1884; she received a B.A. degree from the American College for Girls in Istanbul; she started her career as a writer in various newspapers and magazines; she taught at Teacher's School for Girls in Istanbul; she founded the Girls Schools in Beirut and Damascus. With her husband, she joined the ranks of the nationalists in Ankara, worked in the Ministry of Foreign Affairs, and served in the nationalist armies as corporal between 1920 and 1922. In 1924 she joined the opposition Progressive Republican Party. She left Turkey with her husband to live in exile, served as visiting professor of Turkish Literature at Columbia University, 1931–32, and served in Indian universities until 1936. She returned to Turkey in 1939, was appointed professor of English literature

were the leading advocates of Westernism. They were passionate advocates for the preservation of the sovereignty of the sultan-caliph and the traditional institutions of the Ottoman Empire. They were opposed to the establishment of a new regime based on the sover-' eignty of the people. They argued that following the expulsion of the foreign occupational forces, the principal task of the Grand National Assembly should be to restore the sultan-caliph's sovereign authority within his realm.

Influenced by the arguments of these prominent personalities, the great majority of the deputies of the First Grand National Assembly suggested that all legislative and executive powers should temporarily be concentrated in the assembly. They believed that this action would help to preserve the legitimacy of the sovereignty of the sultan-caliph, and consequently would prevent the establishment of a new regime along the lines of the Soviet system. And concentration of all political power in the assembly would also curb and control Mustafa Kemal's tendency to manage the affairs of the nation single-handedly. Once this objective was achieved, according to Halide Edib, the assembly could shape the future political organization and the economic, social, and educational systems to the pattern of Western models. This is probably why H. Rauf Bey and his associates were identified as Westernists. However, in response to the needs and demands of the conservative and traditionalist people of Turkey, H. Rauf Bey and his supporters favored only gradual political, economic, and social reforms.

Easternism or "the Eastern Ideal" was represented in the assembly by a small minority of idealists. They envisaged the establishment of a new regime along the lines of Marxism and the Soviet system in Russia. They were dedicated to Marxism, which appeared to them as the only means through which the dignity and honor of the people might be restored and the shackles of the oppressive traditional institutions might be abolished. Halide Edib states that Hakkı Behiç Bey, a member of the Representative Committee at Sivas and first the Minister of Finance and later the Minister of Interior of the Grand National Assembly, was the leading exponent of the Eastern Ideal. According to Halide Edib, he "had seriously studied the Marxist philosophy," was a man "born with great heart

---

at the University of Istanbul in 1940, and was elected deputy from İzmir in 1950. She retired from politics in 1954 and died in Istanbul in 1964. She spoke fluent English and French.

ready to share all he had with his kind, and a mind that rebelled against all barriers of class, wealth, race, religion which separated man from man." Halide Edib maintains that Hakkı Behiç Bey was not quite sure how this dream could be realized in Turkey; neither could he propose anything workable. Halide Edib says that "he argued endlessly that Western civilization had outlived its time and was doomed. All over the world something new was struggling to be born, but especially in the East," which was to destroy eventually the whole fabric of the old.[4]

Another idealist who shared the dreams of Hakkı Behiç Bey was a young and highly educated man of upper-class origin — Hikmet (Bayur) Bey. He was the grandson of Kamil Pasha, who was the Grand Vezir during the Young Turks revolutionary period.[5] Hikmet Bey was educated at the Sorbonne and had come from Istanbul to Ankara to join the Nationalist Movement.[6] According to Halide Edib, Hikmet Bey in 1920, "had come very much under the influence of Marxian doctrines, which he now regarded as the means of saving the world: he longed wholeheartedly to see Turkey become Bolshevist." Although Hikmet Bey called himself a com-

---

[4] Halide Edib, *The Turkish Ordeal* (New York: Century, 1928), pp. 171–73.

[5] The Young Turks were young army officers at Salonika and Manastır who rebelled against the absolute rule of the sultan and seized power in Istanbul with a view to restoring the Constitution of 1876 and defending their country against foreign aggressions. They controlled the destiny of the Ottoman Empire from 1908 to 1918. See Lewis, *The Emergence of Modern Turkey*, pp. 200–238.

[6] Hikmet Bey helped in the organization of the Ministry of Foreign Affairs. His thorough knowledge of French together with the thorough knowledge of English of Halide Edib must have been instrumental in eliminating communication difficulties of the Ministry of Foreign Affairs in foreign languages in the early period of the Ministry. Later, Hikmet Bey was appointed as the first Minister to Belgrade of the Republic of Turkey in 1926. Then he was appointed ambassador to Kabul in 1931. Returning from this post, he was appointed Minister of Education from October 1933 to October 1934. He served as deputy in the Grand National Assembly from 1931 to the early 1950s and simultaneously served as professor of history of the Turkish Revolution. He published a large number of articles on the Revolutionary period of Turkey and is the author of the following books: *Son Yirmibeş Yıllık Tarihimize Bakışlar* (Istanbul: Devlet Basımevi, 1938); *Türk İnkilap Tarihi*, 2 cilt (Istanbul: Maarif Matbaası, 1940–1943); *Türkiye Devletinin Harici Siyaseti* (Istanbul: A. Sait Matbaası, 1942); *Atatürk: Hayatı ve Eseri* (Ankara: Aydın Kitapevi, 1962). He was expelled from the Republican People's Party in January 1946. Together with Marshal Fevzi Çakmak and others he founded the Nation Party in July 1948, but resigned from this Party in July 1953. He is now inactive in politics and is engaged in writing.

munist, Halide Edib maintains that he was "Turk enough to want Turkey to be independent not only of the West but of Russia."[7]

In this connection mention also must be made of the *Yeşil Ordu* (Green Army) organization which came into being in the spring of 1920 and found support among the "Easternists" in the Grand National Assembly. It was organized by Hakkı Behiç Bey with the approval of Mustafa Kemal, who viewed it as a means to impress upon Soviet Russia that the nationalists in Ankara were sincere in striving to accomplish a social revolution.[8] The members of the Green Army formed a populist group in the Grand National Assembly which, in addition to Hakkı Behiç Bey, included Nazım Bey, Mehmet Şükrü Bey, and Yunus Nadi Bey.[9] Certain commanders of irregular forces, like Çerkes Ethem, were also members of the Green Army organization, Ethem, due to the growing strength of the Green Army both within and outside of the Grand National Assembly, looked upon his irregular forces (Mobile Forces *Kuvayı Seyyare*) as "a Turkish counterpart of the Russian Red Army"[10] and began to challenge the leadership of Mustafa Kemal and asserted autonomy from the Ankara government.[11] Mustafa Kemal

---

[7] Edib, *The Turkish Ordeal,* pp. 173–74.

[8] See George S. Harris, *The Origins of Communism in Turkey* (Stanford, Calif.: Hoover Institution, 1967), pp. 69–70.

[9]Ibid., p. 74.

[10] Lord Kinross, *Ataturk: A Biography of Mustafa Kemal, Father of Modern Turkey* (New York: William Morrow and Co., 1965), p. 284.

[11] On the quarrels between Mustafa Kemal and Çerkes Ethem, see Mustafa Kemal Atatürk, *A Speech Delivered by Ghazi Mustapha Kemal, President of the Turkish Republic* (trans.) (Leipzig: K. F. Koehler, 1929), p. 403. Hereinafter Atatürk's opus will be referred as *Speech.* Çerkes Ethem was the youngest of three brothers, sons of a Circassian farmer in Emre near Karacabey, who had taken leading parts in the nationalist guerrilla operations. Ethem was born in 1883. He distinguished himself against the Greeks at Salihli and Anzavur Pasha's forces sent by Damat Ferid Pasha to suppress the nationalists (Summer 1919) and in supressing the antinationalist revolts at Düzce and Yozgat (Spring 1920). As commander of Mobile Forces, with his brother Tevfik as deputy, he came into sharp conflict with the regular army of the Western front. Ethem and his brothers, Reşit and Tevfik, and several hundred Circassian guerrillas fled behind Greek lines on January 5, 1921. Following their defeat, Ethem and his brothers went in exile to Greece, Germany, various Arab countries, and eventually to Amman, Jordan. They were denounced as traitors by the Grand National Assembly. Later they were among the 150 persons excepted from the amnesty provisions of the Lausanne Treaty of Peace of 1923. Ethem died of throat cancer in Amman on October 7, 1949. His brother Reşit returned to Turkey in 1950 and died in Ankara in 1951. His other brother Tevfik spent his exile years in Haifa and died soon after his return to Turkey in 1938; see *The Encyclopedia of Islam,* new edition, vol 2. Fasiculies, 23 (London: Luzac and Co., 1960), pp. 25–26.

ordered the disbanding of the Green Army in July 1920 and it was banned in October 1920. However, it was not until the decisive battle of İnönü from January 6 to 10, 1921, against Ethem's forces, which had previously joined the ranks of the Greek armies advancing toward Ankara, that Mustafa Kemal was successful in the liquidation of the Green Army and its adherents.

Although idealists, many of the Easternists were true nationalists and as such had come very much under the influence of the domineering personality of Mustafa Kemal. For example, Hakkı Behiç Bey and Yunus Nadi Bey, upon the request of Mustafa Kemal, disassociated themselves from the Green Army and followed his leadership. Mustafa Kemal was viewing the Eastern Ideal and the activities of the Easternists and the emerging communist organizations from an entirely practical viewpoint. To him the liberation of the nation from the domination of foreign powers as well as from the traditional institutions such as the sultanate-caliphate necessitated cooperation with the anti-imperialist forces, i.e., communists, as well as conservatives. Consequently, he expressed sympathy for the communist cause at a time when the support of Soviet Russia was needed. It was at this critical time of organizing a permanent and regularly functioning government that Mustafa Kemal and his close associates assumed the communist appearance. They wore redpeaked kalpaks, called each other "comrade," and referred to their ministries as "People's Commissariats."[12]

But when the open and secret communist activities posed a serious threat to Mustafa Kemal, he formed his own official Communist Party on October 18, 1920. Hakkı Behiç Bey was designated as the secretary general. This official Communist Party was not only to attract those idealist Easternists into its fold, but also to disqualify other agents of Soviet communism as traitors of the nationalist cause without offending Soviet Russia.[13] Mustafa Kemal

---

[12] Harris, *Origins of Communism*, p. 69; see also Tevfik Biyiklioğlu, *Atatürk Anadoluda, 1919–1921* (Ankara: Türk Tarih Kurumu Basımevi, 1959), p. 68. This practice seems to have created the impression in the European official circles that the Turkish nationalists had gone Bolshevik in their ideas and administration. See the dispatch of the British High Commissioner Rumbold, Great Britain, Foreign Office, 371/6466/E2488/1/44; see also the dispatch dated April 25, 1921, Admiral Bristol to Department of State, U.S. National Archives, Turkey, File No. 867.01/73.

[13] Edib, *The Turkish Ordeal*, p. 175. For a somewhat different interpretation of the motives of Mustafa Kemal, see Lord Kinross, *Ataturk* 14, p. 285.

also hoped that his official Communist Party would serve as a means of facilitating the negotiations between Ankara and Moscow. Incidentally, these negotiations were viewed by Mustafa Kemal as a propitious occasion to remove Ali Fuat Pasha from Ankara and send him to Moscow. It was about this time that the first important confrontation between the two occurred. The issue was the incorporation of the irregular troops into the regular army, which Ali Fuat did not favor. On account of the failure of the offensive against the Greek army in Anatolia, Ali Fuat Pasha was removed from his position as the commander of the Western front and recalled to Ankara. Mustafa Kemal suggested to him that in view of the importance of establishing friendly diplomatic relations with Soviet Russia he should be appointed ambassador to Moscow. Ali Fuat Pasha accepted the offer and went into quasi-exile. Before his departure on November 21, 1920, Ali Fuat Pasha, the first ambassador designate of the government of the Grand National Assembly to Soviet Russia, was given communist credentials by the secretary general of the official Communist Party.[14]

With the backing of the official Communist Party members, Mustafa Kemal began to liquidate the most dangerous Soviet agents in Anatolia, such as Mustafa Suphi[15] and the members of People's Communist Party of Turkey formed by Zinniatulla Navshirvanov and Nazım Bey toward the end of November 1920. They were arrested, tried, and sentenced to long prison terms on April 21, 1921.[16] Thus the struggle between Mustafa Kemal and the communists in Turkey was over once and for all.

But the struggle between Mustafa Kemal and the Westernists led by his old friends was to continue for another four years. This struggle was not only a conflict between conservatism and revolutionism, but also a power struggle for the ultimate leadership. Mustafa Kemal's comrades in arms considered themselves superior to him in culture, education, intellect, and in statesmanship and, therefore, claimed that they deserved leading positions in the govern-

---

[14] See Kılıç Ali, *Kılıç Ali Hatıralarını Anlatıyor* (Istanbul: Sel Yayınları, 1955), pp. 74–75.

[15] On Mustafa Suphi as head of the Turkish Communist movement in Russia, see Ali Fuat Cebesoy, *Moskova Hatıraları* (Istanbul: Vatan Neşriyatı, 1955), pp. 36–37; Edib, *The Turkish Ordeal,* p. 175; Harris, *Origins of Communism,* pp. 50–55, 56–57, 58–60, 64–66.

[16] Harris, *Origins of Communism,* p. 93.

ment of the Grand National Assembly and a leading role in charting the destiny of the Turkish people.

At the outset, Rauf Bey was opposed to Mustafa Kemal's election as the president of the Sivas Congress. Kazım Karabekir Pasha objected to his signing the communiqués and circulars and requested that all communiqués should be signed in the name of the Representative Committee; he questioned the advisability of the rupturing of relations with the Ottoman government in Istanbul.[17] Celalettin Arif Bey, president of the old Ottoman Chamber of Deputies, opposed Mustafa Kemal's election as the president of the First Grand National Assembly but in the end settled for the second presidency. Rauf Bey succeeded in getting a law passed which provided for the election of prime minister and cabinet members by the assembly; he also succeeded in getting himself elected prime minister on July 12, 1922, thereby replacing Mustafa Kemal's man Fevzi Pasha.[18] While in office Rauf Bey, together with Ali Fuat Pasha, Karabekir Pasha, and Refet Pasha, in July 1922 formed an opposition group called the "Second Group" consisting over 100 deputies.[19] Earlier, in May 1921, Mustafa Kemal had organized a political party known as the Defense of the Rights of Anatolia and Rumelia which later was named the Republican People's Party. The group of 200 deputies belonging to the Defense of the Rights of Anatolia and Rumelia, after July 1922, was known as the "First Group."

Although in the darkest days of the War of Independence Mustafa Kemal was given extraordinary powers as commander in chief, limited to a period of three months starting from August 5, 1921, each time the question of the renewal of these powers came up, his old friends expressed strong opposition. In the end, however, Mustafa Kemal was reappointed as commander in chief on July 20, 1922 for an unlimited period of time.[20]

The power struggle between Mustafa Kemal and his old

---

[17] See Rauf Orbay, "Rauf Orbay'ın Hatıraları," *Yakın Tarihimiz* 3, no. 3 (Eylül 20, 1962): 114-15.

[18] See Atatürk, *Speech,* pp. 549–57; Lord Kinross, *Ataturk,* pp. 344–47; "Dispatch," July 16, 1922, High Commissioner Bristol to Department of State, U.S. National Archives, Turkey, File No. 867.002/63.

[19] For the composition of the "Second Group," see Tarık Z. Tunaya, *Türkiye'de Siyasi, Partiler, 1859–1952* (Istanbul: Doğan Kardeş, 1952); and Frederick W. Frey, *The Turkish Political Elite* (Cambridge, Mass.: The M.I.T. Press, 1965), pp. 306–7.

[20] Lord Kinross, *Ataturk,* p. 311.

friends, chiefly Rauf Bey, was approaching its climax just after the final victory over the Greek forces in September 1922. Mustafa Kemal as commander in chief, was holding various meetings with the representatives of the Allied Powers concerning the withdrawal of the Allied troops from Turkey at İzmir. Rauf Bey, as prime minister, informed him that since the military operations had been completed and since the handling of political questions belonged exclusively to the Council of Ministers, he should immediately return to Ankara. At the height of his victory, Mustafa Kemal interpreted this move as an attempt to yank the rug out from under him. He proposed that if the Council of Ministers as a whole or certain ministers wished to reach an understanding with him they should come to see him at İzmir. Rauf Bey and Foreign Minister Yusuf Kemal Bey went to İzmir and took part in the diplomatic negotiations. It was decided that the proposals made to Mustafa Kemal by the Allied representatives would be the same as having them made to the Council of Ministers.[21]

Having lost another round to Mustafa Kemal, it seems that Rauf Bey this time directed his punches against Mustafa Kemal's intimate confidant İsmet Pasha; the occasion was İsmet Pasha's appointment as chief delegate to the Lausanne Peace Conference. This episode deserves particular attention because it not only concerns the power struggle but also foretells something about the political future of İsmet İnönü.[22]

The two principal contenders on the scene, Mustafa Kemal and Rauf Bey, give mutually contradictory accounts of this episode. According to Mustafa Kemal, Rauf Bey volunteered his services and proposed that Mustafa Kemal "should give him İsmet Pasha as an adviser." Mustafa Kemal replied by saying that he did not see what advantage it would be to send İsmet Pasha as an adviser but that he was convinced that İsmet Pasha would render the best services as the chairman of the delegation.[23] On the other hand, Rauf Bey, in his memoirs maintains that his name had been mentioned as the chairman of the delegation but he refused to accept such an assignment on the grounds that it would be inappropriate for him as prime min-

---

[21] Şevket Süreyya Aydemir, *Tek Adam: Mustafa Kemal,* 3 vols. (Istanbul: Remzi Kitapevi, 1963–1965), vol. 3, p. 25.

[22] See Feridun Kandemir, *Siyasi Dargınlıklar* (Istanbul: Ekicigil Matbaası, 1955), vol. 2, pp. 40–46.

[23] Atatürk, *Speech,* p. 570.

ister to attend the Lausanne Conference where other countries were to be represented by their foreign ministers. He goes on to say that he suggested that Yusuf Kemal Bey as foreign minister should be appointed as the chairman of the delegation. However, due to Yusuf Kemal Bey's refusal to accept such an assignment unless he was to accompany Rauf Bey as his foreign minister, Rauf Bey says that he suggested to Mustafa Kemal that İsmet Pasha should be appointed as chairman of the delegation. He says:

> It would be quite appropriate for İsmet Pasha to undertake this assignment since he had conducted successful negotiations at the Mudanya Conference. This proposal of mine was followed by a discussion on the capability of İsmet Pasha to conduct peace negotiations. As far as I was concerned this was not a difficult task, because, we knew beforehand what would be our principal demands at the peace conference. Furthermore, the experts in the Ministry of Foreign Affairs had, in advance of the conference, prepared the necessary documents on the questions that would be raised by us at the conference table. Moreover, the İsmet Pasha delegation would not only be strengthened by the addition of two highly qualified men, like Rıza Nur and Hasan Saka, but also closely be guarded by the instructions to be issued by the Ankara government.[24]

Other sources tend not to confirm Rauf Bey's argument on this issue.[25]

As far as Mustafa Kemal was concerned, Rauf Bey's appointment to that position was out of the question because of his opposition to many of the political ideas and actions of Mustafa Kemal and because of his conservative Westernist orientation and outlook; while İsmet Pasha was Mustafa Kemal's staunchest supporter and a first-class staff officer. Furthermore, it was not easy to handle Rauf Bey but Mustafa Kemal "knew how to control İsmet" Pasha.[26]

Once he had made up his mind, Mustafa Kemal decided that İsmet Pasha should first be appointed as foreign minister and then act as chairman of the delegation. In order to accomplish this, he sent a confidential message to Foreign Minister Yusuf Kemal Bey, asking him to resign from his office and to personally take steps to ensure the election of İsmet Pasha as his successor.[27] Yusuf Kemal

---

24 Rauf Orbay, "Rauf Orbay'ın Hatıraları," *Yakın Tarihimiz* 4, no. 41 (Aralık 6, 1962): 52.

25 See Lord Kinross, *Ataturk,* pp. 388–89; Kandemir, *Siyasi Dargınlıklar,* p. 42; Aydemir, *Tek Adam,* vol 3, p. 40.

26 Lord Kinross, *Ataturk,* p. 389.

27 Atatürk, *Speech,* p. 571.

Bey had no alternative but to resign and, in obedience to Mustafa Kemal's request, to assure the appointment of İsmet Pasha against the will of Prime Minister Rauf Bey. This action not only caused further friction between Mustafa Kemal and Rauf Bey, but also opened a deep mutual disrespect between the latter and İsmet Pasha. Rauf Bey felt insulted by Mustafa Kemal's action and detested the presumptuousness of İsmet Pasha who lacked the qualities of statesmanship and who, after all, was one of the latecomers into the ranks of the Nationalist Movement. Furthermore, it was embarrassing for a prime minister to be compelled to work with a foreign minister who did not like him. Nevertheless, Rauf Bey did not resign in the hopes that İsmet Pasha might commit diplomatic blunders and thus be asked to return to Ankara. The fact of the matter was that Mustafa Kemal was his own prime minister and foreign minister. Eventually he was to replace Rauf Bey with İsmet Pasha. İsmet Pasha was then pushed, at an unexpected moment, into the political limelight, which also assured his rise to the apex of power following the death of his chief.[28]

As was bound to happen, Rauf Bey exhibited strong dissatisfaction with İsmet Pasha's diplomacy at the Lausanne Conference. He endeavored to instill the same feeling of dissatisfaction among the members of his cabinet. İsmet Pasha's reports from Lausanne were interpreted by Rauf Bey and his cabinet as containing a spirit of compromise so disquieting that the only recourse would seem to be his prompt recall. Rauf Bey tried to bring the motion of İsmet Pasha's recall to a vote in one of the cabinet meetings, but through the intervention of Kazım Pasha, Minister of National Defense, this motion was apparently abandoned.[29]

It didn't take long for this same feeling of distrust to arise in the mind of İsmet Pasha against Rauf Bey. He began to look with suspicion at communications which he received that contained the signature of Rauf Bey; he believed that Rauf Bey gave him instructions without Mustafa Kemal's knowledge. He also complained about the unnecessary delays in the dispatch of instructions from the cabinet concerning his particular inquiries. He interpreted these delays as a ploy to place him in a difficult position during his negotiations.[30] He complained, too, that the cabinet allowed him little

[28] Aydemir, *Tek Adam,* vol. 3, p. 40.
[29] Atatürk, *Speech,* p. 635.
[30] Rauf Orbay, "Rauf Orbay'ın Hatıraları," Yakın Tarihimiz, 4, no. 41 (Aralık 6, 1962) : 52.

latitude in directing negotiations as well as carrying them out.[31] Finally, he appealed to Mustafa Kemal, pointing out that since the negotiations had entered a serious and critical stage Mustafa Kemal should personally follow the negotiations. Up until this time, Mustafa Kemal had been kept well posted regarding the reports of İsmet Pasha and the decisions of the Council of Ministers; but he had not concerned himself with the text of the instructions sent by Rauf Bey. After İsmet Pasha had drawn his attention to this matter, he felt compelled to follow the negotiations of the Lausanne Conference in the Council of Ministers and sometimes even to direct the decisions of the cabinet.

When the Lausanne Conference broke up on February 4, 1923, the deputies in the Grand National Assembly chose to vent their growing mistrust of Mustafa Kemal against İsmet Pasha. They tried to blame the failure at Lausanne on İsmet Pasha's lack of ability and on his failure to follow the instructions of the Council of Ministers which insinuated a lack of confidence in the diplomacy of Mustafa Kemal. The attacks on İsmet Pasha began in a secret session of the assembly on February 27 and continued until March 6 with the deputies pouring forth their grievances. They worked on the theme that the victory of the Turkish armies was being sacrificed by İsmet Pasha because of his ineptitude and that the Turkish delegation had become a toy in the hands of the British.[32]

In spite of these bitter criticisms, Mustafa Kemal was not only successful in reopening the Lausanne negotiations, but also in sending İsmet Pasha back to Lausanne for the second time over the objections of Rauf Bey.[33] Concerning the question of the reparations demanded from Greece, there was again a wide difference of opinion between Rauf Bey and İsmet Pasha. Incensed by the obstinacy of İsmet Pasha in making unnecessary concessions to the Greeks, Rauf Bey wrote to İsmet Pasha, calling his attention to the fact that he did not have the power to abandon Turkey's claim for the reparations contrary to his instructions from the Council of Ministers. This bitter criticism led to mutually incriminatory exchanges of messages

[31] Lord Kinross, *Atatürk,* p. 421.

[32] Ibid., p. 411; see also Mümtaz Soysal, *Dış Politika ve Parlamento* (Ankara; Ankara Üniversitesi Siyasal Bilgiler Fakültesi Yayınları, no. 183–165, 1964), pp. 97–99.

[33] Atatürk, *Speech,* p. 601.

between the two.[34] At one time İsmet Pasha threatened to resign from his mission, return home, and let Rauf Bey solve the difficulties encountered at Lausanne.

The majority of the assembly was supporting Rauf Bey's views on this issue. Mustafa Kemal was in favor of İsmet Pasha's argument which, he thought, would assure the conclusion of peace. However, he could not afford to offend Rauf Bey at this time and cause a cabinet crisis which could lead to his political defeat in the assembly and threaten the breakup of the Lausanne Conference. In view of these considerations, Mustafa Kemal decided not to commit himself fully to the support of only one side. He prevented Rauf Bey from exhibiting too strong a critical attitude toward İsmet Pasha and tried to convince him of the necessity of abandoning the reparation claim. He told İsmet Pasha that the decisions of Rauf Bey and the Council of Ministers represented also his own views.[35] Thus a modus vivendi was reached between the prime minister and his foreign minister at least during the Lausanne Conference. However the two had become arch opponents who had a strong mutual dislike. Rauf Bey was of the opinion that İsmet Pasha alone did not succeed in signing the Treaty of Lausanne; therefore he did not deserve all the credit. Rauf Bey also thought that despite his previous assurances to the contrary, Mustafa Kemal unnecessarily intervened in the conduct of the Council of Ministers and exploited his popularity among the members of the National Assembly to his own [Mustafa Kemal's] advantage. Rauf Bey sensed that sooner or later he would be dismissed from his position as prime minister. He frankly told Mustafa Kemal that he could not come face to face with İsmet Pasha anymore and that since İsmet Pasha's views prevailed upon the negotiations and the signing of the peace treaty, he should be designated as the person empowered to put that treaty into effect.

Mustafa Kemal apparently agreed with Rauf Bey only on this last point. He praised Rauf Bey's invaluable contributions to the nationalist cause and said: "Your services to the country are no less than ours." Rauf Bey, upon Mustafa Kemal's expression of his regret for his prime minister's resignation, is quoted as saying: "Do

---

[34] Rauf Orbay, "Rauf Orbay'ın Hatıraları," *Yakın Tarihimiz,* no. 41 (Aralık 6, 1962): 59.

[35] Atatürk, *Speech,* p. 639.

not be sorry, Pasha, you can govern this country with twelve honest men."[36]

Rauf Bey, Kazım Karabekir Pasha, Ali Fuat Pasha, and Refet Pasha continued their opposition to Mustafa Kemal's rule. They vehemently opposed the abolition of the sultanate and the establishment of the republic, knowing full well that the sentiments of the traditionalist majority of the people were on their side. The number of votes cast in the assembly for the election of Mustafa Kemal as president of the republic is indicative of his lack of popularity among the deputies. Announcing the result of the election, İsmet Pasha said: "One hundred fifty-eight deputies have participated in the election of the President of the Republic. By 158 votes they have unanimously elected His Excellency the Gazi Mustafa Kemal Pasha, deputy for Ankara, President.[37] The fact of the matter was, however, that there were almost twice as many deputies in the assembly.[38] There were more than 100 abstentions. Moreover, following the general elections of August 1923, the Second Grand National Assembly was supposed to have been packed by Mustafa Kemal and was expected to be responsive to his will. The result, therefore, cannot be construed as a unanimous vote of approval of the establishment of the republic or as a unanimous vote of confidence in the first president of the republic. However, the fact that no one openly opposed his election indicated that Mustafa Kemal's opponents in the assembly were by this time totally intimidated.

However, the same cannot be said about the conservative majority of the people and their spokesmen, the educated elite, centered in Istanbul. Although they appeared to have accepted the fait accompli in the establishment of the republic, they were not to give up the fight completely. Their only remaining source of hope and strength was the institution of the caliphate, which, if cleverly manipulated, could evoke so strong a religious reaction on the part of the masses that Mustafa Kemal would be compelled to relinquish the state power and agree to a return to the theocratic system of

[36] Lord Kinross, *Ataturk,* pp. 423–24.

[37] Atatürk, *Speech,* p. 672.

[38] Webster maintains that there were 287 deputies in the assembly: see Donald E. Webster, *The Turkey of Ataturk* (Menasha, Wisc.: George Banta, 1939), p. 105; Frederick W. Frey, on the other hand, records the membership of the assembly at 333, *The Turkish Political Elite,* p. 164, table 7.1.

President Kemal Atatürk

government.[39] But it appears that the leadership of the conservative majority once again underestimated the capabilities of Mustafa Kemal and unrealistically expected to see the people of Turkey rise against the victor of the War of Independence. They were once again outmaneuvered by Mustafa Kemal and on March 3, 1924, the caliphate was abolished.

In protest to Mustafa Kemal's demand that all army commanders relinquish their seats in the assembly and return to army posts, Kazım Karabekir Pasha, Ali Fuat Pasha, and Refet Pasha instead relinquished their army commissions. They also resigned from the People's Party and, together with Rauf Bey, Adnan Bey, and other fellow critics of Mustafa Kemal, formed the Progressive Party in November 1924. But only six months later the first oppositional party led by Mustafa Kemal's old friends and comrades in arms was ordered closed by the İsmet Pasha cabinet.

The struggle for power ended in a dramatic scene on the stage of the Independence Tribunal. The scenario was written and directed by Mustafa Kemal and involved an alleged plot against his life. The principal actors were to be accused of taking part in the plot, and once supporting actors were punished severely, the stars of the drama were to be reprimanded and then forgiven. The purpose of the director was to display his benevolence toward the principal stars of the play.

Accordingly, Rauf Bey, Kazım Karabekir Pasha, Ali Fuat Pasha, Refet Pasha, and some other members of the assembly and minor officials were tried in the Independence Tribunal in İzmir in June 1926.[40] Rauf Bey, as mentioned earlier, was tried in absentia for at the time he was in self-exile in Europe. He was sentenced to ten years' banishment. Some of the opponents of minor importance were executed. But old friends of Mustafa Kemal were acquitted. And that was the end of their political careers during Atatürk's lifetime.

The old comrades in arms of Mustafa Kemal were denied a fair share in the management of the affairs of the republic for the very reason that they disagreed with him at times in regard to principles and other times in regard to the methods of adopting and executing political decisions. These disagreements, no doubt,

---

[39] On the views of the conservative leadership, see Atatürk, *Speech*, pp. 683–97.

[40] On these trials see Lord Kinross, *Ataturk*, pp. 483–93.

stemmed from their differences in social backgrounds, upbringing, personalities, and, more importantly, from their political ambitions.

During the National Struggle period, internal checks on Mustafa Kemal's actions came not so much from an elected body, the National Assembly, but from his close associates who advised him against taking drastic innovative actions. Criticisms directed against him by his warrior friends confirmed Mustafa Kemal's conviction that he ought to be extremely careful in avoiding a direct confrontation with the wrong opponent at the wrong time. Thus, he kept the incipient power struggle with his associates under control and within tolerable limits until the achievement of the final military victory against foreign powers. Despite his occasional dictatorial rule, he tolerated bitter criticism and chose persuasion and free discussion as the means of unifying the divergent elements around the primary objective of national survival. He did his best to create the impression that he was not alone on the stage. He appealed to the Westernists' basic emotional feelings toward the sultan-caliph and their sense of participation in the auspicious task of saving the caliph from captivity and saving the country from foreign domination. He deliberately veered away from unduly offending the conservative majority, and he judiciously avoided taking arms against the puppet government of Istanbul and its supporter, the British Empire.

Through the ingenious tactic of encouraging the deputies as well as his close associates to think that they themselves controlled the destiny of the nation and controlled his actions, Mustafa Kemal was able to dominate the unruly and conservative National Assembly and its leading personalities. A strong critic of Mustafa Kemal, Halide Edib's comment is to the point: "I felt that . . . the prevalent belief that he wanted to be the Sultan or the dictator of the new regime was quite groundless. In a strange way I was beginning to feel that he was to be our George Washington."[41]

As far as drastic changes in the political, economic, and social system and structure of the society were concerned, Mustafa Kemal was in agreement with the views of the Easternists, a small minority in the assembly. But he was a realist revolutionary with a steady eye to his future and his realistic objectives. If he had spoken out too much concerning his hopes for the future of Turkey, his objec-

---

[41] Edib, *The Turkish Ordeal,* p. 142.

tives would have been looked upon as mere dreams and would have caused the alienation of close associates and the rest of the people. He was very much concerned with the aggregation of his personal power which would enable him to carry out his objectives. He had the full grasp of the internal and external forces that confronted him. He was convinced that he ought to deal with each problem as it arose and accomplish uncontestable success in its solution and then move on to the next issue.

Through ingenious maneuvering he gained recognition of the legitimacy of the Nationalist Movement, the legitimacy of the government of the Grand National Assembly, and the legitimacy of his rule. When the final military victory was won, it was extremely difficult and dangerous for his opponents to unseat the victor (Gazi Mustafa Kemal) from his power bases: The army and the patriotic people.

His superb strategies and tactics in taking advantage of the opportunities as they presented themselves paved the way for his final triumph over his old friends and enemies. What assured his success, in the final analysis, was his renunciation of the rhetorical legacies which the empty prestige policy of the Ottoman Empire had bequeathed him. He pursued realistic objectives in light of the nature and the amount of power he possessed. He showed courage by avoiding unattainable goals even amid the intoxication of military successes against his opponents.

Those old friends of Mustafa Kemal who challenged his ideas and leadership were replaced by those who were willing to carry out his directives, such as Ali Fethi Bey, Fevzi Pasha, and İsmet Pasha. It appears that Ali Fethi (Okyar) Bey has pursued a very cautious and prudent course. He was a well-balanced man of moderate views and had the abiltiy to make his views respected. He was not mentally subservient to Mustafa Kemal. But, he never attempted to seek the ultimate leadership of the Nationalist Movement, never really challenged Mustafa Kemal's claim to leadership. When he was asked, he served as envoy, prime minister, ambassador, and loyal oppositional leader, and when he was asked to step down from such positions he did so with grace and dignity. Fevzi Pasha never came into the political limelight during the presidency of Mustafa Kemal. He remained as loyal Chief of the General Staff without any political ambition. With few interruptions the political career of İsmet Pasha was always on the ascendancy, and finally he succeeded Mustafa Kemal as president of the republic. The following comparison of the personal characteristics of Mustafa Kemal and İsmet İnönü deserves particular attention:

Ismet was a man with scholarly mind, better read than Kemal. The two shared the same radical ideas and found many opinions in common. . . . Though Kemal and Ismet had similar views and aims they were opposite in temperament as to complement one another. The mind of Kemal moved swiftly and flexibly, with a grasp of broad issues, unorthodox reactions, and a capacity for making bold judgments; Ismet's mind worked within a narrow, more liberal compass, slowly and deliberately, with a laborious attention to detail. Kemal was adventurous in spirit, independent in character, decisive in action; Ismet was cautious, dependent on the views of another, lacking in initiative and hesitant in making decisions. Kemal had an intuitive understanding of human behavior and character; Ismet was an unsure judge of people, whom he treated with reserve and a certain suspicion. Where Kemal was restless, quick-tempered, temperamental, hard-drinking, and promiscuous with women, Ismet was calm, stolid, patient, sober, and a model family man. He was the antithesis of Kemal, hence just the assistant Kemal needed. Ismet was in fact born chief of staff, painstaking and loyal, to whom Kemal could dictate his plans, confident that he would interpret them correctly and carry them out with efficiency. He became Kemal's indispensible "shadow."[42]

Since the death of the charismatic leader of Turkey,[43] the political scene came to be dominated by a few of his lieutenants who unfortunately could not match the spirit, vision, foresightedness, heroics, and dynamism of Atatürk. Yet, thanks to the traditional tendency of the people to submit themselves to the authority of those who wielded state power, first İnönü, and then Celal Bayar, tended to create their own cults of personality under the continuing legacy of Atatürk. But the period since 1938 was again marked by clashes of wills among the lieutenants of the father of modern Turkey.

---

[42] Lord Kinross, *Ataturk,* pp. 119-20.

[43] Cf. Dankwart A. Rustow who maintains: "At most . . . Kemal proved a reluctant revolutionary and a very cautious charismatic." "Ataturk As Founder of a State," in *Prof. Dr. Yavuz Abadan'a Armağan* (Ankara: Ankara Üniversitesi Siyasal Bilgiler Fakültesi Yayınları, no. 280, 1969), p. 521.

Chapter Three

THE STRUGGLE FOR SUCCESSION
TO ATATÜRK

İSMET İNÖNÜ: "THE NATIONAL CHIEF"

It was Atatürk who had set the goals of Turkey. His successor was to carry on the work begun by Atatürk. Would the new leaders be able to meet the requirements of national security and at the same time help modernize the Turkish polity? Apparently the highest echelons of the military establishment and the Republican People's Party saw İsmet İnönü as the man qualified to lead the nation in the difficult times that lay ahead. At the meeting of the parliamentary group of the party on November 11, 1938, İsmet İnönü, by a vote of 322, was unanimously nominated for the presidency of the republic. His election the same day by the Grand National Assembly was again by unanimous vote of 348 deputies present and voting.[1]

İsmet İnönü, at the age of fifty-four, assumed the awesome responsibilities of carrying out the program of modernization and safeguarding the national security at a time when the whole world was in a state of uncertainty and upheaval. But then he was not definitely sure as to his own position in the country. He had always been the chief of staff of Atatürk, his trusted adviser. Yet during the

---

[1] Şevket Süreyya Aydemir, *İkinci Adam: İsmet İnönü,* vol. 2, 1938–1950 (Istanbul: Remzi Kitapevi, 1967), pp. 25–26. The unconfirmed reports circulated at the time of the serious illness of Atatürk mentioned the possibility of Marshal Fevzi Çakmak or Celal Bayar assuming the presidency. See Lord Kinross, *Ataturk,* p. 566.

President İsmet İnönü

last year of the presidency of Atatürk, he had been removed from the prime ministry. Everyone knew also that there were some disagreements between himself and Atatürk. Although he had now been entrusted with the presidency of the republic and the leadership of the party he was, at best, "the second man" in the eyes of many.[2] He could not claim the absolute allegiance of the citizenry. On the other hand, if he were to safeguard the vital national interests of the country as he perceived them, he had to be the president of the republic in his own right and establish his own version of authoritarianism.[3] This would not be a difficult task, for he knew that the people traditionally respected and obeyed those who were in control of the government. He, therefore, assumed that as he entrenched himself in office people would acquiesce to his authoritarian measures and that as time went by, he would be able to create his own political regime.

Atatürk posthumously was given the title of "The Eternal Chief."[4] And it did not take very long for President İnönü to have himself also elevated to the position of highest prestige as "The National Chief." This was done by revising the bylaws of the Republican People's Party.

İsmet İnönü had the national mint issue new coins and banknotes bearing his profile, thus replacing those of Atatürk. A number of statues of him were also erected in various cities and towns. His large-scale portraits were hung on the walls of all the government offices either next to Atatürk's or alone. He estalished "The

---

[2] For an extensive treatment of this point see Aydemir, *İkinci Adam*, vol. 2.

[3] For a similar view, see Karpat who writes: "İsmet İnönü has been one of the most controversial figures in the recent history of Turkey. His enemies have accused him of being the chief architect of the totalitarian policies of the Republican Party. The truth is that after becoming president, he appeared rather doubtful of his own position in the Republican Party and in the country, as contrasted with the undisputed allegiance commanded by Atatürk. He had himself elected permanent chairman of the Republican Party as a result of his doubts." Kemal H. Karpat, *Turkey's Politics: The Transition to a Multi-Party System* (Princeton, N.J.: Princeton University Press, 1959), p. 400.

[4] Nadir Nadi, an eminent journalist, claims that he was the one who first posthumously referred to Atatürk as "The Eternal Chief" in his newspaper on November 14, 1938. And he states that after that day this title found general acceptance. See Nadir Nadi, *Perde Aralığından* (Istanbul: Cumhuriyet Yayınları, 1964), p. 14.

İnönü Award" and "The İnönü Encyclopedia." He had stadiums, streets, avenues, parks, and schools named after him.[5]

Following the general indirect elections in 1939, İnönü packed the Grand National Assembly with those deputies who were loyal to his regime. He appointed and dismissed prime ministers and ministers as he pleased and gathered around him those who were willing to submit to his dictates without any question. He intervened in the minute details of the administration, giving orders to under-secretaries, director generals, and even governors without going through the normal channels of the ministers and the prime ministers. The following anecdote reveals somewhat the nature of the control exercised by President İnönü over his cabinet ministers. Journalist Nadir Nadi writes:

It was at the beginning of 1943, one day I came across Hasan-Âli Yücel, the Minister of Education, in the great reception hall of the Ankara Palace Hotel.
—Good heavens, my eminent master! Why in the world did you have to shave off your beautiful moustache?
—Ah! Don't remind me of it! The National Chief wanted me to shave it off.
—What? The National Chief? Very strange, indeed!
Yes, it was the National Chief who had ordered him to do so. And what is more, not only Hasan-Âli Yücel but all Ministers including Prime Minister Saracoğlu were ordered to shave off their moustaches. Why shouldn't they comply with the wish of the permanent National Chief of the Party? Should they resign their posts because of such a trivial matter? Certainly not![6]

Nadir Nadi calls this "The Moustache Revolution of İnönü."

From the time of his election as president at least until the end of the Second World War İsmet İnönü was, for all practical purposes, a dictator. He could not be criticized by the citizenry, the members of the party, or the press. Martial law and extensive police powers precluded any criticism of President İnönü's policies and actions.[7] He pursued a very cautious and prudent foreign policy which necessitated taking stern measures to control political activities in the internal arena. But during the post-World War II years, President İnönü was confronted with internal and external pressures

---

[5] Ibid., pp. 183–84.
[6] Ibid., pp. 179–80.
[7] Ibid., pp. 183–86.

calling for the relaxation of the stern measures of his authoritarian regime.

Since the founding of the republic, a new elite, educated in and attracted by Western liberal political thought, had grown to maturity. They viewed democracy as the ultimate goal prescribed for Turkey by Atatürk. For them modernization essentially meant Westernization. They, therefore, aspired to the integration of a democratic Turkey in the democratic West. The victory of Western democracies over the Axis powers reconfirmed their belief in the democratic institutions of the West. The dictatorial practices of President İnönü had given rise to serious discontent among the members of the new elite who by 1945 began to express their opposition to İnönü's regime demanding drastic changes in the political system.[8]

A small but resourceful group of deputies, headed by Celal Bayar, Adnan Menderes, Fuat Köprülü, and Refik Koraltan, dared to challenge the leadership of İnönü and his regime. Of these four deputies, Menderes, Köprülü, and Koraltan were expelled from the People's Party. Celal Bayar resigned his seat in the National Assembly and also resigned from the party. On January 7, 1946, these so-called "rebels" formed the Democratic Party and began to campaign against İnönü and his party.[9]

During the last five years of the İnönü administration, the main opposition — the Democratic Party — achieved spectacular success in absorbing the intelligentsia into its ranks and establishing closer ties with the people by paying greater heed to their individual or local interests and by articulating their great many political and economic grievances. The Democratic Party leadership began to press for drastic changes in the politico-socio-economic structure of the society. The replacement of the dictatorship of İnönü's regime with a democratic order ranked as the first and foremost prerequisite of such drastic changes. Quite naturally, Democrats viewed themselves as the true representative of the people and assigned them-

---

[8] C. H. Dodd observes: "The victory of the western democracies persuaded the Turks that democracy was indeed an integral part of western civilization, of which, according to the philosophy of their revolution, the Turks were indisputably part." *Politics and Government in Turkey* (Berkeley: University of California Press, 1969), p. 23.

[9] For a detailed treatment of these developments, see Karpat, *Turkey's Politics,* pp. 140–68; see also Aydemir, *İkinci Adam,* vol. 2, pp. 430–39.

selves the task of the transformation of the Turkish society into a modern democratic order.

Thus in 1945, after some twenty-two years, a bitter intraelite struggle was resurrected, the consequences of which could not be foreseen at the time. The major difference between the old intraelite struggle for power and the new one lay in the fact that the Democratic Party leadership claimed to have the full allegiance and backing of the people.[10] The Democratic Party leadership, long out of political power bases, had an unblemished record. Moreover, it was headed by the last prime minister of Atatürk, Celal Bayar.

As viewed by the Democratic Party leadership and by their ardent supporters, the landslide victory of the Democratic Party in the general elections on May 14, 1950, was a decisive condemnation of President İnönü's authoritarian regime and his outmoded policies and, as such, constituted a clear-cut mandate for drastic changes in the society.[11] The results of the general elections came as a surprise not only to İnönü and his party but also to the leaders of the Democratic Party. They were not really prepared to assume the state power.[12] But when the initial pleasant shock was over, they demonstrated readiness to accept the challenge by swift but smooth actions in taking over the reins of the government.

CELAL BAYAR: "THE DEMOCRATIC CHIEF"

Celal Bayar was elected by the Grand National Assembly with an overwhelming majority as the third president of the republic on May 22, 1950. Bayar was firmly convinced that only he and his close associates in the Democratic Party were capable of providing

---

[10] Cf. Frey, *The Turkish Political Elite,* p. 391, where he says: "Elite unity broke down in pathological form just as the vote was given to the peasant. The intraelite conflict thus became qualitatively different. It was no longer solely *intra*elite. It was transferred, sometimes in violent fashion, to the villages."

[11] For example, Bernard Lewis observes: "The Democratic victory in 1950 was more than a change of party; it was a plebiscite. All who had grievances against the People's Party — and after twenty-seven years there were many — found and took the opportunity to register a complaint against it. After so long a period even a party of angels would probably have been swept out of offfice." *The Emergence of Modern Turkey,* 2nd ed. (London: Oxford University Press, 1968), p. 309.

[12] Ibid., p. 313.

the nation with a dynamic leadership, pulling Turkey out of the stagnation of the era of National Chief İnönü, and motivating the people toward a much brighter future of abundance, prosperity, and greatness through his liberal economic policies and economic development projects.[13] And this is where the trouble started! President Bayar and his prime minister, Adnan Menderes, were to be the victims of their own perceptions of their greatness and indispensability which came into violent and protracted clashes with İsmet İnönü, who may be called the "Rock of Gibraltar of Turkish politics."

Then, too, by the middle of 1954 the national economy began to show signs of depression under the strains and stresses of the mounting inflation, the rising balance of payments deficit in international trade, and the ensuing lack of foreign exchange. Instead of instituting an austerity program and coordinated economic planning, the Democratic Party administration continued to pursue its inflationary policies and even launched more grandiose projects of investment leading to what the oppositional parties, particularly the leadership of the People's Party, called irresponsible and reckless adventurism in economic policy.

Simultaneously important changes began to take place in the infrastructure of the society[14] which created almost insurmountable problems in urbanization, land distribution, education, religion, and in economic and political life which taxed the resourcefulness of the Democratic Party leadership to its limits. The situation was aggravated by the constant criticism and bickering on the part of the oppositional parties which succeeded in creating further dissension

---

[13] See the Democratic Party's 1950 election platform in Karpat, *Turkey's Politics*, pp. 408–14. See also the statments of President Bayar on economic issues in Richard D. Robinson, *The First Turkish Republic: A Case Study in National Development* (Cambridge, Mass.: Harvard University Press, 1963), pp. 144–45. See also Aydemir, *İkinci Adam*, vol. 2, p. 483.

[14] On infrastructural changes one commentator observes: "The 'Menderes Phase' is still difficult to evaluate, partly for the political partisanship attached but equally for the many paradoxes it brought to existence. For instance, the great doses of inflation that seriously imperiled the economy at the same time brought to it a dynamism, volatile yet potentially creative. An investment and entrepreneurial class grew rapidly, knowledge of industrial techniques became much more widespread and a glimpse of the potentialities of the development process was afforded to many hitherto unseeing elements of the population." Dwight J. Simpson, "Development as a Process — the Menderes Phase in Turkey," *The Middle East Journal*, 19 (Spring 1965): 152.

President Celal Bayar

within the ranks of the Democratic Party and discontent among the intelligentsia.

President Bayar and Premier Menderes accused their opponents of obstructionism for the sake of opposition and making the national problem of economic development a political football for the sake of gaining a few electoral votes. Their sensitivity to criticism led to measures of suppressing dissident voices. They reasoned that if modernization was to be achieved in a record period of time then that end would justify authoritarian measures and the muzzling of the opposition. Apparently, President Bayar saw no reason why he should not forego his old promises of consolidating democracy by means of constitutional amendments and special institutions. As far as he was concerned, the solution of the enormous economic and social problems was contingent upon his remaining in power at all cost.

Once this conclusion was reached, the revival of authoritarianism was inevitable. So long as his regime was backed by a great majority of the people, President Bayar reasoned, he could easily suppress the opposition and continue to implement the projects of development of the Democratic Party administration. He reasoned also that repressive measures against the critics of his administration would be of short duration because he was confident of Turkey's brilliant economic future.[15]

President Bayar, in his attempts to deal with the intensified militancy of the opposition, particularly the militancy of the Republican People's Party leadership, committed two simultaneous blunders: One, he underestimated the power of İsmet İnönü and the abilities of İnönü's associates to mobilize the disenchanted and alienated members of the intelligentsia against the government and to create discord and antagonism in the country by exploiting the

---

[15] C. H. Dodd suggests three reasons for the resurgence of authoritarianism during the Democratic Party administration: (1) The Democratic Party leaders "had a long history of active participation in the authoritarian People's Party"; (2) they "left the People's Party because they were unable to unseat İsmet İnönü. . . . When the Democratic Party restricted political freedom it was as much on a personal as on a rational basis. They had İnönü and the People's Party chiefly in mind"; (3) "the Democratic Party got into power and maintained itself in power by victory, often substantial, in the elections; and this gave them the excessive confidence in their own popularity and their own legitimacy. They felt — and rightly — that however illiberal they appeared to intellectuals, the peasants and workers would not care much." *Politics and Government in Turkey*, p. 28.

apparent failures of the Democratic administration in its economic, social, and political policies; and two, Bayar misjudged the loyalty of the officer corps of the armed forces who were asked to quell the student demonstrations.

The Republican People's Party leadership was at this time well equipped to harass the Democratic Party government from all directions at once. The economic, social, and political policies of the government were all wrong; they were simply reckless, irrelevant, inconsistent, and diametrically opposed to secularism, reformism, *étatism,* and republicanism. The government was engaged in a program of destruction of the reforms accomplished during the Atatürk era. The intelligentsia was called to the task of defending the cause of modernization and reform according to Atatürk's ideas. The tactics and strategies of the opposition paid handsomely, for they themselves had been the victims of similar tactics and strategies in the past.[16] What happened between 1954 and 1960 was a virulent struggle among the elite of the Turkish society for political power in general and between İnönü and Bayar in particular.

Exactly ten years and five days after he assumed the office of the presidency, Bayar was taken into protective custody by the military when the Democratic Party government was overthrown by the Committee of National Unity on May 27, 1960. He was taken from the presidential palace at Çankaya and brought to the War College in a military jeep — the kind which Bayar had ridden in when he came to the Grand National Assembly on May 22, 1950, to take the oath of office as president! Later he was transferred to the island of Yassıada where he was detained and tried by a military court. Bayar was indicted in seven different cases for the violation of numerous laws, in particular for the violation of the Constitution.[17] He was sentenced to death three times by unanimous vote of the judges on September 15, 1961. However, on the same day, his death sentences were commuted to life imprisonment by the Committee of National Unity. He was taken to Kayseri prison to serve his sentence. On grounds of ill health he was released a number of times between 1962 and 1964 and returned to prison again.

---

[16] See Frey, *The Turkish Political Elite,* p. 417.

[17] For a brief review of these cases see Walter F. Weiker, *The Turkish Revolution, 1960–1961* (Washington, D.C.: The Brookings Institution, 1963), pp. 30–42.

Finally on July 8, 1966, President Sunay pardoned him. However, he was denied his political rights until 1972.

Celal Bayar, a contemporary of great warriors, such as Atatürk, Orbay, Cebesoy, Karabekir, Çakmak, and İnönü, has had an excellent career as an administrator and was an economist in his own right. As a civilian who has not had much formal education, his rise to prominence, even though to a great extent due to Atatürk's actions and backing, was spectacular. His strong will power and determination to excel among his contemporaries and his strategies and tactics in the game of power politics paid handsomely. After remaining behind the political scene for almost seven years, he came back in full force and made himself president of the republic. Upon reaching the apex of power, he assigned himself the task of the rapid and drastic transformation of Turkey into a modern state. He was determined, at all costs, to accomplish this historic mission. His iron will power, his mastery of power politics, and his dynamic policies and actions, however, were not enough to overwhelm the countervailing forces. Something was missing; whether it was prudence, tactfulness, foresight, cautiousness on his part, or apparent deficiencies in managerial skills of those politicians and administrators around him, it proved to be fatal.

Although President Celal Bayar was the titular head, though not legally the leader, of the Democratic Party and was the head of state in a multiparty democratic system, he nevertheless acted as an authoritarian leader. Every important decision of the government, in the final analysis, emanated from him. General Cemal Gürsel, who succeeded President Bayar as the head of state following the coup d'état, in his letter of May 3, 1960, addressed to the Minister of National Defense, Ethem Menderes, maintained that "there is a general conviction throughout the country that all evil emanates from him [Celal Bayar]."[18]

---

[18] For the text of this letter see Aydemir, *İkinci Adam,* vol. 3, p. 434–37. In this connection Richard D. Robinson observes: "Even high ranking Democratic Party members spoke very bitterly to the author in September 1959 against President Bayar and in off-the-record conversations blamed him for a number of the excesses for which the Party, and members in particular, were identified." *The First Turkish Republic,* p. 193.

Chapter Four
THE GUARDIANS OF THE REGIME

THE MILITARY IN THE POLITICAL ARENA

When the civilian intraelite struggle in general and the clashes of wills between Bayar and İnönü in particular, reached dangerous proportions, the officer corps of the armed forces moved in to restore law and order and to get the reforms of Atatürk back on their authentic track. They removed the Democratic Party government and instituted a number of superstructural changes in the polity.

The unanticipated outcome of these moves, however, was the beginning of yet another power struggle. These moves brought about the direct involvement of the military in the political contests for power: the clashes between the military-civilian moderates and military-civilian militants; the abortive coups d'état; the formation of coalition cabinets; the necessity of the formation of a military-civilian collective leadership; an intense controversy over democratic and authoritarian doctrines including populism, military dictatorship of the left or of the right, socialism, and, above all, "Atatürkism." In brief, the end result was extreme political instability.

However, thanks to the moderating influence, wise counsel, and courageous leadership of General Cemal Gürsel, General Cevdet Sunay, and Admiral Fahri Korutürk, who may be identified as the junior warriors of the War of Independence period, and thanks to the reluctance of the military to take over power, the extremely critical political instabilities were kept from reaching civil war proportions.

The coup d'état of May 27, 1960, was engineered by thirty-eight officers who constituted the Committee of National Unity (CNU).[1] The CNU was composed of five generals, eight colonels, seven lieutenant colonels, twelve majors, and six captains. It was headed by General Cemal Gürsel, who apparently had joined the group or was co-opted by them a few days before the coup d'état.[2]

GENERAL CEMAL GÜRSEL

Until his letter of May 3, 1960, addressed to the Minister of Defense, Ethem Menderes, protesting the maltreatment of student demonstrators by the police and the use of military troops to maintain order, General Cemal Gürsel was virtually unknown outside the armed forces. But in the army he was very well known and was referred to as *Cemal Ağa* because of his "Father Image" and the respect shown to him by the officers as well as by the enlisted men. In that letter of May 3, General Gürsel also had bitterly criticized the conduct of the Democratic Party government against its political opponents and, among other things, had called for the termination of suppressive practices by the government, the resignation of President Bayar, and the formation of a new cabinet. Such a defiance of the authority of the president and his administration had, however, led to the immediate dismissal of General Gürsel from his post as the commander of the land forces. Until May 27, General Gürsel lived in retirement in his home in İzmir. On the morning of May 27, he was flown to Ankara to become the chairman of the Committee of National Unity.

General Gürsel also assumed the position of the head of state and commander in chief of the armed forces. When the first cabinet was formed on May 30, he was designated as prime minister and Minister of National Defense. On June 9, however, he appointed General Fahri Özdilek as his Minister of National Defense.

---

[1] On June 12, 1960, the identity of the members of the Committee of National Unity was revealed. For their names as well as their military ranks see Weiker, *The Turkish Revolution,* p. 119.

[2] See Aydemir, *İkinci Adam,* vol. 3, pp. 480–81.

President Cemal Gürsel

During the most difficult days of structuring the new regime and during the months and years of instability and the feeling of anxiety which followed, General Gürsel played an important conciliatory role in the conflict of interests and clashes of personalities within the CNU and between the CNU and senior officers of the armed forces. He had to contend with the intransigent attitudes and political ambitions of the leaders of the political parties. With the backing of the moderate military officers in the CNU and in the armed forces, as will be explained later, he did not hesitate to take strong and forceful measures to eliminate intermilitary and interparty clashes and to restore common sense and some sort of stability to the political arena.

In the wake of the destruction of the monopoly of power of the Democratic Party leadership a definite power vacuum had come about which created a tantalizing opportunity for those who aspired for state power. Indeed, there were a number of contenders for political power — the military and civilian establishments in general and the military factions and political parties in particular. As of May 27, the state power in fact was in the hands of the CNU. Was it willing to relinquish that power? Its first public statement indicated an affirmative answer. It declared that "the armed forces have taken over the initiative for the purpose of extricating the parties from the irreconcilable situation into which they had fallen and for the purpose of having just and free elections, to be held as soon as possible under the supervision and authority of an above-party administration, and for handing over the administration to whichever party wins the elections."[3] This statement raised an immediate issue: What sort of above-party administration would be responsible for the conduct of just and free general elections?

In his press conference on May 28 General Gürsel already committed himself to the idea of the transfer of power to a civilian government to be installed following the general elections that were to take place within three months. He also stated that he would resign his military commission and disassociate himself from political activities.[4] He also favored the forming of a civilian cabinet, composed of nonpolitical technical experts skilled in the management of the affairs of the state, to function until the end of the general elections. On the other hand, some members of the CNU were in

---

[3] See *Cumhuriyet*, 28 Mayıs 1960, p. 1.
[4] Aydemir, *İkinci Adam*, vol. 3, p. 461.

favor of forming a caretaker cabinet composed of the membership of the CNU. The immediate issue was settled on the basis of a compromise solution in which General Gürsel was instrumental in the formation of a twenty-member cabinet, sixteen of whom were nonparty civilians. Only General Özdilek, the former martial law commander of Istanbul, General Sıtkı Ulay, and General M. I. Kızıloğlu assumed cabinet posts under the premiership of General Gürsel.

A faction within the CNU led by Colonel Alparslan Türkeş was not satisfied with the compromise solution.[5] Colonel Türkeş, his followers in the CNU, and his supporters in the armed forces were not willing to transfer power to a civilian cabinet temporarily or to a new civilian government permanently following the general elections. Instead they were demanding the establishment of a cabinet composed of the membership of the CNU and a military authoritarian regime that would retain power indefinitely, or at least until such time as radical and drastic socio-economic reforms were accomplished.

Colonel Türkeş and his supporters viewed the steps taken by the CNU in revamping the superstructure of the society as inade-

---

[5] Until the first few weeks of the May 27 coup d'état, Colonel Türkeş was known only within his immediate military circles. But since then he has achieved prominence as a right-wing extremist. He was born in Cyprus in 1917 and came to reside in Turkey at the age of fifteen. Türkeş graduated from the War College in Ankara in 1938 and began his military career. He received regular promotions and in 1957 he was appointed military attaché with the rank of colonel and joined the staff of the Turkish Embassy in Washington. Following his return to Turkey in 1958, he is reported to have taken an active part in the formation of a conspiratorial organization against the Democratic Party government. After May 27, 1960, he was appointed counselor to General Gürsel. But because of his extremist ideas he was removed from that position on September 22. On November 13, together with his thirteen other military conspirators he was summarily dismissed from the ranks of the CNU, retired from active military service, and assigned as counselor to the Turkish Embassy in New Delhi. He remained there until December 24, 1962, and upon his return to Turkey he entered the ranks of the Republican Peasant's Nation Party. In 1965, he seized control of the leadership of the party and changed its name to Nationalist Action Party. Following the 1969 general elections he was the only deputy winning the election among the candidates of his party. Colonel Türkeş is known for his super-patriotism, his nationalism, and his dedication to the principles of Kemalism and for his strong anti-Greek and anti-communist feelings. Recently he has organized a right-wing extremist commando establishment to combat leftist organizations. See Weiker, *The Turkish Revolution,* pp. 125–27; see also Ferenc A. Váli, *Bridge Across the Bosporus: The Foreign Policy of Turkey* (Baltimore: The Johns Hopkins Press, 1972), pp. 90–91.

quate and irrelevant in the face of the mounting socio-economic problems of Turkey. However, thanks to the moderating influence exercised by General Gürsel, Colonel Türkeş' militant group apparently agreed in October 1960 to go along with the suggestion of the moderate majority of the CNU with the understanding that "every effort would be made to accomplish certain reforms by October [15] 1961, the date set for the elections," and that if during the interval the necessary reforms could not be accomplished, then the CNU should "ask for a mandate from the people to stay in power for an additional four-year period."[6]

General Gürsel and other senior members of the CNU were convinced that at an opportune moment the Türkeş group would stage a coup d'état and assume the state power in order to institute an authoritarian military regime. To avert such a possibility, with the crucial support of the senior officers of the armed forces, General Gürsel dismissed Colonel Türkeş and thirteen other members of his group from the CNU.[7]

The elimination of the Türkeş group, however, did not restore the image and prestige of the CNU in the eyes of the officer corps, which by this time had begun to express doubt as to the capabilities of the CNU in realizing the objectives of the "May 27 Revolution." Neither did it resolve the issue concerning the nature of the authority of the CNU over the armed forces and the question of the efficacy of turning the government over to the civilian rule following the general elections. What later appeared to be an unwise move on the part of the CNU, the assignment of the chief of the Air Force, General İrfan Tansel, to the Turkish Military Mission in Washington in June 1961 was enough to open a definite breach between the CNU and the officer corps. General Tansel refused to relinquish his post and ordered jet fighters to fly over Ankara in defiance of the order of the CNU. Earlier, in August 1960, the CNU had by decree retired 5,000 officers, including 235 generals, from the armed forces. Apparently, certain senior officers since that time had formed

---

[6] Ergun Özbudun, *The Role of the Military in Recent Turkish Politics* (Cambridge, Mass.: Harvard University, Center for International Affairs, 1966), p. 33. See also Abdi İpekçi ve Ömer Sami Coşar, *İhtilaın İçyüzü* (İstanbul: Uygun Yayınevi, 1965), pp. 426–28; George S. Harris, "The Role of the Military in Turkish Politics," Part II, *The Middle East Journal*, 19 (Spring 1965) : pp. 169–76.

[7] See Aydemir, *İkinci Adam,* vol. 3, p. 511.

a committee called The Union of the Armed Forces. Following the decision of the CNU to transfer General Tansel to Washington, this committee sumitted an ultimatum to General Gürsel concerning the limitation of the powers of the CNU over the armed forces.[8] With the acceptance of the conditions of that ultimatum, the center of power was definitely shifted toward the senior officers of the armed forces. "On June 15 [1961] the Chief of the General Staff, General Cevdet Sunay, for the first time sat in on a meeting of the CNU, a practice which he continued frequently thereafter. Meetings between the CNU and the armed forces commanders also became frequent."[9]

By this time in the civilian sector of the political scene another competition for political power, no less intense, was in the making. In January 1961 when the CNU decreed the opening of political activity, certain opportunistic leaders appeared on the scene who, through the political parties which they formed, tried to capitalize on the bewilderment of the Democratic Party sympathizers. In addition to the Republican People's Party and the Republican Peasant's Nation Party a numer of other potential political power centers emerged: The Justice Party, the New Turkey Party, and the Turkish Labor Party.[10] These political power centers, each denouncing the others and each trying to gain the support of the voters, and each soliciting, in one way or another, the support of the military, increased the already extremely unstable political conditions.

The adoption of the 1961 Constitution added a new dimension to the interparty, intergovernmental, and intermilitary rivalries and clashes of interests. The 1961 Constitution represented a conscious effort on the part of its makers to terminate the contradiction between myth and reality in the exercise of state power. On the one hand, it sought to bring about a better working arrangement between the executive and legislative branches of the government; on the other hand it was also designed to curb any and all tendencies toward an authoritarian regime. The net results of this effort were: the abandonment of the *theory* of concentration of powers and the

---

[8] The text of the ultimatum is in Aydemir, *Ikinci Adam,* vol. 3, p. 547.

[9] Weiker, *The Turkish Revolution,* p. 137.

[10] On the Justice Party see W. B. Sherwood, "The Rise of the Justice Party in Turkey," *World Politics* 20 (October 1967): 54–65.

theoretical supremacy of the legislature over the executive, and the adoption instead of a flexible system of separation of powers and the reciprocal checks between the legislature and the executive; the designation of the members of the CNU as the representatives of the military establishment and the guardians of the new regime. This arrangement, in the final analysis, proved most conducive to a bitter power struggle not only between the two branches of the government but also between the parliament, a representative body, and the military.

And this is what actually happened. The results of the general elections of October 15, 1961, in general and the unexpected showing of the Justice Party in particular were viewed as most alarming by the CNU and by The Union of the Armed Forces. On October 21 ten generals and twenty-eight colonels, believed to have been the members of The Union of the Armed Forces, signed a protocol, calling for the setting aside of the elections, dissolving the parliament, suspending all political activities, closing all political parties and establishing a military dictatorship by October 25.[11] The contents of this protocol were brought to the attention of General Cevdet Sunay, the Chief of the General Staff, and then to the knowledge of İsmet İnönü and to General Cemal Gürsel, the head of state. On October 24 General Gürsel called a meeting at the presidential palace at Çankaya attended by the chiefs of the three armed services, the Chief of the General Staff, party leaders, and the representatives of The Union of the Armed Forces. There it was agreed that the party leaders would not at that time seek an amnesty for the Democratic Party leaders and that they would accept the candidacy of General Gürsel for the presidency of the republic. The party leaders also accepted, among other conditions, the formation of a coalition government, between the Republican People's Party and the Justice Party to be headed by İsmet İnönü.

Thus a possible coup d'état was averted. The Grand National Assembly was convened on October 26, 1961, and at a joint session of its two houses General Cemal Gürsel was elected president of the republic by a vote of 403 of the 607 members. Before this election, however, some threats and arm twisting were employed against the

---

[11] See Özbudun, *The Role of the Military in Recent Turkish Politics*, p. 34.

Justice Party candidate for the presidency, Professor Ali Fuat Başgil. The threats and pressures against Professor Başgil were so intense that in the end he not only withdrew his candidacy but also resigned his seat in the Senate of the Republic.[12]

Yet President Gürsel's problems were not over. There was still dissatisfaction with the civilian coalition cabinet even though it was headed by İsmet İnönü and with the parliament which was being effectively controlled by the Justice Party leadership. The interparty, intergovernmental struggle for power, and the military-civilian rivalry for ultimate power was still going on. The militant army officers, led by a member of The Union of the Armed Forces, Colonel Talat Aydemir, all along had misgivings about the proper working of the civilian government and the parliament, and they were awaiting an opportune time to seize power in order to carry out their plans for drastic socio-politico-economic reforms under a military regime. On February 21, 1962, Colonel Aydemir and his supporters failed in an attempt to overthrow the government. General Gürsel exhibited extreme leniency toward the conspirators. Aydemir was only removed from his post as commander of the War College and dismissed from the army without further punishment. But the coalition cabinet could not survive under the pressure of the military leadership and under the strong criticisms of the Justice Party members in parliament. It resigned on May 30, 1962. İnönü was again given the task by President Gürsel of forming the next cabinet. When İnönü informed the president that he failed in his two-week effort, President Gürsel said that he would not accept İnönü's resignation as premier-designate and that İnönü should try again. After twenty-seven days of difficult negotiations, İnönü finally succeeded in forming a coalition government, this time, composed of the Republican People's Party, the New Turkey Party, the Republican Peasant's Nation Party, and one independent politician.

Political instabilities and power struggle continued. Colonel Aydemir and his supporters, including the cadets of the War College, struck again on May 21, 1963. They failed again. This time Aydemir was brought before a military court and sentenced to death

---

12 See Aydemir, *İkinci Adam,* vol. 3, p. 544. See Ali Fuat Başgil's views on the coup d'état of May 27 and his account of the question of the presidency of the Republic, *Le Révolution militaire de 1960 en Turquie, ses origines* (Geneva: Perret-Gentil, 1963).

together with six fellow conspirators. All cadets of the War College were expelled from their school for complicity in the abortive coup d'état. The second coalition cabinet of İnönü, however, lasted only until December 3, 1963. It again took three weeks for Premier İnönü to form his next coalition cabinet. The new cabinet that was finally formed on December 25, 1963, was composed of the Republican People's Party, independent deputies, and nonparliamentarians. But on February 16, 1965, the third coalition cabinet received a vote of no confidence — the first time in the history of the Republican era — on its budget for 1965. Only after a week could a new cabinet be formed, this time between the Justice Party and three minor parties headed by independent Senator Suat Hayri Ürgüplü, to remain in office until after the general elections in October 1965.

Between 1961 and 1965 when the political situation was approaching a chaotic state of affairs, the Grand National Assembly was the scene of great excitement, activity, and shifting of alliances. Two things prolonged the lives of each of the coalition governments until October 1965: One, the military; and two, the Cyprus crisis in which the military was directly involved. Thus, the actual exercise of constitutional powers either by the Council of Ministers or by the Grand National Assembly was dependent upon the consent of the armed forces and its military leadership. For all intents and purposes the power vacuum that was created in May 1960 was filled by the military. However, in the absence of a charismatic and decisive leader, a group of leaders headed by President Cemal Gürsel exercised the effective state power.

By early 1965, the Justice Party had undergone certain changes in its orientation, outlook, and leadership. It had learned that it could not come to power without the consent of the military establishment and that it could not challenge the legitimacy of the May 27 Revolution. While seeking the release of the imprisoned leaders of the Democratic Party, the Justice Party was thus compelled to create a new image of itself among the high-ranking officers of the armed forces — an image of responsibility and moderation in the conduct of the affairs of the state. Following the death of its leader, General Ragıp Gümüşpala, in the Fall of 1964 a contest for leadership had resulted in the Justice Party. In this contest a young and enterprising engineer with moderate views, Süleyman Demirel, outpolled his conservative rival, Dr. Sadettin Bilgiç. Demirel willingly accepted the dominant role of the military in the affairs of the nation. He "curbed his right-wingers,"[13] and advocated liberal economic and political policies and displayed willingness to subscribe to the political system that was established under the 1961 Constitution.

The military leadership, on its part, permitted free elections in October 1965 which was contested by five major parties: The Republican People's Party, the Justice Party, the Nation Party, the Republican Peasant's Nation Party, and the Turkish Labor Party. The Justice Party obtained absolute majority of 53 per cent of the total vote. The Republican People's Party, on the other hand, did poorly. The military leadership tolerated the formation of a single party government by the Justice Party, giving it a chance to prove itself worthy of such a trust. Süleyman Demirel was appointed prime minister on October 27, 1965, by President Gürsel.

Under the strains and stresses of his office, when every single domestic and foreign policy issue converged and waited solution, in December 1962 President Gürsel suffered a stroke which curtailed his activities considerably. At the end of January 1966 he suffered another stroke which caused partial paralysis. This time he was flown to Washington, D.C. in February for medical treatment. Another and more serious stroke led to a coma on February 8, 1966. President Gürsel was flown back to Ankara on March 25. On the basis of a medical report of the State Board of Health, President Gürsel was declared by the Grand National Assembly on March 28, 1966, no longer capable of exercising the duties of his office. He died in Ankara on September 14, 1966.

Following the serious illness of President Gürsel, the president of the Senate, İbrahim Şevki Atasagun, a retired general, served for fifty-five days as acting president in accordance with the provisions of the Constitution. General Atasagun stepped down when General Cevdet Sunay was elected president.

GENERAL CEVDET SUNAY

The supremacy of the military over civilian government may clearly be seen in the election of General Cevdet Sunay, the Chief of the General Staff, as president to succeed Cemal Gürsel. The

---

[13] Roderic H. Davison, *Turkey* (Englewood Cliffs, N.J.: Prentice-Hall, 1968), p. 163.

armed forces informed Premier Demirel and his party that their candidate was General Sunay and that he was to be elected. General Sunay resigned his commission and was appointed by the acting president Atasagun as senator. Then in a joint session of the two houses of the Grand National Assembly, General Cevdet Sunay was elected unanimously as the fifth president of the republic on March 28, 1966.

From 1960 to 1966, General Sunay, first as the commander of the land forces and then as the Chief of the General Staff, had played a major role in the conduct of the affairs of the state and quite often had warned the civilian political leaders that if they did not cease their interparty quarrels and rivalries the military might have to take over the reins of the government completely.

The Justice Party leadership, thanks to its large popular support and its majority in the parliament, tended to dominate the Grand National Assembly. The Justice Party introduced bills that were designed to further the interests of its own constituency. On major legislation it adopted an uncompromising attitude toward the opposition, which quite often frustrated the leadership of the oppositional parties. Political clashes between the Justice Party and its opposition were intensified both within and outside of the Grand National Assembly. Yet, in dealing with those extremist elements of the counterelite who had begun to abuse their constitutional rights, the Justice Party government pursued a moderate course of action in order to avoid the fate of the defunct Democratic Party. As a result, the political conditions in the country reached the threshold of total anarchy. Even then, the Justice Party leadership disregarded the warnings of President Sunay and the military leaders. Instead, Premier Demirel asserted the supremacy of the Grand National Assembly over other state institutions in matters of public policy on the basis of the provisions of the Constitution and challenged the legality of the intervention of the military in political processes.

In order to end the presumptuousness of Premier Demirel, and in order to guard the regime against irresponsible policies and actions of political institutions, the military leaders, with the consent of President Sunay, removed the Justice Party government on March 12, 1971. Since the dismissal of the government was accomplished by way of the issuance by the military high command of a memorandum, the fall of Premier Demirel's government came to be known as the "Gentle Coup d'État." This was designed to force

President Fahri Korutürk

politicians to meet the political crisis by sinking their differences and creating a strong and respected government capable of ending the chaotic state of affairs and proceeding with "Atatürkist reforms."[14]

But only after fourteen days of intense negotiations between the military and civilian leaders could a government be formed. The new nonpartisan government was headed by a highly experienced political figure and a well-known constitutional law professor, Nihat Erim. After receiving the approval of the Grand National Assembly, the Erim government in April instituted martial law in eleven provinces. A few months later the parliament approved the constitutional amendments proposed by the government limiting some civil rights in light of the national interest and limiting the independence of universities as well as that of the press. Terrorist activities of the extreme leftists were checked by strong measures instituted by the government. However, reform legislation was pigeonholed in the parliament. On December 3, 1971, Premier Erim resigned after half of the cabinet members had quit in disagreement over the pace of reform. Premier Erim formed his second cabinet on December 11 and continued to press for the necessary reform legislation.

In a memorandum to the leadership of political parties on April 3, 1972, President Sunay asked for constitutional revision to give the government the power to rule by decree and to temporarily suspend all political activities. He accused politicians of "bad habits, and obstructionism" which delayed the passage of reform measures.[15] When the four major political parties refused, Prime Minister Erim resigned on April 17. The ensuing political crisis could only be solved when the premier-designate Ferit Melen's cabinet received a vote of confidence in the parliament on June 5, 1972. The new coalition government consisted of ministers from the National Reliance Party, the Justice Party, and the Republican People's Party. The months that followed were marked by intra-party, interparty power struggles and by further clashes between the legislative and executive branches of the government.

ADMIRAL FAHRİ KORUTÜRK

When the seven-year term of office of President Sunay was about to expire, another and more severe political crisis erupted.

---

[14] See *New York Times,* 13 March 1971, p. 1 and the editorial entitled "Self-Deception in Turkey. . . ."

[15] See *New York Times,* 4 April 1972, p. 1.

During the latter part of the 1940s and the 1950s, the struggle for the presidency had been mainly a struggle between the leaders of the Repulican People's Party and the Democratic Party. Once the general elections were won by one party, the leader of the victorious party was elected by the National Assembly in a routine manner. But in the 1960s, the fight over the presidency was not only among the leadership of the political parties but also between the political parties and the military. In the 1960s the military leaders had prevailed over their civilian rivals in parliament.

In the early months of 1973, there was a widespread anxiety within political circles and among the great majority of the members of parliament that the commanders of the armed forces, as they had done in the past, would impose their candidate for president on the Grand National Assembly, thus tarnishing irrevocably the honor and prestige of that representative institution. Their fears and suspicions were based on several facts: The military had thrown the Justice Party government out of office a short while ago; the Melen cabinet was under strong influence of and pressure by the military; eleven major provinces were under martial law which had empowered the military authorities to make wide use of their power in their campaigns against the terrorist activities of the extreme leftists and against the so-called leftist agitation and propaganda, emanating from certain political circles.

Concerning the election of the sixth president of the republic, the leaders of the major political parties and the military leaders were at loggerheads, with each faction refusing to agree to any candidate but its own. The issue, as the political leaders saw it, was whether the democratic process and the free will of the Grand National Assembly would prevail or not. The military leaders, for their part, considered the vital national interests of the country to have priority over procedural matters. As they saw it, only when the security interests of the country are guaranteed could the free will of the Grand National Assembly be meaningfully exercised.

If the fundamental issue had really been to prevent a military intervention in the presidential election, the fragmented political parties could have settled the matter by agreeing among themselves on a compromise candidate. Then the need for military interference in the political process would have been obviated.

The party leaders seemed to be united only in opposing any candidate of the armed forces, and especially General Faruk Gürler, the Chief of the General Staff. But even on this question there seemed to be wide differences of opinion within the ranks of the main oppositional party, the Republican People's Party. The leader of this party, Bülent Ecevit, speaking on behalf of his party, declared that as long as martial law remained in force his party would boycott the election. He maintained that it was unrealistic to suggest that under martial law conditions the Grand National Assembly could express its free will. Yet, Ecevit's own secretary general, Kamil Kırıkoğlu, and a group of thirty-five Republican People's Party parliamentarians seemed to disagree. As it turned out, this group not only took part in the election but also voted for General Gürler.

Ecevit's decision to boycott the election was a salvo aimed at all the candidates. Once the candidates were knocked out of the race, Ecevit was to try to postpone the election for two years, and if that did not work out, then he would introduce his own candidate. In fact, once an impasse was reached, Ecevit proposed that the term of office of President Sunay be extended until March 13, 1975, by way of a constitutional amendment. When the proposal for a constitutional amendment was defeated in the Grand National Assembly by a margin of two votes, Ecevit suggested that the Republican People's Party might end its boycott if everyone concerned agreed on the candidacy of Muhittin Taylan, the president of the Constitutional Court. But, Ecevit's new proposal fell on deaf ears. Finally, at the end of twenty-four days of controversy and bickering, the Republican People's Party leadership reversed itself and ended its boycott. The final outcome suggests that as far as the Republican People's Party leadership was concerned, the idea of the free will of the Grand National Assembly meant that without the consent of the Republican People's Party leadership there would be no new president of the republic.

The same can be said for the attitude of the Justice Party leadership. However, another factor seems to have played an important role in the strategy of the Justice Party leadership: The candidacy of General Faruk Gürler who was directly instrumental in the ouster of the Justice Party government in March 1971. Yet, prudence called for avoiding any clashes with General Gürler on a personal basis. Therefore, the Justice Party leadership camouflaged its opposition against General Gürler under the mantle of the concept of the exercise of the free will of the parliament in electing the next president. Moreover, it declared that it had an excellent candi-

President Cevdet Sunay

date of its own, namely, Tekin Arıburun, the president of the Senate.

The Justice Party votes, however, were not enough to elect its candidate as president. It needed the support of the other parties. But the other parties were determined to vote against the candidate of the majority party. In the final stages of the war game, the Justice Party proposed a number of alternative solutions to break the deadlock: To initiate new and fresh efforts to find a candidate acceptable to all concerned from among the membership of the parliament; to hold the general elections earlier than October 1973 as previously scheduled, and to postpone the presidential election until after the general elections; and to amend the Constitution so as to provide for the election of the president by the general public. In the absence of affirmative response to the last two proposals, the Justice Party renewed its efforts to find a compromise candidate.

The former right-wing dissidents of the Justice Party had been organized as the Democratic Party under the leadership of Ferruh Bozbeyli. They were determined to oppose all other candidates and vote for their own leader. True to their resolve, they cast their votes for Bozbeyli until the very end.

The Republican Reliance Party, which was formed following the merger of the National Reliance Party and the Repulican Party in March 1973, was composed of the former dissident members of the Republican People's Party. Its strategy was to follow a middle course in the power struggle, that is, to support a candidate to be nominated from among the memership of the parliament which, of course, included General Gürler since his appointment to the Senate.

Although committed in principle to the democratic ideal, the majority of the high-ranking officers of the armed forces, including the Chief of the General Staff and the commanders of armed services, had come to view the position of the Chief of the General Staff as a steppingstone to the presidency. As guardians of the legacies of Atatürk and the republic, they wished to be actively involved in public affairs so as to protect the vital national interests of Turkey. On the other hand, they were genuinely reluctant to take over power completely except as a last resort, both for the sake of Turkey's international image and because of the internal opposition to a military regime. In their opinion, the election of the Chief of the General Staff as president would not only obviate a military takeover but at the same time would help to institute a strong guarantee against irresponsible foot dragging and squabbles among politicians; it would also help to facilitate the adoption of necessary reforms in the country. They, as well as President Sunay, Prime Minister Melen, and the members of his cabinet, had hoped that General Gürler would receive enough votes in the parliament for his election.

On election day, March 13, 1973, there were then three candidates: General Faruk Gürler, who on March 5 had resigned his commission as the Chief of the General Staff and then had been appointed senator by President Sunay; Tekin Arıburun; and Ferruh Bozbeyli.

Interestingly enough, Tekin Arıburun had served as commander of the air force between 1959 and 1960 under the Celal Bayar administration. General Arıburun had been dismissed from his command post and confined at Yassıada for trial together with his wife Perihan Arıburun, a Democratic Party deputy, following the May 27, 1960 coup. In 1964 General Arıburun entered into politics and was elected to the Senate on the Justice Party ticket. As president of the Senate, General Arıburun had taken a strong stand against the ouster of Premier Demirel in March 1971. At the time of his candidacy for president, General Arıburun was sixty-eight years old.[16]

Ferruh Bozbeyli, at forty-six was the youngest and the only truly civilian candidate. He had been a Justice Party deputy from 1961 to 1970. He served as president of the National Assembly in 1965, 1967, and 1969. In 1970 he resigned from the Justice Party and subsequently formed a new political party, the Democratic Party.

The Constitution required a two-thirds majority, or 422 votes, for the election on the first and second ballots. After that, a simple majority, or 318 votes, was sufficient. The first ballot, with more than 600 parliamentarians meeting in the assembly hall, gave 149 votes to General Gürler and 293 to his opponent General Arıburun. Bozeyli had only forty-eight votes. The second ballot, like the first one, was inconclusive, producing only minor changes. The next two ballots taken the same day produced only one result, namely, a tense political impasse — an unprecedented political development in the history of the republic. It was clear, however, that General

---

[16] *Devir,* no. 23, 9 Nisan 1973, p. 19.

Gürler lacked the necessary votes to get himself elected. Shortly thereafter, both General Gürler and General Arıburun withdrew their candidacies.

For the next twenty-two days the parliament tried ten more times to elect the next president of the republic. On March 28 the term of office of President Sunay expired. He stepped down and in accordance with the constitutional provisions he joined the ranks of the upper house as senator. Simultaneously, the president of the Senate, General Arıburun, again in accordance with the provisions of the Constitution, assumed the position of the acting president of the republic.

Meanwhile, top military commanders urged the leaders of the political parties that they should end this critical state of affairs by electing an independent parliamentarian soon. Otherwise, they were warned, according to press reports, it would be difficult to stem discontent and restlessness in the armed forces. Realizing the seriousness of the situation, the leaders of the major parties renewed their efforts to agree on a compromise candidate.

In the end, the Justice Party, the Republican People's Party, and the Republican Reliance Party leaders reached an agreement on the candidacy of Senator Fahri Korutürk. Candidate Korutürk also received the approval of the military leaders.

A career naval officer, Korutürk had been promoted to admiral in 1957 and served as the commander of the navy from 1957 to May 27, 1960. Upon his retirement from his post, he was appointed ambassador to Moscow by the head of state, General Cemal Gürsel. When he was transferred to Madrid, Admiral Korutürk refused to accept his second ambassadorial post and retired in 1964. Four years later Admiral Korutürk was appointed senator by President Sunay. At the time of his nomination for president, Admiral Korutürk was serving as the spokesman for the fifteen presidential-appointees in the Senate.

The seventy-year-old Senator Korutürk was regarded as an honest and courageous military figure as well as an astute soldier-statesman, and as such he was highly respected within military and political circles. An Associated Press dispatch from Ankara identified Admiral Korutürk as "the perfect compromise candidate for leaders of Turkey's 'military democracy'." The report went on to say: "He is known as a moderate and has scrupulously avoided affiliation or close ties with any party, making him acceptable 'or at least equally unacceptable to all,' as one senator said."[17]

The fifteenth and final ballot was taken on April 6, 1973, in the Grand National Assembly. At the time some twenty-five top generals, including the Chief of the General Staff, Semih Sancar, and the commanders of land forces, navy, and air force were present in the assembly hall. Senator Korutürk received 365 votes and thus was elected as the sixth president of the republic. As for the former candidates, General Gürler received 87 votes, Bozbeyli 56, and General Arıburun 17.[18]

The election of Admiral Korutürk was hailed as a victory for both the Grand National Assembly and the guardians of the Republican regime. Although the latter had applied pressure on the political leaders in parliament, they had shown patience and prudence and had acted wisely. Their rational judgments prevailed over their emotions and they resisted the temptation to move in even when the political leaders dragged their feet and entered into prolonged bargaining sessions. The political leaders had successfully withstood the pressure and refused to permit overt interference by the military in the political processes. Nevertheless, their resolve was also tempered with cautious wisdom, moderation, and pragmatic considerations. By selecting an admiral with a distinguished military record, they averted the necessity for the military leaders to test their dedication to the preservation of "Turkish democracy."[19]

In taking the oath of office, President Korutürk pledged to guard the Constitution, Turkish independence, Turkish democracy, and to remain neutral, with all his strength. In a brief statement afterward, President Korutürk said that he would do his best to carry out his task with the cooperation of the parliament, the nation, and the institutions of state — an indirect reference to the military establishment. He added that his oath would be his guide in carrying out his duties.[20]

October 29, 1973, would mark the fiftieth anniversary of the founding of the Republic of Turkey. President Korutürk took over

[17] *Lubbock Avalanche-Journal,* 7 April 1973, p. 2. See also *New York Times,* 7 April 1973, p. 3.

[18] *Devir,* no. 26, 16 Nisan 1973, p. 11.

[19] *Middle East Intelligence Survey,* April 15, 1973, p. 16.

[20] *Devir,* no. 26, 16 Nisan 1973, p. 11.

the helm of the Turkish ship of state which had nearly run aground through the discord and dissension among the officers and crew. Admiral Korutürk assumed the command of the ship with determination to make it seaworthy. He accepted the resignation of Premier Melen and on April 15 appointed Naim Talu as Prime Minister. Talu was an independent senator who had served in the previous two cabinets as Minister of Commerce. Talu formed a caretaker coalition cabinet to remain in office until the results of the October 1973 general elections were in.

Premier Talu, after receiving a vote of confidence, secured parliamentary approval of a number of measures favored by the military. These included the establishment of state security courts, a greater degree of governmental control over universities, and an agricultural reform law.

President Korutürk, presiding over the Supreme Military Council, made a number of changes in the high command of the armed forces with a view of removing a few "activist" generals, including the commander of the air force, Muhsin Batur, who had been the only remaining commander on active duty of the four commanders who caused the ouster of Premier Demirel. President Korutürk was also able to defuse the emotionally-charged and intense political struggle among the politicians during the longest governmental crisis in the Turkish history which followed the general elections.

The October 14 general elections resulted in a political stalemate. The right-wing votes were split three ways among the Justice Party, the National Salvation Party, and the Democratic Party. The centrist Republican Reliance Party was also badly hurt. The left-of-center Republican People's Party had pulled far ahead with a plurality that nevertheless was short of an absolute majority. Under these circumstances a coalition government had to be formed. On October 27 President Korutürk entrusted the formation of the new government to Bülent Ecevit, the leader of the Republican People's Party. But, Ecevit's efforts to form a coalition with the National Salvation Party, a religious conservative party, came to nothing. Subsequent efforts by Demirel and Talu also failed. Then, Ecevit was asked a second time to try to form the new government. After ten days of intensive efforts and bargaining which were closely watched by Korutürk, Ecevit succeeded in bringing the leadership of the National Salvation Party into a coalition. This was a strange alliance between two parties that were committed to opposite goals and policies. The Republican People's Party, founded by Atatürk, under Ecevit's leadership stands for technological and scientific progress, westernization, secularism, and economic and social reforms in the infrastructure of the society, whereas its coalition partner, founded only in 1972, stands for religious revival and restoration of the traditional institutions and a return to the old way of life. President Korutürk not only helped these two parties to form a coalition but also helped them to reach a compromise by dropping a number of their campaign promises or postponing pet ideas and schemes. He was thus able to end the eighty-two-day-long government crisis on January 25, 1974.

A Second Atatürk

At this point an assessment of the political power struggle in Turkey is in order. During the authoritarian regimes of Atatürk and İnönü, overt and forceful opposition against them was a practical impossibility. However, once the dictatorial regime of President İnönü was liberalized in the latter part of the 1940s, the personal rivalries of prominent political personalities gave way to bitter contests for political power. These contests first led to the defeat of İnönü at the polls in 1950 and then led to the violent overthrow of Bayar and his administration in 1960.

The 1960s were marked by further liberalization of the political system which facilitated the expansion of the elite and the rising of expectations of the general public as well as that of the enlarged elite class. Most important of all, however, the period since 1960 has been marked by the absence of a leader like Atatürk who could handle effectively the ever-increasing socio-politico-economic problems. There was a definite power vacuum. There were a number of aspirants, but no one could rest his claim to the state power on his personal spectacular accomplishment. Instead, the struggle for power was waged in the name of the parliament, the military, and the general public. In this struggle, particularly in the latter part of the 1960s, not only was the number of combatants increased but the area was expanded to include the city streets and the rural areas.

It is interesting to note that all three presidents of the republic since 1960 were moderate military leaders who, prior to their election to the presidency, had had no political experience. They had been co-opted by the military or military-civilian leaders.

As presidents of the republic, General Gürsel, General Sunay, and Admiral Korutürk have demonstrated a strong determination to prevent the domination of the political arena by any extremist elements that could emerge from among the ranks of the military and political elites. They were also able to maintain the instabilities of the Turkish polity within tolerable limits. But they seemed to be unable to exhibit the qualities of a charismatic leader like Atatürk.

II

Foreign and Domestic Policy Goals

> *"Only those who possess power can claim humane, just, and generous treatment."*
>
> ATATÜRK

Chapter Five

INTRODUCTION

At the height of its power, the Ottoman Empire had a direct influence in the shaping of the international system and structure. However, by the time the West was awakened under the impact of the Renaissance and Reformation, compartmentalized as it was into nation-states though unified in purpose, it managed to check the Ottoman conquest of Europe and in turn launched an unceasing campaign against the Ottomans that was to last for almost two and a half centuries.

Unlike the nation-states of the West, the Ottoman Empire was basically a heterogeneous and religious polity. The masters of the empire, the Turks, constituting a small minority, had sunk their separate identity in the Islamic community and in the Ottoman dynasty. They had retained but few memories of their pre-Islamic past. Only during the latter part of the nineteenth century did they begin to recall their Turkish identity. But by that time their empire was in the final stages of its decline. The empire was weakened from within by the *Millet* system and by administrative and political corruption. It was also weakened by the capitulatory privileges that were granted to foreign powers. In terms of military power, science, and technology, it was far behind the European powers. The heads of the Ottoman Empire, sultan-caliphs, and the military establishment, the Janissary order, had lost their warrior spirit and thus were hopelessly at the mercy of foreign powers.

Sultan Selim II, Mahmut II, and Abdülmecit had introduced a series of reform measures which were designed to transform the superstructure of the state from the sultan's household to a modern state and thus solve the dilemma of security and survival brought about by the repeated military defeats at the hands of European powers. However, the reforms of the nineteenth century did not bring about an appreciable modernization of the state, nor relief from foreign threats and pressures. The reform movement of the nineteenth cenutry, known as the *Tanzimat,* according to Davison "represented the views of a small bureaucratic and intellectual elite, and not even all that elite." Because of its coming from the top down, Davison argues, it was "less likely to achieve success than reform that has vigorous popular supports." He maintains that the *Tanzimat,* which changed only the external forms and not the substance, was also "backward." "For instance," he says, "the parliamentary procedure was introduced into the central government in the Supreme Council in 1839, the principle of representation in the same body in 1856, but actual election of representatives — and then only indirect — first with the Constitution of 1876."[1] Even after the *Tanzimat,* the central government was unable to forge a viable political order; neither could it prevent further defeats, this time at the hands of the formerly subject peoples of the Balkans. Only the skillful diplomacy of the Ottoman statesmen and the balance of power system of Europe could help to sustain the life of the empire until 1914.

But, then, the grandiose political and military schemes of the leadership of the Committee of Union and Progress gave way to the crushing defeat of the Ottoman Empire in the First World War. The Allied Powers, particularly Great Britain, were resolved to destroy the Ottoman Empire first through the armistice agreement of October 30, 1918,[2] and later through the Peace Treaty of Sèvres of August 10, 1920. Soon after the signing of the armistice agreement, the Allied forces began to occupy the capital as well as the various Anatolian provinces of Turkey in order to implement the secret wartime agreements among themselves.[3]

---

[1] Roderic H. Davison, *Reform in the Ottoman Empire, 1856–1876* (Princeton, N.J.: Princeton University Press, 1963), p. 406.

[2] For a detailed study of the armistice negotiations, see Ali Türkgeldi, *Moudros ve Mudanya Mütarekelerinin Tarihi* (Ankara: Güney Matbaacılık, 1948). Türkgeldi was the secretary of the Ottoman delegation.

[3] See Metin Tamkoç, "Allied Occupations of the Ottoman Empire Following the Armistice of Mudros of October 30, 1918." (Ph.D. diss. Georgetown University, 1960).

However, at the time, a group of young Turkish military officers, led by Mustafa Kemal Pasha, were preparing plans for saving their motherland from dismemberment and annexation. These young warriors were convinced that in view of the limited military capabilities of the Turks living in Anatolia and in eastern Thrace, they could not restore the sovereignty of the Ottoman Empire in territories inhabited by the Arabs and occupied by the Allied Powers. Therefore, they strove toward and succeeded in awakening the nascent nationalism of the Turks. Simultaneously they called the Turks to arms and launched the Turkish War of Independence with a view to creating a small but culturally and politically homogenous nation-state. In the end, the defeat of the Ottoman Empire, as far as the Turks were concerned, was turned into a solid victory which sealed the right of the Turks to soverign, independent existence.

The Turkish warriors made a second successful transition of the Ottoman polity from a theocratic and heterogeneous empire into a Turkish nation-state whose political system was based on the theory of constitutional democracy. The first phase of the Turkish revolution — the creation of an independent state — was an unqualified success. But there remained the equally difficult task of assuring the progressive development and modernization of the Republic of Turkey, the second phase of the Turkish revolution.

Although Davison's observations, previously quoted, concern the *Tanzimat* period, they also seem to be quite valid for the Republican period. The transformation of the Turkish polity during the Republican era, on the whole, reflected the political beliefs of the ultimate decision makers and their principal advisers, the governing elite. Secondly, the governing elite paid greater attention to superstructural rather than infrastructural changes. Thirdly, they were primarily concerned with the outer form rather than with the substance of the politico-economic organization of the polity. As a result, particularly during the last two decades when democratic and authoritarian systems were transposed, the Turkish polity was very nearly shaken to its foundations.

The modernization of the society was viewed by Kemal Atatürk as a matter of utmost importance for the national security objective as well as a significant end in itself. Thus, national security and the need to bring Turkey to the level of contemporary civilization were set by him as inseparable twin goals of the Republican regime. However, the presidents of the republic have displayed greater commitment to the problems of foreign policy in general and to the questions of national security in particular than to the issues of the rapid and drastic socio-economic changes in the society.

Chapter Six
PRIMACY OF FOREIGN OVER
DOMESTIC POLICIES

The primacy of foreign over domestic policies may be attributed to three important factors: The tradition of mostly warlike contacts with foreign peoples and states on the part of the Turks; the geopolitical position of Turkey; and the military background of the Turkish leaders.

First, the Turks as a people have always been on the move. They moved from the steppes of central Asia in search of new frontiers, settled in the Middle East, and then moved to central Europe. They have been in contact and inevitably at war with foreign peoples for centuries. They have borrowed extensively from foreign cultures and civilizations and, in turn, they have left the imprints of their political, military, administrative, and legal systems in the conquered lands. Although in the twentieth century the Turks lost their empire, once one of the greatest in history, and reconciled themselves to the fact that theirs was now a small state, they nevertheless aspired to achieve greatness in terms of political and economic status. They wished to be considered an equal partner of the modern nations of the West.

Secondly, a small country like Turkey, located at the crossroads of international politics and in an area of the world where western and eastern ways of life and interest overlap and where constant crosscurrents of violent upheavals and wars have shaped the destinies of the people, could not isolate itself from the external arena. Moreover, the Turkish leaders were aware of the fact that the international system and structure in general and the powerful states in particular influence the foreign and domestic policy orientations of small states and that the more cohesive and centralized an international structure, the less latitude of choice remains for the weaker states.[1] The geopolitical position of Turkey, particularly her proximity to the Soviet Union and the presence of great sea powers in the Middle East region, made it absolutely essential for the Turkish warrior diplomats to try to minimize the impact of the international system and structure and the influence of the powerful states upon their foreign and domestic policies and to try to pursue an independent course in international affairs.

Thirdly the leaders of Turkey were professional soldiers, warriors, whose military background and experiences obliged them to keep a vigilant eye on Turkey's frontiers and beyond, to keep up with the policies, actions, and capabilities of foreign powers, to engage in constant re-evaluation of the international developments so as to devise the necessary and right strategies and tactics. As members of the military establishment, they represented the most modern segment of the society which was to draw the rest of the people toward the modern way of life. The Turkish warrior diplomats were much more successful in external rather than in internal affairs, even though the latter were naturally much more familiar to them and the former entailed much greater risks and uncertainties. It seems as though their successes in foreign affairs reinforced their commitment to matters of foreign policy.

It is generally recognized that in times of national emergency and external danger national leaders concentrate their energies and efforts on matters of foreign policy and attribute secondary importance to domestic issues, unless the latter seem to have direct bearing on the question of national security. This proposition is no less true for the Turkish leaders. In fact, the Turkish leaders, since the beginning of the twentieth century, except for very brief periods of tranquility and peace, have been in the midst of constant national emergencies and great political upheavals. They had to mobilize the human and material resources of the country and conduct military operations in order to protect and preserve the territorial integrity and independence of their country in the Balkan Wars, in the First

---

[1] On this concept see K. J. Holsti, *International Politics: A Framework for Analysis,* 2nd. ed. (Englewood Cliffs, N.J.: Prentice-Hall, 1972), p. 354.

World War, and in the War of Independence. Then they had to face the threats posed to Turkey's national security by the revisionist great powers during the 1930s; this was followed by the Second World War, taking place in the immediate vicinity of the Turkish borders. And then, they had to find solutions to the questions of national security and survival in the face of the threatening gestures of the Soviet Union. Under these circumstances the Turkish leaders could not help focusing their attention on foreign policy questions.

In this connection the following developments may be noted. During the War of Independence period, the nationalist leader Mustafa Kemal wisely decided to postpone the settlement of such domestic questions as the legal status of the sultan-caliph and his government in Istanbul, the authority of the caliph over the Moslem population of Turkey, and the question of the legitimacy of the new regime in Ankara. With a view to achieving unity of purpose against the external and internal opponents, Mustafa Kemal also appeared to remain loyal to the sultan-caliph and to the traditional political and religious institutions.

The new regime in Ankara, in fact, acquired legitimacy and permanancy only after the decisive military victories of the national-ist forces. The territorial limits of new Turkey and the nature and extent of her sovereignty were first determined on the battlefields. On the basis of his realistic assessment of the actual capabilities of new Turkey and of the policies and powers of Turkey's foes and friends, Mustafa Kemal agreed, under the provisions of the Lausanne Peace Treaty, to make certain concessions to the Allied Powers which had important domestic implications. For instance, Turkey's claims over the Mosul and Hatay regions were left unde-cided. Turkey's sovereignty over the Turkish Straits was limited because of the internationalization and demilitarization of the Dardanelles and Bosporus. The legal and educational systems of new Turkey were also subjected to certain restrictions. The question of the legal status of the foreign-owned and foreign-operated industrial-commercial enterprises, and communication and trans-portation systems was left unsettled. During his presidency, Mustafa Kemal Atatürk was preoccupied with these questions as well as with the question of creating new bases for friendly relations with the old enemies.

It is important to note also that the internal reforms introduced by Atatürk were primarily designed: to create a strong and modern state which without external assistance could defend its territorial integrity and political independence against external aggression; and to make Turkey a full-fledged member of the western European community of nations on an equal basis. These two foreign policy objectives seemed to have occupied the minds of Atatürk as well as all the succeeding presidents.

Until quite recently the Turkish intelligentsia, the counterelite in particular, had raised no objection to the fact that the governmental leaders were preoccupied with the questions of foreign policy. However, during the latter part of the 1960s, once threats to Turkey's national security seemed to dissipate and once international tension seemed to be relaxed, their attention was focused more and more on domestic matters and domestic consequences of foreign policy commitments. They argued that excessive outside influence in foreign policy matters had led to similar interference in domestic economic, social, and political policies, the end result being the gradual surrendering of the right to formulate and execute domestic policies and programs. They also questioned the wisdom of the maintenance of close ties with NATO and the United States, which, according to their view, paved the way for the foreign influence on domestic policies of Turkey.

It is hardly conceivable that the Turkish warrior diplomats should be willing to trade Turkey's independence and sovereignty for joining the western alliance system. It may be, on the other hand, that theTurkish warrior diplomats, as realistic practitioners of power politics, were willing to tolerate some outside influence on domestic policies without, however, relinquishing their right to make independent foreign and domestic policy decisions.

Concerning the impact of the international system and the influence of foreign powers on internal policies of small powers like Turkey, first, it may be said that the very nature of the political system of Turkey between 1920 and 1923 and the Atatürk regime were the necessary corollaries of the international principle of national self-determination. Second, the transformation of Turkey from a "one-party dictatorship" or a "constitutional democracy" into something resembling a "multiparty parliamentary democracy" was not unrelated to President İnönü's strong commitment to the goal of making Turkey an equal member of the western community of democratic nations. Third, strong criticism of the foreign policy of governments was raised only four or five years after the adoption of the ultrademocratic Constitution of 1961 which coincided with the relaxation of international tension and the diminishing of the threats to Turkey's national security. And finally when such strong criticisms, compounded by the subversive activities of the leftist extremists, began to be viewed by the governmental leaders as constituting dangerous threats to national security, the top military leaders took stern measures to suppress irresponsible opposition. This point will be elaborated upon later. It suffices here to note that foreign policy considerations of the warrior diplomats have had direct influence on domestic political developments.

Chapter Seven

THE NATIONALIST ORGANIZATION
AND THE ESTABLISHMENT
OF THE REPUBLIC

When Mustafa Kemal set foot in Anatolia at Samsun on May 19, 1919, there were certain local resistance movements created by a cross section of the local elite under the name of "Association for the Defense of Rights" of various provinces such as İzmir, Trabzon, Diyarbakır, Erzurum, etc. These local resistance movements had sprung up on the basis of the assumption that the dismemberment of the Ottoman Empire was imminent and that before that eventuality occurred it was better to save what was worth saving. Initially they tried to remind the Allied Powers' representatives that their regions were geographically, historically, and demographically Ottoman and Moslem and that these regions should not be taken away by non-Moslem minority groups or annexed by other states. But when these modest claims remained unheeded, in the face of the armed invasion of İzmir by the Greek army and in the face of the forceful attempt to create an Armenian state by the French occupational forces in southeastern Anatolia, the local resistance movements resolved to defend their legitimate rights through guerrilla activities conducted by their "national militia forces."

Mustafa Kemal, Rauf Bey, Ali Fuat Pasha, Kazım Karabekir Pasha, and Colonel Refet considered it imperative to coordinate the sporadic and as yet disorganized resistance movements and to transform them into a regular nationalist fighting force under the supervision, direction, and control of a political organization. With the exception of Karabekir Pasha, they met secretly at Amasya on June 21, 1919, and prepared a circular calling for the centralization of the resistance movement and the convening of a national congress at Sivas which would take charge of the destiny of the nation. Eroğlu maintains that this circular, which was sent in cipher to civil and military authorities in Anatolia, was tantamount to a "declaration of revolution" and that it signaled the "commencement of the Anatolian Revolution."[1]

Meanwhile the Erzurum branch of the Association for the Defense of Rights of the Eastern Provinces was to convene a congress upon the call of Karabekir Pasha on July 10. The organizing committee invited Mustafa Kemal to assume the presidency of the executive committee of the association. Due to the difficulties encountered in getting together a sufficient number of delegates, the congress was not convened until July 23 with fifty-four delegates.[2] At its first session, Mustafa Kemal was elected president of the congress despite some opposition. At the time, he was no longer holding a military position; he had been dismissed by the Ottoman government from his position as the inspector general of the Ninth Army and he himself simultaneously had resigned his duties and his commission in the army on July 8.

After prolonged discussions and debate, the congress adopted the following important principles: (1) the foreign occupation of the eastern provinces would be resisted; (2) the defense of the Ottoman Empire and the caliphate constituted the fundamental objective; (3) in the event of the Ottoman government being obliged to cede some of the provinces under a peace treaty, a provisional government would immediately be proclaimed in the eastern provinces so that at a later date these provinces might be brought into the confines of the empire; in the event of the creation of such a provisional and autonomous government, this fact would be communicated to all foreign powers and an administrative commission would assume the task of convening a general congress which would

---

[1] Hamza Eroğlu, *Türk Devrimi Tarihi* (Ankara: Kardeş Matbaası, 1967), p. 59.

[2] See Cevat Dursunoğlu, *Erzurum Kongresi Sırasında Atatürk'ün Düşünceleri* (Ankara: Türk Tarih Kurumu Basımevi, 1967), pp. 247–48; see also *Atatürk'ün Söylev ve Demeçleri* (Ankara: Türk Tarih Kurumu Basımevi, 1961), pp. 3–7. For the names of the delegates attending this congress see *Cumhuriyet*, 23 July, 1967, p. 5.

take the necessary steps for the establishment of a definite governmental machinery; (4) the return of the Greek and Armenian emmigrants to the eastern provinces was to be prohibited; (5) no mandate or protection of a foreign power should be accepted.[3]

On August 8 a special committee of the Congress prepared a twelve-page booklet describing the nature of the organization to be created. It also contained the principles adopted by the Congress. The booklet was to be distributed to civil and military authorities throughout the eastern provinces.[4] It contained the following information with respect to the early organization of the Nationalist Movement: All political parties and associations hitherto established would be unified under the name of the Association for the Defense of the Rights of Eastern Anatolia. All Moslems would be natural members of this association. Each province and its subdivision would have its branch organizations. In each province a representative committee and an administrative committee would be elected. Each subdivision of provinces would have its own representative and administrative committees. On July 23 of each year, a General Congress would be convened at a place to be decided upon by the Representative Committee of the Congress after consultation with the administrative committees of provinces, to be attended by delegates from each administrative committee of each province. The General Congress would be empowered to review the decisions and actions of the Representative Committee of the Congress and would adopt policy decisions and direct the activities of the Representative Committee. All decisions of the General Congress would be final and as such had to be accepted by the people. The Representative Committee of the General Congress would be elected from among its membership or from outside and would be composed of at least nine memers, but not to exceed sixteen. One member of the Representative Committee of the General Congress would be elected as its president. The Representative Committee of the General Congress would be authorized to take all necessary measures to protect

---

[3] See Atatürk, *Speech,* p. 50; for a general review of the proceedings of the Congress see Cevat Dursunoğlu, *Milli Mücadelede Erzurum* (Ankara: Ziraat Bankası Matbaası, 1946).

[4] For the original and English translations of this booklet, which apparently was also obtained by the British authorities, see Great Britain, Foreign Office, 371, Political, Turkey, File 521/136062.

the country and to make all necessary decisions affecting the destiny of the empire.

Although this booklet does not identify its author or authors, there is no doubt that it was written by Mustafa Kemal. It contains, in no uncertain terms, the ideas Mustafa Kemal held concerning the need for the establishment of a permanent legislative body and an executive organ. In this respect the contents of this booklet may be considered as the provisional Constitution of the Nationalist Movement which was replaced by the provisional Constitution of 1921 of the regime of the Grand National Assembly of Turkey.

Before its adjournment on August 7, the Erzurum Congress elected a Representative Committee headed by Mustafa Kemal to act in the interim of the prospective annual meetings of the General Congress. Other members of the committee included: Rauf Bey; Raif Efendi, ex-deputy of Erzurum; İzzet Bey, ex-deputy of Trabzon; Servet Bey, ex-deputy of Trabzon; Fevzi Efendi, the Sheyh of the Order of Naksibend of Erzincan; Bekir Sami Bey, ex-governor of Beirut who joined the committee later at the Sivas Congress; Sadullah Efendi, ex-deputy of Bitlis; and Hacı Musa Bey, chief of the Mukti tribe.[5]

Following the preliminary deliberations of the Erzurum Congress, Mustafa Kemal was busy trying to extend the roots of the Nationalist Movement. In order to prepare the groundwork of the Sivas Congress, he left Erzurum on August 29 and arrived at Sivas on September 2. Two days later the Sivas Congress was opened in a classroom of the Sivas High School building. Although some 200 delegates were expected only thirty-six showed up. This means that at that time only a handful of people had any real faith in the success of "the National Struggle," any real hope of the ascent of the phoenix!

Of these thirty-six delegates, six represented Istanbul; three delegates had come from Denizli, Eskişehir, and Kayseri respectively; Afyon, Samsun, Bursa, Çorum and Niğde were represented by two delegates each; and one delegate had come from each of the following provinces: Alaşehir, Erzurum, Erzincan, Hakkari, Kastamonu, Nevşehir, Saruhan, Tokat, and Yozgat. The origin of two delegates is not known. Seven of these delegates were military officers, four businessmen, three religious leaders, two ex-deputies,

---

[5] See Aydemir, *Tek Adam,* vol. 2, pp. 114–15.

two ex-governors, two university students, a mayor, a lawyer, a teacher, a civil servant, and a tribal leader. Of these thirty-six delegates the professions of eleven are not identified in the available sources.[6] Of the nine members of the Representative Committee of the Erzurum Congress only Mustafa Kemal, Rauf Bey, Raif Efendi, and Fevzi Efendi had come to take part in the Sivas Congress.

Despite some strong opposition to his candidacy, Mustafa Kemal was elected president of the Congress. And after prolonged deliberations and debate, the Congress issued a declaration on September 11 which called for: (1) a firm stand on the territorial integrity of the Ottoman Empire as defined under the terms of the Armistice of Mudros; (2) preservation of national independence and to that end the deployment of the national forces; (3) opposition to the formation of an independent Armenia or independent parts of Greece in western Anatolia; (4) discontinuance of privileges of non-Moslems; (5) safeguarding the sultanate-caliphate by all necessary means; (6) a meeting of the Ottoman parliament to take action in safeguarding the interests of the nation; (7) the recognition of the legitimacy of theAssociation for the Defense of the Rights of Anatolia and Rumelia; (8) the prosecution of the national cause by the Representative Committee of the Association.[7]

The decisions of the Congress were to be put into effect by a Representative Committee again headed by Mustafa Kemal. The Congress added six new members to the committee elected by the Erzurum Congress. There appeared to be conflicting reports, however, as to the composition of the new Representative Committee. Mustafa Kemal did not disclose the list of the members of the committee, probably because he did not really believe in the efficacy of such a collective body other than its propaganda value as having an ostensibly representative character. In his memoirs, Rauf Bey is quoted as naming the following as members of the committee: Mustafa Kemal; Rauf Bey; Colonel Refet; Raif Efendi, ex-deputy of Erzurum; İzzet Bey, ex-deputy of Trabzon; Servet Bey, ex-deputy of Trabzon; Fevzi Efendi, the Sheyh of the Order of Naksibend of Erzincan; Bekir Sami Bey, ex-governor of Beirut; Mazhar Müfit,

---

[6] For the list compiled by Vehbi Cem Aşkun see his *Sivas Kongresi* (Istanbul: İnkilâp Kitapevi, 1963), pp. 148–49.

[7] See Sabahattin Selek, *Anadolu İhtilali* (Istanbul: Istanbul Matbassı, 1963–1965), vol. 1, p. 240. For the text of the Sivas declaration see U.S. Congress, 66th Cong., 2nd Sess., Senate, Document No. 266, Exhibit E, pp. 38–39.

ex-governor; Ömer Mümtaz, ex-deputy of Ankara; Hakkı Behiç, ex-governor; Hüsrev Sami and Ratıpzade Mustafa.[8] In the list of another writer, the name of Colonel Refet is replaced by Kara Vasıf Bey; also excluded are the names of İzzet, Servet, Sadullah, and Hacı Musa who are reported as being members of the committee selected by the Erzurum Congress.[9] Aydemir, in addition, mentions the names of Süreyya (Yigit) Bey and Alfred Rüstem.[10] The latter is identified by a British intelligence agent as "a well-known renegade of Polish extraction, who crowned a disreputable career by becoming a Turkish ambassador in Washington, having quit that post at the request of the United States Government."[11] The same source describes Bekir Sami Bey, who was to be appointed as the first Minister of Foreign Affairs of the Ankara government, as "a Circassian who has held high administrative posts," and goes on to say that "he was presumably called in to give an air of Constantinopolitan respectability to the movement which might otherwise suffer the reproach of being the creation of swashbuckling adventurers."[12]

Be that as it may, the Representative Committee was in fact a one-man government of Mustafa Kemal who at times consulted with his close friends such as Rauf Bey, Ali Fuat Pasha, Karabekir Pasha, and Colonel Refet. The committee never functioned as a collective body. Roughly half of its members returned to their hometowns following the closing of the Sivas Congress. It was Mustafa Kemal who communicated with the civil and military officials in Anatolia, with the Ottoman Government in Istanbul, and with the foreign powers and their representatives in Turkey. He signed these communications using the title "President of the Representative Committee" to preserve the fiction that they were issued by a representative body.[13] Mustafa Kemal later revealed his

---

[8] Rauf Orbay, "Rauf Orbay'ın Hatıraları" *Yakın Tarihimiz* 3, no. 31 (27 Eylül 1962): 148.

[9] Aşkun, *Sivas Kongresi,* p. 149.

[10] Aydemir, *Tek Adam,* vol. 2, p. 201.

[11] Great Britain, Foreign Office, 371, Political, File 521/146626. His name is shown as Ahmed Rüstem Paşa by Hamit Aral in his *Dışişleri Bakanlığı 1967 Yıllığı* (Ankara: Ankara Basım ve Ciltevi, 1968), p. 943. Aral states that Ahmed Rüstem Paşa served as ambassador of Turkey in Washington from May 22, 1914, to October 4, 1914.

[12] Great Britain, Foreign Office, 371, Political, File 521/146626.

[13] See Lord Kinross, *Ataturk,* p. 224.

misgivings that he held during and after the Erzurum Congress about the advisability of relying on a collective body like the Representative Committee for the management and direction of the Nationalist Movement. He said: "I admit that I had no confidence in the ability of any representative body to carry through the principles and decisions . . . that were adopted by the [Erzurum] Congress."[14]

When the Representative Committee transferred its center from Sivas to Ankara on December 27, 1919, few of its members accompanied Mustafa Kemal. These included Rauf Bey, Mazhar Müfit Bey, Süreyya Bey, Hakkı Behiç Bey, and the immediate staff: Rüstem Bey, Cevat Abbas, Hüsrev Bey, and Dr. Refik.

It is reported that when Mustafa Kemal and other members of the committee set out from Erzurum to Sivas they had only 100 Turkish liras among them, but a retired major donated his lifetime savings of 900 TL to the Representative Committee. This money was given to Mustafa Kemal to cover their travelling expenses and the expenses of the Sivas Congress.[15] In this respect it is also interesting to note that when the members of the Representative Committee set out to go to Ankara from Sivas they had only enough money to purchase twenty eggs, one kilo of cheese, and ten loaves of bread.[16] This may be an exaggeration of the meagerness of the material resources of the nationalist leaders. However, it dramatizes their resolve to overcome the almost insurmountable difficulties that were to confront them.

Among numerous difficulties, the hostility of the Istanbul government toward the nationalist leaders deserves special attention. Mustafa Kemal thought that by establishing communication and contact with the government in Istanbul he could convince it of the legitimacy of his cause which in turn could enhance his power and prestige in the eyes of those whom he identified as reactionary conservatives and in the eyes of the general public. Thus, following the resignation of Damat Ferid Pasha's cabinet, the arch enemy of the nationalists, and the appointment of Ali Rıza Pasha as Grand Vezir, contact was established between Istanbul and Mustafa Kemal, which led to a meeting for three days between him and a group of representatives of the Istanbul government headed by Min-

---

[14] Atatürk, *Speech,* p. 53.
[15] Aydemir, *Tek Adam,* vol. 2, p. 113.
[16] Aşkun, *Sivas Kongresi,* p. 137.

ister of Marines Salih Pasha from October 20 to 22, 1919, at Amasya. During these negotiations the following agreements were made: (1) the provinces inhabited by Turks shall not be ceded to enemies under any condition; (2) that no mandate or protectorate shall be accepted; (3) that no privileges shall be granted to non-Moslems; (4) that the Istanbul government shall recognize the legality and legitimacy of the Association for the Defense of the Rights of Anatolia and Rumelia; (5) that only those delegates approved by the Representative Committee shall be sent to the peace conference; (6) that the impending session of the Ottoman Parliament shall not be opened in Istanbul.[17] This agreement, called the Amasaya Protocol, was a clear-cut political victory for Mustafa Kemal over his rivals in Istanbul. It left no doubt as to the legitimacy of the National Struggle and as to who was to determine from then onward the destiny of the nation.

Following the general elections, resulting with the victory of the nationalist candidates, the last Ottoman Parliament convened in Istanbul on January 12, 1920, because the Istanbul government chose to violate the last provision of the Amasya Protocol. On January 28, the principles proclaimed in the Sivas Declaration, which came to be known as the National Pact, were adopted by the Chamber of Deputies.[18] This was another victory for the nationalists in Anatolia, particularly a victory for Mustafa Kemal.

The National Pact was an instrument of ratification of the declaration of independence of the Turks in Anatolia. Its historical importance does not lie so much in the specific points, which were framed to meet a temporary situation, as in the spirit which inspired its authors, principally Mustafa Kemal. There is no doubt the authors had in mind the western concept of the right of national self-determination. The nationalist leaders knew very well they had been defeated in the First World War. Accordingly, they resigned themselves to losing the Ottoman provinces inhabited by non-Turkish majorities, but they insisted on the application of the principle of national self-determination to the inhabitants of Anatolia, the Turks.

---

[17] Tevfik Bıyıklıoğlu, *Atatürk Anadoluda: 1919–1921,* p. 56; Atatürk, *Speech,* pp. 205–10.

[18] For the English translation of the text of the National Pact see J. C. Hurewitz, *Diplomacy in the Near and Middle East* (Princeton, N.J.: D. Van Nostrand, 1956), vol. 2, pp. 74–75.

Meanwhile the Allied authorities in Istanbul decided to inflict a counter blow by formally occupying the capital of the empire.[19] Long before the formal occupation of Istanbul, Mustafa Kemal had had reason to believe that eventually the Allies would help his cause by resorting to such an act. In order to augment his power and prestige, he had urged his colleagues to support his candidacy for the presidency of the Chamber of Deputies of the Ottoman Parliament without his going to Istanbul. Mustafa Kemal thought that in the event of the occupation of Istanbul by the Allies he could, as the president of the Chamber of Deputies, call the deputies to Ankara and re-establish the parliament there. His associates had agreed and assured him that they would help him to get elected. But then much to his surprise he heard that, with the exception of one or two of his friends, the others did not even open their mouths to say a word on the subject.[20] The Allied occupational authorities did for Mustafa Kemal what his friends could not have done! The occupation of Istanbul helped Mustafa Kemal to solidify and strengthen the Nationalist Movement.

On March 19, 1920, Mustafa Kemal in the name of the Representative Committee[21] issued a circular to all provinces and all officers commanding army corps in which he stated that in view of the occupation of Istanul and the attack upon the Ottoman Parliament by the Allied forces it had become imperative to convene an assembly at Ankara with extraordinary powers to be composed of elected representatives as well as the members of the last Ottoman Parliament, so that this assembly might help secure the independence of the nation and the liberation of the country.

Considering religion as a powerful unifying factor, Mustafa Kemal decided to take advantage of the religious feelings of the

---

[19] For the text of the proclamation issued on the day of occupation by General H. F. M. Wilson, see Great Britain, Foreign Office, 371 Political Affairs, 3238/3/44. See also High Commissioner Admiral Bristol to Department of State, "Report on Political Conditions in Turkey," April 10, 1920, U.S. National Archives, Turkey, File No. 867.00/1258.

[20] Atatürk, *Speech,* p. 312.

[21] Some members of the Representative Committee had left for Istanbul to attend the sessions of the Ottoman Parliament as deputies when it convened on January 12, 1920. The composition of the Representative Committee was, therefore, changed. According to one report it included: Mustafa Kemal, Hüsrev Sami, Hakkı Behiç, Recep (Peker), Bekir Sami, Eyub Sabri. This report also mentions Ali Fuat Pasha attending its meetings; see Intelligence Report, May 6, 1920, Great Britain, F. O. 371/5052, E 7721/3/44.

people. Prior to the opening of the Grand National Assembly in Ankara, he issued a proclamation on April 21, 1920, in which he stated that the opening of the assembly would take place on Friday, April 23, a holy day in Islam. The ceremonies would be initiated, he said, by a solemn prayer in the Hacı Bayram Mosque to be attended by all "honorable deputies," in the course of which "the light of the Koran and the call to prayer will be poured forth over all the believers." Following the end of the Friday prayer, the proclamation read, sermons would be delivered on the importance and sacred character of the National Struggle and on the obligation to everyone to do his patriotic duty. This would be followed, said Mustafa Kemal, by a solemn ceremony of congratulations in every town.[22]

The next day Mustafa Kemal issued a circular to all army corps and provinces, informing them that from the date of April 23 the Grand National Assembly would be the lawful authority to which all civil and military authorities and the entire nation must turn.[23] The Grand National Assembly opened on April 23, 1920, with strict adherence to the sacred ritual, in a building formerly belonging to the Union and Progress Party. The building, one of the largest and sturdiest in Ankara, was decorated with flags and flowers.

There were three principal groups of deputies who were expected to attend the meetings of the Grand National Assembly: ninety-two deputies who were transferred from the Chamber of Deputies of the Ottoman Parliament; fourteen deputies who had returned from exile; and 330 deputies who were elected in the two-stage elections from sixty-six constituencies. However, almost 10 per cent of the elected deputies found it personally too risky to participate in the Grand National Assembly and a number of deputies resigned for the same reason.[24] According to a survey

---

[22] Atatürk, *Speech,* pp. 375–76.

[23] Ibid., p. 376.

[24] Frey, *The Turkish Political Elite,* p. 163. There are conflicting reports as to the exact number of deputies attending the first session of the assembly. For example Fevzi (Çakmak) Pasha in his communication to Nureddin Pasha states that "A Grand National Assembly of 300 members has been formed. . . ." See Intelligence Report, Great Britain, F. O. 371/5049, E 5858/3/44. Lord Kinross on the other hand gives the number as 369. (*Ataturk,* p. 250.) Another writer Frederick W. Frey maintains that there were 437 deputies in the assembly. Frey says he derived this figure from *T.B.M.M. 25 ci Yıl Dönümü Anış Albümü* (Ankara: T.B.M.M. Basımevi, 1945).

on the occupational composition of the assembly, a large portion of deputies, 17 per cent, were men of religion, and governmental employees constituted 23 per cent of the deputies, and other professions were represented as follows: military 15 per cent, law 13 per cent, medicine 5 per cent, education 5 per cent, trade 12 per cent, agriculture 6 per cent, banking 1 per cent, journalism 2 per cent and other professions 2 per cent, and 15 per cent unknown.[25]

Following the ceremonial meeting on Friday, April 23, the Grand National Assembly of Turkey[26] met at 10:00 A.M. Saturday under the presidency of Şerif Bey, the deputy from Sinop. The assembly first examined and approved the reports dealing with the election of deputies. Then, Mustafa Kemal gave an account of the important events that took place from the Armistice of Mudros to the opening of the assembly. The same day, he presented a motion advocating the creation without delay of a government and stated that the present assembly was not merely a deliberating body controlling the affairs of the government, but a body that would actually deal from day to day with the destiny of the nation and one that would assume direct responsibilities to that end. He added, however, that since the whole assembly could not conduct the affairs of the nation it appeared imperative that it should elect a council composed of the deputies of the assembly to manage the functions of government in its own name and that the members of this council should be individually and collectively responsible to the assembly. He suggested further that the president of the assembly should be considered ex-officio chairman of the executive council and should be held responsible for his actions to the assembly. Recalling the primary objective of the Nationalist Struggle as the liberation of the sultan-caliph and the restoration of his rightful powers as the head of all Moslems, Mustafa Kemal maintained that there could be no question of designating a head of a provisional government, or a regent-sultan in Anatolia. He concluded:

---

[25] Frey, *The Turkish Political Elite,* table 7.5, p. 181.

[26] On the adoption of the name *Türkiye Büyük Millet Meclisi* Halide Edib writes: "Hamdullah Subhi Bey proposed Kurultay (*Assembly* in old Turkish); Jelaleddin Arif Bey proposed 'Mejliss-i-Kebir-i-Milli" *Grand National Assembly* in Arabic; but one was too archaic and the other was Arabic. Then someone proposed 'Büyük Millet Meclisi' (*Great National Assembly* in Turkish), and this was accepted." *The Turkish Ordeal,* p. 144.

"We are therefore obliged to form a government without a head of government."[27]

Mustafa Kemal's motion was adopted. Then the assembly decided to elect its officers. Mustafa Kemal was elected president by a vote of 110. Celalettin Arif Bey with 109 votes was elected second president. Hacı Bektaş Çelebisi Cemalettin Efendi and Abdul Halim Çelebi were elected vice presidents.[28]

After a long and acrimonious debate, the assembly adopted the Law Concerning the Election of the Council of Ministers of the Grand National Assembly on May 1, 1920. Two days later the members of the Council of Ministers were elected one by one by the assembly. It consisted of the following: Mustafa Fehmi Efendi (Religious Affairs); Cami (Baykurt) (Interior); Celalettin Arif (Justice); İsmail Fazıl Pasha (Public Works); Bekir Sami (Kunduk) (Foreign Affairs); Dr. Adnan (Adıvar) (Public Health); Yusuf Kemal (Tengirşenk) (Economics, Commerce, Agriculture); Fevzi (Çakmak) Pasha (National Defense); Hakkı Behiç (Finance); Dr. Rıza Nur (Education); Colonel İsmet (İnönü) Chief of the General Staff). Mustafa Kemal was to be the ex-officio chairman of the Council of Ministers.

The program of the Council of Ministers was read before the assembly by Dr. Rıza Nur who outlined the objectives to be pursued in the name of the assembly. In the field of foreign relations, the program emphasized the objective of guaranteeing respect on the part of the Allied Powers of the territorial integrity and independence of the country in accordance with the National Pact.[29]

On April 30, Mustafa Kemal, in the name of the Grand National Assembly, dispatched communications to the governments of the Allied and Associated Powers stating that since the Grand National Assembly considered the sultan-caliph a prisoner of the Allies all decrees and *fetvas* emanating from Istanbul would have no legal or religious validity whatsoever and that all contractual engagements entered into by the Istanbul government would be null

[27] *Atatürk'ün Söylev ve Demeçleri.* I (Ankara: Türk Tarih Kurumu Basımevi, 1961), pp. 60–62.

[28] See Türkiye Büyük Millet Meclisi, *Zabıt Ceridesi,* Devre 1, vol. 1, pp. 42–44; see also Great Britain, Foreign Office, 371, 5049, E 5858/3/44.

[29] For the text of the program see Kazım Öztürk, *Türkiye Cumhuriyeti Hükümetleri ve Programları,* pp. 13–17.

and void. Mustafa Kemal's communication also stated that the Turkish nation was resolved to conclude only an equitable and honorable peace by delegates appointed by the Grand National Assembly and not by any other authority.[30]

The new government not only had to operate under primitive conditions, but also lacked sufficient funds to manage the affairs of the nation, raise armies, and wage a war of independence. According to one report, when the Representative Committee moved to Ankara it had practically no funds left. The Association for the Defense of Rights branch at Ankara provided it with some 800 liras donated by Müftü Rıfat (Börekci) Efendi, a religious leader. Later the same organization contributed 1,000 liras every month to Mustafa Kemal enabling him to meet the expenses of the Representative Committee in Ankara.[31] The new government was dependent upon local contributions and gifts until it could draw on the revenues obtained from other provincial centers of Anatolia. The budget of the Ankara government was not passed until the end of the fiscal year on February 28, 1921, with a deficit of 14 million liras out of a total of 60 million liras.[32] At the time one pound sterling was equal to five Turkish liras. Twenty-eight million liras of the budget were allocated for the defense. The Ankara government was not even able to pay the salaries of its employees.

After nine long months of deliberations and much bittter controversy between Mustafa Kemal and his conservative opponents who constituted the majority in the assembly, the provisional Constitution of the new regime was adopted on January 20, 1921. Article 1 of the Constitution set forth the fundamental principle of the new regime. It read: "Sovereignty is vested unconditionally in the nation. The system of administration is based on the principle that the people personally and effectively direct their own destinies." Under Article 2 the legislative and executive powers were to be concentrated in the hands of the Grand National Assembly as the true and only representative of the nation. The government, under Article 3, was to be called the Government of the Grand National

---

[30] For the original text sent to Lord Curzon, see Great Britain, F. O. 371/5051, E 7090/3/44.

[31] Aydemir, *Tek Adam,* vol. 2, p. 201.

[32] See Sabahattin Selek, *Anadolu İhtilali,* pp. 106–15.

Assembly of Turkey. The Constitution for the first time created the institution of the chairmanship of the Council of Ministers. The chairman was to be elected by the members of the Council of Ministers from among its members. However, the president of the Grand National Assembly was to be ex-officio president of the Council of Ministers. The Constitution further stated that the assembly was to give directives to the ministers in the exercise of their duties and that if need be it could dismiss the individual ministers. In the field of foreign relations the assembly explicitly reserved the right to conclude conventions and peace treaties and to declare war.

The Constitution of 1921 did not contain a provision concerning the powers and duties of the head of state in deference to the existing sultan-caliph in Istanbul who was considered by the conservative majority of the assembly as the head of the Ottoman state. Instead the Constitution stated that the president of the Grand National Assembly was authorized to sign the official papers in the name of the assembly and to ratify the decisions of the Council of Ministers. Moreover, the Constitution contained a clause to the effect that "The provisions of the Constitution of 1876, which are not contradictory to the principles herein, remain in effect."[33] As these points clearly indicated, this constitution reflected the prevailing currents of thought in the assembly and as such was a compromise of the conflicting views of the conservatives and Mustafa Kemal. Conservatives as well as Mustafa Kemal, for reasons diametrically opposed to each other, viewed the Constitution, the assembly, and its Council of Ministers as provisional.

Up until the final military victory, the question of the sultanate remained dormant. The Allied Powers, who invited both the Istanbul and Ankara governments to the peace conference at Lausanne, inadvertently helped the cause of Mustafa Kemal in abolishing the sultanate. The refusal of the British to recognize the Ankara government as the sole representative of the nation created considerable indignation among the deputies of the Grand National Assembly. Mustafa Kemal immediately seized the opportunity and proposed the abolition of the sultanate together with its government in Istanbul. Even then, Mustafa Kemal had at times to threaten

---

[33] Article 10. For the text of the Constitution of 1921 see *Resmi Gazete* (Official Gazette), no. 1, February 7, 1921.

and at other times cajole his conservative opponents. In the end, on November 1, 1922, the resolution was unanimously adopted. It contained two articles. The first declared that "the Turkish people consider that the form of government in Istanbul resting on the sovereignty of an individual had ceased to exist on March 16, 1920, and had passed forever into history"; the second declared that, though the caliphate belonged to the Ottoman Empire, it rested on the Turkish state, and that the Grand National Assembly would choose as caliph "that member of the Ottoman house who was in learning and character most worthy and fitting."[34]

Later, Abdülmecid was appointed as the new caliph to replace Sultan Vahdeddin (Mehmet VI), who sought the protection of the Allied Commander in Chief General Harington. On November 16, the Grand National Assembly accused Vahdeddin of high treason and ordered him and his cabinet ministers to be placed on trial. Once again the British inadvertently came to the aid of Mustafa Kemal. On November 17, Vahdeddin was secretly removed from his palace and transferred to Malta on *H.M.S. Malaya*.[35] "The Ottoman dynasty has produced 36 Sultans, great and weak, good and bad" wrote one of the newspapers in Istanbul, "but hitherto there has been known none so pusillanimous as Vahdeddin, who has now turned his back upon the sepulchres of his ancestors, and is about to start on who knows what adventures."[36] That was the end of the sultanate in Turkey.

The first assembly was elected for the conduct of the affairs of Turkey during the emergency period. It had thus outlived its usefulness by the end of the War of Independence. The approval of the peace treaty and the adoption of internal reforms were contingent upon the existence of an assembly which would be much easier to manage. This question was discussed at an emergency meeting of the Council of Ministers where Mustafa Kemal explained the necessity for the dissolving of the National Assembly without divulging his own motives. He also induced the National Assembly to dissolve itself on April 1, 1923, and go to new elections.

---

[34] Text in A. Şeref Gözübüyük ve Suna Kili, *Türk Anayasa Metinleri* (Ankara: Ankara Üniversitesi Siyasal Bilgiler Fakültesi Yayınları no. 75–57, 1957), pp. 90–91.

[35] For text of Vahdeddin's letter see Sir Charles Harington, *Tim Harington Looks Back* (London: John Murray, 1940), p. 125.

[36] Quoted in E. G. Mears, *Modern Turkey* (New York: Macmillan, 1924), p. 570.

On April 8, Mustafa Kemal issued a nine-point election plat-form of the Association for the Defense of Rights of Anatolia and Rumelia, in which he also revealed that this political organization would be transformed into a full-fledged political party. The People's Party, succeeding the Association for the Defense of Rights, was formally founded on October 23. The People's Party was identified by Mustafa Kemal as a school for the political training of the Turkish people.[37]

Meanwhile, the elections resulted in victory for Mustafa Kemal and his supporters. The Second Grand National Assembly, packed by Mustafa Kemal, convened on August 11 and on August 14 elected Ali Fethi Bey as the new prime minister. To underscore the resurgence of a new Turkey, it was decided to transfer the capital from Istanbul to Ankara, already the seat of the nationalist govern-ment. A bill to that effect was introduced by İsmet Pasha and to the dismay of many it was adopted on October 13, 1923.

On October 27 Mustafa Kemal precipitated a government crisis by asking Ali Fethi Bey to resign. Mustafa Kemal hoped that the assembly responsible for the election of ministers was not going to be able to agree on a list of ministers. He would then suggest that the system of government be changed. As was expected, for two days the assembly could not produce a list of ministers acceptable to all concerned. Mustafa Kemal and İsmet Pasha submitted a set of amendments to the Constitution. At the end of the first article the sentence "The form of the government of the Turkish state is a republic" was added. Other amendments dealt with the election of the president of the republic and the selection of the members of the Council of Ministers. On October 19, the amendments were submitted to the People's Party caucus which debated them the whole day; the proposals were finally adopted. At 6:00 in the evening, the Constitutional Law Committee of the National Assem-bly began to examine the motion for the amendment of the Consti-tution, and at 8:30 P.M. the National Assembly voted to accept the motion for the amendments and thus the republic was born. Having adopted this motion the assembly elected Mustafa Kemal as the first president of the Turkish Republic.[38]

---

[37] See Naki Cevat Akkerman, *Demokrasi ve Türkiyede Siyasi Partiler Hakkında Kısa Notlar* (Ankara: Ulus Basımevi, 1950), p. 36. For the initial program of the People's Party see Webster, *The Turkey of Ataturk,* pp. 173–80, 307–18.

[38] See Atatürk, *Speech,* pp. 664–65.

Following the establishment of the republic, the hopes of the conservative elite were centered on the institution of the caliphate to arrest further drastic reorganization of the state and the society. It was hoped that the caliphate could also be used in returning to the traditional system of government. Aware of the threats posed by the caliphate to the Republican regime and to his personal prestige and power, Mustafa Kemal decided to abolish that institution as well.

In order to test his strength once again within the ranks of the military establishment, Mustafa Kemal organized military exercises in January 1924 in the İzmir region. During the maneuvers he broached the question of the abolishing of the caliphate with his top military leaders, including the Chief of the General Staff Fevzi Pasha, and Minister of Defense Kazım Pasha. They all agreed on the necessity of that move. When they returned to Ankara, three bills were introduced in the National Assembly. After lengthy and at times bitter debate, all the proposals of Mustafa Kemal were adopted on March 3, 1924. The caliphate was abolished. The Caliph Abdülmecid was declared deposed and all members of the deposed Ottoman dynasty were henceforth forbidden to reside within Turkey.[39] The Ministry of Religious Affairs and the pious foundations were disestablished.

Then, a new and permanent Constitution was adopted on April 20, 1924, which incorporated the principles contained in the 1921 Constitution as well as the subsequent amendments to that provisional organic law.[40] The new Constitution defined the powers and functions of the three branches of the government and the rights and duties of the Turks in more elaborate fashion. The Constitution declared that "sovereignty belongs unconditionally to the nation" and that the Grand National Assembly exercises sovereignty in the name of the people. The Constitution provided for the concentration of the legislative and executive powers in the hands of the National Assembly. The president of the republic was to be elected for a term of four years by the assembly. As head of state,

---

[39] See Atatürk, Speech, p. 701. See also William L. Westerman, "The Abolishing of the Ottoman Phantom Caliphate," Asia 24 (May 1924): 349–52; Constantin Brown, "The Tragicomic Exit of the Ottoman Dynasty," Asia, 24 (June 1924): 449–53.

[40] See Bülent Nuri Esen, Türk Anayasa Hukuku, Birinci Fasikül (Ankara: Ayyıldız Matbaası, 1968), pp. 54–70; The Turkish Information Office, New York, The Turkish Constitution, n.d.

the president was empowered to preside over the assembly during special occasions, and at the beginning of each of the annual sessions of the assembly he was to deliver an address regarding the activities of the government during the past year and the measures recommended for the coming year. The president was authorized to designate the Prime Minister from among the members of the assembly, approve the membership of the cabinet as chosen by the prime minister, and submit the list of the members of the Council of Ministers to the assembly for its approval. The Council of Ministers was required to submit its program to the assembly within one week and request a vote of confidence. As chief executive, the president was authorized to preside over the Council of Ministers and to participate actively in the adoption and implementation of internal and external policies, but without any political responsibility. He was authorized to appoint the diplomatic representatives of Turkey and to receive foreign envoys. The assembly was empowered to conclude conventions and treaties of peace with foreign powers and to declare war.

The Nationalist Movement and the National Struggle had freed theTurks from foreign domination and had laid the foundations of a new sovereign independent nation-state. After four years of struggle against external enemies and internal foes, Mustafa Kemal was successful in accomplishing drastic superstructural changes in the Turkish polity. These changes were: (1) to destroy the traditional politico-religious institutions; (2) to educate the people in self-government; (3) to secularize the process of further development of the society; and (4) to create a modern outlook for the Turkish polity.

The adoption of a new Constitution may be said to have marked the completion of the first phase of the Turkish Revolution. The Turkish people, under the provisions of the new organic law, had obtained the right to participate in the affairs of the state. However, such participation was to be guided by the president of the republic until such time as the Turkish society was transformed in the image of modern societies.

It is highly interesting that after the 1960 coup d'état, instead of introducing sweeping infrastructural reforms in the society, with a view to supplementing the reform measures of Atatürk, the Committee of National Unity and the intelligentsia chose to replace the 1924 Constitution of Atatürk with a new one and to undertake a thorough reorganization of the executive, legislative, and judicial branches of the government. To this end, the Committee of National Unity convened a Constituent Assembly on January 6, 1961, composed of two houses, the upper house containing the membership of the Committee of National Unity, and a lower house, the Representative Assembly. The Constituent Assembly was given the task of preparing and adopting a new constitution and a new electoral law. The new Constitution as worked out by the Constituent Assembly was submitted to the approval of the electorate. Sixty-two per cent of the eligible voters approved the new Constitution which was promulgated on July 20, 1961.[41]

The main provisions of the 1961 Constitution may be summarized as follows. Preceded by a somewhat flowery preamble, the first part, among other provisions, declared that "The Turkish State is a Republic" and that it "is based on the principles of human rights and is a national, democratic, secular, social state bound by the rule of law." The second part contained one of the most comprehensive set of democratic and civil liberties as well as social and economic rights. The Constitution appears to have abandoned the concept of concentration of powers in the hands of the legislature and adopted instead the theory of flexible separation of powers. In addition it contained a number of innovations: (1) It established a bicameral system: the National Assembly and the Senate of the Republic; (2) it limited the number of elected senators to 150 and deputies to 450; (3) it provided for appointed as well as lifetime senatorships, that is presidential appointees and the members of the Committee of National Unity respectively; (4) it set the term of the president as seven years, overlapping the terms of the Senate and the National Assembly, six and four years respectively; (5) it made the president ineligible for re-election; (6) it opened the way for the appointment of ministers from outside the Grand National Assembly; (7) it granted the president limited power under certain circumstances to dissolve the National Assembly; (8) it created a High Council of Judiciary responsible for the promotion or removal of judges; and (9) it created a Constitutional Court to review the constitutionality of legislative acts.

Under the 1961 Constitution, the president is elected by the two houses of the Grand National Assembly, the Senate of the Republic and the National Assembly, in a joint session from among

---

[41] The text in *Resmi Gazete,* 20 Temmuz 1961, no. 10859.

the members of either house. The candidates are required to be forty years of age or older and to have completed university level education. As head of the executive, the President presides, whenever he deems it necessary, over the Council of Ministers. He appoints the diplomatic representatives of Turkey and receives the representatives of foreign powers. Upon the approval of the Grand National Assembly, he ratifies and promulgates international agreements, conventions, and treaties. The president is not accountable for his actions connected with his duties. All decrees emanating from the president must be countersigned by the prime minister, and the relevant ministers. The latter are responsible for the enforcement of these decrees. The president has limited veto power over legislation: He may request a fresh discussion on a bill, other than budget bills and constitutional amendments, by referring it to the Grand National Assembly within ten days; he is empowered also to initiate action in the Constitutional Court against a bill which he thinks is contrary to the Constitution.

The president appoints the prime minister from among the members of the Grand National Assembly. The ministers are nominated by the prime minister from among the members of the Grand National Assembly or from among those qualified for election as deputies appointed by the president. The cabinet, or the Council of Ministers, thus formed presents its program to the Grand National Assembly and must seek and obtain a vote of confidence in the lower house, the National Assembly. The prime minister ensures cooperation and harmony between the ministries and supervises the conduct of the general policy determined by the Council of Ministers.

It seems that the framers of the 1961 Constitution had hoped that once they had drastically reorganized the governmental structure and set new broad principles and guidelines for further modernization of the society, the newly constituted Grand National Assembly, the Council of Ministers, and the leadership of political parties would be able at last to accomplish those reforms left undone by the authoritarian leaders of the past. It seems that the military and civilian leaders of Turkey had hoped that the new Grand National Assembly would launch the second phase of the Turkish Revolution by enacting all the legislation necessary for altering drastically the socio-economic fabric of the society. Thus, the new regime which was labeled, at least for a while, as "The Second Republic" was created in an atmosphere of great expectations.

Chapter Eight

THE MODERNIZATION
OF TURKEY

A Traditional Society Channeled
Toward Modernity

The process of transformation of the Turkish polity from the fall
of the Ottoman Empire until today may be studied under the
following headings: (1) Authority Reforms; (2) Nation Building;
(3) Secularist Reforms; (4) Participation Reforms; and (5) Social
and Economic Reforms.

Authority Reforms

The authority of the Ottoman rulers was based upon the fact
that as ghazi leaders they had had absolute control over the military
establishment. Legitimacy of their authority was derived from their
monopoly of power. Traditionally, the Ottoman sovereigns regulated
all politico-socio-economic affairs of the society through their house-
holds. The Ottoman sultan-caliphs could make or remake the ruling
institutions and determine the membership of the religious, bureaucratic, and military establishments.

By the beginning of the nineteenth century, the Ottoman head
of state, for all practical purposes, had lost his control over the
institutions of the empire, such as the Janissary order, the *Ulema*,

the bureaucracy, feudal lords, the local dynasties and the *Ayan*.[1] At this time there were two competing centers of power: One was operating in the capital where formal authority was still vested in the sultan but real authority had shifted to the *Ulema,* the military, and the bureaucratic establishments; the other was functioning in the provinces where effective power and control was seized by the provincial notables and feudal lords.[2] Once the monopoly of power, particularly temporal power, of the sultan was challenged and taken over by the military and bureaucratic order, which came in the wake of military defeats in the West, the state was no longer master of its own destiny.

The emergence of the Nationalist Movement despite abortive attempts at its suppression by the central government in Istanbul, the successes of the nationalist leaders in carrying out the National Struggle against the external enemies as well as against the sultan's government can be explained by the fact that the central government in Istanbul had no effective control in the interior of Anatolia. Furthermore, the nationalist leaders wisely utilized the effective power of the provincial notables, feudal lords, and religious leaders over the peasantry. Without such an alliance between Mustafa Kemal and his associates and the provincial notables, the conduct of the National Struggle would probably have been an impossible undertaking.

After the victory against foreign powers, in order to destroy the competing centers of temporal power, and to restore the authority (formal power) and control (effective power) of the state over the politico-socio-economic activities of the citizenry, Mustafa Kemal decided to change the superstructure of the Ottoman Empire drastically. As noted earlier, the sultanate was abolished, the capital was transferred to Ankara, the republic was proclaimed, and a new organic law was adopted. These drastic changes were followed by steps in creating greater differentiation, functional specificity, and integration of all governmental institutions. In addition to the governmental agencies in the provinces and the military establishment throughout the country, the Republican People's Party was given the task of disseminating the principles of nationalism, repub-

---

[1] See Bernard Lewis, *The Emergence of Modern Turkey,* p. 134.

[2] For the dichotomy of "formal" power (authority) and "effective" power (control) see Fred W. Riggs, *Administration in Developing Countries: The Theory of Prismatic Society* (Boston: Houghton Mifflin, 1964), p. 281.

licanism, reformism, *étatism,* populism, and secularism so as to bring about greater public understanding and support of the authority of the state. With the establishment of control and direction of the bureaucracy by the Republican People's Party, the coalescing of party and state was fully realized.

It was not until 1937 that the regime was able to deal effectively with the aggitation and propaganda of the religious fanatics, the traditionalist counterelite, and the pacification of the dissident minority groups such as the Kurds. In response to Kurdish insurrections in February 1925, March 1930, and August 1937, the government took stern measures, even to the extent of undertaking large-scale military operations. During the political, religious, and racial disturbances, the government exercised dictatorial powers under martial law. However, the Republican regime never created an atmosphere of terror in order to establish its authority and control throughout the country. Martial law was also declared during the Second World War and on numerous occasions of civil disturbance in the years that followed, such as in 1955, 1960, 1961–1963, 1970, and 1971. Although state authority was fully instituted throughout the land from 1923, the regime was not immune to serious challenges even to the extent of organized violence on the part of the reactionary and dissident groups.

The most serious threat to state authority was, of course, posed by the military on May 27, 1960, when it overthrew the government of the Democratic Party. Following the seizure of state power by the Committee of National Unity, the military directly exercised state authority until October 20, 1961, at which time it turned power over to an elected civilian government: The three attempted coups, in November 1960, February 1962, and May 1963, instigated by extremist elements in the armed forces were quickly suppressed.

The latter part of the 1960s and 1970 and 1971 witnessed further defiance of state authority by the extremists on the left and right. In order to reinstate the authority of the state and to protect and preserve law and order in the land, the top military leaders, the Chief of the General Staff and the commanders of the ground, air, and naval forces issued an ultimatum to the government and to the legislature on March 12, 1971, in which they claimed that the policies of the government and the parliament had led the country into a state of anarchy, and they demanded the resignation of the Justice Party cabinet and called for the establishment of a nonpartisan government capable, "within the framework of the democratic principles," of ending the current spate of violence and accomplishing the necessary reforms. They made it quite clear that if such a government were not organized the armed forces would "seize power to protect the republic" against internal instability and disorder bordering anarchy.[3] It seems that throughout the history of the Turkish Republic the authority of the state was upheld, protected, and enforced by the disciplined armed forces and their officer corps.

NATION BUILDING

Loyalty to the new political community was in the long run contingent upon the development of fealty to the Turkish nation on the part of the Anatolian people. The Ministry of Education, the Turkish Historical Society, the Republican People's Party as well as the members of the intelligentsia engaged in a massive campaign to re-educate and indoctrinate the Turks in a sense of pride for their past accomplishments and a desire to achieve greater things in the future, and to develop in them a knowledge of their identity and worth as a people. The new history books which emphasized Turkey's contributions to past civilizations, and accomplishments, the new language which revived old Turkish words, the flag, patriotic stories, poems and music, political slogans, pictures and statues of the national hero, Mustafa Kemal Atatürk, were devices effectively used in building a genuine and homogeneous Turkish nation.

This fostering of a sense of nationhood was probably the most successful and enduring of the reforms of the Republican regime, encouraging the common man to regard himself as a Turk first and then a Moslem. If the Turkish leaders, the intelligentsia, even the man in the street, subscribed to a new set of values, the idea of "Turkish Nationalism" merits being called an ideology.

SECULARIST REFORMS

Universalism of Islam and its jurisdiction over all phases of the life of the believer were not compatible with the new nationalism

---

[3] See *New York Times,* 13 March 1971, p. 1.

of the Turks and their nation-state. In order to direct the loyalties
of the people from the religious to secular institutions, the caliphate
was abolished, the Ottoman dynasty was banished, religious semi-
naries and religious orders and courts were closed and suppressed,
wearing of the *fez* was forbidden, the *Derviş* order and religiously
significant tombs were closed, the article of the Constitution declar-
ing Islam the national religion was repealed, and the state was
declared secular.

Such secularist reforms were not accomplished overnight, however, but were undertaken over a span of some thirteen years. Then,
too, these changes involved only the outward manifestations of the
Islamic faith. No attempt was made to reform the fundamental
precepts of the religion or to reform the belief system that rested
essentially on the faith itself.

On the other hand, the initial democratization of the tutelary
regime in 1946 necessitated, of course, for political reasons, the
loosening of the tight grip over religious activities beginning in
November 1948. First, religious lessons in elementary schools were
allowed. Preachers and worship leaders' schools were opened, followed by the establishment of the Faculty of Theology at the
University of Ankara. The *Derviş* meeting places and religiously
significant tombs were opened, and the ban on religious radio
programs was lifted, including the reading of the Koran on the air
by the state radio in July 1950.

Such compromises in the secular reforms and tolerance of the
religious institutions by politicians hoping to secure the support of
the peasant majority have had important repercussions on the body
politic in recent years and have created a resurgence of traditional
religious practices.

Participation Reforms

The legitimacy of the new regime in Turkey was derived from
the principle of popular sovereignty. It was therefore absolutely
essential to change the status of the individual from that of "subject
of the sultan" to that of "free citizen." Here again, it is instructive
to note that such transformation was accomplished gradually from
1924 to 1946. Step by step the people were granted the right to
participate in the affairs of their government and permitted to demand the rendering of services by the government to meet their
needs. First, the electoral law was amended in April 1924 to elim-

inate the requirement that electors, candidates, and voters be tax-payers and to extend the vote to all male citizens over eighteen. Women were given the right to vote in municipal elections in 1930 and four years later they were permitted to vote in the national elections and to become deputies in the Grand National Assembly. The adoption of "populism" as one of the cardinal principles of the Constitution in 1937 was followed in May 1946 by the enact-ment of a new electoral law providing for direct, universal suffrage and secret ballots, which replaced the two-stage election system of the past.

The formal aspects of the participation reforms were success-fully materialized when almost 90 per cent of the electorate took part in the general elections of May 1950 that were contested by a number of political parties. Since the 1950s, the general public and the counterelite have not only managed to organize themselves into political parties and exercise a definite influence over govern-mental policies and programs, but have also begun demanding greater governmental outputs in line with their socio-economic needs. These demands were partially met by responsive govern-ments. For example, restrictions on public religious activities were discontinued; the establishment of organizations based on religious, class, or economic interests was permitted by modifying the law of societies; domestic and external economic policies were liberalized; village institutes were closed; new mosques were built by state funds; large sums of money were allocated as agricultural credits. Further-more, the adoption of a new liberal Constitution in 1961, in theory, put an end to dictatorial practices and facilitated greatly the exer-cise of freedom of conscience, of political beliefs, of assembly and press, of the right to form political and cultural organizations, poli-tical parties, and labor unions. In this atmosphere of freedom and liberty, all sorts of moderate and extremist socialist ideas, "Marxist-Leninist-Maoist" doctrines, religious fanaticism, chauvinism, which were totally banned in previous decades, were let loose. The end result of such permissive, liberal acts and policies was political violence within the ranks of the elite.

SOCIAL AND ECONOMIC REFORMS

It appears that the changes that were introduced by the regime dealt a heavy blow only to the symbolic aspects of the socio-economic life. To illustrate, the following reform acts may be cited: The international calendar and system of time, the international numbering system, the Latin alphabet, and the decimal system of measurement were adopted between 1925 and 1931; the Turkish Language Society was organized in 1932 to institute linguistic reforms; a modern civil code was adopted in 1926; family names were ordered adopted and all titles and hereditary positions were abolished in 1934; women were given equal rights in 1934; elementary, secondary schools, and universities were organized along modern and secular lines, including the establishment of the now defunct village institutes. In the economic sphere, a new commercial code was introduced in 1926; private enterprises were promised concessions and governmental support to encourage the growth of the private sector of the economy; the first five-year development plan was instituted in 1934; a new labor law was adopted in 1935 to regulate working conditions; the principle of *étatism* was incorporated into the Constitution in 1937; a law imposing a wealth tax was enacted in 1942; the organization of labor unions was allowed in 1947; the economic development was tied in with the foreign economic aid in 1948; numerous liberal laws designed to encourage foreign capital investment were adopted in the 1950s; and in order to institute a rational and efficient economic development, the State Planning Organization was established in 1960.

The Republican regime always emphasized the absence of social and economic classes and the solidarity of the Turkish nation. Note the slogan *imtiyazsız sınıfsız bir milletiz* (We are one nation without any separate or privileged classes). The Anatolian peasant was always identified as the backbone of the nation, the lord and master of the regime. Yet, the regime did very little, aside from building a network of roads between rural and urban centers, to elevate the economic, social, and educational status of the peasantry. For example, in 1927, 89.4 per cent of the population, (12,536,774 persons) were illiterate; in 1970, 44.5 per cent of the population remained illiterate. In 1970 there were more illiterate persons (13,148,398) than in 1927. Again in 1970 there were almost a million children between the ages of seven and twelve who were not attending elementary schools.[4] As Lewis observes, "Legal termination [of the traces of feudalism] was, however, insufficient, and a number of great landowners, notably in the south

---

[4] See *Cumhuriyet,* 16 August 1972, p. 5.

and east, still enjoyed the status of almost *derebeys* in the provinces. Even in the more advanced parts of the country, the large land-owner in the towns, with his ally or dependent the rich peasant in the village, still wielded enormous power over the peasantry."[5]

Every government in Turkey in its program as submitted to parliament has declared land reform to be its primary objective, yet no government including the "nonpartisan government" of Dr. Nihat Erim, which was installed by the military leaders, was able to carry out any measures entailing such far-reaching consequences for the Turkish society.

Admittedly, the above-mentioned socio-economic reforms have brought about appreciable changes in the outward manifestations of the socio-economic life. But, they did not raise the lifestyles of the great majority of the people to the level of modern societies. Neither did they penetrate deep into the traditional culture and improve the qualities of the socio-economic institutions nor help to develop better human relationships. Instead, the rising desires and expectations of the people — as articulated by the elite — led to increased frustrations and eventually to political violence of immense proportions.

Why did the leaders of Turkey neglect substantive cultural changes? Answers to this question may be found in the characteristics of the society and its traditional political culture.

THE CONCENTRIC SOCIETY

In terms of modernity and in terms of the exercise of actual political power, the Turkish society can be said to consist of three concentric circles: the elite; the intermediates; and the peasantry.[6]

Even though deep in their hearts they subscribe to the commands of the traditional culture, the elite display a modern outlook. However, from the standpoint of their political power, the elite usually fall into one of two groups: conservatives and revisionists. The actual political behavior of each of these groups is directly related to the distance of each from the center of state power.

---

[5] Lewis, *The Emergence of Modern Turkey*, p. 468.

[6] On Daniel Lerner's typology see his *The Passing of Traditional Society: Modernization in the Middle East* (New York: The Free Press, paperback ed., 1964), pp. 136–66.

In the Turkish polity, the state power, constitutional provisions notwithstanding, is concentrated in the hands of the chief executive and emanates from the person of the president. The absolute power of the sultans of the past has been replaced in the Republican era by the almost absolute power of the president.[7] The president and his close associates — the top military leaders and the prominent personalities of the party in power — comprise the highest echelon of the conservative group. They tend to do everything possible to preserve their dominant political positions so as to modernize the society from the top of the political structure downward by gradually introducing the necessary reforms. Since these reforms are to be implemented by the bureaucracy and the intelligentsia, the president and his close associates consider it imperative that they exercise complete control over the acts of the political and non-political elite and help them to achieve a modern status. They believe that if the loyalty of the elite and its modernization can be assured, it would be a simpler matter to minimize the opposition of the peasantry to formal or substantive changes, since the elite exercised undisputed control over the conduct of the peasantry.

The revisionists, on the other hand, are those who, not being in possession of state power, are dissatisfied with the existing unequal distribution of political power and strive for it. Their demands for drastic and rapid politico-socio-economic changes appeal primarily to the intermediates, thereby increasing their chances for obtaining state power. While in opposition, the revisionists appear much more idealistic and dogmatic about the questions of modernization. They often accuse the power holders of betraying the letter and spirit of the principles of Atatürkism. Yet, when the revisionists come to power they also begin to display conservative tendencies, and thus seem to emulate their opponents. For example, during the İnönü era the revisionists demanded the liberalization of the internal system of government, during the 1950s since the "ins" (conservatives) had changed role with the "outs" (revisionists), the leadership of the Republican People's Party (now revisionists)

---

[7] Speaking of the actual powers of Presidents Atatürk and İnönü, Lewis shares the same view. *The Emergence of Modern Turkey,* pp. 370–71. It must be recalled that it took a coup d'état to remove President Bayar from the presidency. However, since 1961, a collegium of military-civilian leadership at Çankaya seems to have replaced the absolute authority of the president.

called for the termination of what they called "the authoritarian practices" of the Democratic Party and the modernization of the infrastructure of the society; during the latter part of the 1960s the revisionists, again the Republican People's Party, began to intensify their advocacy of the replacement of the traditional political beliefs with that of modern democratic values, including the concept of social justice.

As the struggle between the revisionists and conservatives was converted into acts of political violence in the 1960s, the elite were split four ways: moderate conservatives, moderate revisionists, militant conservatives, and militant revisionists. The latter were usually identified as "militant revolutionaries" or "urban guerrillas." The militancy of the conservatives was proportionate to the extent and nature of the unauthorized political violence resorted to by the militant revisionists who constituted a very small, but apparently well-organized and disciplined, core of extremists. The moderates in most instances formed a common front because of their overlapping interests in opposing extremism in general and extreme measures of political violence in particular. They exercised a moderating influence over the actions of the militant groups.

The conservative elite, particularly since the 1950s, have found their power bases essentially in the support of the conservative peasantry — the silent majority — whereas the revisionists have relied on the support of the intermediates. The latter, a distinct product of the Republican era, are those who live in urban centers and who aspire to political and economic elite status. They include the university students, junior military officers, and civil servants as well as the entrepreneur class. The intermediates, because of their level of education and proximity to the elite, are more acculturated to the modern way of life than the peasantry. They — the second of the concentric circles — enter the ranks of the elite.

On the other hand, the peasantry — the third and largest circle in the society — are deeply committed to the traditional way of life and patiently await the satisfaction of their limited needs. They are at times the beneficiaries of the intraelite struggles and at times they become the victims of such clashes.

In short, the first circle — the elite, sometimes referred to as the "self-appointed modernizers" — had dominated and continues to dominate the political scene. They determine the pace and scope of the process of modernization.

TURKISH POLITICAL CULTURE

ITS SALIENT FEATURES

Although it is beyond the scope of this study to engage in an extensive treatment of Turkish political culture, which constitutes an integral part of the general Turkish culture, a brief discussion of the more salient features of the Turkish political beliefs[8] which condition the political life may shed some light on the process of modernization. The fundamental characteristics of the political beliefs held by the Turkish citizens may be generalized as follows.

The individual regards himself first and foremost as a Turk, endowed with special qualities, powers, and obligations to protect and preserve the motherland and the Turkish polity. Almost equal in importance, however, is his belief in himself as a Moslem, which to his way of thinking is very nearly synonymous with the word Turk. His strong sense of identity extends to his parochial ties of family, village, and region from which he derives his greatest feelings of immediate security and belonging. These sources of immediate security comprise his intangible assets and constitute a strong emotional investment. For the protection of his life, freedom of action, and the satisfaction of his other desires and expectations — since internal and external security is guaranteed by the state — he believes in the necessity of cultivating the support of politico-socio-economic power holders. For financial security he places his trust in guaranteed assets such as land, immovable properties, and precious metals.

The need for security stems from the belief that he lives in an environment of harsh natural conditions as well as in an environment of bitter struggle and hostility brought about by natural forces beyond his control and by strangers *(yabancılar)* — those who live outside the immediate circle of parochial associations — and by foreigners usually identified as *gavurlar,* (e.g. *Moskof gavuru*) bent upon exploiting the human and natural resources of his motherland. It may, therefore, be said that a deep-rooted distrust and cynicism

---

[8] On general political beliefs see Sidney Verba, "Comparative Political Culture" in *Political Culture and Political Development,* ed. Lucian W. Pye and Sidney Verba (Princeton, N.J.: Princeton University Press, paperback ed. 1969), pp. 518–44.

toward his fellowmen in general and toward strangers and foreigners in particular permeates the thinking of the individual citizen. And yet the essentially pragmatic mind of the individual, in the main, regulates his attitude toward his fellowmen and strangers and foreigners. Note the proverb: "One must deal with the devil until one crosses over the bridge" *(Köprüyü geçene kadar ayıya dayı denir)*.

The feeling of suspicion and distrust precludes confidence in fellow political actors and the possibility of accommodation of differences of views through amicable processes. This suspicion is most clearly visible in intraelite encounters. Those who are in power positions both in political parties or in government do not tolerate opposition to their authority or their policies. Here are some examples: (1) the conservative majorities of the Erzurum and Sivas Congresses and the Grand National Assembly vehemently opposed Mustafa Kemal's plans in creating a new regime in Anatolia; (2) Mustafa Kemal himself did not tolerate the formation of an opposition party, the Progressive Party; (3) the president and the party leader İnönü demanded the expulsion of Bayar, Menderes, Köprülü, and Koraltan from the Republican People's Party. These opposition leaders in turn established the Democratic Party; (4) the dissident elements within the Democratic Party were expelled and they in turn founded the Nation Party; (5) the Nation Party was dissolved by court order in 1954; (6) the nineteen deputies who were expelled from the Democratic Party established the Freedom Party in 1955; (7) when the Democratic Party was abolished by court order in 1960, it was succeeded by the Justice Party; (8) the military kept the Justice Party out of power until 1965 and in 1971 the Justice Party government was dismissed; (9) the forty-eight deputies who opposed the secretary general of the Republican People's Party and the "Left of Center" platform were compelled to resign from the party and they in turn established the Reliance Party in 1967; and (10) the Turkish Labor Party was abolished by court order in 1971. Among many others, these examples of political struggle and intolerance of political opposition since the 1920s demonstrate the fact that in interparty, intraparty, and intergovernmental affairs the opposition groups and parties usually do not identify themselves with or have trust in those who are in power positions and that the power holders lean toward wresting obedience to their will by resorting to coercive methods. Finding no other peaceful alternative to obtaining power, the opposition groups or opposition party leadership tend to encourage conspiratorial activities which in turn reinforce the antagonism of those in power.[9]

Nonetheless, a strong belief in moderation — a distinct feature of Turkish political culture — conditions the political behavior of the power holders against their political opponents. Recent political history is replete with examples of temperance on the part of governmental leaders.

Since authority and decision making are perceived as having been concentrated in the hands of those leaders who do not deserve confidence and who lack competence, opposition groups and parties usually center around personalities with charisma (real or assumed) or with broad politico-economic power bases rather than around

---

[9] Ergun Özbudun seems to concur in this view. He writes: "Despite the low ideological content of party politics in the 1950s, Turkish political life in general has been characterized by deep and hostile partisan feelings. This antagonism has led the successive governments (Union and Progress, Republican People's Party, and Democratic Party) in recent Turkish history to view the opposition parties not as acceptable alternative governments but as subversive organizations engaged in treasonable activities." *Batı Demokrasilerinde ve Türkiye'de Parti Disiplini* (Ankara: Hukuk Fakültesi Yayınları no. 235, 1968), p. 261. We note that the Democratic Party leadership particularly from 1957 to May 1960 considered the Republican People's Party as a conspiratorial organization. On this point see Aydemir, *İkinci Adam,* vol. 3, pp. 355–449. It was reported in Zafer newspaper (April 6, 7, 1960) that the government had intercepted orders from the Republican People's Party headquarters to all party branches calling upon them to be prepared to go underground. Then on April 18, 1960, the National Assembly, controlled by the Democratic Party, established a committee to investigate the activities of the Republican People's Party. General Cemal Gürsel's letter to the leader of the Justice Party, General Gümüşpala, in July 1961, also supports the above-mentioned point. In this letter Gürsel said: "If there is no basic cleaning-out of your party, if it does not turn back from the road which the whole nation recognizes as evil, and turn to honorable ends which the democratic system demands, it will not even be possible for me to recognize you as a legitimate political party." Quoted in Walter F. Weiker. *The Turkish Revolution,* p. 97; see also *Ulus,* July 26, 1961. Also, at the XVI Congress of the Republican People's Party in December 1962, İnönü demanded the expulsion of Kasım Gülek, Nihat Erim, Avni Doğan, and Turgut Göle for their alleged conspiratorial activities and connections with the abortive coup d'état of February 1962, which were aiming at implicating the Republican People's Party in "another adventure of a new military regime." Exactly a year later Kasım Gülek, Avni Doğan, Kenan Esengin, and Celal Sungur were also accused of being directly involved in activities leading to the abortive coup d'état of May 1963. On these developments see Özbudun, *Batı Demokrasilerinde ve Türkiye'de Parti Disiplini,* pp. 227–28.

a definite set of ideas and programs. Before broadening the basis of their support, prominent political personalities are usually called by the conservative attentive public to the task of demonstrating their invincibility against the established authority.

The belief in authoritative practices and coercion in case of noncompliance with the will of the power holders is deeply rooted in the minds of the general public. According to Savcı, the principle of authoritarianism, originating in the steppes of central Asia and developing further in the sanded wastelands of Islam, has been the most enduring feature of the Turkish statecraft.[10] Submission to the will of the ruler has been the fundamental principle of government not only in the ghazi society of the Ottomans, but also in the Turkish society brought into being by Gazi Mustafa Kemal. The governed have always had a preference for order over anarchy, no matter which leader held the power.

The social as well as political power structure is autocratic in character and functions from top down, each stratum exercising domineering power and influence backed by coercive sanctions over the inferior one. The family, the school, parties, and government all teach the doctrine of quietism, acquiescence, and obedience to the will of the powerful. The lessons in the family, in school and in nonpolitical as well as political experience stress authority because of its monopoly of power — whether duly constituted and legitimate or not!

Since political activity as well as intragovernmental affairs and personal relations are essentially based on mutual fear and suspicion, authority is rarely delegated to subordinates nor is undue responsibility assumed by them. The results are extreme red tape, inefficiency, and waste of human and material resources. In order to avoid undue responsibility, the administrators show a strong tendency toward subscribing to the legal formalities; they tend to perform their functions according to the rules of the book but when confronted with persons of power they do not hesitate to interpret the rules liberally so as to meet the demand. It appears that in public administration time is the most abundant commodity expended free of charge!

---

[10] Bahri Savcı "Modernleşmede Devlet Başkanımızın Rolü," *Prof. Dr. Yavuz Abadan'a Armağan* (Ankara: Ankara Üniversitesi Siyasal Bilgiler Fakültesi Yayınları no. 280, 1969), p. 207.

His political experiences reconfirm the belief of the individual that the government represents a paternal and coercive authority, like that found in the home. No wonder, then, that the government's main functions are to maintain internal and external security and to render justice. These functions are acceptable to the citizen because, as the proverb goes, "The finger cut by justice will not smart."

On the other hand, the politician is considered an ambitious and opportunistic person bent on personal aggrandizement or enrichment or both. He is viewed with much cynicism: "He who holds the honeycomb licks his finger."

The formal legislation notwithstanding, the three concentric circles accept their hierarchical stratification. Rustow illustrates this point by referring to the everyday speech and etiquette.[11] A person of lower social status is expected to use the formal address form, the second person plural; a person of higher social status utilizes the informal form of address when speaking to a person of lower social status. Then, too, the "illegal" titles that usually follow the proper name are also indicative of the prevailing social distinctions. In descending order of prestige and social position, for example, Osman might be referred to as *Muhterem* Osman *Beyefendi,* Osman *Paşa,* Osman *Beyefendi,* Osman *Bey,* or Osman *Ağa.* If he is of rather low estate or a youngster or child, he would be addressed as Osman *Efendi,* or just plain Osman! These forms of address are prevalent and still accepted by the people.

The political elite look upon themselves as having the inherent right to lead the general public and protect and preserve the Republican regime and to act as the guardians of the principles of Atatürkism. This feeling of superiority reinforces the belief that it is the elite in general and the governing elite in particular who will bring Turkey to the level of contemporary civilization.[12]

---

[11] Dankwart A. Rustow, "Turkey: The Modernity of Tradition." *Political Culture and Political Development,* ed. Lucian W. Pye and Sidney Verba (Princeton, N.J.: Princeton University Press, paperback ed., 1969), p. 181.

[12] Cf. Kemal H. Karpat, bemoans this fact. He writes: "Bureaucracy and the intelligentsia emerged as distinct social groups and viewed themselves as superior to other social groups. They took upon themselves the duty of guiding other groups, not through free discussion, but through the force of state power. This situation is the greatest disaster that can befall a society." *Political and Social Thought in the Contemporary Middle East,* ed. Kemal H. Karpat (New York: Frederick A. Praeger, 1968), p. 344.

Correlative to cynicism and authoritarianism is the belief in a high degree of "formalism" and "legalism" which demand that politico-socio-economic life comply with the traditional forms and rules of etiquette and that rights and obligations be delineated under strict rules of conduct. In this regard, more respect and consideration are given to "form" and outward appearance. In matters of education, it is the accumulation of degrees and social and professional titles rather than practical experience and knowledge that guarantees higher status and prestige for the individual. In economic life, immovable property, gold coins, jewelry, custom-made clothing, cars, and of late, television receivers are the tangible items of higher prestige and social status. In governmental affairs, first priority is given to the enactment of laws and by-laws and recruitment of personnel instead of the introduction of efficient methods for better public service. Construction of impressive establishments, such as modern public buildings, monuments, and factories far removed from sources of raw materials, are regarded as symbols of modernity.

An important feature of Turkish political culture is the belief in the principle of expediency and pragmatism on the part of the holders of political power and an equally profound belief in the principle of theoretical perfection (idealism) on the part of those lacking political power. However, as noted earlier, the elite essentially display a high degree of commitment to the principle of moderation in dealing with opponents and in seeking political objectives.

ATATÜRKISM AS "IDEOLOGY"

In recent years, particularly since the 1950s, principles which formerly were considered as the fundamental ingredients of "Kemalism" and ideas and ideals of Atatürk about the past, present, and future of the Turkish polity have become the most cherished and favored ideology of the educated classes. Atatürk's personality and his image have acquired a somewhat sacred nature. His sayings and pronouncements have assumed an aura of absolute truth. The leadership of political parties and the intelligentsia demanded strict and passionate adherence to the ideas and ideals of Atatürk.

Atatürkism itself has become the major value to be defended and expanded.[13]

However, writings of the intelligentsia display great differences of opinion about the general principles of Atatürkism. Such differences have often caused bitter debate within the ranks of the intelligentsia and have led to an artificial division of the educated classes into basically two groups: Those who consider the ideas and principles of Atatürk as essentially pragmatic concepts that must be understood within their given historical context and that must be applied and interpreted liberally so as to meet the exigencies of the time; and those who consider Atatürkism as a system of tenets, true and valid at all times, which constitute the only set of guides to the modernization of the Turkish society. No wonder, then, that those who argued that these principles and some other ideas of Atatürk were merely expedient formulas to meet the needs of a given situation have been labeled as "reactionary traditionalists," "advocates of socio-economic status quo," "lackeys of imperialists," and worst of all "anti-Atatürkists." Yet, one cannot fail to detect a definite tendency of those who call themselves "true Atatürkists" to relate their own ideas and values to that of Atatürk. On this point Harris observes: "Cloaking their appeals with the mantle of Kemalism, the socialists attempted to gain increased legitimacy by claiming Atatürk as one of their own."[14]

If Atatürkism is to be called an ideology, that ideology is fundamentally different from most other "isms" in that it only calls upon the Turkish people to look toward the future expressing full confidence in the capabilities of the Turks to fulfill their own ever-expanding desires. Atatürkism, as Berkes observes, lacks a doctrinal, dogmatic basis; it does not contain the blueprints of a perfect and prosperous Turkish society.[15] The remarkable achievements of Atatürk and other leaders in terms of closing the gap between the past and present were precisely the result of their

---

[13] As recently as June 1971, a special commission on the principles of Atatürk was created; its task is to perpetuate the image of Atatürk and spread "Atatürkism" as the ideology of Turkey.

[14] George S. Harris, *Troubled Alliance: Turkish-American Problems in Historical Perspective* (Washington, D.C.: American Enterprise Institute for Public Policy Research, 1972), p. 96.

[15] Berkes, *The Development of Secularism in Turkey*, p. 52.

pragmatic orientation and outlook and their tendency to veer away from drawing an ideological blueprint.[16]

Be that as it may, how can one explain the fact that Atatürkism is the most favored ideology? One reasonable explanation may be sought in the nature of global environment. More than ever before, the world is in the midst of ideological struggles. Today ideology is the "in" thing. It may, therefore, be that the Turkish intelligentsia is responding to the requirements of the time. Another reason might be that while the Islamic way of life, together with its values, may not be the most perfect instrument to raise Turkish society to the level of contemporary civilization, neither are any of the foreign ideologies. Neither Western democracy nor socialism nor Marxism of the so-called communist countries appears to be suitable to the aspirations and expectations of the Turkish people. The intelligentsia it seems are after a new cultural synthesis and in this task they find their greatest inspiration in the ideas and ideals of Atatürk. They seem to keep in mind what Atatürk had said some time ago: "But it is not our making, if we do not resemble either democracy or socialism, nor for that matter resemble anything. Gentlemen, we should be proud of defying comparison! Because, gentlemen, we resemble ourselves."[17] It may, therefore, be said that the Turkish intelligentsia view Atatürkism as an alternative to foreign ideologies, including that of the Islamic way of life.

Atatürkism appears both as an independent value (end), and a dependent value (means). It first of all fulfills the need to have an indigenous set of ideas as the basis for the future way of life for the Turks and, second, it serves as an instrument for the elite to help modernize society. Then, too, in the intraelite struggles the single most important issue, i.e., deviation from or conformity to Atatürkism, appears to be the most useful and effective instrument in bringing the downfall of the ruling elite. The fate of the Democratic Party in 1960 and the Justice Party in 1971 are cases in point. These two cases, among many other similar situations, lead one to ask: Is democracy a myth or a reality in Turkey?

---

[16] See Richard D. Robinson, *The First Turkish Republic,* p. 87.

[17] Türk İnkilap Tarihi Enstitüsü, *Atatürk'ün Söylev ve Demeçleri* (Ankara: Türk Tarih Kurumu Basımevi, 1961), p. 196.

The Myth of Democracy

There has always been an inconsistency between the theoretical framework and actual functioning of the political system in Turkey, between the constitutional powers of the governmental agencies and their actual practices, in short, between the "outer appearance," (form) and the "essence." Under the 1924 Constitution, the legislative and executive powers were concentrated in the hands of the National Assembly. But, as Soysal observes, in actual practice the two powers were separated and the weight shifted heavily in favor of the executive branch of the government.[18] Balta expresses essentially the same view. He writes: "In practice, the Constitutional principle granting superiority to the National Assembly over the executive was never materialized; instead the executive had come to dominate the legislature." Although he does not identify the political regime of Turkey as a "dictatorship" he nevertheless admits that "in our system of government the executive has always been stronger and more effective than the legislature. In fact, a strong and effective executive has always been the traditional practice in Turkey."[19]

The reasons for this practice are found in the personal qualities of the warrior leaders like Atatürk and İnönü and in their power based on the single party regime which they have instituted and maintained. Their regular election at four-year intervals during the single party regime was a matter of form. Even though Celal Bayar was elected president during the multiparty regime, he controlled an overwhelming majority in the National Assembly. He could be dislodged from his office only through a coup d'état. It is a truism to say that until 1960 the presidents of the republic determined who was to be the deputy in the National Assembly, who was to occupy the office of prime minister and what would be the composition of the Council of Ministers. These officials remained in their offices at the pleasure of the presidents. During the years from 1923 to 1960, twenty-three cabinets were formed, headed by only nine prime ministers. İsmet İnönü held the post for thirteen years and eight months; Adnan Menderes served for ten years.

---

[18] Soysal, *Dış Politika ve Parlamento,* p. 104.
[19] Tahsin Bekir Balta, *Türkiye'de Yürütme Kudreti* (Ankara: Ajans-Türk Matbassı, 1960), pp. 13–14.

During the same period only one prime minister died in office, Refik Saydam, in 1942; one prime minister was voted out of office as a result of the general elections in 1950, Şemsettin Günaltay; and one prime minister was forced out of office by a military coup, Adnan Menderes.

Most important of all, none of these twenty-three cabinets ever received a vote of no confidence in the National Assembly, causing their resignation. Although the Grand National Assembly is said to be the supreme repository of governmental authority and is always identified by many adherents of the democratic ideal as being a truly democratic institution, representing the sovereign will of the nation, it never exercised that authority against the authoritarian practices of the presidents.[20]

Similar discrepancies between theory and practice are readily available in the period since the adoption of the 1961 Constitution. The most recent confrontation between the top military leaders, the cabinet, and the Grand National Assembly is a case in point. When the popularly-elected Justice Party cabinet was summarily dismissed and replaced by a "nonpartisan cabinet" of Dr. Nihat Erim, the latter received an overwhelming vote of confidence from the assembly (321 for and 46 against with 3 abstentions, 74 deputies not taking part in the voting).[21] The ex-Premier Demirel in a realistic appraisal of the situation is quoted as saying that the Justice Party could not oppose the army by calling in the forces of national militia.[22]

As long as the Atatürk reforms were to be carried forward by fiat rather than by the consent of the governed, was it necessary to adopt an elaborate constitutional frame and call the new regime "The Second Republic"? How can one reconcile the government by fiat with a multiparty parliamentary system, with "constitutional democracy"? How can one explain this apparent paradox? The governing elite, evidence indicates, see no contradiction between the authoritarian methods they advocate in order to achieve moderni-

---

[20] Frederick W. Frey suggests that the deputies in the Grand National Assembly "probably constituted a major portion of the wielders of disproportionate *real power*, not formal authority, in Turkish society." *The Turkish Political Elite,* p. 6.

[21] *Cumhuriyet,* 27 Mart 1971.

[22] Ibid., 7 Nisan 1971.

zation and the functioning of the democratic institutions, since they view the latter as the essential ingredients of modernized status. As long as they do not impede the achievement of the ultimate objective, the governing elite protect and preserve the democratic institutions and processes. But when strict adherence to these institutions and processes seems to appear as an obstacle to the ultimate goal, the governing elite hasten to put them aside. In a nutshell, as far as the governing elite are concerned, democracy may be something desirable to have but not necessarily essential in reaching the greater end. In the hierarchy of values, democracy is given a lower position than the goal of modernization, and the apparent paradox is resolved. On the other hand, the political counterelite, in their hierarchy of values, place democracy and modernization on the same footing and view the former as an immediate end. Being in the opposition, the counterelite appear more outspoken in their defense and their advocacy of democracy; but when they in turn come to power they do not hesitate to emulate their opponents. Recent events bear testimony to this fact. It will be interesting to see if Prime Minister Bülent Ecevit and his associates who in the past have acted as the standard bearers of democracy will be able to reverse the practice and succeed in achieving drastic and rapid socio-economic changes through democratic processes.

The foregoing description of the nature of reforms and of Turkish political culture shows that political democracy, not to mention social democracy, as yet remains a myth in Turkey. Even if one were to argue that the formal aspects of the political democracy of the West[23] have been transplanted in Turkey, one must remember that the political democracy of the West has its own socio-economic infrastructure, its own traditions, its own function and meaning based on its fundamental belief system, and that in cultural exchanges, form or outer appearance is more easily assimilated than function and meaning. The Turkish reformers were aware of this fact, and perhaps this is why they have opted for the superstructural changes and changes in the outer appearance of the society.

---

[23] For a critical review of "Western democracy" see Robert A. Dahl, *Democracy in the United States: Promise and Performance,* 2nd. ed. (Chicago: Rand McNally, 1972), pp. 23-53. The political regimes in thirty-two countries which are commonly referred to as "democracies" are described by Dahl as "polyarchies"—regimes that appear to approach "ideal democracy" but fall short of it by a considerable and significant margin.

The infrastructural and cultural differences between the Turkish polity and Western polities tend to be obscured by the vast quantities of verbiage that emanate from among the ranks of the idealist counterelite. The unsophisticated but politically astute peasant, on the other hand, is less likely to be fooled by the existence of a democratic façade when he experiences every evidence of the powerful few imposing their will on the vast majority. His heritage of traditional authoritarianism teaches him to accept the political system and the goal of modernization as devised and defined by the elite.

THE NATURE AND EXTENT OF THE "TURKISH REVOLUTION"

Indeed, Turkey underwent a superstructural revolution, or the first phase of the "Turkish Revolution." If the Turkish warriors had been willing to shoulder greater risks, they would have introduced drastic, rapid, and forceful changes in the socio-economic life of Turkey. The second phase of their revolution would have uprooted traditional values and beliefs, and recast the socio-economic infrastructure of the society by forceful and violent methods.

Mustafa Kemal, a product of the Turkish traditional culture, but a dynamic leader oriented toward modern ways of life, did not attempt to dismantle the socio-economic structure of the society in one forceful blow. He did not initiate a revolutionary program of sweeping infrastructural changes to be carried out by force. The same may be said for the leadership of the Committee of National Unity during their rule in 1960 and 1961. At the time of the coup d'état on May 27, 1960, the whole armed forces as well as a considerable segment of the intelligentsia were wholeheartedly on the side of the CNU leadership.[24] They could have launched the second phase of the Turkish Revolution, but they did not. As noted earlier, they preferred to revise the superstructure of the society by introducing a new Constitution. However, by delegating the task of legislating socio-economic reforms to the new Grand National

---

[24] See Weiker, *The Turkish Revolution,* pp. 19-20; Davison, *Turkey,* pp. 155-56; Geoffrey Lewis, *Modern Turkey,* 3rd ed. (New York: Praeger Publishers, 1974), pp. 153–57.

Assembly, they not only postponed indefinitely the necessary infrastructural reforms, but also made their enactment a virtual impossibility. Those elected deputies and senators would certainly not find it in their interest to alienate their conservative constituencies by advocating or enacting measures contrary to the beliefs and values of the conservative majority of the people. In fact, the reform bills introduced by the nonpartisan cabinets of Nihat Erim, Ferit Melen, and Naim Talu, since April 1971, were revised so drastically in the parliament that the proponents of "necessary reforms in the infrastructure of the society" could hardly identify the enacted measures as "reform measures."

Therefore, social upheaval did not take place in Turkey simply because the warrior diplomats did not wish to resort to methods of revolutionary change. They preferred instead to achieve modernization gradually through a series of careful changes. They decided to modernize Turkey step by step, partly because of the restraining influences of the traditional culture discussed above and partly because of their pragmatic orientation. Atatürk's and his successors' chief strategies for accomplishing external and internal objectives were based on the principle of striking a balance between ends and means. These warrior leaders formulated their goals in accordance with the realities of international and domestic life and on the basis of a realistic assessment of the human and material resources of Turkey, as well as that of the cultural heritage of the people. They were never fully committed to the idea of drastic and rapid cultural change. Instead, they were determined to borrow selectively and cautiously from the treasures of Western institutions and political philosophies with a view to creating an original synthesis composed of the Turkish traditional values and those "forms" borrowed from the West. They have opted for evolutionary processes of change because they, as well as the great majority of the people, were deeply attached to traditional institutions and beliefs, which at one time had helped the Turks create a glittering civilization. Then, too, sweeping and rapid infrastructural changes could be brought about through measures of mass imprisonment, deportations, and executions to be carried out in an atmosphere of general terror. No Turkish leader was willing to pay such a high premium to achieve revolutionary changes!

The reason for the apparent neglect of drastic and substantive cultural changes seems to lie also in the fact that Atatürk, İnönü, and their successors were preoccupied with the questions of national security, internal cohesion, and stability. Social and economic questions seem to have attracted their attention only to the extent of their direct bearing on the question of national security.[25] Moreover, the leadership of Turkey was motivated by a strong desire to avoid firm commitment to any foreign ideologies, including that of the extreme ideologies of the Right or the Left, in order to minimize the chances of foreign intervention in the domestic affairs of Turkey.

If this analysis is correct, then, it may be suggested that, contrary to the opinion of those writers who in their studies of the domestic affairs of the last fifty years speak about an ongoing Turkish Revolution, Turkey is in a state of transformation (reform) rather than revolution. The term "Turkish Revolution" does not accurately reflect nor does it describe the realities of domestic politics, for the second phase of the Turkish Revolution was never intended to take place. The term Turkish Revolution may only reflect the aspirations and expectations of those counterelite who are not satisfied with the existing distribution of political power, prestige, and influence. It may also be that some of the idealists in this age of revolutions are hoping to emulate the so-called revolutionary movements in the external arena!

But how can one explain the extreme tension, political unrest, and violence that swept the country during the 1950s and which in the latter part of the 1960s brought about an atmosphere of revolution? It must be remembered that with the opening up of the tutelary regime of İnönü a serious split occurred within the ranks of the intelligentsia. As Frey aptly puts it, "The Kemalist unity . . . has been fractured. . . . That elite unity which permitted mobilization of the society for rapid reform had degenerated into the war of each against all. . . ."[26] The relaxation of international tension in general and the so-called "gestures of friendship" displayed by the Soviet Union caused the diversion of the attention of the intelligentsia from the external to the internal scene. There, the

---

[25] Dankwart A. Rustow maintains that Mustafa "Kemal indeed displayed little interest in social and economic change as these terms have to be understood since the Mexican, Russian and anticolonial revolutions. For him, economic improvement and bridging of class differences were practical requirements of national solidarity and international stature, rather than deeply felt needs of human justice and dignity." "Atatürk as Founder of a State," in *Prof. Dr. Yavuz Abadan'a Armagan*, p. 569.

[26] Frey, *The Turkish Political Elite*, p. 391.

counterelite found, suddenly and as though by black magic, a "great gap" between the superstructure and infrastructure in terms of their modernity. This great gap was made glaringly real under the provisions of the 1961 Constitution which brought about sweeping changes in the organization and structure of the state, including the establishment of the Second Republic. The same organic law also instituted further democratic safeguards against the authoritarian practices of the past.

Since May 1960, within the ranks of the elite, the idea of revolutionay socio-economic change under the auspices of the true Atatürkists has constantly clashed with the idea of necessary reforms under the direction of military-civilian leadership. Because of the idiosyncracies of Turkish political culture, such clashes of ideas led to further division of the elite into splinter groups and to political violence organized and directed clandestinely by the leadership of the revisionist opposition parties and their adherents within the elite and intermediate segments of the society.

Moreover, the absence of a strong charismatic leader — military or civilian — who could create common consensus among the intelligentsia and unify them behind his reform policies and programs has intensified the division and dissension within the military-civilian elite. In fact, not since 1938 has there been a leader who, in the eyes of the general public as well as the intelligentsia, has measured up to the qualities of the charismatic personality of Atatürk. Particularly since 1950, the country has been run first by the collective leadership of the Democratic Party, Bayar and Menderes, then by the Committee of National Unity, and then by coalition governments and/or a collegium of military-civilian leaders. It may be said that since Atatürk's death in 1938, Turkey has been plagued by a "crisis of decisive leadership."

In the years of political violence, the governmental leaders maneuvered delicately and avoided taking stern measures against the instigators of violence and perpetrators of acts of terrorism. No doubt the traditional belief in moderation as well as the ultra-democratic provisions of the 1961 Constitution played an important role in their reactions against the extremists and terrorists. The latter, however, interpreted the restraint that was clearly visible in governmental reactions as weakness and increased their attacks against the established authority, thinking that the time was ripe for revolutionary restructuring of the Turkish polity.

But in March 1971 when the situation appeared to have slipped out of the control of the government, the top military leaders moved in once again and installed a nonpartisan cabinet. Since then, martial law has been instituted, perpetrators of terrorist acts have been apprehended and tried by military authorities, and the Constitution has been amended a number of times to prevent any more abuse of political and civil rights on the part of extremists.

These latest moves of the military indicated in clearest terms that the basic assumptions of the 1961 Constitution were unfounded. In fact Premier Erim, former professor of public law at Ankara University, has strongly criticized the Constitution as "a luxury for Turkey."[27] It seems that for those who wield power in directing the course of the Turkish ship of state, the constitutional arrangement of power distribution among various branches of the government is of little more than academic value. The important mission of modernization may, at times, necessitate the violation of the provisions of the organic law. This is what the warriors have done in recent years, which revealed once again the true nature of the political regime in Turkey: "Government for the People and by the Militarized Elite." The militarized elite is composed of the top military leaders, the warriors in civilian clothes, and the "militarized civilians"[28] — the ardent guardians of the legacies of Gazi Mustafa Kemal and of the republic.

BUT NO SECOND REVOLUTION

The main points of the second part of this study may be summarized as follows. The prevailing international system and structure have been directly instrumental in the growth and ultimate dismemberment of the Ghazi Ottoman society and the Ottoman Empire and in the birth and transformation of the Republic of Turkey.

The warrior leaders of Turkey, having won the War of Independence, considered modernization as the best and surest means

---

[27] *Milliyet,* 2 Mayis 1971. See also Nihat Erim, "The Turkish Experience in the Light of Recent Developments," *The Middle East Journal,* 26 (Summer 1972): 248.

[28] This phrase is borrowed from Richard J. Barnet, et al. *American Government Today* (Del Mar, Calif.: CRM Books, 1974), p. 152.

to create and sustain a viable Turkish society and to guarantee its independent existence. Thus, they set the protection of national security and the reaching the level of contemporary civilization as their twin goals.

For these leaders modernization meant political reforms in the superstructure of the society which, if carried out successfully, would not only usher in an era of continued growth and development but would also enhance the power, prestige, and stature of Turkey in the international arena, thus justifying her claim to equal sovereign status with the modern democratic states of the West.

Due to the idiosyncracies of Turkish political culture, modernization was initiated from the top of the political structure by the warrior leaders and carried out by the ruling elite. The process of modernization, because of pragmatic considerations, entailed step by step innovations, and because of preoccupation with the questions of national security, little attention was paid to socio-economic changes. The leaders created an original political system which is a synthesis of the Turkish traditional authoritarian practices and the borrowed forms of the democratic institutions of the West.

At present, the attention of the intelligentsia more than ever before is focused on socio-economic problems. The extremist elements of the counterelite, taking advantage of the liberalization of the political system under the 1961 Constitution, in recent years have resorted to methods of political violence with a view to changing drastically the infrastructure of the society. Due to the absence of a charismatic leader and because of the ultrademocratic provisions of the Constitution, governments at times seem to have been unable to cope with the political violence of the extremists. However, the collective military-civilian leadership has repeatedly helped to restore the authority of the state and impose law and order in the country. In light of the developments in the 1960s and the most recent actions of the governments, one is led to believe that the military-civilian collective leadership of Turkey seems to possess a remarkable amount of political wisdom, prudence, temperance, and foresight, and that at critical junctures leaders are capable of subordinating their own personal political ambitions and even their ideological commitments to the twin goal of national security and modernization.

Pragmatic orientation, realism, and moderation in seeking political objectives — all enduring features of the Turkish political culture — may be identified as the most important stabilizing forces in domestic politics, and have so far prevented the otherwise chronically unstable condition — a necessary consequence of the process of modernization — from reaching civil war proportions.

One is also led to believe that the present military-civilian collective leadership, like its warrior predecessors, is determined to minimize the inherent instabilities of modernization and close the gap between the superstructure and infrastructure, between the past and present by introducing further socio-economic reforms as circumstances permit.

III

The Warriors
And Their Diplomacy

*"Diplomacy is to do and say the
nastiest thing in the nicest way."*

Isaac Goldberg

Chapter Nine

THE SUMMIT DIPLOMACY
OF THE PRESIDENTS:
AN OVERVIEW

As Mustafa Kemal saw it, the foreign policy objectives of the
nationalists would have to be formulated and executed from one
center and the military and diplomatic campaigns be directed at
the summit of political power. Accordingly, during the War of
Independence period, as much as circumstances permitted, he almost
singlehandedly managed the military, diplomatic, and political
affairs of the government of the Grand National Assembly of
Turkey. He insisted on negotiating agreements with the emissaries
of foreign powers and communicating with foreign heads of governments. He received foreign envoys, appointed, and, when necessary,
dismissed the representatives of the Ankara government. As president of the republic, Mustafa Kemal not only set the fundamental
foreign policy goals of Turkey but also continued to act as the chief
diplomat of his country.

The summit diplomacy of warrior chief Mustafa Kemal was
not something new for Turkish statecraft.[1] Its roots are deep in the
traditional political system of the Turkish ghazi states and the
Ottoman Empire where the head of state determined the goals of
foreign policy and, in most instances, directly managed foreign

---

[1] For the nature and scope of summit diplomacy, see Elmer Plischke,
Summit Diplomacy: Personal Diplomacy of the President of the United States
(College Park, Md.: Bureau of Governmental Research, University of Maryland,
1958).

affairs. This practice was carried over into the Republican era. Under the provisions of the Constitution, the president of the republic is the head of state and as such represents the republic. He is empowered to preside over the meetings of the Council of Ministers where domestic and foreign policies are formulated, to appoint the diplomatic representatives and to receive foreign envoys, to ratify and publish international agreements, to welcome foreign heads of state, to send messages of greetings, congratulations, and condolences, and to take part in summit conferences of heads of state. But in fact the presidents of the republic have had much greater powers than such symbolic functions.

The history of the last fifty years of the republic suggests that the presidents have had the final say in the questions of domestic and foreign policies, including the questions of war and peace and the deployment of the Turkish armed forces outside the territorial limits of Turkey. For example, Lord Kinross reports that during a meeting with the Italian ambassador Atatürk suggested that instead of urging the Italian students to demonstrate in front of the Turkish Embassy in Rome for the cession of the Antalya region to Italy, Mussolini should land troops in Antalya to be followed by a battle between the Turkish and Italian forces and that the side which won the battle should have Antalya. Upon the Italian ambassador's inquiry as to whether this was "a declaration of war," Atatürk is quoted by Lord Kinross as saying: "I am speaking here as a mere citizen. Only the Grand National Assembly can declare war in the name of Turkey. But try to remember that, when the time comes, the Grand National Assembly will take into consideration the feelings of mere citizens like myself."[2] It may also be noted that following the end of the Second World War a motion was unanimously adopted by the Grand National Assembly which commissioned twenty deputies with "the pleasant and joyous mission" of personally conveying to "His Excellency President İnönü" the indebtedness and deep gratitude of the assembly as well as the people for his leadership and guidance during the most difficult and dark hours of the war.[3] Five years later President Bayar, following his private conversations with his prime minister and defense minister, decided to send 5,000 Turkish troops to Korea to participate

---

[2] Lord Kinross, *Ataturk,* p. 545.

[3] See Soysal, *Dış Politika ve Parlamento,* p. 105.

in the Korean War. At the time, the other members of the Council of Ministers and the Grand National Assembly were kept uninformed about such a dramatic and important action.[4]

The documents in foreign archives, the memoirs of Turkish statesmen and officials indicate that foreign policy decisions were made in the presidential palace, the *Köşk,* at Çankaya, in the Dolmabahçe palace in Istanbul, in the resort palaces at Florya and Yalova, and at times on the Presidential yacht, *Savarona.* Close associates and trusted advisers of presidents, such as the prime ministers, other cabinet officers, top military leaders, and close friends were often called in to these places to consider foreign policy issues and to review alternative courses of actions and plans. However, at the end of such deliberations, the presidents formulated policies and gave instructions for their prompt implementation.

It is also known that matters of foreign policy and the nature and scope of the conduct of Turkish diplomacy were also reviewed and discussed at secret sessions of the caucuses of the parties in power and at the executive sessions of the Grand National Assembly. The records of such meetings, however, are still secret and therefore unavailable to the general public.[5]

The State of the Nation speeches of the presidents before the National Assembly were almost the only avenues through which the legislature as well as the general public could obtain information from the head of state on the foreign relations activities of the Turkish government. However, a content analysis of these speeches would reveal the fact that they contained only broad and general statements about Turkey's foreign relations. It appears that the presidents preferred to keep foreign powers as well as the Grand National Assembly guessing as to their strategies and tactics. These speeches, which were delivered in person by the presidents on March 1 of each year until 1924, and on November 1 from 1924 to 1960 provided pompous occasions whereby the presidents appeared in their stately splendor before the representatives of the people and the diplomatic corps and explained their general views

---

[4] On this issue see the statement of Fahri Belen, then the Minister of Public Works, in Ibid., pp. 201–2.

[5] Soysal maintains that during the years from 1923 to 1959 the Grand National Assembly was convened in seven extraordinary sessions to consider the foreign relations activities of the governments. *Dış Politika ve Parlamento,* pp. 106–8, 235–36.

about the affairs of the nation. The State of the Nation speeches usually contained brief remarks expressing the desire of Turkey for peace and friendly relations with small and great powers alike. Occasionally they referred to the international agreements that were signed with foreign powers, the state visits of foreign heads of state and heads of government, and the visits of the Turkish officials to foreign capitals.[6] This practice has been discontinued since the adoption of the 1961 Constitution.

As far as providing the legislature and the general public with information on foreign affairs of Turkey is concerned, the programs of cabinets,[7] the occasional foreign policy statements of the prime ministers and foreign ministers made before the plenary sessions of the Grand National Assembly or at its committee hearings,[8] and press conferences[9] may be mentioned. Needless to add, such official statements, in the main, disclosed only those broad outlines of foreign policy strategies.

The state visits of the presidents and the visits of foreign heads of state as well as the official visits of the Turkish prime ministers and foreign ministers to foreign capitals, and the visits of foreign heads of governments and other foreign state officials have shown a steady increase since the 1950s. It is significant to note that neither Atatürk, İnönü, or Gürsel, as presidents of the republic, paid state visits to foreign countries, whereas Presidents Bayar and Sunay engaged extensively in the practice of state visits and acted as host to an increasing number of foreign heads of state.

It was President İnönü who for the first time attended a summit conference outside of Turkey. He met with President F. D. Roosevelt and Prime Minister W. S. Churchill in Cairo from December 4 to 7, 1943. Since then Presidents Bayar and Sunay attended a number of summit conferences. What actually transpired in such summit meetings is still a closely guarded state secret and the records of these conferences are, unfortunately, unavailable.

When the presidents considered it necessary, which was not infrequent, they withheld information from the Grand National

6 For the texts of these speeches see *Atatürk'ün Söylev ve Demeçleri,* and the November 2 issue of the official gazette, *Resmi Gazete.*

7 See Kazım Öztürk, *Türkiye Cumhuriyeti Hükümetleri ve Programları.*

8 See T.B.M.M., *Zabıt Ceridesi "Tutanak Dergisi"* (Ankara: T.B.M.M. Matbaası, 1920–1970).

9 See *Dışişleri Bakanlığı Belleteni,* 1964–1971.

Assembly and the general public alike on the grounds that publication of the contents of communications and executive agreements was contrary to national security and public interest. Because of the heavy blanket of secrecy covering the foreign policy decision-making process and the conduct of foreign relations of Turkey, one can only form a somewhat hazy picture of this otherwise colorful subject by piecing together related data reported in memoirs and in journals and newspapers. Indeed, the process of putting such data into meaningful form and shape is like working jigsaw puzzles.

Be that as it may, there will be an attempt to describe the summit diplomacy of the Presidents Atatürk, İnönü, Bayar, Gürsel, Sunay, and Korutürk and a review of the personal relations of these warrior diplomats with their chief foreign policy advisers, the prime ministers and foreign ministers.

Chapter Ten
GAZİ MUSTAFA KEMAL ATATÜRK

Mustafa Kemal's Diplomacy During The War of Independence Period

His Early Diplomatic Contacts

Even before his departure from Istanbul on May 15, 1919, Mustafa Kemal was exploring the possibilities of establishing some sort of contact with the occupation authorities with a view to sounding out their feelings toward the possible emergence of a nationalist movement in the interior of Anatolia.

His erstwhile adversary, Italian High Commissioner Count Carlo Sforza, incensed by the treatment of Italy by the British and French over the question of the establishment of an Italian sphere of influence in the İzmir region, was also in search of a helping hand. Their mutual animosity toward Britain and France seems to have brought Count Sforza and Mustafa Kemal temporarily together in order to exchange views on the prevailing conditions in Turkey. It is reported that Count Sforza arranged a meeting with Mustafa Kemal and told him that if and when a nationalist government was formed in the interior of Anatolia, he could count on Italian support for his actions and that if he was in trouble he could seek the assistance of the Italian Embassy.[1] Count Sforza, in his version, reports that Mustafa Kemal, on being informed

---

[1] See Lord Kinross, *Ataturk,* p. 167.

about the possibility of his deportation from the country, inquired of the Italian High Commissioner as to whether he could count on his support; Count Sforza assured Mustafa Kemal that "an apartment was at his disposal at the Italian Embassy."[2]

Mustafa Kemal was also seeking out British authorities in order to gain an appointment to a position of prestige, such as governorship of a province, from which he could organize a nationalist movement. With this objective in mind, he established contact with a British newspaper correspondent, G. Ward Price, in Istanbul. Mustafa Kemal is reported to have told Price that in view of the expected division of Anatolia by the Allies the Turks would prefer a British administration over a French one, that they, the Turks, were "particularly anxious to keep the French out of Asia Minor" and that "if the British are going to assume responsibility for Anatolia they will need the cooperation of experienced Turkish governors to work under them." Price goes on to say that Mustafa Kemal concluded his remarks by inquiring as to the proper authority to which he could offer his services as a governor. Then Price writes: "I gave an account of this conversation to Colonel Heywood. He dismissed it as unimportant. 'There will be a lot of these Turkish general looking for jobs before long' he said."[3] Little did the British know! Mustafa Kemal also offered his services to that sultan-caliph whom he deposed and banished from Turkey!

In this connection, a report of an English intelligence officer concerning Mustafa Kemal's views of the recent developments in Turkey as told him by Dimitri Atchkoff, a deputy in the Bulgarian Parliament from 1903 to 1908, deserves mention. The intelligence officer identified Dimitri Atchkoff as a personal friend of Mustafa Kemal, an ardent Kemalist, and Mustafa Kemal's "agent and propagandist in Bulgaria." To substantiate his assertion that they were close friends, the intelligence officer says that in one of his visits Atchkoff had shown him a signed photograph and a sword presented by Mustafa Kemal. According to this report Atchkoff and Mustafa Kemal had become good friends when the latter was the Turkish military attaché in Sofia, and in January 1916, after the battle of Anafarta, Mustafa Kemal had come to Sofia on a

---

[2] Count Carlo Sforza, *Makers of Modern Europe: Portraits and Personal Impressions and Recollections* (Indianapolis: Bobbs-Merrill, 1928), p. 365.

[3] G. Ward Price, *Extra-Special Correspondent* (London: George G. Harrap, 1957), pp. 104–5.

month's leave and stayed in Atchkoff's house as his guest. And then at a later date they were together again in Istanbul. Then, in March 1920 Atchkoff, obtaining permission from French authorities to go to Anatolia ostensibly for business purposes, paid a visit to Mustafa Kemal. And since then Atchkoff communicated with Mustafa Kemal and last received a letter from him in September 1920.[4] According to Atchkoff, Mustafa Kemal desired above all "to come to an agreement with Great Britain — other countries, France, Italy, etc., did not count. . . . Mustafa Kemal was not interested in the Arab question, but only in territories where the population was Turkish. . . . Mustafa Kemal would recognize and guarantee racial minorities, so long as they did not conspire against the sovereignty of Turkish State. An independent Turkey *must* exist and Great Britain should return to this policy. As regards Bolshevism Mustafa Kemal's attitude was this: Bolshevism could take no root in Turkish soil: religion and traditions alike were against it. But he would readily make use of its assistance in order to attain the ideals of Turkish Nation."[5]

The intelligence report also contains the conclusions of Dimitri Atchkoff, that Great Britain would derive infinitely more advantages from an understanding with Mustafa Kemal and his nationalist government than from Greece and that such an understanding would put an end to the "unnatural collaboration between the Turks and the Bolsheviks."[6]

During the Erzurum Congress, Mustafa Kemal met with Colonel A. Rawlinson, the British control officer at Erzurum in charge of disarming the Turkish troops under the terms of the Armistice of Mudros. However, no account of this contact can be found. Following the Sivas Congress, a copy of the declaration of the Congress was sent to Colonel Rawlinson. And as a reprisal against the deportation of the nationalists in the Ottoman Parliament by the British authorities, Colonel Rawlinson, together with other British officers in Anatolia, was arrested and imprisoned for eighteen months. At the end of that time, an agreement was reached between the nationalist and British authorities on the exchange of prisoners

---

[4] This intelligence report dated November 20, 1920, is in Great Britain, F. O. 371/5291, E 15358/14574/44.

[5] Ibid.

[6] Ibid.

and Colonel Rawlinson was released. He then tried to inform the British authorities as to future capabilities of the Nationalist Movement in Anatolia. But his efforts in this direction were of no avail.[7]

It is reported that with the help of the Karakol Society, organized in the latter part of 1918 in Istanbul by a group of nationalists to conduct guerrilla resistance operations and supplying the nationalists in Anatolia with arms and intelligence information, the ground was prepared for a meeting between Mustafa Kemal and Soviet Colonel Semen Mikhailovich Budenny. According to intelligence reports, Colonel Budenny had been sent to Istanbul to report on the situation in Anatolia. The meeting between Mustafa Kemal and Colonel Budenny is said to have taken place between May 25 and 28, 1919 at Havza.[8] The meeting seems to have been exploratory in nature as to possible Soviet-Turkish cooperation. A student of Turco-Soviet relations states that "Colonel Budenny is also reported to have urged the acceptance of Bolshevik ideology by Turkish nationalists, and Mustafa Kemal Pasha to have avoided a direct answer by stating that such changes required time and much educational work among the people, and that there existed more urgent questions of defense for Turkey at present."[9]

In his memoirs, Ali Fuat Cebesoy reports that two months after the Sivas Congress, the commander in chief of the Caucasian Bolshevik armies, General Shalva Eliava, had traveled secretly to Istanbul to report on the latest situation in the Ottoman Empire and while in Istanbul he established contact with nationalist agents from Anatolia and had promised them that Soviet Russia would recognize and support the Turkish Nationalist Movement.[10] However, Cebesoy does not disclose whether General Eliava actually had met Mustafa Kemal.

---

[7] A. Rawlinson, *Adventures in the Near East: 1918–1922* (London: Andrew Melrose, 1923), p. 234.

[8] On the Karakol Society and its activities see George S. Harris, *The Origins of Communism in Turkey*, pp. 47–48.

[9] İbrahim H. Karal, "Turkish Relations with Soviet Russia during the National Liberation War of Turkey, 1918–1922." (Ph.D. diss. University of California, 1967), p. 99; see also Sabahattin Selek, *Anadolu İhtilali*, p. 56; Fethi Tevetoğlu, "Atatürk'ün Kapattırdığı Kızıl Teşekkül: Yeşilordu," *Türk Kültürü* 5, no. 49 (Kasım 1966): 62.

[10] Ali Fuat Cebesoy, *Moskova Hatıraları*, p. 60; see also Harris, *The Origins of Communism*, p. 47.

During the early months of the Nationalist Movement, Mustafa Kemal lost no opportunity in explaining the nature and the objectives of the movement to those foreigners who came to eastern Anatolia. An American newspaperman, Louis E. Browne, representing the *Chicago Daily News,* personally observed the proceedings of the Sivas Cogress and conducted a number of interviews with Mustafa Kemal. Yet, at the time his reports did not make much headway in the official circles of the United States and served only the interests of those few readers curious about the ways in which the Armenians were being treated in Anatolia.[11]

Another contact of Mustafa Kemal with an American took place on September 22, 1919, at Sivas. The United States had sent a military mission to eastern Anatolia to investigate the military problems of a possible American mandate over Armenia. This military mission headed by General James G. Harbord came to Sivas to meet the leader of the Turkish Nationalist Movement. Mustafa Kemal had a long conversation with General Harbord about the aims of the movement, its organization, and its attitude toward the non-Moslem elements in Anatolia. Mustafa Kemal submitted a memorandum to General Harbord describing the events which led to the convening of the Erzurum and Sivas Congresses and the establishment of the Association for the Defense of Rights of Anatolia and Rumelia; he concluded his remarks by saying that the assistance of a powerful and impartial foreign nation which would save the Turks from the iniquitous oppression and hasten their development would be favorably received.[12]

Mustafa Kemal in his famous *Speech* of 1927 makes passing reference to his conversation with General Harbord. He particularly recalls the inquiry of General Harbord as to the things he would do if it came to pass that, despite every imaginable effort and sacrifice

---

[11] Lord Kinross maintains that at the suggestion of Halide Edib (Adıvar) Mr. Browne was sent to the Sivas Congress "ostensibly as the correspondent of the *Chicago Daily News,* but in fact rather as Mr. Crane's personal emissary." *Ataturk,* p. 218. Mr. Charles R. Crane was a member of the American Section of the International Commission on mandates in Turkey; on this commission's activities see Zeine N. Zeine, *The Struggle for Arab Independence: Western Diplomacy and the Rise and Fall of Faisal's Kingdom in Syria* (Beirut: Khayat's, 1960), pp. 93–94.

[12] U.S. Congress, 66th Congress, 2nd Session, Senate, *Document No. 266 A Report of the American Military Mission to Armenia* by Maj. Gen. James G. Harbord, 1920, p. 33.

made by the nation, it should all end in failure. Mustafa Kemal states that under such circumstances there would be no other way but victory for independence and freedom.[13]

The French high commissioner of Syria, Georges Picot, came to visit Mustafa Kemal on December 8, 1919, while he was at Sivas. Two days of talks between the two centered around the French position in southeastern Anatolia and possible Franco-Turkish cooperation in maintaining peace and security in the area and eventual friendship between the two nations.[14] Georges Picot claimed that he represented the French government in his talks with Mustafa Kemal. This was a unique opportunity for Mustafa Kemal to inform Georges Picot of the growing strength of the Nationalist Movement and call his attention to the fact that the Turks in the French occupied zone were determined to be the masters of their own region and did not wish to see the imposition of an Armenian rule with the help of French forces. As far as Mustafa Kemal was concerned, the visit of the French high commissioner showed the weakness of the French position in southeastern Anatolia. This visit, therefore, strengthened the morale and the convictions of the nationalists and enhanced the power and prestige of Mustafa Kemal in the eyes of all concerned. Lord Kinross maintains that "Picot was impressed" by the firm determination of Mustafa Kemal to resist force by force, "comparing it favorably with that of the government in Constantinople," and says: "Not long afterwards the Paris Press began to reflect certain Nationalist sympathies."[15]

The early contacts of Mustafa Kemal with the representatives of foreign powers seem to serve as: a means of exploring the alternative courses of action open to the nationalists; a means of assessing the policies and possible counteractions of the Allied Powers against the nationalists; a method of gaining foreign material and moral assistance; and a vehicle of propaganda in order to gain favorable response for the nationalist cause. Indeed, as later develop-

---

[13] Atatürk, *Speech,* p. 144; for a dramatic portrayal of this question and answer see Lord Kinross, *Atatürk,* p. 219, where he concludes: "Harbord was impressed by his resolution, his spirit. 'I had taken everything into account,' he said, 'but not that. Had we been in your place, we should have done the same thing'."

[14] Aydemir, *Tek Adam,* vol. 2, pp. 407–8.

[15] Lord Kinross, *Ataturk,* p. 234.

ments clearly indicate, Mustafa Kemal utilized these early contacts as a testing ground for his political and military objectives and thus sought to establish an equilibrium between his objectives and the means to realize them. His objectives in each of his actions seem to have been commensurate with the power he possessed.

DIPLOMATIC RELATIONS WITH SOVIET RUSSIA

During the first few weeks of his landing in Anatolia, Mustafa Kemal was busy not only in assessing the situation in Anatolia but also in reviewing the developments in Caucasia where the Azerbaijanis, Georgians, and Armenians were trying to achieve their independence from Soviet Russia. He thought that direct contact and the establishment of ties of friendship with the Bolshevik leaders of Russia would not only open up avenues of cooperation against the common enemy — the West — but also would help check a possible invasion of Anatolia by Bolshevik forces after their conquest of Caucasia.

Accordingly, he began sounding out the opinion of army commanders in eastern Anatolia, particularly Kazım Karabekir Pasha, concerning the establishment of direct contacts with the Caucasians and the Soviets. He asked Karabekir Pasha to send a few trusted men into the Caucasus region. The first contacts with the Bolsheviks were made by Dr. Fuat Sabit sent by Karabekir Pasha to Baku. In view of his previous experiences in the Caucasus region, Mustafa Kemal urged Halil (Kut) Pasha to undertake the mission of establishing diplomatic contacts with the Bolsheviks and securing arms and financial assistance from them.[16]

---

[16] See "Intelligence Report," September 25, 1920, Great Britain, F.O. 371/5178, E 14638/345/44. Halil Pasha was the uncle of Enver Pasha who served as the Minister of War during 1914–1918. He was a classmate of Mustafa Kemal in the War College. He had achieved a distinguished service record during the Tripoli and Balkan Wars and was an active member of the Committee of Union and Progress at Salonica. During the First World War he had served in the Caucasus region and in Iraq. He had taken General Townshend prisoner of war in the Iraq campaign. He was later sent to the Caucasus region once again and appointed commander of the 3rd and 9th Armies. Following the armistice upon the demand of the British authorities in Istanbul he was arrested but later managed to escape in August 1919. On September 10, he proceeded to Ankara, then he went to Sivas where he met Mustafa Kemal his old friend. See Cebesoy, *Moskova Hatıraları*, p. 134.

Halil Pasha arrived in Moscow in May 1920 and met with G. V. Chicherin, the Soviet Commissar for Foreign Affairs. Presenting himself as the representative of the Turkish nationalist forces,[17] he asked Chicherin what financial and military aid the Soviets could render to the nationalists. Chicherin is reported to have told Halil Pasha that, following investigation of the state of the transportation facilities, the Soviets would render some assistance to the Turkish nationalists.[18]

Mustafa Kemal himself wrote to Chicherin on April 26, 1920, soon after the opening of the Grand National Assembly, proposing that the two governments enter into regular diplomatic relations and join hands in their struggle against the imperialists powers. Mustafa Kemal stated that if the Bolshevik forces overcame the resistance of Georgia or succeeded in the expulsion of the British forces from Georgia the Turkish forces would simultaneously strive to overcome the resistance of Armenia and would ensure the inclusion of Azerbaijan within Soviet Russia. He then suggested that in order to realize these objectives, Soviet Russia should provide the nationalist government of Ankara with 5 million pieces of gold and military supplies.[19] Mustafa Kemal's letter was forwarded by Kazım Karabekir Pasha by way of a courier sent from Trabzon on May 8, 1920, and given to Halil Pasha who transmitted it to the Soviet government.

In his reply of June 2, 1920, Chicherin agreed to the establishment of diplomatic relations between Moscow and Ankara and assured Mustafa Kemal that the Soviet government remained faithful to its principle of recognizing the right of all peoples to self-determination, and that it followed with great interest the heroic struggle which the Turkish people were waging for their independence.[20]

It is reported also that Mustafa Kemal dispatched another note on June 19, 1920, to the Soviet government with a delegation

[17] Tevfik Bıyıklıoğlu, *Atatürk Anadoluda, 1919–1921,* p. 19.

[18] Cebesoy, *Moskova Hatıraları,* p. 136.

[19] Text of this note in Louis Fischer, *The Soviets in World Affairs* (London: J. Cape, 1930), vol. 1, p. 390. *International Affairs* (Moscow) in the November 1963 issue refers to this letter as one addressed to V. I. Lenin and reproduces a part of the text, p. 111.

[20] Text of this note in Jane Degras, ed. *Soviet Documents on Foreign Policy,* vol. 1, 1917–1924 (London: Oxford University Press, 1951), pp. 187–88.

headed by Staff Major Nazım Bey. In this note, Mustafa Kemal stated that Major Nazım Bey was given detailed verbal instructions concerning the nature and scope of his conversations with Soviet officials, but he also reminded the Soviet government that the Turkish nationalist forces were "waging a war of national defense in accordance with the humanitarian principles proclaimed by the Bolsheviks against the continued aggressions of Christianity . . . against this modern crusade," and that if the Soviet government desired the cooperation of the nationalists and the entire Moslem world, it should send necessary military supplies without delay.[21]

Even before Chicherin's reply to his letter of April 26, Mustafa Kemal decided to send a delegation to Moscow to negotiate a treaty of friendship with the Soviet government and to obtain military and financial assistance. The delegation headed by Minister of Foreign Affairs Bekir Sami Bey included the following members: Yusuf Kemal Bey, Minister of Economy; Dr. Colonel İbrahim Tali (Öngören); Osman Bey, deputy from Trabzon; and Staff Lieutenant Colonel Seyfi (Düzgören). The Bekir Sami mission left Ankara on May 11 and after a long journey of sixty-nine days arrived at Moscow on July 19, 1920.[22]

The negotiations commenced on July 24 and lasted until August 24, at which time a draft treaty of friendship was initialed by Bekir Sami Bey and Chicherin. Under this draft treaty, the Soviet government agreed not to recognize as valid any agreement not approved by the government of the Grand National Assembly of Turkey; it also agreed to consider all previous agreements between Russia and the Ottoman Empire null and void. The two governments decided to take all necessary measures to establish and maintain rail communications between the two countries and to convene an international conference of the littoral states to determine the

---

[21] "Intelligence Report," July 22, 1920, Great Britain, F.O. 371/5170, E 10014/262/44.

[22] Cebesoy, *Moskova Hatıraları*, pp. 61–62. The above-mentioned British "Intelligence Report" transmitting a copy of Mustafa Kemal's letter to Chicherin of July 19 quotes Mustafa Kemal as referring to "the treaty concluded last autumn." Similarly, several writers assert that by April 1920, the Ankara and Soviet governments had already concluded a military assistance pact. However, these writers do not cite documents. See, for example, Harold Armstrong, *Turkey in Travail* (London: 1925), p. 116; Arnold J. Toynbee, *The Western Question in Greece and Turkey* (London: Constable and Co., 1922), p. 367; A. J. Toynbee in *Survey of International Affairs*, 1920–1923, p. 365, mentions even earlier agreements of December 1919, and March 1920.

international regime of the Turkish Straits and of the Black Sea and to establish diplomatic and consular relations between the two countries.[23]

A few days after initialing the draft treaty, Chicherin demanded the transfer of Van and Bitlis provinces to Armenia and stated that the Soviet military and financial assistance to the Ankara government was contingent upon its acceptance of this demand.[24]

On account of the Soviet territorial demands and the ensuing deadlock on further negotiations, Bekir Sami Bey instructed Yusuf Kemal Bey to take the draft treaty and his report on the Moscow talks to Ankara. Returning to Trabzon, Yusuf Kemal Bey on September 18 transmitted the text of the draft treaty and Bekir Sami Bey's report to Mustafa Kemal.

Under these circumstances the nationalist forces in the East had to be deployed against the Armenians before the Soviet forces entrenched themselves in Armenia. Mustafa Kemal, therefore, ordered Kazım Karabekir Pasha, commanding the nationalist forces in eastern Anatolia to commence the military operations against Armenia which had been suspended during the time of the exchange of letters between Ankara and Moscow. On September 28 Sarıkamış, and two days later, Kars, was captured by Karabekir Pasha's forces. On November 6 the Armenians sued for peace. Negotiations leading to the Treaty of Gümrü commenced on November 26 and concluded on December 3, 1920.

Meanwhile, on October 16 following careful deliberations in the Council of Ministers over the draft treaty, Mustafa Kemal sent new instructions to Bekir Sami Bey and asked him to inform the Soviet government in clear and precise terms that in view of the existence of a strong Turkish-Moslem majority in Van and Bitlis provinces, as certified by the reports of foreign and domestic experts, the demand of cession of these territories in favor of Armenia could only be construed as the reflection of an imperialist ambition, and that the nationalist Ankara government could hardly conceive that Soviet Russia would entertain such aspirations of territorial aggrandizement. However, Mustafa Kemal called Bekir Sami Bey's attention to the fact that if and when the Soviet government renounced its claims he should sign the final treaty of friendship and the secret

---

[23] Text of this draft in Cebesoy, *Moskova Hatıraları,* pp. 80–81.

[24] Bıyıklıoğlu, *Atatürk Anadoluda,* p. 68.

letters to be exchanged on behalf of the government of the Grand National Assembly.[25]

At the same time Mustafa Kemal also decided to send a second delegation to Moscow together with a diplomatic mission in order to iron out the differences between the two governments and to establish normal diplomatic relations. For the task of negotiations with the Soviet leaders, he chose Yusuf Kemal Bey, Minister of Economy, and for the establishment of an embassy in Moscow he chose Ali Fuat Pasha.[26] Ali Fuat Pasha left Ankara on November 21, later followed by Yusuf Kemal Bey's mission. However, when Bekir Sami Bey returned from Moscow to Ankara toward the end of December, almost empty-handed, and informed Mustafa Kemal that the Soviet leaders were still pressing for territorial concessions in return for Soviet aid, Mustafa Kemal ordered Yusuf Kemal Bey and Ali Fuat Pasha's missions not to proceed beyond Kars.[27]

Just about this time Budu Mdivani, the Soviet representative commissioned to go to Ankara, arrived at Kars and immediately got in touch with Kazım Karabekir Pasha, Yusuf Kemal Bey, and Ali Fuat Pasha and informed them in writing that the Soviet government had renounced its territorial claims. Then the Turkish delegation was authorized to depart for Moscow on January 20, 1921. The Turkish delegation consisted of four groups: plenipotentiaries; military advisers; political advisers; and a study group. The plenipotentiaries included: Yusuf Kemal Bey, Minister of Economy and deputy from Kastamonu; Dr. Rıza Nur Bey, Minister of Education and deputy from Sinop; and Ambassador Ali Fuat Pasha. The mili-

---

[25] Cebesoy, *Moskova Hatıraları*, p. 90. In answer to Chicherin's letter on July 2, 1920, Mustafa Kemal is said to have sent another letter to Chicherin on October 22, 1920. According to *International Affairs* (Moscow) Mustafa Kemal in this letter emphasized the common struggle of Turkey and Russia against the "imperialists of the West," and made no mention of the request of Turkey for military assistance from the Soviets. See November 1963, pp. 112–13.

[26] On his way to Moscow, Ali Fuat Pasha is reported to have made the following statement: "Personally I desire agreement with Entente on condition that Turkey is re-instated and Angora Government recognized. Otherwise we shall be driven into closer relations with Bolsheviks with whom we have little in common." Great Britain, F.O. 371/6465, E 1710/1/44. This statement seems to confirm Ali Fuat Pasha's "Westernist" orientation.

[27] Hikmet Bayur, "Birinci Genel Savaştan Sonra Yapılan Barış Antlaşmalarımız," *Belleten* 30, no. 117, part II (Ocak 1966): 149; Cebesoy, *Moskova Hatıraları*, p. 111.

tary advisory group included: Staff Lt. Colonel Seyfi (Düzgören); Staff Major Saffet (Arıkan), military attaché of the embassy; Staff Captain Mithat (Erman), deputy military attaché of the embassy; and Captain Kemal, deputy military attaché. The political advisory group consisted of the representative of northern Caucasia, Staff Colonel Bekir Sami, and his aide de camp, Captain Selahattin (Yurdoğlu), representative of Azerbaijan Memduh Şervket (Esendal), representative of Georgia, Staff Colonel Kazım (Dirik). The study group was composed of the members of the Grand National Assembly which included: Dr. Tevfik Rüştü (Aras), chairman of the group; Fuat (Carım); İsmail (Soysaloğlu); and Tashin (Baç) the secretary of the group.[28] The last group, the four trusted aides of Mustafa Kemal and members of the "official" Communist Party were ostensibly charged with the task of studying the feasibility of the application of the Bolshevik ideas and institutions in Turkey. In order to eliminate all doubts as to the Ankara government's sincere interest in Bolshevik principles, the chairman of the study group was instructed to apply for membership in the Communist International.

Official talks between the Turkish delegation and the Soviet leaders, following preliminary discussions with Foreign Affairs Commissar Chicherin, commenced on February 26, 1921, in Moscow. The negotiations were conducted on two separate subjects, one dealing with the political matters and the other involving questions of military assistance. According to Yusuf Kemal Bey, the treaty of friendship was signed either on March 22 or on March 23, 1921. However, in his memoirs Yusuf Kemal Bey states that he had suggested to Chicherin that the new Turco-Soviet friendship agreement should carry the date of March 16, 1921, as the date of its signature so as to mark the opening of a new era of friendship between the two former enemies on the first anniversary of the formal occupation of Istanbul by the Allied Powers. He adds that Chicherin accepted his proposal.[29] On the other hand, Ali Fuat Pasha, who also signed the treaty, maintains that upon the request of Chicherin it was agreed to publish the text of the treaty on March 18 without changing its date of signature.[30]

---

[28] Cebesoy, *Moskova Hatıraları*, pp. 102–3.

[29] Yusuf Kemal Tengirşenk, "Milli Mücadelede Ruslarla İlk Temaslarımız" *Yakın Tarihimiz*, 4, no. 43 (December 20, 1962): 97.

[30] Cebesoy, *Moskova Hatıraları*, p. 155.

Under the treaty of friendship, which followed the general lines of the draft treaty of August 24, 1920, with certain modifications, each of the contracting parties solemnly agreed not to recognize any international agreement imposed upon one another by force. Soviet Russia agreed that the term "Turkey" meant the territories specified in the National Pact and promised not to recognize as valid any treaty that was imposed upon Turkey against the will of the government of the Grand National Assembly of Turkey. Furthermore, Soviet Russia renounced all its capitulatory rights in Turkey that were granted to tsarist Russia by the Ottoman Empire in the past. Soviet Russia and Turkey decided to entrust the final elaboration of the regime of the Black Sea and the Straits to a special conference of delegates of the littoral states on the condition that any decisions that may be arrived at should not involve any derogation of Turkey's complete sovereignty or of the security of Turkey and her capital, Istanbul. Each of the contracting parties further agreed not to permit the formation or existence on their respective territories of organizations and groups whose aim was to overthrow the government of the other party. The two governments promised to maintain and develop, as rapidly as possible, all means of communication and transportation between the two countries. Soviet Russia promised to repatriate all Turkish prisoners of war and civilians found in Russia. Under this treaty, Batum was to be turned over to the Soviets, and Kars and Ardahan were to remain within Turkey.[31]

It was agreed during the negotiations that the amount and the nature of the Soviet financial and military aid should be finalized through the exchange of secret letters and that these letters should be considered an indispensable part of the treaty of friendship. Ali Fuat Pasha reports that during the negotiations the Soviet government had agreed to send to Turkey 10 million gold rubles and arms enough to equip two whole divisions.[32]

Despite the prolonged, and at times frustrating, negotiations in Moscow from August 1920 to March 1921, inexperienced na-

---

[31] Text in Degras, *Soviet Documents on Foreign Policy*, pp. 237–42. For the specific views of the Turkish delegations prior to the signing of this treaty see Cebesoy, *Moskova Hatıraları*, pp. 146–49. The treaty of friendship came into force on September 13, 1921, following the exchange of the Instruments of Ratification at Kars.

[32] Cebesoy, *Moskova Hatıraları*, p. 149.

tionalist diplomats neatly passed the acid test of dealing with the Bolshevik leaders. The Moscow treaty of friendship was a major diplomatic achievement for Mustafa Kemal and for the government of the Grand National Assembly which secured favorable and stable eastern frontiers and strengthened its diplomatic and military position vis-à-vis the Allied Powers.

The opening of the formal diplomatic relations between Ankara and Moscow had preceded the signing of the treaty of friendship. A large mansion in Moscow, formerly belonging to a sugar industrialist, was designated by the Soviet government as the Turkish Embassy building. The embassy staff headed by Ambassador Ali Fuat Pasha included the following: First Secretary Aziz (Meker), Second Secretary Osman Kemal, Attachés Captain İdris (Cora), Captain Saim (Önhan), clerk Feridun Hotinli, and accountant Tahsin. Aziz Bey and Osman Kemal Bey are reported to have had a thorough knowledge of Russian. In addition, the embassy included the Office of the Military Attaché headed by Staff Major Saffet (Arıkan) and a number of other officers who were to arrange the shipment of Soviet military aid and the repatriation of the Turkish prisoners of war in Russia.[33]

In view of the continued violent upheavals in Russia and disturbances in Moscow, it was considered prudent by the Ankara government to send a platoon of soldiers along with the embassy staff. Upon his arrival at the embassy ground, Ali Fuat Pasha found out to his surprise that he and his staff were to be well protected by the secret police agents disguised as servants, gardeners, and cooks, headed by a custodian of the embassy building evidently in charge of all the other secret police agents. However, after some delicate maneuvering by Ambassador Ali Fuat Pasha, these Soviet personnel were removed from the embassy grounds.

Not long afterwards, however, a raid by the Soviet secret service agents on the Turkish military attaché's office and their confiscation of a briefcase containing Turkish documents caused a serious diplomatic crisis, threatening the friendly relations between the two countries. After a frantic exchange of notes between the Soviet and Ankara governments, the Soviet ambassador to Ankara, Aralov, on June 19, 1922, extended the apologies of the Soviet government for the unfortunate incident and thus the rupture of

[33] Ibid., pp. 102–3.

diplomatic relations was averted. However, prior to the delivery of the Soviet note, Ambassador Ali Fuat Pasha had left Moscow on May 10 and returned to Ankara, apparently on the grounds that he personally would no longer be useful in the performance of his diplomatic functions in the Soviet capital.[34] Until the appointment of Ahmet Muhtar (Mollaoğlu), a one-time acting Minister of Foreign Affairs, on December 9, 1922, the Turkish Embassy in Moscow was headed by a *charge d'affaires ad interim*.

The first formal Soviet diplomatic mission headed by Counselor I. Upmal-Angarskii was sent to Ankara on October 4, 1920. And the first Soviet Ambassador Sergey Petrovich Natsarenus was received by Mustafa Kemal on May 31, 1921. The full text of Natsarenus' speech and Mustafa Kemal's reply are given below, first to show the contrast concerning their points of emphasis and second, to provide the reader with an example of the first diplomatic reception speech of Mustafa Kemal. Ambassador Natsarenus' speech reads as follows:

His Excellency, The President.

Please permit me to salute you and the heroic Turkish nation. The development of the world events has formed a bloody struggle between a big group of nations. The Treaty of Love [Fraternity] and Friendship concluded between the great Russian and Turkish nations on March 16, 1921, show and guarantee that neither Russia nor Turkey will accept slavery.

These two nations are the first to hoist the flag of revolution. So they will save the whole world by being a glorious example of the great revolution.

After breaking the chain of capitalism the Russians have destroyed a bloody and corrupt heritage. They have annulled all the treaties concluded by the Czarist Regime and have brought a radical change into their foreign policy.

The Russian nation has annulled the capitulations which formed an unbearable load for small nations and has put in its place the independence of nations. Colonies have been replaced by free states. Privileges have been replaced by freely concluded treaties. By denying its past Russia has become a natural ally of the nations who fight for their independence. It was not the Russian nation that desired to siege Constantinople — it was the despotic Czarist government. For these reasons the treaty signed in Moscow must and

---

[34] On the detail of this episode see Ibid., pp. 329–43. Aralov, on the other hand, maintains that Ali Fuat Pasha had taken a Turkish spy under his protection and that when this spy was caught red-handed while delivering secret documents to a British agent Ali Fuat Pasha was considered responsible for this incident and he was recalled by the Ankara government. *Bir Sovyet Diplomatının Türkiye Hatıraları*, p. 137.

indeed shall be the bright star of the two nations, who for the first time see a possibility of knowing each other.

The Turkish and Russian nations have more difficult roads to travel. The heroic struggle which is being carried on by the Turks and of which an example cannot be met within all history has already broken some of the chains with which the Turkish nation was bound. The time is not far when the Turks, whose fighting ability astounded the world in the past, will break all these chains and proudly and victoriously decide and plan their life themselves. This is the sincere wish of the Russian nation.

I beg His Excellency to accept these wishes of the Russians which I am commissioned to communicate.[35]

In his reply, while echoing to the full Natsarenus' remarks as to the cooperation between Soviet Russia and Turkey, Mustafa Kemal made no mention of the words "revolution" and "capitalism" nor did he refer to anything in the nature of world revolution. Mustafa Kemal made it perfectly clear that, as far as Turkey was concerned, the fundamental objective was the protection of the right of national existence. His language throughout his speech was that of a conscious equal and ally and not that of a grateful client. It is significant to note also that he made no reference to the Bolshevik regime in Russia and no reference to change in the politico-socio-economic structure of Turkey to the likeness of the Soviet system. His speech reads as follows:

His Excellency the Ambassador.

I thank you for the kind words you used for the Turkish nation and for myself. I am glad to salute you and Russia.

It is desirable that this alliance continue forever to prevent conquest. Our nations whose right to life and independence were threatened have entered a struggle to protect their rights. The causes which have created this uprising and this struggle have also brought to existence this brotherhood of which our nation is glad. The example of struggle against tyranny and oppression set by our nations has undoubtedly been a warning for all oppressed nations. Our nation highly appreciates the good will shown by the Russians by annulling the capitulations forced upon small nations by the Czarist government.

Our nation also refused the capitulations and has reformed itself on a new basis of freedom.

---

[35] Translation from *Peyam-l Sabah* of July 11, 1921, by staff of the U.S. High Commission, "Report" dated July 18, 1921, U.S. High Commissioner Mark L. Bristol to Department of State, U.S. National Archives, Turkey, File No. 701. 6167/12.

The harmony formed by the new Russia's annulling the old ties and Turkey's breaking the ties of the old Ottoman Empire has brought to existence the friendship between Russia and Turkey.

The Treaty of Moscow concluded on March 16, 1921, is a document which will unite the two nations. The importance of this Treaty, which represents the new ideals of both nations, is great. I call to memory the difficulties with which both nations met and appreciate greatly the sacrifices made by them. I also estimate the difficulties to be met with in the future and believe most firmly that we shall succeed. The restrictions put on the Ottoman Empire have caused our decline day by day. Now a death sentence is imposed under the name of the Treaty of Sèvres. I thank you heartily for believing that we shall succeed in our cause. I hope that in your person we shall find the maximum of help in strengthening the friendly relations between the two nations. I assure you that we shall do all we can to help you in this mission.[36]

A few months later negotiations were conducted at Kars between the representatives of Soviet Russia, the Caucasian Soviet Republics, and the Ankara government. The Turkish delegation headed by Kazım Karabekir Pasha included Veli Bey, deputy from Burdur, Ahmet Muhtar Bey, and Memduh Şevket (Esendal). The negotiations culminated in the signing of the Treaty of Kars on October 13, 1921, which in many respects duplicated the provisions of the Treaty of Moscow.[37]

On the subject of the Soviet financial and military assistance to the war effort of the Turkish nationalists, no exhaustive study has been published up to the present. The amount and nature of such assistance has not officially been disclosed either by the Soviet or the Turkish governments. In his *Speech,* Mustafa Kemal makes no direct reference to the Soviet aid. However, a British intelligence report dated June 27, 1921, and several other sources indicate that since the beginning of direct contact between Moscow and Ankara, the latter had requested the payment of a lump sum of 50 million gold rubles and that in view of the Soviet unwillingness to agree on such a large sum Ankara in August 1921 expressed its willingness to accept 20 million gold rubles instead.[38]

---

[36] Ibid. Translation in the original document. For a different and somewhat slanted translation of this speech see *International Affairs* (Moscow) November 1963, p. 113.

[37] Cebesoy, *Moskova Hatıraları,* pp. 258–59.

[38] See copy of an official note of the Ministry of Foreign Affairs dated August 17, 1921, in Ibid., p. 247.

On the amount of Soviet financial aid the Turkish sources contain the following figures:

(1) Halil Pasha, the first semiofficial representative of the Ankara government in Moscow, is quoted as saying that he had handed over to Cavit Bey, the division commander at Karaköse, some 100,000 Turkish liras worth gold bullion in May 1920 which was given to him by the Soviets.[39]

(2) Yusuf Kemal Bey, returning from his first Moscow mission headed by Bekir Sami Bey, is said to have brought back to Turkey 1 million gold rubles in September 1920.[40]

(3) In his memoirs, Yusuf Kemal Bey says that following the signing of the Moscow treaty of March 1921, he brought to Turkey 400,000 gold rubles and while he was in Moscow sent 100,000 gold rubles to the Turkish agents in Germany with Staff Major Saffet (Arıkan) for the purchase of war materials.

(4) Şevket Süreyya Aydemir maintains that the Ankara government had requested from the Soviets 10 million gold rubles each year for the continuation of the War of Independence and that during 1920 approximately 5 million gold rubles were transferred to Turkey and from 1921 to 1922, 10 million gold rubles were also received.[41]

According to Karal, Soviet sources indicate the delivery of the following amounts of financial aid to Turkey:[42] In September 1920, 1 million gold rubles and 200.6 Kilogram gold were brought to Erzurum by Counselor I. Upmal-Angarskii; in April 1921, Yusuf Kemal Bey received 4 million gold rubles; during May and June 1921, deputy Military Attaché Saffet (Arıkan) was given 1.4 million gold rubles; in November 1921, General Frunze brought with him to Trabzon 1.1 million gold rubles; in May 1922, Ambassador Aralov brought with him to Ankara 3.5 million gold rubles. Again according to Karal, the Minister of Finance, Hasan Fehmi (Aytaç)

---

[39] Ibid., p. 137; also Bıyıklıoğlu, *Atatürk Anadoluda,* p. 19.

[40] Cebesoy, *Moskova Hatıraları,* p. 82.

[41] Aydemir, *Tek Adam,* vol. 2, p. 433.

[42] Karal, "Turkish Relations with Soviet Russia . . . ," pp. 270–71. İbrahim H. Karal cites the following sources: *Dokumenty Vneshnei Politiki SSSR,* III (Moscow, 1959), p. 675; *International Affairs* (Moscow) July 1960, pp. 120–22; Kazım Karabekir, *Istiklal Harbimiz* (Istanbul: 1960), pp. 882, 953; Sabahattin Selek, *Anadolu İhtilali,* vol. 1 (Istanbul: 1963), pp. 112–13; *Yakın Tarihimiz* (Istanbul), vol. 1 (1962), p. 100.

gave to Ambassador Aralov a receipt for the full 10 million gold rubles upon the latter's delivery of the last installment.[43]

A British intelligence report dated November 21, 1921, cites the following amounts of assistance received by the Ankara government during the period of March 1920 to October 1921:

July 1920,	20 *poods* of gold (about £ 50,000 sterling) as the first installment of a projected loan of 50 million gold rubles
November 1920,	2 million gold rubles
April 1921,	40 million gold rubles, plus 1 million gold rubles sent to Turkish agents in Germany
September 1921,	500 *okes* of gold (about £90,000 sterling)[44]

As to the nature and amount of the Soviet military aid to the Turkish nationalist forces, there is hardly any reliable information.[45] It is reported that of the almost 10,000 prisoners of war taken by the Russians during the First World War, only 1,200 men were returned. And these men were subjected to an intensive program of indoctrination by the Soviet authorities and sent to Anatolia in the winter of 1920–1921. Ali Fuat Pasha states that they were later deployed on the Western front and despite their previous program of indoctrination served the nationalist cause with distinction.

The Soviets, for reasons of their own, also have offered the Red Army units in the defense of Anatolia against the Greeks. The Bolshevik commander of the Red Army units in Caucasia approached Kazım Karabekir Pasha about July 20, 1921 and said that he was prepared to send his troops to Anatolia. After careful consideration of this matter during a secret session of the Grand National Assembly, it is reported that Mustafa Kemal instructed Karabekir Pasha to communicate the deep appreciation of the Ankara government to the Soviet commander for his friendly and generous offer of assistance and then state that at the time, however, the nationalist government did not think that it was in need of the

---

[43] Karal, "Turkish Relations with Soviet Russia . . . ," p. 300, footnote 48.

[44] Great Britain, F.O. 371/6537, E 13700/143/44.

[45] On the amount of military aid requested by Ankara from the Soviets, see Cebesoy, *Moskova Hatıraları,* pp. 144–45, 247–48, Great Britain Foreign Office, 371/6537, E 13700/143/44; Aralov, *Bir Sovyet Diplomatının Türkiye Hatıraları,* pp. 17–18; Harris, *The Origins of Communism,* pp. 59–60.

proffered assistance but should it become necessary in the future it would avail itself of the gallant offer of help.[46]

Later a similar offer was made by General M. V. Frunze, the commander in chief of the Ukrainian forces during his visit to Ankara between November 25, 1921 and January 15, 1922. This offer was also turned down politely by Mustafa Kemal.[47] However, Mustafa Kemal went to extraordinary lengths to assure him of the existence of strong ties of friendship between the Bolsheviks and Turkey and expressed his thanks to Soviet Russia for the invaluable assistance it had rendered up until then to the nationalist cause in Anatolia.[48]

While General Frunze was in Ankara, a treaty of friendship between Turkey and the Ukraine was signed on January 2, 1922. General Frunze's mission was followed by the arrival of Soviet Ambassador Semion Ivanovich Aralov on January 29, 1922. Ambassador Aralov in his memoirs states that he had received a most friendly welcome by both the Ministers of Foreign Affairs, Yusuf Kemal Bey, and Mustafa Kemal himself. He also relates the stories of festive gatherings in the Soviet Embassy often attended by Mustafa Kemal and his close associates, during which serious matters, such as Turco-Soviet relations and military operations in Anatolia, were also discussed. It appears that Aralov might have been received coolly by Prime Minister Rauf Bey and his "Westernist" friends, which must have been reciprocated by him with a certain feeling of resentment. As noted earlier, Aralov, in his memoirs, does not have a nice word to say about Rauf Bey. He accuses Rauf Bey of being disloyal to the nationalist cause and identifies him as an enemy of Mustafa Kemal and the Republic of Turkey.[49]

---

[46] See "Intelligence Report," Great Britain, F.O. 371/6537, E 13700.143/ 44.

[47] Bıyıklıoğlu, *Atatürk Anadoluda,* p. 72.

[48] See Türk Devrim Tarihi Enstitüsü *Atatürk'ün Söylev ve Demeçleri,* vol. 2 (1918–1937) (Ankara: Türk Devrim Tarihi Enstitüsü Yayınları, 1961), pp. 18–20; Harris, *The Origins of Communism,* p. 107. See also Mustafa Kemal's speech on accepting the credentials of the Ambassador Extraordinary of the Ukrainian Soviet Socialist Republic, General M. V. Frunze, in *International Affairs* (Moscow) November 1963, pp. 114–15.

[49] Aralov, *Bir Sovyet Diplomatının Türkiye Hatıraları,* pp. 220–21.

RELATIONS WITH THE WESTERN POWERS

THE TURCO-ITALIAN RELATIONS. Such seemingly warm and friendly relations between Mustafa Kemal and Soviet officials during the period of 1920 to 1922, however, did not prevent Mustafa Kemal from searching avenues of understanding and cooperation with Italy and France when opportunities presented themselves.

When the promises made by Britain and France under the secret wartime agreements were not fulfilled in 1919, the general feeling in Italy was that they had been swindled out of the rewards of victory. This feeling of bitterness was instrumental in Italy's tendency toward understanding and friendship with Turkey.[50] It is reported that on September 5, 1920, Galip Kemali Bey, an unofficial representative of Mustafa Kemal in Rome, was approached by an official of the Italian Ministry of Foreign Affairs asking him to transmit a message to Mustafa Kemal. In this message the Italian government is said to have expressed its readiness to help iron out the differences between Turkey and the other Allied Powers.[51]

The British intelligence agents report that even before the evacuation of the Antalya region on July 5, 1921, the Italian authorities there were extremely helpful in arranging the transmission of messages and the transportation of arms and men between Ankara and Italian ports.[52] It seems that the Ankara government had, at least by June 1920, established a center of communication at Antalya.[53]

The port of Antalya was also being used freely by the nationalists for the transport of arms and goods to such an extent that British High Commissioner Horace Rumbold, one time in his secret report to London, bitterly complained about the Italian cooperation with the nationalists in these words: "To all intents and purposes the port of Adalia [Antalya] is in the hands of the Nationalists,

---

[50] See Count Carlo Sforza, *Diplomatic Europe Since the Treaty of Versailles* (New Haven, Conn.: Yale University Press, 1928), pp. 51–66.

[51] See "Intelligence Report," Great Britain, F.O. 371/5058, E 15089/3/44.

[52] See "Intelligence Report," March 8, 1921, Great Britain, F.O. 371/6466, E 2919/1/44.

[53] See Galip Kemali Söylemezoğlu, *Hariciye Hizmetinde 30 Sene, 1892–1922* (Istanbul: Maarif Basımevi, 1955), p. 393–95.

aided and abetted by the Italian official authorities."[54] High Commissioner Rumbold also informed London that Azmi Bey, a representative of the Ankara government, once came to Antalya in the Fall of 1919 from Italy in an Italian ship bearing a passport to which his name was appended by the Italian commander after Azmi Bey had landed at Antalya.[55]

When the nationalist delegation, headed by Bekir Sami Bey, came to Antalya on its way to the London Conference, according to reports, they were given a royal treatment there, and then brought aboard an Italian destroyer for the voyage from Rhodes to Brindisi. They held private, friendly talks with Count Sforza in Rome before leaving for London.[56]

Mustafa Kemal must have been in personal contact with Count Sforza in Istanbul, for it is reported that in June 1920 Lieutenant Colonel Fago, with credentials from Count Sforza, was sent to Ankara for the purpose of concluding an agreement with the Ankara government.[57] However such démarche of Count Sforza seems to have failed to lead to an agreement. But, Bekir Sami Bey negotiated an agreement with Count Sforza on March 12, 1921, which was repudiated by Mustafa Kemal.[58] Yet, with a view to reinstating that agreement it was reported that Count Sforza and Cami Bey, the nationalist representative in Rome, "were negotiating a secret informal agreement whereby Italy was to send munitions in the value of 50 million Italian liras in exchange for ratification of 'the Bekir Sami-Sforza agreement'."[59] This report adds, however, that "the agreement had almost been completed when Sforza held up shipment of arms — according to Sforza because the British and the Greeks had heard the agreement." The report maintains that the real reason why Mustafa Kemal also renounced such an agree-

---

[54] "Secret Report of December 2, 1920, by Horace Rumbold," Great Britain, F.O. 371/5058, E 15529/3/44.

[55] Ibid.

[56] "Dispatch" of February 21, 1921 by the British Ambassador in Rome, Great Britain, F.O. 371/6466, E 2495/1/44.

[57] "Intelligence Report" of July 1, 1920, Great Britain, F.O. 371/5070, E 8567/262/44.

[58] Text of the agreement in Count Carlo Sforza, *Diplomatic Europe Since the Treaty of Versailles,* pp. 104–5.

[59] See "Dispatch" of April 30, 1921, U.S. Ambassador in Rome to Secretary of State, U.S. National Archives, Turkey, File No. 767.68/89.

ment was because he viewed it as a further attempt to achieve economic concessions for Italy.[60]

Several British intelligence reports mention certain direct personal contacts between Mustafa Kemal and Italian authorities at Antalya and also at Rhodes. One such report, dated November 13, 1920, claims that Mustafa Kemal "is said to have secretly been to Adalia [Antalya] to confer with the Italian military authorities regarding Nationalist operations against the Greeks."[61] Another such report advances an astonishing assertion that Mustafa Kemal in September 1920 paid an unexpected visit to the island of Rhodes. This fact, which has never been recorded in any of the published material, if it is true, sheds further light on Mustafa Kemal's diplomacy during the War of Independence. It proves that in order not to rely completely on the Soviet financial and military aid Mustafa Kemal was willing to exhaust all avenues in obtaining material and moral support from Western powers during the most critical period of the Nationalist Struggle against Britain and its proxy Greece and against the Istanbul government. The above-mentioned "Intelligence Report" reads as follows:

In addition to Adalia [Antalya], the Island of Rhodes is also an important link in the chain between Rome and Angora [Ankara]. On September 8th [1920] Staff Major Ashit [Aksit] Efendi left Angora with certain other Nationalist officials and proceeded to Adalia where he was met by the Italian Commander. As a result of the interviews that took place, Major Ashit Efendi telegraphed to Mustafa Kemal who immediately proceeded to Adalia with a bodyguard of about 200 men. From Adalia Mustafa Kemal went to Rhodes in the S.S. "Galicia" of the Lloyd Trestino line. He remained at Rhodes for three days, during which period he met the following persons:
  (a) Ahmet Dino and certain other Turks of the same colour
  (b) A representative of the Sublime Porte
  (c) Two Italian political emissaries.[62]

At this time the nationalist representatives in Rome were also busy purchasing arms from Italy and actively engaging in propa-

---

[60] Ibid.

[61] "Intelligence Report" of November 13, 1920, Great Britain, F.O. 371/5058, E 14781/3/44.

[62] "Intelligence Report" of December 2, 1920, Great Britain, F.O. 371/5058, E 15529/3/44.

ganda on behalf of the nationalist cause. Lieutenant Colonel Edib
Bey, alias Servet Vedat Bey, is identified in intelligence reports as
the accredited agent of Mustafa Kemal in Rome and Galip Kemali
(Söylemezoğlu) as political representative of the Ankara government.[63]

On September 4, 1920, Mustafa Kemal appointed Cami
(Baykurt), his one-time close associate and the first Minister of
Interior of the Ankara government, as the first official representative
of the government of the Grand National Assembly in Rome.[64]
It is reported that in order to increase Italian sympathy for the
nationalist cause Cami Bey suggested the formation in Italy of an
Italo-Turkish Chamber of Commerce in connection with the Italian
Eastern Institute, the invitation by Ankara of an Italian economic
mission, and a cordial demand for a permanent Italian representative to Ankara.[65] Apparently these suggestions had fallen on deaf
ears in Ankara because of the fear that they might entail economic
concessions in Anatolia in favor of Italy. In one of his reports dated
August 10, 1921, Cami Bey proposed to the Ministry of National
Defense that funds should be sent to Rome for the purchase of
munitions, and stated that 200,000 rifles and from 10 to 20 million
rounds of small arms ammunitions were made available by Skoda
factories.[66]

It may be gathered from the intelligence reports of this period
that the nationalist representatives in Italy, with the connivance of
the Italian government, were successful in purchasing large quantities of arms and ammunitions and transporting them to Antalya.
However, the nature and exact quantity of this arms traffic cannot
be ascertained because of either the lack of or secrecy of official
records.

Again according to the information contained in the British
and American intelligence reports, the nationalist representatives in
Rome established their "legation" at the Piazza dell 'Esquilino

---

[63] Ibid.

[64] See Hamid Aral, comp., *Dışişleri Bakanlığı Yıllığı, 1964–1965* (Ankara: n.p., n.d.), p. 348. Galip Kemali, however, identifies him as an unofficial
representative. *Hariciye Hizmetinde 30 Sene*, p. 442.

[65] "Intelligence Report" of September 10, 1921, Great Britain, F.O.
371/6474, E 10261/1/44.

[66] Ibid.

No. 8, posing as a newspaper agency and publicly identifying themselves as correspondents for Istanbul newspapers.[67]

The representatives of the Ankara government in Rome are reported to have carried on an extensive propaganda campaign in Italy and in other European capitals which included the following activities: The Italian press was given the communiqués of the Anatolian Agency, the official news agency of the Ankara government. These communiqués were being printed in French in Ankara and sent to Italy through the branch office of the Anatolian Agency at Antalya; certain Italian newspapers were subsidized to print news favorable to the nationalists; a periodical entitled "Turkey" edited in Rome by A. M. Nüzhet Bey and published monthly by the Turkish Congress at Lausanne was distributed in Italy and in other European countries.[68]

THE FRANCO-TURKISH RELATIONS. Mustafa Kemal reports that toward the end of May 1920, a French mission, headed by Monsieur Du Quest, the deputy high commissioner of Syria, came to Ankara and on May 30, a twenty-day armistice agreement was signed. He considers this agreement as a de facto recognition of the Ankara government by a principal Allied Power.[69]

However, from June 1920 to February 1921, there was no direct diplomatic contact between France and the Ankara government. Following the unsuccessful London Conference, Foreign Minister Bekir Sami Bey signed a separate agreement with Aristide Briand on March 11, 1921, under the terms of which the hostilities between France and the nationalists were to cease and the French were to be given preference in enterprises for the economic develop-

---

[67] "Memorandum on Kemalist Activity in Italy" by John F. Carter, Jr., private secretary of the U.S. Ambassador in Rome, dated March 10, 1921, U.S. Ambassador in Rome to Department of State, U.S. National Archives, Turkey, File No. 867.00/1395.

[68] "Dispatch" of January 31, 1921, U.S. Ambassador Richard W. Child, Rome, to Department of State, U.S. National Archives, Turkey, File No. 867.20265/–. In addition the following publications were also distributed in Italy: (1) L'Assasinat d'un Peuple, by Ghalip Kemaly Bey; (2) Un Discours de Moustapha Kemal Pacha Sur La Bataille de la Sakaria et la Situation Politique Actuelle de la Turquie; (3) Atrocités Grecques Documents et Rapports Officiels; (4) Une Enquete en Anatolie—Rapport de M. Gehri, Deleque de la Croix—Rouge Internationale; (5) L'Accord Franco-Turc, by Nihad Rechad; (6) Rapport du Parti National Egyptien sur les Règles de l'Accord Anglo-Egyptien; (7) A Angora auprès de Mustapha Kemal by Aleaddine Haidar.

[69] Atatürk, Speech, pp. 391–92.

ment of the districts evacuated by their forces.[70] Mustafa Kemal maintained that this agreement was contrary to the letter and spirit of the National Pact and therefore he considered it null and void. But in order not to offend unduly the *amour propre* of France, he instructed Dr. Nihat Reşat (Belger), his unofficial representative in Paris, to issue a statement to the press saying that the Ankara government, after careful study of the contents of the agreement, accepted it in principle, but certain "modalities" involved therein roused such serious objections that the Council of Ministers, fearing total rejection of the agreement by the assembly, decided not to present it to the latter and that the Council of Ministers drafted a counterproposal for submission as promptly as possible to the French government.[71]

Bekir Sami Bey thereupon resigned because he could not, as the original author of the agreement, countersign the proposed modifications nor undertake the presentation of them to the French government. Yet, he was again assigned the task of entering into further negotiations with the Italian and French officials. But at about the time of his departure for Rome, Henri Franklin-Bouillon, the chairman of the Senate Foreign Relations Committee of the French Parliament, arrived in Istanbul on May 24, 1921, once again shifting the scene of diplomatic maneuvering to Anatolia. Mustafa Kemal decided to handle the negotiations directly with the French statesman. Permission was obtained by Mustafa Kemal's representative Hamid Bey for Franklin-Bouillon to proceed to Ankara. On his trip to Ankara, Franklin-Bouillon was accompanied by Lt. Colonel Sarrou, who had served in the Ottoman gendarmerie prior to the First World War, who also spoke fluent Turkish and is reported to have had a number of friends among the nationalist leaders. Hamid Bey, in his message to Yusuf Kemal Bey, the Minister of Foreign Affairs, described Franklin-Bouillon as a person "whom it was very easy to convince" with respect to the settlement of the Cilician question.[72] At a special meeting of the Council of Ministers, chaired by Mustafa Kemal, the nationalist policy

---

[70] Text of the agreement is in *Oriento Moderno* 1 (July 15, 1921): 79–81.

[71] See the report of the British Ambassador to Rome, dated July 6, 1921, Great Britain, F.O. 371/6471, E 7731/1/44.

[72] "Intelligence Report" of October 1921, Great Britain, F.O. 371/6475, E 11169/1/44.

toward France in general and the Cilician question in particular was viewed, and the general outlines of the tactics to be followed in the forthcoming negotiations with Franklin-Bouillon were set. The latter came to Ankara on June 9.

Following the preliminaries of diplomatic courtesy extended to the French statesman and his party, the serious business of negotiations commenced on June 13 and lasted for two weeks. Fevzi Pasha, the prime minister, and Yusuf Kemal Bey took part in the negotiations between Mustafa Kemal and Franklin-Bouillon. Although Mustafa Kemal was successful in establishing a close personal relationship with Franklin-Bouillon and the two worked out the basic principles of an agreement, he had sensed that Franklin-Bouillon was still searching for tangible proof of the permanency of the Ankara regime before he could finalize an agreement with it. The victory of the nationalist forces at the battle of Sakarya resolved the doubts of the French statesman as to the military power of the Ankara government.[73]

Meanwhile Bekir Sami Bey was conducting negotiations in Paris. But on August 26 he was recalled by Mustafa Kemal, who apparently was of the opinion that Bekir Sami Bey's talks in Paris with the French governmental officials and his extremely soft attitude toward the French had complicated his own conversations with Franklin-Bouillon in Ankara.[74]

Uninformed about the nature of and the developments in the negotiations that had taken place between Mustafa Kemal and Franklin-Bouillon, Bekir Sami Bey held the conviction that he had persuaded the French government to agree to the principles of the National Pact and that he was rendering useful service to the nationalist cause. Upon being recalled he thought that Mustafa Kemal was once again yanking the rug out from under him. He returned from his last diplomatic mission totally disgusted about the whole affair. He then joined the ranks of the opposition to Mustafa Kemal.

In the latter part of October, Franklin-Bouillon returned to Ankara as the emissary of Quai d'Orsay ready to sign the agreement on Mustafa Kemal's terms. The treaty called "The Agreement for

---

[73] See Atatürk, *Speech,* pp. 523–26.

[74] "Intelligence Report" of September 13, 1921, Great Britain, F.O. 371/6474, E 10503/1/44.

the Promotion of Peace: France and the Nationalist Government of Turkey," usually referred to as the Ankara Agreement or the Franklin-Bouillon Agreement, actually was signed on October 20, 1921, by Yusuf Kemal Bey and Henri Franklin-Bouillon.[75] This agreement was hailed in Ankara as another diplomatic victory for the nationalists.

The Ankara Agreement provided that the state of war between France and Turkey would cease immediately, the prisoners of war and detainees would be repatriated, and a new frontier between Turkey and Syria would be established which would incorporate Cilicia and most of the Baghdad railway line into Turkey. The agreement also provided that a special administrative regime would be established for the district of Alexandretta (Hatay) and that the inhabitants of this district would enjoy every facility for their cultural development where the Turkish language would be officially recognized.

The significant feature of this agreement is the implied recognition of the Ankara government by France which once again brought into the open the grave differences of policy between Great Britain and France concerning the question of the Turkish settlement. It constituted a separate peace with the nationalist government, and this was what the British government objected to most of all. But by the begining of 1922 the British officials were having second thoughts about their hostile attitude toward the Ankara government. They also thought that they should come to grips with the realities of the situation in Anatolia.

An interesting and amusing episode in the Anglo-French rivalry over Turkey deserves particular mention here. In February 1922, Mustafa Kemal instructed Yusuf Kemal Bey to go to Paris and London by way of Istanbul in order to find out what steps were being contemplated by the French and British governments concerning the peaceful settlement of the Greco-Turkish War. Having been informed of Yusuf Kemal Bey's intended visit to Istanbul, the French authorities decided to steal a march on their British colleagues, and arranged to have a destroyer on hand at İzmit to transport Yusuf Kemal Bey the remainder of the journey in comfort. It was agreed that Hamid Bey, the representative of the

---

[75] Text of the Ankara Agreement in J. C. Hurewitz, *Diplomacy in the Near and Middle East,* vol. 2, pp. 98–100.

Ankara government was to be aboard the destroyer when it arrived at İzmit in order to meet the nationalist foreign minister. However, due to a misunderstanding on the part of the captain of the French destroyer, Hamid Bey was not permitted on board. When Yusuf Kemal Bey met the destroyer at İzmit and learned that Hamid Bey was not aboard, he refused to embark, fearing treachery. Meanwhile Hamid Bey had gotten in touch with the British authorities and informed them of the miscarriage of the French plans. The British officials quickly took advantage of the situation and hastily formed a special train which was sent from Haydarpaşa to İzmit, with a British officer in command and Hamid Bey on board. They brought Yusuf Kemal Bey safely to Istanbul, much to the chagrin of the French high commission there. In reporting this incident, the American high commissioner comments: "Here we see France and Great Britain vying with each other to show courtesy to a Turkish nationalist representative whom two years ago they would probably have exiled if they could have put their hands on him."[76]

Meanwhile in accordance with the provisions of the Ankara Agreement on December 1, 1921, the French authorities turned over the civil administration to the nationalist representatives in Cilicia, but retained military control in important centers until January 4, 1922. The military evacuation which began on December 4 was completed within one month.

The British intelligence sources report that immediately following the signature of the Ankara Agreement negotiations were started between France and the Ankara government for the supply of arms on an "extensive scale" from France and from depots in Cilicia. These sources also indicate that a military commission con-consisting of Refet Bey, Captain Sıdkı, and Major Cemal Bey, all on the staff of the Ministry of National Defense, arrived in Paris on October 29, 1921. The commission was charged with ordering war materials, including airplanes, on an agreed system of deferred payments.[77]

When the Turkish forces and their Commander in Chief Mustafa Kemal entered İzmir on September 9 and 10, 1922,

---

[76] "Dispatch" of February 22, 1922, High Commissioner Bristol to Department of State, U.S. National Archives, Turkey, File No. 867.00/1497.

[77] "Intelligence Report," December 5, 1921, Great Britain, F.O. 371/6537, E 14125/143/44.

General Pelle, the French high commissioner, came to İzmir for the purpose of meeting Mustafa Kemal and inquiring as to his next military-diplomatic move. At the time a serious crisis was begining to take shape in the Çanakkale region; the Turkish forces were approaching Dardanelles which were held mainly by the British troops. General Pelle advised Mustafa Kemal not to allow his troops to enter the so-called neutral zone in the Dardanelles and Bosporus regions. A few days later, on September 23, Henri Franklin-Bouillon appeared once again on the scene urging Mustafa Kemal, as the emissary of France, Great Britain, and Italy, not to move toward the Dardanelles lest he precipitate a direct military confrontation, if not with all three Allied Powers, at least with Britain. At this time, the Allied Powers in their note dated September 23 asked for the cessation of hostilities and the opening of negotiations leading to a final peace settlement. Mustafa Kemal reasoned: If the enemy's troops could be induced to evacuate the whole of eastern Thrace as far as the Turkish national frontiers, further military operations would automatically become unnecessary.[78]

THE TURCO-BRITISH RELATIONS. As far as can be ascertained, the earliest diplomatic contacts between the Ankara and British governments took place at the time of the London Conference of February 1921, which was convened to review the possibilities of modifying the stillborn Treaty of Sèvres of August 10, 1920, in view of the nationalist victories in the Eastern and Western fronts. The Allies, upon inviting the Ottoman government to the conference, stated that its participation was contingent upon the presence of nationalist representatives in its delegation.

Upon being informed of this indirect invitation, Mustafa Kemal did not miss the opportunity to reassert his claim that the Ankara government was the only legitimate authority in Turkey by dispatching copies of his communication with the Grand Vezir Tevfik Pasha in Istanbul to the Allied governments and by stating that a direct invitation for such a conference would be favorably received.[79] It appears that before asking for a separate invitation from the Allied Powers, before revealing the nature of the London

---

[78] Atatürk, *Speech,* p. 568.

[79] See "Dispatch," British High Commissioner Sir H. Rumbold, Great Britain, F.O. 371/6465, E 2021/1/44 and E 14448/1/44.

Conference to the Grand National Assembly, and before the impasse with the Istanbul government on the composition of the Turkish delegation, Mustafa Kemal had already decided to send a separate delegation to London.[80]

The Ankara delegation, headed by Foreign Minister Bekir Sami Bey, included Yunus Nadi Bey, deputy of Aydın; Hüsrev (Gerede), deputy of Trabzon; Zekai (Apaydın) Bey, deputy of Adana; and Cami (Baykurt) Bey, the representative of the Ankara government in Rome. The delegation also included a group of experts: Mahmut Esat (Bozkurt), deputy of İzmir; Vehbi Bey, deputy of Karesi; Sırrı (Belli), deputy of İzmit. Muvaffak (Menencioğlu), deputy of Saruhan and director of the Anatolian News Agency, and Staff Captain Yumni Salih were also attached to the delegation as advisers.[81]

At the London Conference, which opened on February 21, 1921, the Ankara and Istanbul delegations' head, Grand Vezir Tevfik Pasha, yielded the floor to Bekir Sami Bey as the only spokesman for Turkey. Because of his disillusionment with the things he saw in Moscow and because of his westernist orientation, Bekir Sami Bey was willing to consider, with certain reservations, the

---

[80] This may be deduced from the contents of Bekir Sami Bey's note to the Allied governments. For a translated version of the text of the note see Great Britain, F.O. 371/6465, E 1678/1/44. This note asks the Allied Powers to postpone the opening of the conference for a few days in order to enable the Ankara delegation to reach London on time.

[81] Yunus Nadi Bey was the editor of *Anadoluda Yeni Gün* newspaper, an eminent journalist in his own right and a close associate of Mustafa Kemal. Apparently, because of his membership in the "official" Communist Party he is identified in a British intelligence report as "a particularly poisonous and unscrupulous journalist, whom both we and [the] French wanted arrested." The report goes on to say that "he edits *Yeni Ghazi [Yeni Gün]* newspaper at Angora, and was some months ago too extreme for government there. He was Socialist, and stood strongly for Bolshevik alliance, though not for introduction of Bolshevism as such." The report maintains that "selection of Yunus may be due to desire to give representation to Extreme Left in the Grand National Assembly." "Intelligence Report," Great Britain, F.O. 371/6465, E 2031/1/44. Hüsrev Gerede was again a close associate of Mustafa Kemal. Later he served as minister and as ambassador in Budapest (1924–1926), Sofia (1926–1930), Tehran (1930–1934), Tokyo (1936–1939) and Berlin (1939–1942). Zekai Apaydın also served later as minister and as ambassador in London in 1924 and in Moscow (1925–1927). Mahmut Esat Bozkurt, Sırrı Belli, and Vehbi Bey later assumed ministerial posts in various cabinets of Fevzi Pasha, Rauf Bey, and İsmet Pasha. See also Galip Kemali, *Hariciye Hizmetinde 30 Sene,* pp. 493–94.

modification of the Treaty of Sèvres.[82] However, thanks to the refusal of the Greek delegation to accept any modification in the Treaty of Sèvres, the Turkish delegation was spared the necessity of turning down the Allied proposals which were considered contrary to the principles of the National Pact. The London Conference thus could not produce any concrete results. However, in addition to his agreements with the French and Italian representatives, Bekir Sami Bey signed another agreement with Lloyd George concerning the exchange of prisoners of war. But this agreement was also repudiated by Mustafa Kemal.

Following some preliminary contacts between the emissaries of General Harington, the commander in chief of the Allied forces, and Mustafa Kemal at İnebolu,[83] on July 5, 1921, General Harington sent Major Henry and an official of the British high commission to İnebolu bearing a letter to Mustafa Kemal. In this letter, General Harington states that in view of the previous exchanges between their emissaries he understood that Mustafa Kemal desired to "lay before" him "certain views as one soldier speaking to another," and he goes on to say that "If this is the case I am authorized . . . to proceed in the battleship Ajax to Inebolu or Ismid to meet you any day convenient to you and . . . I am authorized to listen to Your Lordship's views and report them to the British Government for their consideration." While he reminds Mustafa Kemal that he is not "empowered to negotiate or speak on behalf of the British Government," he proposes that the "interview should take place on board the British battleship when Your Lordship will be received appropriately and enjoy full liberty until you land."[84] In his reply, Mustafa Kemal makes it absolutely clear that it was not he who originally asked for a meeting, but that he was, nevertheless, prepared to negotiate with General Harington provided that the complete independence and territorial integrity of Turkey would be recognized in advance. In order to convey the

---

[82] For example, Count Sforza writes: "I . . . tried to use my influence over Bekir to make him adopt a moderate attitude. I was fortunate enough to succeed. He showed himself more willing than the Greeks to place himself in the hands of an impartial arbitrator." *Diplomatic Europe Since the Treaty of Versailles,* p. 63.

[83] See Atatürk, *Speech,* p. 541 and "Dispatch," July 8, 1921, Great Britain, F.O. 371/6472, E 7866/1/44.

[84] Great Britain, F.O. 371/6471, E 7656/1/44.

idea that he was the chief representative of a sovereign nation, Mustafa Kemal also asked General Harington to come ashore to meet him on Turkish soil and on his own terms. In his last paragraph Mustafa Kemal states: "If Your Excellency has no other purpose in view than to exchange opinions about the situation, I shall send my comrades for the interview."[85] This amounts to a direct snub at the commander in chief of the Allied forces, stating in effect that "if you are not willing to talk serious business, an inferior officer of the nationalist government would be a suitable person to chat with!" Needless to say, no reply was made to Mustafa Kemal's letter and the prospective meeting did not take place. Acting British High Commissioner Rattigan interprets Mustafa Kemal's refusal to meet General Harington as an indication of the fact that "either he is virtually a prisoner of extremists in which case his value is unimportant," or "merely a pretext which would appear to lend colour to the possibility that the whole proposal is a strategem to gain prestige." Then he states: "If he [Mustafa Kemal] does hold reins and seriously intends to make some reasonable offer then he should have no difficulty in meeting General Harington at some point on the coast."[86] Concerning Mustafa Kemal's demand for complete independence of Turkey, Rattigan declares: "Kemalists appeared to have taken leave of their senses in formulating such a demand."[87]

However, a few months later, General Harington once again sent Major Henry to İnebolu to negotiate with Colonel Refet concerning the exchange of prisoners of war. Apparently, this time, an agreement was reached and the exchange of prisoners took place in İnebolu.[88]

During Bekir Sami Bey's second mission in Europe he approached the British Embassy in Paris and inquired into the possibilities of conducting talks with the British government. In view of what the Foreign Office called "the disrespectful conduct of the Angora Government in repudiating the agreement" concluded between Bekir Sami Bey and Lloyd George, the British government was not willing to accept Bekir Sami Bey as the representative of

[85]Atatürk, *Speech,* p. 542.
[86] Great Britain, F.O. 371/6471, E 7108/1/44.
[87] Great Britain, F.O. 371/6472, E 7866/1/44.
[88] Lord Kinross, *Ataturk,* p. 329.

the nationalist government. The Foreign Office, in its instructions to the Paris Embassy concerning this matter, stated that the

hostile and almost insolent attitude of Mustafa Kemal, with respect to meeting with General Harington in Black Sea, also renders us skeptical of the advantage of meeting a representative of his, of the exact measure of whose authority we are completely uncertain and who is probably not a representative at all.[89]

Ambassador Sir Cheetham was advised, therefore, to discourage Bekir Sami Bey from visiting London.

There were some other diplomatic contacts between the Turkish and British officials in Moscow. Talks between Ambassador Ali Fuat Pasha and R. M. Hodgson, the head of the British trade delegation, were arranged by Chicherin, the Soviet Commissar for Foreign Affairs, in August 1921. However, these talks were inconclusive and, in the main, entailed exchanges of views between Ali Fuat Pasha and Mr. Hodgson concerning matters of mutual interest.[90]

Before the final offensive of the Turkish forces in the latter part of August 1922, Mustafa Kemal, in his search for the realization of the objectives defined in the National Pact by peaceful means, dispatched his Minister of Foreign Affairs, Yusuf Kemal Bey, to Rome, Paris, and London in February 1922; he later sent Ali Fethi Bey, Minister of Interior, to the same European capitals. These attempts were, however, to no avail. In Ali Fethi Bey's case, he was even denied an audience with Lord Curzon in London.

Just before the final drive against the Greeks, General Townshend once again appeared on the scene, this time as a member of the British Parliament. He held private talks with Mustafa Kemal in Konya on June 24, 1922, and with Prime Minister Rauf Bey in Ankara. Nothing, however, came out of these conversations.[91]

Upon the retreat of the Greek armies from western Anatolia the Turkish nationalist forces next turned their attention to the

---

[89] "Instructions to Ambassador Cheetham," July 12, 1921, Great Britain, F.O. 371/6472, E 7888/1/44.

[90] See Cebesoy, *Moskova Hatıraları,* pp. 255–60; "Dispatch," September 6, 1921, Great Britain, F.O. 371/6475, E 10539/1/44.

[91] See Rauf Orbay, "Rauf Orbay'ın Hatıraları," *Yakın Tarihimiz,* 3 (15 Kasım 1962): 371–72; Aralov, *Bir Sovyet Diplomatının Türkiye Hatıraları,* p. 135.

Allied, particularly the British, forces at Çanakkale on the southern shores of the Dardanelles. They had come to the neutral zone established by the commander in chief of the Allied forces in 1921 and were ready to cross the Dardanelles and pursue the Greek forces in eastern Thrace. General Sir Charles Harington was instructed by the British government: to hold Gallipoli at all costs; to hold Çanakkale as long as he could without endangering his forces; to evacuate the İzmit Peninsula when forced to by threats of serious attack; and to evacuate Istanbul when forced to do so.[92]

The British high commissioner in Istanbul informed his Allied colleagues on September 8 that British policy in Turkey had not changed due to the nationalists' victory over the Greeks, and that the British government was prepared to send large forces to fight the nationalists if necessary in order to hold the Straits.[93] General Harington asked the French and Italian high commissioners to assist him with additional troops. However, the French and Italian governments did not approve the affirmative response of their high commissioners and ordered their detachments to be withdrawn from Çanakkale.[94] The attitude of these two governments in 1922 was that Greece, backed by Great Britain, had been fighting a war of conquest and had lost; that during this war in which the Allied governments had formally declared neutrality, Greece had been allowed to use Istanbul as a base; now that the Turks were in a position to carry the war into Thrace, they demanded that the Allies allow them to cross the neutral zone.

General Harington rushed nearly all his troops from the İzmit Peninsula, Istanbul, and the Çatalca lines to Çanakkale. In order to preserve order in Istanbul, General Harington asked American High Commissioner Bristol whether he would use American sailors to assist the British authorities in maintaining order in Istanbul. But he was refused assistance.[95] General Harington,

---

[92] Sir Charles Harington, *Tim Harington Looks Back,* p. 117; see also General Harington's Dispatch to War Office, *Orient News* (Istanbul), November 5, 1922.

[93] "Telegram," September 11, 1922, High Commissioner Bristol to Department of State, U.S. National Archives, Turkey, File No. 767.68/306.

[94] Harington, *Tim Harington Looks Back,* p. 111.

[95] "Dispatch," September 23, 1922, High Commissioner Bristol to Department of State, U.S. National Archives, Turkey, File No. 767.68/363.

on September 26, sent a message to Mustafa Kemal asking him to withdraw the Turkish troops outside the neutral zone.[96] In reply, the next day, Mustafa Kemal disclaimed any knowledge as to the existence of a neutral zone and called upon General Harington to desist from intervening between the Turkish forces and the Greek army, promising that the Ankara government would observe the freedom of navigation over the Straits. The same day General Harington wrote back and said that in order to prevent a possible clash between Turkish and British forces at Çanakkale Mustafa Kemal should withdraw any appearance of threat to the British forces. He then said: "Should there be any points of misunderstanding between us, I would be prepared to meet you in any place mutually agreed upon between us. . . . It is . . . an immense relief to me to hear that you have no aggressive intentions against my troops."[97] The two generals played their hands cautiously: General Harington ignored his government's ultimatum calling for the withdrawal of the Turkish forces from the neutral zone and Mustafa Kemal chose not to provoke his opponents. Thus a new military confrontation was averted.

THE ARMISTICE OF MUDANYA. The next encounter between Mustafa Kemal and the Allies took place at the Mudanya Armistice Conference which was convened on October 3, 1922. Although it had been called essentially for the purpose of arranging an armistice between the Turkish and Greek forces and avoiding a clash between the Turkish and British forces, it became evident that Mustafa Kemal's representative İsmet Pasha was to draw the Allied generals into a discussion of political questions. For this reason, the conference dragged on for nine days. İsmet Pasha insisted on the immediate restoration of Thrace to the Ankara government up to the right bank of the Maritza River, including the city of Edirne. Under instructions from Mustafa Kemal, İsmet Pasha held out as long as he could, but then yielded to the demands of the Allied generals that the transfer of eastern Thrace to the Ankara government should take place in stages, in order to avoid

---

[96] "Intelligence Report," September 28, 1922, High Commissioner Bristol to Department of State, U.S. National Archives, Turkey, File No. 867.00/1550.

[97] Ibid. See also Col. D. I. Shuttleworth, "Turkey, From the Armistice to the Peace," *Journal of the Central Asian Society*, 11 (1924): 61–62.

a possible war with Britain.[98] The armistice agreement was signed on October 11, 1922.

The Armistice of Mudanya fixed a line behind which the Greek forces were to withdraw from Thrace and settled the mode of evacuation of the Greek troops and administration, and of installing the administraton and gendarmerie of the Ankara government. It also provided for the control of the region by the Allies during the period of transition for the purpose of maintaining order and tranquility.

The Armistice of Mudanya was a political victory for Mustafa Kemal coming in the wake of his military victory. It secured eastern Thrace without firing a shot and it compelled the Allies to treat the Ankara government as the real government of Turkey. American High Commissioner Admiral Bristol remarked: "The humiliation of the British during this Conference is obvious when, with a large part of the Atlantic fleet anchored in the Bosporus and the Dardanelles . . . General Harington was forced to make concessions to the Turks which a month ago the British would not have dreamed of making, and he was forced to witness British prestige suffer a defeat from which it will take many years to recover."[99] Winston S. Churchill called it a humiliation of not only the British but more so of the Allies as a whole. He wrote:

Nowhere had the victory been more complete than over Turkey; nowhere had the conqueror's power been flaunted more arrogantly than in Turkey; and now, in the end, all the fruits of successful war, all the laurels for which so many scores of thousands had died on the Gallipoli Peninsula, in the deserts of Palestine and Mesopotamia . . . was to end in shame. Victory over Turkey absolute and unchallenged had been laid by the armies upon the council table of the Peace Conference. Four years had past, and the talkers had turned it into defeat. . . . All the fine pretentions of Europe and the United States, all the eloquence of their statesmen, all the hiving and burrow-

---

[98] On the details of the negotiations see Türkgeldi, *Moudros ve Mudanya Mütarekelerinin Tarihi,* pp. 164–70, and Harington, *Tim Harington Looks Back,* pp. 118–29. Text of the armistice agreement in "Dispatch," October 16, 1922, High Commissioner Bristol to Department of State, U.S. National Archives, Turkey, File No. 767.68119/69.

[99] "Report on Recent Events of Political Interest," October 16, 1922, High Commissioner Bristol to Department of State, U.S. National Archives, Turkey, File No. 767.68/500.

ing committees and commissions had led the erstwhile masters of overwhelming power to this bitter and ignominous finish.[100]

The decision to deliver eastern Thrace to the Ankara government had reduced the position of the Istanbul government to a still lower ebb of ineffectiveness than before. Now, its attitude toward the nationalist government in Ankara was *Morituri te salutamus.* However, in order to obtain some guarantees of their capitulatory privileges from the Istanbul government, the Allied Powers wished to attribute some legitimacy to it by inviting the Sublime Porte to a peace conference in Lausanne as an equal to the Ankara government. Such an invitation, however, led to only one result — the abolition of the sultanate by the Grand National Assembly of Turkey.

On October 9, 1922, Mustafa Kemal had appointed his old friend Refet Pasha as the governor general of eastern Thrace responsible for taking over that region in the name of the Ankara government. Following the abolition of the sultanate, Refet Pasha was ordered also to take over the administration in Istanbul. Refet Pasha promulgated a series of regulations concerning the transfer of jurisdiction to the Ankara government and acted as though there were no Allied occupation authorities in Istanbul.[101] The Allied high commissioners, however, maintained that they were resolved to "maintain order and security in the zone occupied by the Allied armies," and that this mandate included also the administration of the occupied zone (Istanbul province) by themselves as they had done since November 1918, and that the administrative changes that were introduced in Istanbul had been carried out without their knowledge and, therefore, constituted a violation of the Mudanya Armistice Agreement.[102] The Ankara government, on the other hand, called upon the high commissioners to cease their interven-

---

[100] Winston S. Churchill, *The Aftermath* (New York: Charles Scribner, 1929), p. 445.

[101] On these developments see *Orient News* (Constantinople) November 7, 1922; "Intelligence Report," November 21, 1922, High Commissioner Bristol to Department of State, U.S. National Archives, Turkey, File No. 867.00/1576; see also "Dispatch," November 8, 1922, File No. 867.00/1574.

[102] For the Allied note to the Ankara government see "Dispatch," November 21, 1922, High Commissioner Bristol to Department of State, U.S. National Archives, Turkey, File No. 767.68119/306.

tions in the domestic affairs of Turkey but also declared that it had had confidence in the conciliatory sentiments of the Allied Powers.[103]

The Allied authorities in Istanbul were faced with an extremely ambiguous situation. They were not quite sure whether they were representing victorious or defeated powers. Their authority in the so-called occupied zone was constantly being challenged by the measures introduced by Refet Pasha.[104] The Allied generals went to see Refet Pasha with a view to easing the situation. They were able to induce him to modify some of the administrative measures.[105] Ultimately, a feeling of understanding and cooperation came to prevail between the Ankara government and the Allied high commissioners concerning the assumption of primary responsibility on the part of the representatives of the Ankara government in the administration and control of the Istanbul province.

THE CONFRONTATION OF THE TURKISH AND WESTERN DIPLOMACIES AT LAUSANNE

The Lausanne Conference marked the first and most important confrontation between the Turkish and Western diplomacies on equal terms. The Treaty of Sèvres which was imposed upon the Ottoman government on August 10, 1920, was long a dead letter. Now, the warrior diplomats of the Nationalist Movement, unyielding on the principles for which they stood, were called upon to consider the consequences of the previous eight years in all its ramifications and to establish a new status quo in the Middle East based on mutual respect of sovereignty and independence. The representatives of the government of the Grand National Assembly were no longer spokesmen for "The Sick Man of Europe." The fact of the matter was, however, that the Allied Powers were still unwilling or unable to accept Turkey as their equal. That equality

---

[103] The text of the Turkish note in Ibid.

[104] On the feelings of the Allied authorities as described by General Harington in his dispatch to the British War Office see *Orient News* (Constantinople), November 5, 1922.

[105] See "War Diary," December 1, 1922, High Commissioner Bristol, U.S. National Archives, Turkey, File No. 867.00/1596.

won on the battlefields, as one observer put it, "was to be completed by no less notable victories at Lausanne."[106]

For this task Mustafa Kemal chose his intimate associate İsmet Pasha as the head of the Turkish delegation. He was to be assisted by Dr. Rıza Nur Bey, the Minister of Public Health and deputy from Sinop; Hasan Bey, ex-Minister of Economy and deputy from Trabzon. The delegation included a group of political advisers: Zekai Bey, deputy from Adana; Celal Bey, deputy from Saruhan; Zülfi Bey, deputy from Diyarbakır; and Veli Bey, deputy from Burdur.[107] Münir Bey, Mustafa Şerif Bey, Tahir Bey, Muhtar Bey, Tevfik Bey, and Reşit Safvet Bey were also members of the Turkish delegation.[108]

It seems that İsmet Pasha showed some reluctance in accepting the grave responsibilities of his new assignment. After all, throughout his career he was a military man, and aside from the negotiations which he had undertaken at the Mudanya Conference he had no previous experience in the art of diplomacy. Furthermore, he regarded his experience at the Mudanya negotiations as having been extremely strenuous and somewhat distasteful, even though it had been a military conference in which military men participated. He was now asked to take an essentially diplomatic task and deal with "European diplomacy, with its artful commanders and its armory of unknown and insidious weapons."[109] However, despite his plea that he was no diplomat, as a good soldier, he obeyed the order of his Commander in Chief Mustafa Kemal to face up to the skillful practitioners of European diplomacy, particularly that Bismarckian diplomat, Lord Curzon, the foreign secretary of Great Britain.

Not only did İsmet Pasha lack the self-assurance of a career diplomat and experience in European conference diplomacy, he was not sure that he would have the solid backing, in his negotiations with the Allied representatives, of the members of the cabinet headed by Rauf Bey. He knew very well that any small concessions

---

[106] Harry N. Howard, *The Partition of Turkey* (Norman, Okla: University of Oklahoma Press, 1931), p. 277.

[107] Soysal, *Dış Politika ve Parlamento*, p. 93.

[108] Joseph C. Grew, *Turbulent Era: A Diplomatic Record of Forty Years, 1904–1945* (Boston: Houghton Mifflin, 1952), vol. 1, p. 481.

[109] Lord Kinross, *Ataturk*, p. 403.

he had to make in order to reach a satisfactory peace settlement would be subject to severe criticism on the part of those, including Rauf Bey, who did not favor his appointment. The members of the Grand National Assembly were expecting from his delegation as solid a diplomatic victory as the military victory achieved by the Turkish forces.

Consequently, as İsmet Pasha set out to go to Lausanne he was handicapped by his own lack of diplomatic experience, doubts clearly expressed by his opponents as to his capabilities in the intricacies of European diplomacy, the rigidity of his instructions concerning the goals he was asked to achieve, close scrutiny of his statements at the conference table by Mustafa Kemal and by his opponents, and finally the determination of the experienced Allied diplomats in denying Turkey the fruits of her military victory. The chief difficulty to be encountered by İsmet Pasha and his delegation was the handling of the presumed superiority complex of their opponents. The Allied statesmen and diplomats were out to crush the Turkish delegation with steam-roller methods. They hoped that they could induce the Turkish delegation to sign a treaty of peace within a few weeks.

According to one Western writer, İsmet Pasha's principal opponent Lord Curzon "seemed to look upon him as one of his subjects in India."[110] This attitude exasperated İsmet Pasha and his delegates, for the Turkish delegation had not come to Lausanne, hat in hand, begging for peace, but with a victorious army behind them. His was not the same delegation on which the ignominious Treaty of Sèvres was imposed two years before.

The question of the recognition of Turkey's complete sovereignty and independence was the cardinal issue upon which the success or failure of the Lausanne Conference depended. İsmet Pasha stood on the National Pact, and Turkish sovereignty was his major weapon in combatting any measure of foreign control over the internal affairs of Turkey. "Turkey was acutely sensitive on this matter, and her fears were unfortunately well-founded," said İsmet Pasha, "for up to the present day Turkish sovereignty had always been infringed on the plea of humanitarian considerations. The integrity of Turkey had frequently been guaranteed by means of promises from the highest authorities and also by solemn treaties,

---

[110] Ibid., p. 404.

and yet Turkish sovereignty had repeatedly been violated."[111] Lord Curzon, on the other hand, is reported to have viewed the whole emphasis on sovereignty as a ridiculous obsession. Describing one of his conversations with İsmet Pasha, Lord Curzon is quoted as saying: "İsmet, you remind me of nothing so much as a music-box. You play the same old tune day after day until we are all heartily sick of it — sovereignty, sovereignty, sovereignty."[112]

The whole proceeding of the conference was marked by the contrast between Lord Curzon's flamboyant brilliance and eloquence, his domineering personality, his superiority complex, and İsmet Pasha's timorous but obstinate stand. The American ambassador to Italy, R. W. Child, attending the conference as an observer describes İsmet Pasha in these words: "He is forty years old and looks fifty. He is deaf and his health is not good. His face has in it suffering, anxiety, slyness and sweetness. . . . In private conversation he indulges in long silences of apparent meditation and then suddenly breaks forth, often on a wholly new subject. In fact this method is one he uses constantly in order to change the subject. His sense of humor is excellent and he has a hearty laugh, but the two, I find, are not connected always because I have heard him laugh when he was not amused and known of his amusement when he did not laugh."[113] No doubt the uncompromising and at times threatening attitude of İsmet Pasha was primarily due to the tremendous difficulties he was encountering in his negotiations with the Allied diplomatic wizards. Another observer of the conference provides further glimpses of the state of mind of İsmet Pasha. Ambassador Joseph C. Grew writes: "The more I study those apparently baneful eyes of İsmet Pasha, the more I believe that they are expressive merely of nervousness, anxiety, ill-ease."[114]

As Lord Curzon attempted to disallow İsmet Pasha's proposals concerning the procedure with a gesture of indignant, regal authority but with suavity of manner and splendid flow of beautiful

[111] Great Britain, *Turkey no. I (1923). Lausanne Conference on Near Eastern Affairs, 1922–1923.* Cmd. 1814, p. 219. This contains the proces-verbaux and acts of the Lausanne Conference.

[112] Grew, *Turbulent Era,* vol. 1, p. 524.

[113] Richard Washburn Child, *A Diplomat Looks at Europe* (New York: Duffield and Co., 1925), p. 96.

[114] Grew, *Turbulent Era,* vol. 1, p. 493.

English İsmet Pasha dug himself in for a prolonged contest of wills. İsmet Pasha thought that his greatest asset was time. He sensed that his opponents were seeking a quick and somewhat dictated peace settlement. He sensed, too, that the Allies had no inclination to force their claims. They were, furthermore, unaccustomed to dealing with the representatives of an Eastern country with an independent spirit and national pride, demanding sovereign equality and willing to fight for it. İsmet Pasha, therefore, prepared his plans for a prolonged siege, patiently working toward his goal.

From the very opening hours of the conference, he let the European diplomats know what he was up to. Following the opening speech of the president of Switzerland, Haab, welcoming the delegates to his country, to which Lord Curzon replied, İsmet Pasha rose and delivered a speech which was interpreted by Western diplomats as "a most tactless address, controversial and threatening in tone."[115] But İsmet Pasha let everyone concerned there know that he was there to fight for his rights. According to Ambassador Grew, at the first business session at the Hotel du Château, İsmet Pasha raised various objections to the draft of procedure drawn up by the three Allied Powers. For example, he demanded that the presidency of the Territorial, Financial, and Economic Committee be assigned to his delegation. He asked that a member of his delegation be appointed as assistant secretary of the conference. These moves were interpreted by the Allies as obstructionism. He did not make quick and witty replies, of which his opponent Lord Curzon was a master. He always reserved his right to reply to comments and allegations at a later time. He demanded time to prepare his statements. He demanded time to confer interminably with his experts or to consult with Ankara. When he did reply, he was slow, methodical, and read from prepared statements in French or from notes dictated in Turkish to his secretary; he spoke with ostensibly calm feeling and a slow voice that was barely audible. At times he was touchy, quick to suspect affronts to his country's dignity and threats to her sovereignty. At other times, he pleaded deafness, which he used as a stratagem to gain time, but he always heard what he wanted to hear.[116] As another observer put it: "It is said that İsmet's deafness contributed largely to his

---

[115] Ibid., p. 489.
[116] Ibid., pp. 491–92.

success at Lausanne, because it permitted his remaining in the room after certain delegates had reflected improperly upon Turkey in phrases which, if he had heard them, must have so affronted his patriotism and self-respect as to force his withdrawal."[117] Ambassador Child describes the contest of wills between Lord Curzon and İsmet Pasha vividly in these words:

İsmet is a complex mentality blanketed under the veneer of extreme simplicity. To Curzon he appears as a rather ignorant and rough little man who at moments when Curzon wants him to yield something becomes inexpressive or merely reiterates some sentence he has said a dozen times before. In personal contact this creates in Curzon a kind of tempest of inner rage and a sense of his total lack of power to proceed. Curzon believes that the whole phenomena comes from İsmet's stupidity. I am certain that when İsmet's mind ceases to function openly it is functioning marvelously within. İsmet knows the value of simple stupidity. Curzon talks like a schoolmaster, occasionally is insulting at the Conference table. İsmet makes no protest. He frowns — gazes in blank amazement or wears a sheepish smile. He knows, I believe, that Curzon will, in a rage, someday say something foolish. And he will! Already the victory in this contest between two men rests more with İsmet than with Curzon, for Curzon has taken positions from which he has been forced to recede.[118]

İsmet Pasha knew that Lord Curzon's outbursts and bullying methods, unless backed up by a willingness to fight, were mere bluffs which could be ignored. He was, therefore, wholly untouched by Lord Curzon's diplomatic oratory. The conference dragged on week after week and month after month and thus İsmet Pasha gained concession after concession, for he was never willing to bargain on the principles of sovereignty and territorial integrity of Turkey.

İsmet Pasha also took advantage of the apparent differences of policy among the three Allied Powers. He also took advantage of the Turco-Soviet friendship in his adamant refusal to accept any infringement of Turkish sovereignty; he made it quite clear that "Turkey could look to the East and the North as well as the West" if the West was unwilling to accept Turkey as a sovereign European power.

---

[117] C. H. Sherrill, *A Year's Embassy to Mustafa Kemal* (New York: Methuen and Co., 1934), pp. 145–46.

[118] Child, *A Diplomat Looks at Europe,* p. 95.

Particularly, on the question of the Straits, he used the backing of Commissar Chicherin as a threat against Western interests in the Straits and the Black Sea. On the other hand, İsmet Pasha avoided dependence on Soviet Russia. As one commentator put it, İsmet Pasha "placed the new Turkey in an advantageous position between the West and Russia. Though the decision on the Straits [concerning its demilitarization and its free use by all nations] is sometimes represented as Curzon's triumph in splitting Turkey from Russia, it was as much İsmet's triumph in avoiding dependence on Russia."[119]

On January 31, 1923, Lord Curzon formally presented to İsmet Pasha a draft treaty, which he had put into French and had practiced reading until there could be no misunderstanding his pronunciation. When Lord Curzon finished reading the text, İsmet Pasha merely cupped his ear and said, "Pardon me, but I am very deaf: would you mind reading that again?"[120] Although flabbergasted and outraged by this remark, Lord Curzon made a supreme effort to cool his temper and read the text again. İsmet Pasha in a brief reply pointed out that the draft treaty contained not only articles that had been agreed upon but also articles that had not been agreed to in committees; in addition the draft treaty contained some entirely new proposals which had never been discussed previously. He therefore asked for a period of eight days to enable his delegation to hold conversations with the Allies in an effort to agree upon the terms of peace. On February 4, in his final encounter with Lord Curzon, İsmet Pasha submitted a draft treaty containing only those clauses which had been agreed to and stated that these clauses constituted a sufficient basis for peace, and that other matters could be settled later.[121] Thus an impasse was reached and Lord Curzon left Lausanne the same day, forcing the adjournment of the conference without reaching a settlement. Three days later İsmet Pasha and his delegation left for Ankara.

On March 8 İsmet Pasha, in his note to the Allies, described the minimum conditions under which a peace settlement could be achieved. These conditions included: (1) complete abolition of

---

[119] Roderic H. Davison, "Turkish Diplomacy from Mudros to Lausanne," *The Diplomats: 1919–1939,* ed. Gordon A. Craig and Felix Gilbert. (Princeton: Princeton University Press, 1953), p. 203.

[120] Webster, *The Turkey of Atatürk,* p. 100.

[121] Grew, *Turbulent Era,* vol. 1, p. 550.

the Capitulations; (2) postponement within a fixed time of the Mosul question and the economic clauses; (3) acceptance of the Karaagac clause, abandoning the Turkish claim to the 1913 frontier west of the Maritza delta; (4) insistence on the claim for Greek reparations for damages in Anatolia; (5) acceptance of all other points settled at Lausanne; (6) immediate evacuation of occupied territories by the Allies after peace; and (7) acceptance of the internationalization of the Straits.[122] Upon expression of willingness by the Allied Powers to discuss these points, the Lausanne Conference reconvened on April 23, 1923. However, this time Lord Curzon was absent; his place was taken by the British high commissioner in Istanbul, Sir Horace Rumbold.

The second session of the conference lasted for three months, during which İsmet Pasha refused any concessions on the principles of the National Pact. He knew what he wanted and what he was prepared to give, such as the renouncement of the reparations from Greece in return for restoration of Karaagac to Turkey. When the Treaty of Lausanne was finally signed on July 24, 1923, together with seventeen annexes, İsmet Pasha had achieved a major diplomatic victory in compelling the Western Powers to acknowledge that the relations between Turkey and the Allies were to be based on mutual respect for independence and sovereignty.

The peace treaty of Lausanne provided for the boundaries outlined in the National Pact, for the demilitarization of the Greek islands nearest the coast of Anatolia, and for recognition of Italy's claim to the Dodecanese Islands, renouncing all claims to territories outside the boundaries defined in the National Pact. It confirmed the status of territories in the Middle East formerly controlled by the Ottoman Empire but now under Allied control. It confirmed the status of the Straits as a demilitarized zone, and provided for freedom of passage through the Straits. It contained provisions concerning the protection of the human rights of minority peoples remaining in Turkey. It secured the recognition of the abolition of the Capitulations; foreign residents, businesses, and economic concessions were to be subject to Turkish law. The Mosul questions

---

[122] Howard, *The Partition of Turkey,* p. 280; the texts of the note and the draft in France, Ministère des affaires étrangères. *Documents diplomatiques. Conference de Lausanne sur les affaires du proche-orient 1922–1923, Recueil des actes de la conference,* Ier Serie, tome 4, pp. 26–33; see also *Oriento Moderno.* 2 no. 11 (April 15, 1923): 643-59.

were left to bilateral negotiations between Turkey and Great Britain.[123]

Upon the signing of the Treaty of Lausanne, Mustafa Kemal, in his telegram to İsmet Pasha, congratulated him on his historic achievement. He said:

You have brought the new mission entrusted to Your Excellency by the nation and the government to a happy conclusion. You have thus crowned with a historic success a life which consists of a series of eminent services rendered to your country. At a moment when, after long struggles our country at last enjoys peace and independence, I address my most thankful congratulations to Your Excellency for your brilliant services, to Riza Nur Bey and Hasan Bey, your honorable colleagues, as well as to all members of the Delegation who have helped you in your task.[124]

The Grand National Assembly approved the Treaty of Lausanne on August 23, 1923, and the evacuation of the Allied troops commenced the following day and was carried out according to a program ending on October 2.

On the day of the signing of the Treaty of Lausanne, General Harington, commander in chief of the Allied forces paid a visit to the Turkish military governor of Istanbul, Selahaddin Adil Pasha, and "requested him to assist in establishing old traditions which have existed formerly between the British and Turkish armies, so that incidents might be avoided." General Harington also confirmed his respects for the Turkish forces "either as friend or foe" and informed Selahaddin Adil Pasha that "the usual compliments paid between armies" will be observed "as regards to the Turkish forces."[125] Now, the past was to be forgotten and a new spirit of mutual respect and understanding was to prevail.

RELATIONS WITH THE NEUTRAL POWERS

Following the return of the United States representatives to Istanbul in the early months of 1919, an anomalous diplomatic

---

[123] Text of the Treaty of Peace of Lausanne in League of Nations, *Treaty Series*, 28 (1924): 11ff; see also Great Britain, Foreign Office, *Treaty Series, No. 16 (1923) Treaty of Peace with Turkey, and Other Instruments signed at Lausanne on July 24, 1923, Cmd. 1929.*

[124] Atatürk, *Speech*, p. 654.

[125] See *Orient News* (Constantinople), 5 November 1923.

situation developed in the relations between the Ottoman Empire and the United States. During the First World War, these two powers were not at war with each other, but due to the declaration of war by the United States upon Germany, the Ottoman Empire broke off its diplomatic relations with the United States on April 17, 1917. For the purpose of protecting its interests in Turkey, the United States government reopened its diplomatic mission in Istanbul in January 1919 without re-establishing formal diplomatic relations with the Sublime Porte.

Thus, for a period of almost eight years, despite the presence of a considerably large diplomatic mission in Istanbul and a strong detachment of naval vessels in Turkish waters, no formal diplomatic relations existed between the United States and either the Istanbul government or the National government in Ankara.[126] However, on account of his pro-Turkish sentiments, the United States high commissioner in Istanbul from 1919 to 1927, Rear Admiral Mark L. Bristol, was able to protect American interests in Turkey without offending the pride and prestige of the nationalist leaders in Ankara.

Aside from the meeting between Mustafa Kemal and General Harbord in September 1919, no significant contact between the American representatives in Istanbul and the Ankara government took place until February 1922. On February 18, 1922, Foreign Minister Yusuf Kemal Bey met with Admiral Bristol in Istanbul and raised the question of the resumption of diplomatic relations between Turkey and the United States without the burden of Capitulations.[127] At the time, however, the United States was not prepared to recognize the Ankara government. Formal discussions leading to the signing of two separate treaties between the two countries were conducted during the Lausanne Conference to which the United States had sent observers.

During the second phase of the Lausanne Conference, İsmet Pasha met with Ambassador Joseph C. Grew and proposed to enter into treaty relations with the United States. He argued that an early settlement with the Allies would be promoted by a prior agreement with the United States. He wanted to restore diplomatic

---

[126] For an extensive treatment of this subject see Metin Tamkoç, "The Question of the Recognition of the Republic of Turkey by the United States," *The Turkish Yearbook of International Relations* 1 (1960): 92–120.

[127] See "Dispatch," February 22, 1922, High Commissioner Bristol to Department of State, U.S. National Archives, Turkey, File No. 867.00/1497.

relations under a treaty of friendship and commerce, which would be supplemented by declaratory pledges from the Turkish government offering protection of American missions and schools in accordance with Turkish law and guaranteeing fair treatment of Americans in trade and in the courts.[128] In his letter to Ambassador Grew on May 5, 1923, İsmet Pasha proposed immediate talks for treaties of amity, reciprocal consular relations and conditions of residence for respective nationals, and commerce. Formal negotiations between İsmet Pasha and Mr. Grew commenced on June 1 and concluded on August 6, 1923, at which time a general treaty and an extradition treaty were signed.

Under the terms of the general treaty, formal diplomatic relations were to be resumed following the exchange of the instruments of ratification of the treaty. However, strong opposition to the treaty on the part of the Greek and Armenian minority groups in America and their supporters in the United States Senate caused the postponement of the consideration of it by the Senate of the United States until January 18, 1927. On that date the Senate, after an executive session, rejected the treaty by a vote of fifty in favor and thirty-four against, just six votes short of the two-thirds majority required by the Constitution.

Meanwhile, pending the consideration of the general treaty by the United States Senate, Admiral Bristol and the Minister of Foreign Affairs, Dr. Tevfik Rüştü (Aras), had signed a modus vivendi according mutual most-favored-nation treatment in customs matters for a period of six months, on February 17, 1926, in Ankara. This period was extended for another six months on July 20, 1926.[129]

Upon the rejection of the general treaty by the United States Senate, Admiral Bristol, under instructions from his government, entered into negotiations with Dr. Tevfik Rüştü (Aras) with a view to the resumption of diplomatic relations between the two countries. As a result of the exchange of notes on February 17, 1927, the two governments entered into formal diplomatic relations.

The president of the United States, on May 20, 1927, appointed Undersecretary of State Joseph C. Grew as the United

---

[128] U.S. Department of State, *Papers Relating to the Foreign Relations of the United States,* vol. 2 (1923) (Washington: Government Printing Office, 1938), p. 897.

[129] See U.S. Department of State, *Papers Relating to the Foreign Relations of the United States,* vol. 2 (1926) (Washington: Government Printing Office, 1941), pp. 990–1000.

States ambassador, and a week later the United States government agreed to the appointment of Ahmet Muhtar Bey as Turkish ambassador to the United States.[130]

Following the signing of the Treaty of Lausanne, the question of the presence of a considerably large number of American war vessels (twenty-three) in Turkish waters was yet to be settled. Although friendly toward the United States, Mustafa Kemal had to demonstrate fully the independence and sovereignty of Turkey by requesting that the United States recall all American war vessels from Turkish waters even before the withdrawal of all war vessels of the Allied Powers. He instructed his representative in Istanbul, Dr. Adnan (Adıvar) Bey, to approach Admiral Bristol and raise the question of the removal of the American war vessels from Turkish waters. Admiral Bristol told Dr. Adnan Bey that American ships had not come to Turkish waters as a part of the occupying naval force, that they were visiting Turkish waters in the same way that they visited the ports of other countries, and that American vessels had been cordially received in all ports of Turkey. At the same time, Admiral Bristol contended that the Straits convention was not yet in operation; until the peace treaty with the Allies was ratified, the Ankara government was at liberty to take any action it liked with regard to ships remaining in Turkish ports, except that under a declaration of the Ankara government the Allies were permitted to have a cruiser and two destroyers in the Straits until the peace treaty was ratified or not later than December 31, 1923. Adnan Bey expressed his conviction that the independence and sovereignty of Turkey could only be properly demonstrated by having all American war vessels leave Turkish ports before the evacuation of the Allies or at the same time. He wanted to have a definite time set for the departure of American vessels and suggested that it should be within two weeks. He also stressed the point that if Admiral Bristol wished to keep his guard ship *Scorpion*, its crew

---

[130] It is interesting to note that when Mr. Grew arrived at Istanbul on September 8, 1927, his appointment was not yet confirmed by the Senate. The opponents in the Senate to the general treaty with Turkey were able to exercise pressure which held up the confirmation until April 6, 1928. On the other hand, the Turkish Ambassador Ahmet Muhtar Bey, lest he be subject to an attempt at assasination by Greek or Armenian minority groups, arrived in Washington from New York on November 29, 1927, under police protection. See Grew, *Turbulent Era,* pp. 772 and 784.

should be civilian. In the end it was agreed that the *Scorpion* and a supply ship should stay a short time longer without any definite time being set.[131]

Following such informal talks, upon the recommendation of Admiral Bristol, the United States withdrew all its war vessels from Turkish waters. On the day of the entry of the Turkish troops into Istanbul, October 6, 1923, there was no American war vessel in the Bosporus.[132]

During the initial phase of the Nationalist Movement, Mustafa Kemal initiated an active propaganda campaign among the Arab nationalists in Syria for the collaboration of the Arabs and the Turks against the French and British occupations; for this reason he sent certain emissaries to Syria.[133] An Arab historian reports that as a result of this propaganda campaign a "wave of pro-Turkish sympathy" reasserted itself within the ranks of Arab nationalists, "skillfully fed by Turkish circulars issued by the Mustafa 'Kemal Party' in Aleppo. . . ."[134] He then quotes one of these circulars which reads:

> Mustafa Kemal's proclamation to the Syrians.
> As a co-religionist I pray you not to heed the strife stirred amongst us and which has separated us; we must remove all misunderstanding and let us all aim our arms against the treacherous parties who want to divide our country. . . .
> The Mujahids (Fighters for a religious cause) who trust in the Right will soon be the visitors of their Arab brethren, and will scatter away the enemy. Let us live as brethren in religion and may our enemies perish.[135]

It appears that on account of such propaganda activities, prominent Arab nationalists, particularly those who had served in the Turkish army prior to the Arab revolt against the Ottoman Empire in 1916, sought to enter into negotiations with the Turkish nationalists. In January 1920, the Syrian Arab government decided

---

[131] "War Diary," September 26, 1923, High Commissioner Bristol, U.S. National Archives, Turkey, File No. 867.00/1732.

[132] "Dispatch," October 25, 1923, High Commissioner Bristol to Department of State, U.S. National Archives, Turkey, File No. 867.00/1729.

[133] "Intelligence Report," March 23, 1920, Great Britain, F.O. 371, E 3494/3/44.

[134] Zeine N. Zeine, *The Struggle for Arab Independence*, p. 123.

[135] Ibid.

to send two emissaries to Istanbul to contact the representatives of Mustafa Kemal there. However, when Emir Faisal arrived in Beirut from Paris on January 7, 1920, where he was negotiating with the Allied leaders for the independence of the Arabs, he asked that the mission to Istanbul be canceled. He was then persuaded to go along with this idea "apparently on the understanding that Turkish opposition to him as ruler of Syria would cease. . . ."[136] Said Haidar, a prominent member of *Hizb al-Istiglal* of the General Syrian Congress, and Badi' Bekdash, son-in-law of the president of the Ottoman Senate, Rifat Bey, then went to Istanbul where they met with the representatives of Mustafa Kemal. A four-point agreement was reached which included the following provisions: "(1) certain modifications to be introduced in the northern boundary of Syria, particularly in the region of Mosul; (2) a unified front to be organized against the Western Powers, 'from Ma'an to the Black Sea'; (3) the Turkish and Arab armies to be placed under a unified command; (4) in the event of the successful outcome of their efforts against the West, the Arabs and the Turks will live side by side in two independent states but their relations will be nearly on the same lines as the relations of Austria and Hungary in the Pre-War Austro-Hungarian Empire. This relationship will be governed by a treaty to last for fifty years."[137] But when this agreement was brought to the attention of Faisal in April 1920, he refused to approve it for fear of placing the Arab destiny once again under the control of the Turks.[138] Thus, no cooperation with the Arabs could be materialized against the French occupation forces. The Franco–Turkish agreement of October 1921 in the final analysis was detrimental to the interests of the Arabs in Syria which, though tacitly, placed Syria in the French sphere of influence.

Meanwhile, upon the formal occupation of the seat of the empire on March 16, 1920, Mustafa Kemal issued a proclamation to the entire Moslem world on March 19. Although he did not

---

[136] Laurence Evans, *United States Policy and the Partition of Turkey, 1914–1924* (Baltimore: Johns Hopkins Press, 1965), p. 247.

[137] Zeine, *The Struggle for Arab Independence,* p. 148.

[138] Evans, *United States Policy and the Partition of Turkey,* p. 247; Lord Kinross, *Ataturk,* p. 240. An intelligence report, however, claims that Mustafa Kemal was "as late as June 1920 in treaty with various Arab chiefs, to whom he made certain proposals, which were afterwards laid before Faisal and accepted by him." Great Britain, F.O. 371/5170, E 10708/262/44.

have much hope in rallying the Moslem world behind the Turkish Nationalist Movement, whose ostensible objective was identified as rescuing the sultan-caliph from the hands of the infidel occupants of Istanbul. Nevertheless, he thought that such an appeal to the Moslems now living outside the jurisdiction and sovereignty of the sultan-caliph might provoke resistance against the Western Powers, which in turn might lead to the lessening of the British and French pressure against the Turkish Nationalist Movement.[139] But, Mustafa Kemal's proclamation fell upon deaf ears.

One of the earliest agreements concluded by the Ankara government was the treaty of friendship signed by Yusuf Kemal Bey and the ambassador of Afghanistan in Moscow on March 1, 1921. Under the provisions of this treaty, Afghanistan recognized Turkey as the standard bearer of Islam. The two countries were also to form a common front against Great Britain. Turkey was to provide the Afghan army with military instructors. Afghanistan was the second country to establish a permanent diplomatic mission in Ankara headed by Sultan Ahmed Khan. In order to emphasize the importance of a friendship with Afghanistan, Mustafa Kemal personally participated in the ceremony of hoisting the Afghan flag in the embassy grounds on June 10, 1921. During this ceremony, he recalled the old ties of friendship between Turkey and Afghanistan and expressed his sincere thanks to Ambassador Sultan Ahmed Khan for Afghanistan's feelings of close friendship during these days of the National Struggle of Turkey.[140] In 1920 the nationalist government had already sent Abdurrahman Bey as its representative to Kabul and later on June 26, 1922, appointed Fahrettin (Türkkan) Pasha as its first ambassador to Afghanistan.

In March 1921 Mustafa Kemal had approved the idea of convening a pan-Islamic Congress in Sivas which was originally suggested by Sheikh Ahmed es-Sherif es-Senusi of Cyrenaica, then visiting Ankara. However, Mustafa Kemal soon realized that such a Congress might in the long run be more harmful than useful to the nationalist cause and therefore he changed his mind and disapproved such a gathering of representatives of Moslem countries.

---

[139] For the translation of the original proclamation by the British intelligence authorities see Great Britain, F.O. 371, E 3243/3/44.

[140] See Great Britain, F.O. 371/6472, E 8222/1/44.

Mustafa Kemal's Principal Advisers

As mentioned before those people in the leading positions of the Nationalist Movement who viewed their capabilities as on a par with or superior to Gazi Mustafa Kemal's[141] and thus tended to challenge and criticize Mustafa Kemal's decisions and actions were relieved of their important posts in the Ankara government at the first opportune moment. These people included Rauf (Orbay) Bey, Kazım Karabekir Pasha, Ali Fuat Pasha, Refet (Bele) Pasha, Celaleddin Arif Bey, Dr. Adnan (Adıvar), Halide Edib (Adıvar), Bekir Sami (Kunduk), Cami Bey, Nazım Bey, Hakkı Behiç Bey and scores of others.

Among the first six old friends and nationalist leaders, Ali Fethi (Okyar) assumed the position of prime minister twice. Upon Mustafa Kemal's request, he resigned just before the establishment of the republic. And upon İsmet Pasha's resignation, ostensibly because of his ill health, Ali Fethi Okyar reassumed the prime ministry in November 1924. On account of the disturbances in eastern Anatolia, Okyar resigned once again in March 1925 and was succeeded by İsmet Pasha. At the time, one foreign observer compared the two in these words: "Fethi Bey gives the impression of a man fitted to meet the difficult duties of prime minister of Turkey at the present time. He is essentially a well-balanced man of moderate views and with a distinct ability to make these views respected. That he is an abler man than İsmet Pasha seems to be unquestionable. For one thing, he is not mentally subservient to Mustafa Kemal Pasha as was İsmet Pasha. The latter, even as

---

[141] As noted earlier, until he assumed the family name Atatürk, Mustafa Kemal preferred to use the title "Gazi." Before his formal reception by Gazi Mustafa Kemal, the U.S. Ambassador Joseph C. Grew in 1927 was requested by the Ministry of Foreign Affairs to alter the address on President Coolidge's letter of credence from "Mustafa Kemal Pasha" to "Gazi Mustafa Kemal." Ambassador Grew comments on this point saying: "Of course I can't break the great seal of the United States but will make the change on the envelope and they can return the letter for correction after it has been opened by them, if they wish, but the address is another matter; a man has a right to be called by his correct name." He was also asked to make a number of changes in his proposed speech: Two references to his "residing near the Turkish Government" were to be changed to "residing near His Excellency the President." Again Ambassador Grew's reference to his hope for the President's "co-operation" was to be altered to "support." Grew, *Turbulent Era*, pp. 719–20.

prime minister regarded his relations to the president as similar to that of Chief of Staff to his general; namely, that it was his duty to make practical arrangements to carry out the wishes of his commanding officer. Fethi Bey entirely rejects this theory and intends to be prime minister in all sense of the word."[142] It is no wonder then that İsmet Pasha remained in office the longest among the prime ministers of Atatürk. However, during İsmet Pasha's prime ministry, Atatürk intervened, even in minute detail, in the management of the affairs of the state which was legally the domain of the Council of Ministers. Atatürk criticized the conduct of the ministers and gave them orders over the head of the prime minister. Problems relating to the implementation of his internal reforms, internal security, and particularly the conduct of foreign relations were considered by Atatürk as matters falling within his own jurisdiction and authority. As time went by, İsmet Pasha began to feel uneasy about such interventions and at times he was exasperated by the constant supervision and control of his conduct by Atatürk. He was doing his best in carrying out directives on domestic and external affairs. As directed, he was visiting foreign capitals in order to foster close cooperation and understanding with the neighboring countries, and he was concluding regional defensive pacts. Yet, as far as Atatürk was concerned, he had serious short-comings, such as his fussiness, his cautiousness, his slowness in reaching decisions, his concern over formal arrangement of things, his lack of initiative and dynamism, and above all his pedantry and presumptuousness. It appears that on account of these shortcomings of İsmet Pasha, during the last few years of Atatürk's life their relations had become somewhat strained. The final break between the two is said to have occurred due to matters of foreign policy. On the question of full cooperation with the League of Nations Conference decisions at Nyon, concerning the institution of an international patrol against piratical acts of the Italian submarines, Atatürk and İsmet Pasha stood in opposite corners. İsmet Pasha's cautious attitude on the Hatay question also seemed to have angered Atatürk.[143] Atatürk then decided to replace İsmet Pasha with Celal

---

142 "Political Report," December 18, 1924, High Commissioner Bristol to Department of State, U.S. National Archives, Turkey, File No. 867.002/81.

143 See Lord Kinross, *Ataturk,* p. 552; Maurice Pernot, "Position de la Turquie," *L'Europe Nouvelle,* November 7, 1937, pp. 1145f.

Bayar, who was to be much more amenable to his will and thus easier to handle.

Celal Bayar was known also as having liberal ideas on the question of the economic development of Turkey. İsmet Pasha had all along favored statist policies on economic questions. Incidentally, the conflict over economic and political policies of İsmet Pasha and Celal Bayar were to surface in full force some eight to ten years after the death of Atatürk.

After fifteen years of service as foreign minister and prime minister, İsmet Pasha was dismissed on October 25, 1937, but served as prime minister until the appointment of Celal Bayar to that position on November 1, 1937. Celal Bayar, in his speech outlining the program of his cabinet, displayed his intention to pursue the directives of the Republican People's Party program as determined by Atatürk. He said: "Party governments, like ours, do not possess programs of their own other than the program of the Party. The program which we are to implement is the realistic and dynamic program of the Party . . . which verbalizes the collective will and wishes of this great Turkish nation. The government, in the light of the directives given by the Chief [Atatürk] from this rostrum, has undertaken the responsibility of carrying out the program of the Party which may simply be defined as one aiming at making Turkey more powerful, prosperous, free and independent." Concerning the foreign policy of Turkey, Bayar said: "The permanent features of Turkey's foreign policy is known by all. The foreign policy of Turkey has always found its source in the will and enlightening and inspiring mind of Atatürk. Its course has been charted. And, as ever, it will continue to pursue the road to peace, friendship and vigilance."[144] Celal Bayar served as Atatürk's prime minister for only one year and nine days.

From 1920 until his death, five foreign ministers served Atatürk. These, in order of their appointment, included Bekir Sami Kunduk, Yusuf Kemal Tengirşenk, İsmet İnönü, Şükrü Kaya, and Dr. Tevfik Rüştü Aras. They were given the task of implementing Atatürk's foreign policy decisions and, at times, serving as principal foreign policy advisers. Atatürk often acted as his own foreign minister, particularly in negotiating agreements with foreign envoys

---

[144] Öztürk, *Türkiye Cumhuriyeti Hükümetleri ve Programları*, pp. 211–12. For the full text of Bayar's speech see also pp. 167–214.

in Turkey. He never went abroad for diplomatic negotiations or for state visits. For diplomatic negotiations he sent his foreign ministers. Among his five foreign ministers, only İsmet İnönü and Dr. Tevfik Rüştü Aras seem to have had his full confidence. Atatürk had encountered extensive opposition and challenge from his first foreign minister, Bekir Sami Bey. The differences of views on matters of foreign policy between the two were due partly to the difference in their social, educational, and cultural backgrounds and partly due to the existing circumstances and the ongoing power struggle within the ranks of the nationalist leaders.

Bekir Sami Bey was a member of an upper-class family. His father was a tsarist and later an Ottoman general. He was first educated in a conservative family atmosphere and was graduated from Galatasaray Lisesi and then from the Political Science Faculty of the University of Paris. He joined the Ottoman foreign service and later he was appointed governor, serving in a number of provinces. Although Bekir Sami Bey had joined the Nationalist Movement during its inception and had worked closely with Mustafa Kemal as member of the Executive Committees of the Erzurum and Sivas Congresses, he was at heart a monarchist, primarily concerned with the restoration of the sovereignty of the sultan-caliph and with the preservation of the traditional institutions. When the Grand National Assembly was opened in Ankara, Bekir Sami Bey sided with the Westernists and their leadership.[145]

---

[145] An interesting sidelight of Bekir Sami Bey is to be found in the report of a British intelligence officer which identifies him as a man of moderate political views and reads: "He is exceedingly fond of comforts of life, on which he spends freely. He is also a confirmed gambler, so that it is not surprising that he has been at times exceedingly short of money. On one occasion when he was Vali of Aleppo he was compelled to borrow 100 liras from either an American or British charitable institution." The report goes on to claim that it was through his constant need of money that the nationalist leaders were able to keep him on their side. This insinuation of bribery does not seem too likely if one is reminded of the financial difficulties encountered by the nationalists. See "Intelligence Report," March 3, 1921, Great Britain, F.O. 371/6466, E 291/9/1/44.

American Consul General Hollis describes Bekir Sami Bey as a man, "who, under a most elaborate and carefully cultivated exterior of high European civilization, conceals his true character in such a successful manner that he has many times deceived the most astute European and other statesmen." Then, Hollis claims to reveal Bekir Sami Bey's true character in these words: "I have seen him in his office, at his recreation, and at his club, under many different conditions, and I can assure the Department that, notwithstanding his very plausible exterior, he is, at heart, an Ottoman Moslem, of the type of Abdul

According to Mustafa Kemal, while in office as foreign minister, Bekir Sami Bey maintained that it was possible and in a way indispensible to come to terms with the Allied Powers. He advocated the conclusion of peace. His idea of peace at any price seems to have been based on his anti-Bolshevik sentiments and his fears of Soviet domination over his native land the Caucasus, over Turkey, and ultimately over the whole world.[146]

In terms of their outlook and orientation, and in terms of the understanding of the fundamental objectives of the nationalist movement, Mustafa Kemal and Bekir Sami Bey were in opposite corners. And yet, as a pragmatic power politician, Mustafa Kemal did not wish to dismiss Bekir Sami Bey and open a serious breach within the ranks of the leading nationalists until such time as he was strong enough to do so.

As instructed by Mustafa Kemal, Bekir Sami Bey headed the Turkish delegation to negotiate the opening of friendly relations with Soviet Russia in Moscow. After prolonged negotiations he initialed the first draft treaty of friendship on August 24, 1920. However, he returned to Ankara toward the end of December without signing the agreement. Then, he was sent to London to represent the Ankara government at the London Conference in February 1921. Bekir Sami Bey negotiated and signed agreements with Great Britain, France, and Italy during his European trip from February 1921 to April 1921. But the contents of these agreements led Mustafa Kemal to think that his foreign minister was either not sincerely committed to the objectives sought by the nationalist Ankara government or he had become a victim of the idea of peace at any price. Therefore, Mustafa Kemal declared these agreements as null and void. The ostensible reason for such a declaration was that Bekir Sami Bey was not authorized to conclude such agreements.

By this time, the treaty of friendship with Soviet Russia had been signed, the eastern borders of Turkey had been secured, the

---

Hamid, absolutely unscrupulous, unreliable and not to be trusted." Hollis thinks that the Ankara government must have been in desperate straits to appoint such a man as Bekir Sami to be its Minister of Foreign Affairs. See U.S. High Commissioner Mark L. Bristol to Department of State, "Dispatch," February 25, 1921, U.S. National Archives, Turkey, File No. 867.00/1391.

[146] See Atatürk, *Speech,* pp. 498–500.

nationalist armies had thrown back the Greek offensive in the second battle of İnönü, and Allied Powers had begun to exhibit a conciliatory attitude toward the Ankara government. Mustafa Kemal felt that he was in a strong enough position to dismiss a leading member of his conservative and Westernist opponents. On May 8, 1921, he asked Bekir Sami Bey to step down.[147]

At the time, a number of speculative ideas concerning the dismissal of Bekir Sami Bey were advanced. One explanation is to be found in Halide Edib's work. According to Halide Edib, who was a prominent member of the Westernists in the Grand National Assembly, while Bekir Sami Bey was in London he expounded his fears of Bolshevik oppression in the Caucasus to Lloyd George in a private meeting and suggested that with the help of Great Britain the Caucasus region should be united with Turkey to form a federal buffer state between Russia and the West, and that, if necessary, all Caucasians should be unified under Turkey to fight the Bolshevik regime in Russia.[148] Halide Edib suggests that the reason why Bekir Sami Bey was forced to resign was because somehow a copy of the verbatim report of his private meeting with Lloyd George, which was later shown to her by Bekir Sami Bey, had reached Chicherin, the Soviet Commissar for Foreign Affairs, who sent a harsh note to the Ankara government demanding an explanation for the unfriendly attitude of its Minister of Foreign Affairs.[149] In his *Speech* Mustafa Kemal refers to the existence of Bekir Sami Bey's report but he says that it could not be located among the files of the Ministry of Foreign Affairs.

Another explanation of the reason for Bekir Sami Bey's resignation was advanced by the British acting high commissioner in Istanbul, Frank Rottigan, who, in his dispatch dated June 8, 1921, suggested that Bekir Sami Bey's fall was really due to the fact that he was responsible for the arrangement with Great Britain for the exchange of prisoners of war, whereby an important group of the members of the Union and Progress Party were released; they subsequently joined the ranks of the opponents of Mustafa Kemal in the National Assembly, thus further weakening his position.

---

[147] Ibid., p. 499.

[148] Halide Edib, *The Turkish Ordeal,* pp. 254–55.

[149] Ibid., p. 255.

Rottigan comments: "The latter could not openly oppose the release of Turkish prisoners, but was incensed by the folly of Bekir Sami in thus effecting a reinforcement of his opponents, and therefore withdrew from him the support of the Kemalist Party."[150] However, the United States High Commissioner Mark L. Bristol's views on this issue seem to be more plausible. Bristol attributes the fall of Bekir Sami Bey to the ascendancy of what he calls "the uncompromising faction" of the nationalists in the National Assembly over the moderates and conservatively oriented faction.[151] This is probably why Mustafa Kemal had asked his conservative and Westernist Minister of Foreign Affairs to resign. Among others, the following statement of Bekir Sami Bey may be cited as proof of his Westernist views. During his conversation with the British ambassador to Rome on June 26, 1921, Bekir Sami Bey is reported as saying: "If only His Majesty's Government held out [a] helping hand to him [the] moderate party to which he belonged would soon get the upper hand and there would be an end to all Bolshevik influence."[152]

Bekir Sami Bey, despite his dismissal from his post, was once again sent to Rome and Paris from June to August 1921 as an unofficial representative of the Ankara government. His task was to dissipate certain prejudices against the nationalists, to explain fully the motives for the action of the government of the Grand National Assembly in rejecting the agreements signed by him, and to prepare the ground for friendly understanding with the Allied Powers. While in Paris, Bekir Sami Bey issued a statement explaining his feelings of friendship toward France. He said that he firmly hoped to arrive at an agreement with France, which was always regarded among the Turks as a traditional friend of Turkey. He added that the agreement which he had signed with France had not been definitely rejected by the Grand National Assembly, and he hoped that a modified treaty could be worked out between the two countries. He went on to say that the Turks desired not only

---

[150] Great Britain, F.O. 371/6471, E 6786/1/44.

[151] U.S. High Commissioner Mark L. Bristol to Department of State "Dispatch," May 25, 1921, U.S. National Archives, Turkey, File No. 867.00/1421.

[152] Great Britain, F.O. 371/6471, E 7281/1/44.

independence of strictly Turkish territory, but also financial and economic independence. He then said: "France need have no fear of any interference by us in Syria, Mesopotamia, or elsewhere (these regions not being Turkish), nor of action by us on the Cilician front." In regard to the Soviet-Turkish friendship he said: "As for the help which Moscow may have been led to offer us in critical circumstances, we have a proverb which says 'a man fallen into the sea will even grasp at serpents'."[153]

Following the resignation of Bekir Sami Bey, Fevzi Pasha served as acting foreign minister for a week and on May 16, 1921, Mustafa Kemal appointed Yusuf Kemal Tengirşenk as Minister of Foreign Affairs. Yusuf Kemal Bey had started his career as a teacher in a private secondary school and following his graduation from the Istanbul law school he was employed as instructor of Criminal and Private International Law at his alma mater. In 1908 he entered into politics; then he was employed in the Ottoman civil service, and in 1919, he joined the ranks of the nationalists in Ankara. There he served first as Minister of Economy and later as Minister of Justice until he was designated as Minister of Foreign Affairs.

However, apparently because of his conservative outlook and orientation and because of his close ties with Rauf Bey, he was asked to relinquish his post on October 26, 1922, at the time when the Lausanne Conference was to open.[154] He was succeeded by İsmet Pasha. The fourth foreign minister of Mustafa Kemal was Şükrü Kaya. He had acquired legal training and had served as a civil servant in the Ottoman government. During the War of Independence, Şükrü Kaya was arrested and detained at Malta by the British. Upon his escape he joined the nationalist ranks and for a while he served as mayor of İzmir. In 1924 he was appointed Minister of Agriculture and in November 1924 he joined Ali Fethi Okyar's cabinet as Minister of Foreign Affairs. He lost his post when Ali Fethi Okyar's cabinet resigned.

The next and last foreign minister of Mustafa Kemal was Dr. Tevfik Rüştü Aras. He was a close friend of Atatürk since their

---

[153] "Interview with Rome Correspondent of 'Matin'," Great Britain, F.O. 371/6471, E 7093/1/44.

[154] See Atatürk, *Speech*, p. 571. For a detailed account of the replacement of Yusuf Kemal Bey by İsmet Pasha see Chapter I of this book.

youthful days at Salonica.[155] Dr. Aras served the longest among the
foreign ministers of the republic — thirteen years, seven months and
six days. Since Dr. Aras signed so many treaties and pacts during
this period, according to one former Turkish diplomat, he came to
be regarded as "Pactomaniac."[156]

Dr. Aras was an ardent admirer and loyal lieutenant of
Atatürk. He accepted Atatürk as his wise, infallible, inspiring, and
benevolent "Chief." He told this writer in the exquisitely decorated
reception hall of the famous Ankara Palas Hotel, that it was his
good fortune that he could serve this great man.[157] Incidentally, in
the old days, the Ankara Palas Hotel was the entertainment center of
Atatürk, where lively receptions of the government and of foreign
dignitaries were held, where foreign heads of states, presidents, kings,
and emperors temporarily resided during their state visits, and where
Atatürk, his prime ministers, and other cabinet members and deputies were regular customers. The hotel was just a few steps away
from the Grand National Assembly across from the boulevard.
Dr. Aras said that, since his retirement from public life, whenever he
came to visit Ankara from Istanbul he stayed in the Ankara Palas.
This was apparently due to his longing for the good old days of the
Atatürk era. However, he said he had chosen to live on the shores of
the Bosporus, for the integrity of which Atatürk and he had worked
hard. He underlined the fact that he was born in Çanakkale, the
western end of the Turkish Straits and that he wished to rest
eternally on the shores of the Bosporus. He added further that the
great majority of the nationalist leaders were born in Rumelia and
that they always cherished the hope to see Rumelia united once
again. He maintained that in order to realize this aspiration Atatürk
had instructed him to work diligently toward the establishment of
closer ties between the Balkan countries. Expressing his views on the
Balkan Pact, he made it understood that the concept of the unity
of Rumelia had a different meaning in the 1930s. It was no longer

[155] Lord Kinross in his biography of Atatürk reports that during those
early days Atatürk had prophetically designated his friend Tevfik Rüştü for the
post of Minister of Foreign Affairs in his government of the future Turkish
state. *Ataturk,* p. 461. But, Lord Kinross does not explain why Mustafa Kemal
waited until 1925 to appoint Dr. Aras as his foreign minister.

[156] Yakup Kadri Karaosmanoğlu, *Zoraki Diplomat: Hatıra ve Müşahade*
(Istanbul: Inkilap Kitapevi, 1955), p. 97.

[157] The interview took place on December 26, 1967.

possible or even desirable to return to the arrangements of the past. The unity of Rumelia was to be based on sovereign equality of the Balkan states and their sincere cooperation for the protection of their respective sovereignty and independence. In a nutshell, Dr. Aras said: "The thing which is attainable is the ideal and the rest is nothing else but fiction," implying that foreign policies must find their roots in the facts of international life.

Dr. Aras was not born to be a diplomat, but he was willing to listen and to learn the lessons of the art of diplomacy from Atatürk. His rather vague and radical views on external affairs, which he had held prior to this appointment as foreign minister, had taken definite shape and had become more concise, studied, and intelligent as a result of his constant contact with Atatürk and as a result of his continued tenure of office.[158] He had a flexible mind and had gained insight into the pragmatic and flexible mind of his tutor. He viewed his job as fulfilling the directives of Atatürk. At times he misunderstood them, thus causing some confusion in his relations with foreign diplomats. He occasionally perplexed foreign diplomats by retracting his previous promises and statements or by reversing his decisions. One Western diplomat, for example, expressed his amazement over this unorthodox method of conducting foreign relations. He wrote: "In most countries, the Minister of Foreign Affairs speaks authoritatively and finally for the government, unless he makes some reservations before committing himself; this is distinctly not the case with Tevfik Rüştü Bey; he commits himself and the government and then reverses himself and the government later or doesn't even bother to rectify his statement. A new kind of diplomacy for me. It is at least an interesting study."[159] This was no doubt due to the fact that Dr. Aras was receiving further instructions on his negotiations with foreign diplomats from Atatürk.

As far as the appointment and dismissal of the Turkish diplomats was concerned, Atatürk also held the ultimate authority. Many of Atatürk's old friends and close associates were sent abroad, mostly for political reasons, on diplomatic missions. One may

---

158 For the appraisal of personal qualities of Dr. Aras by Sheldon L. Crosby, an American diplomat, see "Dispatch," October 13, 1928, Ambassador Grew to Department of State, U.S. National Archives, Turkey, File No. 711.6712 Anti-War/28.

159 Grew, *Turbulent Era,* p. 770.

mention the following men: Ali Fuat Pasha, Cami (Baykurt) Bey, Bekir Sami Bey, Yusuf Kemal Bey, Celaleddin Arif Bey, Ali Fethi Bey, Hüsrev Gerede, Ruşen Eşref Ünaydın, Memduh Şevket Esendal, Yusuf Hikmet Bayur, Ahmet Muhtar, Tevfik Bıyıklıoğlu, Vasfi Çınar, and İbrahim Tali. When it was considered necessary, they were relieved of their diplomatic duties. The dismissal of Hüsrev Gerede, a close lieutenant of Atatürk, may be cited as an example.

In June 1934 Ambassador Gerede had accompanied the Shah of Iran on his state visit to Turkey. During this state visit one day Dr. Tevfik Rüştü Aras asked Ambassador Gerede to come and see him in his suite at the Tokatlıyan Hotel in Istanbul. According to Gerede, the first thing Foreign Minister Aras said to him was: "His Excellency the Gazi has instructed me to tell you that you must resign from your Tehran post." Gerede, upon hearing this unexpected demand for his resignation, attempted to inquire into the reasons behind such an abrupt dismissal. But he received no explanation from Aras. Then he politely told Aras that he could not do anything on this matter before he had the opportunity of having an interview with Prime Minister İsmet İnönü, who at the time was also staying in the same hotel. Gerede asked İsmet Pasha to explain why he was being dismissed. İsmet Pasha also declined to give a satisfactory answer. On the contrary, İsmet Pasha reminded him of the inadvisability of resisting the decision of the Gazi and he said that "if he were him [Gerede] he would immediately tender his resignation without making much fuss about it."[160] So he did.

PRESIDENT ATATÜRK AND THE QUESTIONS OF MOSUL, THE STRAITS, AND HATAY

Because of the unbridgeable differences between İsmet Pasha and the Allied diplomats at the Lausanne Conference over the question of the Mosul province, the peace treaty had left open the delimitation of the Turco-Iraqi boundary. The second paragraph of Article 3 of this peace treaty provided that if Turkey and Britain failed to reach an agreement within nine months through direct

---

[160] Hüsrev Gerede, "Hatıralar," *Yakın Tarihimiz* 1, no. 6 (5 Nisan 1962): 163.

negotiations, the Mosul question should be referred to the Council of the League of Nations.

Bilateral and direct negotiations commenced in Istanbul on May 19, 1924. Since İsmet Pasha was prime minister at the time, Atatürk appointed Ali Fethi Okyar as the head of the Turkish delegation. The Istanbul Conference, however, adjourned on June 5, 1924, without finding a solution to the dispute.[161]

The matter was then submitted to the Council of the League of Nations on September 30, 1924. Turkey was once again represented at the council meetings by Ali Fethi Okyar who refused to accept a final decision on the question by the League of Nations. The council determined a provisional boundary line between Turkey and Iraq on October 29, and two days later appointed a commission to go to Mosul to investigate conditions and bring back a report. The report of the commission given to the council on September 3, 1925, favored uniting Mosul with Iraq, provided that the latter be under the mandate of Great Britain for twenty-five years.[162] Dr. Tevfik Rüştü Aras, representing Turkey before the council, maintained that Turkey could not accept the report of the investigation commission, did not recognize the mandate over Iraq, and insisted that Mosul belonged to his country. He also raised the question concerning the competence of the council. Then, the question of competence was brought before the Permanent Court of International Justice. On November 21, 1925, the court handed down an opinion recognizing the right of the council to decide the fate of Mosul. Turkey was not represented before the court. Professor Gilbert Gidel rendered advisory legal opinion for Turkey.[163] Turkey not only rejected the advisory opinion of the court, but also refused to participate in any further meetings of the council when that body adopted the opinion of the court. The council awarded Mosul to Great Britain on December 16, 1925. At the time, Foreign

---

[161] For the procès verbal of the conference, see Turkey, Ministère des affaires étrangères, *Le livre rouge. La question de Mossoul* (30 Octobre 1918–1 Mars 1925), pp. 180–200.

[162] See Turkey, *La Question de Mossoul a la 35me session du conseil de la Societé des nations.* September 3, 1925 (Lausanne: Imprimerie de la societé suisse de publicité, 1925).

[163] See Gilbert Gidel, "L'avis consultatif de la cour permanente de justice," *L'Europe nouvelle* 28: 608–10; see also Nihat Erim, "Milletlerarası Daimi Adalet Divanı ve Türkiye: Musul Meselesi," *Ankara Üniversitesi Hukuk Fakültesi Dergisi* 3, no. 2–4, (1946): 328–43.

Minister Aras was in Paris negotiating with the Soviet Commissar for Foreign Affairs, Chicherin. These negotiations led to the conclusion of the Treaty of Friendship and Neutrality of December 17, 1925.[164]

Since the signing of the Treaty of Lausanne, these were the most critical days in the relations between Great Britain and Turkey. War seemed to be inevitable. On December 18, 1925, the cabinet of İsmet Pasha, presided over by Atatürk, decided to meet every eventuality.[165] However, despite the general feeling in favor of a showdown with Great Britain, Atatürk was not going to endanger the ongoing internal reforms of Turkey for the sake of Mosul. He had played all his cards by rejecting the report of the investigation commission, refusing the competence of the council on this matter, disagreeing with the advisory opinion of the World Court, denying the validity of the decision of the council, and condemning the League of Nations as the instrument of the powerful. There were two alternative courses of action left: one, to go to war against Britain; and, two, to show a spirit of reconciliation in reconsidering the Mosul question by renegotiating. Atatürk chose the second alternative and instructed Dr. Aras to reopen the negotiations with a view of obtaining the best terms he could from Great Britain. The negotiations in Ankara ended on June 5, 1926, with the signing of a treaty recognizing the mandate of Iraq and accepting the decision of the Council of the League with mutually agreeable minor modifications.[166] Under the terms of the treaty, Iraq was to pay Turkey a 10 per cent royalty on oil rights in Mosul or pay, if Turkey so desired, £ 500,000 in lieu of 10 per cent royalty rights. On June 17, Turkey decided to accept the lump sum payment.

The net result of the Mosul question was the postponement of Turkey's membership in the League of Nations. Dr. Aras made this point clear when he stated: "It is only after having found a solution which satisfies both our own requirements and the methods used by the League that we shall be able to join that body."[167] Dr. Aras

---

[164] See League of Nations, *Treaty Series,* No. 3610, vol. 157 (1935), pp. 353–69.

[165] See *Current History,* February 1926, p. 765.

[166] For the text of the treaty see Great Britain, *Parliamentary Papers,* 1930, Treaty Series, no. 7, Cmd. 3488.

[167] See Institute of International Relations, Faculty of Political Science, University of Ankara, *Turkey and the United Nations* (New York: Manhattan Publishing Co., 1961), p. 32.

also revealed that among the reasons why Turkey declined to enter the League was the fact that Turkey was not offered a seat in the council of the League.[168] Another important consideration on this question was the negative attitude of the Soviet Union, Turkey's closest neighbor, toward the world organization.[169] Furthermore, under the directives of Atatürk, Dr. Aras let it be known within the Assembly of the League that Turkey would consider joining the League upon its specific invitation to that effect.[170] In fact, only upon the unanimous invitation of the Assembly, dated July 6, 1932, did Turkey express her willingness to join the world organization.[171]

Once the Mosul question was settled, Atatürk wished to restore friendly relations with Great Britain and tried to obtain its assistance in the revision of the provisions of the Treaty of Lausanne concerning the Turkish Straits. He was never satisfied regarding the demilitarization of the Straits. And, as Italy launched the invasion of Ethiopia and rattled its arms in the Mediterranean, as Germany marched into the Rhineland, and as threatening clouds began to gather over Europe, there was almost nothing that would prevent the Turkish troops from marching into the demilitarized zone of the Straits and presenting the world with another fait accompli. However, the major reason why Atatürk did not wish to resort to force was that he could, under the existing conditions, achieve what he wanted through negotiations and thus continue to remain on good terms with Great Britain, the nearest great sea power, and with the Soviet Union, the nearest great land power. Atatürk instructed Dr. Aras to approach the British and Soviet governments and obtain their backing of the Turkish desire for the revision of the Treaty of Lausanne. Dr. Aras, together with the Turkish ambassador to London, Ali Fethi Okyar, discussed this problem with Foreign Secretary Anthony Eden and received favorable response from him.[172] On April 11, 1936, Dr. Aras sent a note to all signatories,

---

[168] See Mehmet Gönlübol and Cem Sar, *Atatürk ve Türkiyenin Dış Politikası, 1919–1938* (Istanbul: Milli Egitim Basımevi, 1963), p. 73.

[169] Ibid., p. 92.

[170] Ibid., where reference is made to a statement by Cemal Hüsnü Taray, former Turkish minister at Bern during 1930–1936, in *Cumhuriyet* newspaper.

[171] See Mehmet Gönlübol and Türkkaya Ataöv, *Turkey in the United Nations* (Ankara: Publications of the Institute of International Relations of the University of Ankara, no. 14, 1960), p. 9.

[172] See Anthony Eden, Earl of Avon, *The Memoirs of, Facing the Dictators* (Boston: Houghton Mifflin Co., 1962), p. 471.

calling for the convening of a conference to discuss the question of the revision of the provisions of the Treaty of Lausanne concerning the regime of the Turkish Straits. Upon receiving favorable replies, Dr. Aras and the secretary general of the Ministry of Foreign Affairs, Numan Menemencioğlu prepared a draft which was reviewed by the Council of Ministers and by Atatürk. Numan Menemencioğlu was then sent to London to explain the draft to the British Foreign Office. At a meeting in Geneva, Dr. Aras reached an agreement on the date and the place of meeting of the proposed conference with the British and Soviet foreign ministers.[173] The Montreux Conference was convened on June 22, 1936, and was attended by the representatives of Turkey, Great Britain, Australia, Bulgaria, France, Greece, Japan, Romania, the Soviet Union, and Yugoslavia; it led to the signing of the Montreux Convention on July 20, 1936, setting up a new regime for the Turkish Straits.[174] Under this convention, Turkey assumed the functions of the International Commission which supervised the previous regime of the Straits, while a separate protocol authorized Turkey to remilitarize the Straits. Moreover, if threatened with imminent danger of war or if actually engaged in war, Turkey was to have the legal right to permit or prevent the passage of war vessels through the Straits. Thus, the limitations on Turkey's complete sovereignty and jurisdiction over the Straits were lifted.

Having accomplished this important diplomatic victory, Atatürk turned his attention yet to another unsettled question, the Hatay problem. At this time Atatürk's personal power and prestige were at its peak. The country was moving steadily along the road of modernization and had gained an enviable position of power among its neighbors in the Balkans and the Middle East. Turkey had established close ties of friendships with the Balkan powers which culminated in the signing of the Balkan Pact on February 9, 1934. With Iraq, Iran, and Afghanistan, Turkey had concluded the Sa'dabad Pact of July 9, 1937. These pacts, however, were preceded by intense diplomatic activities and by personal contacts between Atatürk and the heads of government and heads of state of these neighboring powers. King Amanullah Khan of Afghanistan

---

[173] On the preliminaries of the Montreux Conference see Dr. Tevfik Rüştü Aras, *Görüşlerim* (Istanbul: Semih Lütfü Basımevi, 1945), 1:126–27.

[174] For complete text of the Montreux Convention see League of Nations, *Treaty Series,* no. 4015, vol. 173 (1936–1937), pp. 213–41.

had paid a state visit to Turkey in May 1928; Greek Prime Minister Eleutherios Venizelos had visited Ankara in October 1930; Prime Minister Nuri al–Said of Iraq had paid a visit to Ankara in August 1931; King Faisal I of Iraq had come to Turkey in June 1932; Prime Minister Tsaldares of Greece had visited Ankara in September 1933; King Alexander of Yugoslavia had visited Istanbul in October 1933; Mohammad Riza Shah Pahlavi of Iran had paid an official visit to Turkey in June 1934; and the prime minister of Yugoslavia, Milan Stoyadinovich, had come to Turkey in October 1936.

Under the Ankara Agreement of October 20, 1921, a special administration was established by France in Hatay. The Treaty of Lausanne had confirmed the special status of Hatay. On September 9, 1936, a Franco-Syrian agreement was reached according to which the French mandate of Syria was to end in 1939. There was no direct reference, however, to the status of Hatay. Syria, on the other hand, considered Hatay as a part of its territory. Turkey vehemently objected to such claims over Hatay. France maintained that separation of Hatay from Syria would in effect mean dismemberment of Syria, which France was not willing to see happen. After a lengthy exchange of notes between Turkey and France, it was decided that the matter be submitted to the Council of the League of Nations. It was about this time that Atatürk took a personal hand in the dispute. He is quoted as saying: "I am not interested in territorial aggrandizement. I am not a habitual peacebreaker. I only demand our rights, based on treaties. If I do not obtain these, I cannot rest in peace. I promise my nation I will get Hatay."[175] On the basis of his assessment of the general situation in Europe, Atatürk seems to have concluded that France was in no position to fight against Turkish pressure over Hatay while she was preoccupied with greater threats posed by Germany and Italy. Thus he ordered the movement of troops to the Syrian border on January 7, 1937, in an attempt at a show of force. This maneuver produced the expected result: The French were willing to reach an agreement with Turkey. Meanwhile the League Council had dispatched a neutral commission to Hatay. On the basis of the report of the neutral commission, an agreement was reached on January

---

[175] See Altemur Kılıç *Turkey and the World* (Washington, D.C.: Public Affairs Press, 1959), p. 64.

27, 1937, according to which Hatay was to form a separate political entity, but its financial and foreign affairs were to be linked with Syria, and Turkish and Arabic were to be its official languages.

The Hatay problem had become a major national issue. The intensive official and unofficial propaganda and the editorials, news reports of the press had roused the nationalist feelings of the Turks to the point that they were willing to go to war against Syria and France in order to protect their brothers in Hatay who, the reports had said, were being subjected to untold atrocities.

Under intense pressure, France finally agreed to conclude with Turkey an agreement establishing a new status quo in Hatay. The Treaty of Amity of July 3, 1938, proclaimed Hatay as a Franco-Turkish condominium. Turkish contingents marched into Hatay on July 5, pending the result of a general election. In September 1938, elections were held and the Turks gained a majority in the Hatay assembly which promptly proclaimed the establishment of the Republic of Hatay. The Turkish troops crossed into Hatay on April 5, 1939, and on June 23, 1939, France and Turkey concluded a nonaggression pact, and France agreed to the incorporation of the Republic of Hatay into Turkey. And the final phase of the Hatay problem was settled when the assembly of the Hatay Republic voted for union with Turkey on June 29, 1939.[176] Atatürk, however, did not see the final phase of the Hatay problem. But his promise to his nation was kept.

---

[176] For a detailed treatment of the Hatay question see Mehmet Gönlübol, Cem Sar, "1919–1938 Yılları Arasında Türk Dış Politikası " *Olaylarla Türk Dış Politikası (1919–1965)* (comp.) M. Gönlübol, C. Sar, A. S. Esmer, O. Sander, H. Ülman, A. S. Bilge, D. Sezer (Ankara: Dışişleri Bakanlığı Matbaası, 1968), pp. 119–25.

Chapter Eleven
İSMET İNÖNÜ:
"THE NATIONAL CHIEF"

İNÖNÜ'S SUMMIT DIPLOMACY

Although he had, in the past, proven himself to be a man who could handle the sword and the implements of diplomacy, İsmet İnönü as president of the republic was to demonstrate his diplomatic and military skills without the guidance of a superior leader and to lead the nation in an extremely critical period second only to the dangerous and eventful years from 1919 to 1923.

In this chapter attention will be focused mainly on the strategies of İnönü to keep Turkey out of the Second World War and on his responses to the threats posed to Turkey's national security by the Soviet Union during the post-World War II period.

Inasmuch as her revisionist claims had been satisfied by the middle of 1939, Turkey had become a status quo power. As such, her interests seemed to coincide with the major status quo nations of Europe, namely France and Great Britain. However, such a stand did not preclude the possibility of maintaining friendly relations with the revisionist powers like Germany, Italy, and the Soviet Union as long as they were to respect the territorial integrity and independence of Turkey. Therefore, President İnönü initiated moves toward strengthening friendly relations with both the status quo and revisionist powers. Following the commencement of the Second World War, İnönü sent a delegation headed by Foreign Minister Şükrü Saracoğlu to Moscow with a view to negotiating and signing a pact

The Turkish cartoonist Ramiz's perception of the relations of Turkey with the major powers during the Second World War. Translation of captions from left to right reads: The Comrade of Germany; The Sweetheart of America; The Ally of Britain; The Neighbor of Russia; The Protector of Peace; The Friend of the World.

of mutual assistance or a treaty of nonaggression which could establish a bridge between the Soviet Union and Britain and France.

The preliminary negotiations on such an agreement had been worked out during the visit of M. V. Potemkin, the Soviet vice Commissar for Foreign Affairs, to Ankara in April 1939. Although the negotiations between Saracoğlu and V. Molotov commenced on

September 26, the Moscow talks dragged on for nearly a month and terminated on October 17 without any result. During these negotiations, Molotov, among his other demands, called for the revision of the Montreux Convention in favor of the Soviet Union and the closing of the Turkish Straits to non-Black Sea powers. These demands were totally unacceptable to Saracoğlu.[1] He was given a warm sendoff, however, from Moscow, and his party boarded a Soviet warship at Crimea which took them to Istanbul. The Kremlin leaders also were careful to avoid the impression of an open breach with Turkey. The official Moscow communiqué spoke about the cordial atmosphere which, it was said, had dominated the Molotov-Saracoğlu talks and the friendly relations between the two countries.[2]

In his State of the Nation speech on November 1, 1939, President İnönü also utilized conciliatory language in describing the Moscow negotiations. He said "the mutually advantageous agreement which we hoped to conclude with the Soviet Union could not be reached at this time. Nevertheless, you are aware that the friendship between the two neighbors is based on firm foundations. The unusual conditions and the difficulties of this period should not be permitted to undermine such a friendship. In the future, as was the case in the past, we shall sincerely follow the friendly course of the Turco-Soviet relations."[3]

Meanwhile, with a view to maintaining close ties with Great Britain and France against possible Italian and German ambitions over Turkey, İnönü had instructed Prime Minister Refik Saydam to initiate negotiations with the representatives of these powers for the purpose of establishing a treaty of mutual assistance.[4] The treaty was signed on October 19, 1939.[5] İnönü took pains to stipulate

---

[1] For an extensive treatment of these negotiations see Feridun Cemal Erkin, *Türk-Sovyet İlişkileri ve Boğazlar Meselesi* (Ankara: Başnur Matbaası, 1968), pp. 135–56; see also Türkkaya Ataöv, *Turkish Foreign Policy, 1939–1945* (Ankara: Ankara Üniversitesi Siyasal Bilgiler Fakültesi Yayınları no. 197–179, 1965), pp. 56–65.

[2] See *Ayın Tarihi, no. 71* Ekim 1939, pp. 66–72.

[3] *Resmi Gazete,* 2 Kasım 1939, no. 4351, p. 1.

[4] Prior to these negotiations, bilateral declarations between Turkey and Britain, May 12, 1939, and between Turkey and France, June 23, 1939, were issued concerning the security of the Balkans and the Mediterranean regions.

[5] Text in League of Nations, *Treaty Series,* no. 4689, vol. 200, pp. 167–89; see also *Ayın Tarihi,* no. 71, Ekim 1939, pp. 88–91.

in all negotiations leading to the signing of the treaty and also in the text of the same that in no case would Turkey become belligerent toward the Soviet Union. The second protocol attached to this treaty stated that the obligations undertaken by virtue of the treaty could in no way compel Turkey to take action having as its effect, or involving as its consequence, entry into armed conflict with the USSR. İnönü described this treaty as one "not directed against any other country but designed to contribute to international peace and security in areas that are within the reach of the effectiveness of Turkey, and by this way designed to protect Turkey's security." To prevent any misunderstanding on the part of the Soviets as to the peaceful intentions of Turkey, İnönü had kept Moscow informed about the negotiations leading to the tripartite treaty.[6]

The National Chief was determined to pursue an extremely cautious and correct policy toward the belligerents. He was ready to fight if Turkey was attacked, but did not consider his armies sufficiently equipped for offensive action against the Axis Powers.[7] When Italy declared war on France, İnönü did not go to the assistance of his ally. Neither was he willing to risk a war with the Axis Powers when Italy invaded Greece in October 1940.[8] In either situation, the fear of a possible Soviet attack on Turkey deterred İnönü from supporting the Allies. His sympathies were with the Allies, but he was adamant in keeping Turkey out of the war unless she was attacked by either the Axis Powers or the Soviet Union. This policy of İnönü was called "belligerent neutrality" or "non-belligerency."[9]

When Yugoslavia and Greece were invaded by German forces, İnönü reiterated Turkey's belligerent neutrality. Prior to the invasion of Yugoslavia, British Foreign Secretary Anthony Eden had come to Ankara on February 26, 1941, to confer with Foreign

---

[6] See Nihat Erim, "The Development of the Anglo-Turkish Alliance," *Asiatic Review,* October 1946, pp. 347–351; Cevat Açıkalın, "Turkey's International Relations," *International Affairs,* October 1947, pp. 477–91.

[7] See Franz von Papen, *Memoirs* (New York: E. P. Dutton, 1953), p. 472.

[8] See Türkkaya Ataöv, *Turkish Foreign Policy, 1939–1945,* pp. 73–75.

[9] Gerhard von Glahn calls this anomalous status of a neutral power "nonbelligerency" in his *Law Among Nations* (New York: Macmillan, 1965), p. 619. See also Robert R. Wilson, " 'Non-Belligerency' in Relation to the Terminology of Neutrality," *American Journal of International Law,* 35 (1941): 121–23.

Minister Saracoğlu on the Balkan situation. The three-day talks were followed up in Cyprus on March 18 between Eden and Saracoğlu and led to the identity of views over Turkey's neutrality.

At this time Turkey was being subjected to German pressures for the repudiation of the Tripartite Pact with Britain and France and for granting transit rights for military assistance to Iraq where Rashid Ali al-Gaylani had overthrown the government and had established a pro-Axis regime in May 1941. İnönü turned his deaf ear to German demands. He took his time in giving conditional response to German requests for troop movement through Turkey, hoping that by the time an agreement was reached the British would have suppressed the Rashid Ali regime in Iraq. Sure enough, the pro-Axis regime of Iraq was overthrown and İnönü was thus relieved of the awesome possibility of agreeing to German demands.

Furthermore, İnönü was successful also in extracting a favorable treaty from the so-far victorious Germany, in that the Turco-German Treaty of Friendship and Non-Aggression of June 18, 1941, contained a clause which stated that the "already existing engagements of each party" would not be affected by the treaty, thus reserving Turkey's 1925 agreement with the Soviets and 1939 pact with Britain.[10] The National Chief kept the British ambassador well informed as to the nature of the negotiations between Saracoğlu and Ambassador von Papen leading to the Turco-German treaty. This, however, was no secret; von Papen reluctantly had agreed to have the Turkish Ministry of Foreign Affairs inform the British ambassador, Sir Hughe Knatchbull-Hugessen.[11]

İnönü's constant concern over Soviet designs on Turkish territories including the Straits, as they were clearly evident during the Molotov-Ribbentrop negotiations on November 12 and 13, 1940, and the possibility of joint Russo-German operations against Turkey were eliminated as a result of the Turco-German treaty and as a result of the German offensive against the Soviet Union on June 22, 1941. Yet President İnönü left no doubt as to Turkey's neutrality in the Russo-German War, even though the general public opinion and the unofficial views of the Turkish governmental leaders favored an eventual German victory over the Soviet Union.

---

[10] Text of the treaty in *Resmi Gazete,* no. 4849, 2 Temmuz 1941.

[11] See Sir Hughe Knatchbull-Hugessen, *Diplomat in Peace and War* (London: John Murray, 1949), Chapter 13.

The Russo-German War had brought about a very strange alliance between the Soviet Union and Britain, and had created an extremely delicate situation for the Turkish leader to handle. Each new Allied success during the war had made it more difficult for İnönü to withstand Allied pressure on him to enter the war.

İnönü was more concerned with Turkey's future relations with a victorious Soviet Union than with participation in the war. According to İnönü a status quo country such as Turkey could not expect any benefit from a possible victory. This is why he had declined the offer of territorial concessions made by both Germany and by the Allies.[12] Furthermore, if Turkey had entered the war and were subjected to aerial bombardment and enemy occupation, who would guarantee that at the end of the war Turkey was not going to be another victim of the "liberating" Red Army of the Soviet Union? This was the crux of the matter when Allied leaders pressured İnönü to join their ranks in the Adana and Cairo Summit Conferences.

President Roosevelt and Prime Minister Churchill had agreed at the Casablanca Conference in January 1943 that Churchill should do everything possible in order to bring Turkey into the war.[13] Then Churchill in his message to İnönü, without divulging the Anglo-American plans concerning Turkey's entry into the war, asked him if he would consider a secret meeting in order to discuss the matters affecting general defensive security of Turkey and said that "Cyprus would afford a completely sine and secret meeting-place for a friendly talk about the general situation."[14] President Roosevelt also sent a message to İnönü, urging him to meet with Churchill. In his reply to President Roosevelt dated January 26, 1943, İnönü accepted his suggestion and expressed his pleasure for Roosevelt's support of the proposed meeting. Apparently Roosevelt's letter had been an important factor in İnönü's decision to meet with Prime Minister Churchill.[15]

---

[12] On this point see Şevket Süreyya Aydemir, *İkinci Adam: İsmet İnönü,* vol. 2, pp. 161–62, 248; see also Knatchbull-Hugessen, *Diplomat in Peace and War,* p. 178.

[13] Cordell Hull, *The Memoirs of Cordell Hull,* (New York: Macmillan, 1948), vol. 2, p. 1365.

[14] Winston S. Churchill, *The Hinge of Fate* (Boston: Houghton Mifflin Co., 1950), p. 701.

[15] Hull, *The Memoirs of Cordell Hull,* p. 1365.

Several suggestions were made concerning the place of the secret rendezvous. One plan was that Churchill should come to Ankara. This suggestion was strongly opposed by the British Foreign Office, particularly in view of what the Foreign Office called "the lack of security," as had been shown by the secret attempt to assassinate the German Ambassador von Papen by a Soviet agent on February 24, 1942.[16] Another suggestion was that the meeting should take place in Cyprus on January 31 between Saracoğlu and Churchill. But Churchill was not inclined to meet with the second man in command in Turkey; he wished to see İnönü. Then İnönü asked Churchill to come to Adana. Finally arrangements were made for a meeting on board the special "White Train" of President İnönü switched to a siding of the Adana railroad station. Absolute secrecy prevailed over the whole affair and the movement of the White Train containing President İnönü and his staff and the British and American ambassadors.

On January 30, President İnönü received Churchill and his staff with utmost cordiality on board the White Train. Several

---

[16] Churchill, *The Hinge of Fate*, p. 705. The attempt at the assassination of von Papen is worth mentioning here, because had the culprits not been promptly apprehended by the Turkish authorities the incident could very well have led to the breaking of the diplomatic relations between Turkey and Germany. This is how the incident occurred. The Soviet Embassy in Ankara knew that it was von Papen's habit to take morning walks. In order to help deteriorate the Turco-German relations, the Soviets instructed one of their agents to assassinate Franz von Papen with a pistol and then throw a bomb, which would emit a smoke screen facilitating his escape from the scene of the crime! On the morning of February 24, the Soviet agent, apparently because of his nervousness, exploded the bomb a fraction of a second before firing the shot. The "smoke bomb" proved to be a real explosive and blew the agent into pieces. Von Papen was not even hurt. Reaching the scene of the crime immediately after the explosion of the bomb, the Turkish police conducted a thorough investigation and within a matter of hours arrested the accomplices of the would-be assassin, two Russians and two Moslem Macedonians. They were put on trial despite Soviet intervention on their behalf. The two Russians were sentenced to sixteen years and eight months and the two Macedonians to ten years each. The Soviet government exerted tremendous pressure for the release of the convicted but to no avail. This incident increased the tension between the two countries. However, a week after the breaking of the diplomatic relations between Turkey and Germany, the convicted Soviet agents were released from prison on August 9, 1944. On this important spy thriller see von Papen, *Memoirs,* pp. 485–487; *Cumhuriyet,* 26 February and 6 March 1942. Needless to point out, during the war Ankara and Istanbul had become important centers of international espionage and intrigue. On the story of a German spy known as Cicero who had successfully stolen documents from the British Embassy in Ankara, see L. C. Moyzisch, *Operation Cicero* (New York: Bantam, 1952).

saloon carriages had been put on the train to accommodate the British delegation. The Turkish and British delegations spent two nights in the White Train, having long, serious discussions and very convivial conversations at mealtimes.

President İnönü had with him Marshal Fevzi Çakmak, Chief of the General Staff, Prime Minister Saracoğlu, Foreign Minister Menemencioğlu and a group of special military and political advisers. Prime Minister Churchill had Sir Harold Alexander, Sir Henry M. Wilson, Sir Alan Brooke, Sir Wilfred Lindsell, and Sir Alexander Cadogan for the Foreign Office, and Sir Hughe M. Knatchbull-Hugessen, ambassador to Ankara. Apparently talks were held between Saracoğlu and Churchill, with President İnönü keeping a close eye over the discussions. Conversations centered around the likelihood and desirability of Turkey's taking an active part in the war during 1943. Saracoğlu made it quite clear that Turkey should be adequately prepared before any steps were taken for her entry into the war.[17] He maintained also that "all Europe was full of Slavs and Communists. All the defeated countries would become Bolshevik and Slav if Germany was beaten."[18] He pointed out that Turkey was obliged to be prudent about the Soviet attitude toward Europe in general and toward Turkey in particular. İnönü and Saracoğlu made it known that they did not share the optimistic views of Churchill concerning the postwar relations between the Western Powers and the Soviet Union. İnönü tried to impress Churchill with his ideas concerning the possible course of developments in the future. He went so far as to suggest the need for bringing the war to a prompt end long before the unconditional surrender of Germany which would certainly give the Soviet Union the chance to dominate central Europe and to strive to move toward the Mediterranean region. His offer of mediation was unacceptable to Churchill, for he appeared to be much less pessimistic about the future intentions of the Soviet Union.[19]

---

[17] Aydemir, *İkinci Adam,* vol. 2, p. 261; Erkin, *Türk-Sovyet İlişkileri ve Boğazlar Meselesi,* p. 199.

[18] Churchill, *The Hinge of Fate,* p. 710.

[19] Ibid. A similar suggestion was previously made by President İnönü to Franz von Papen for the termination of the war between Germany and the Western Powers. See Aydemir, *İkinci Adam,* vol. 2, p. 163, and von Papen, *Memoirs,* p. 300.

During the general political conversations, military talks were conducted between the British and Turkish general staffs concerning the provision of equipment for the Turkish forces, "prior and subsequent to any political move by Turkey."[20]

The Adana summit meeting between President İnönü and Prime Minister Churchill was inconclusive on the political matters of utmost importance, namely Turkey's entry into the war. The official communiqué issued after the end of the talks referred to the identity of views between the two leaders and stated that Churchill had viewed Turkish policy with sympathy and understanding.[21] The only positive result of the summit meeting, however, was the agreement reached between the military leaders concerning the setting up in Ankara of a joint Anglo-Turkish military commission to "improve communications for the transit of munitions."[22]

The British commanders in the Middle East came to Ankara on February 26 to implement the Adana agreement and started talks with Marshal Çakmak and his staff. Marshal Çakmak put forth such extensive demands for military assistance that the British could not fulfill them without jeopardizing their offensive against Germany. These talks were again inconclusive.

However, the British did not give up hope. The next round of Turco-British talks was conducted at the ministerial level. Foreign Secretary Anthony Eden asked Foreign Minister Menemencioğlu to meet him in Cairo for talks. İnönü instructed Menemencioğlu not to yield to British pressure for Turkey's contribution to the war efforts of the Allies. Menemencioğlu was accompanied by Cevat Açıkalın, the secretary general of the Ministry and other foreign ministry officials. The Eden-Menemencioğlu talks commenced on November 3, 1943, and lasted for three days. Eden raised the question of Turkey's immediately making air bases available to the Allies and entering the war.[23] But Menemencioğlu turned a deaf ear to such demands once again. Eden later wrote: "My persuasions were the less effective as both the foreign minister and Acikalin seemed to be particularly deaf, and, at one point, when I appealed to the

---

[20] Churchill, *The Hinge of Fate,* p. 712.

[21] *Ayın Tarihi,* no. 111, Şubat 1943, pp. 110–11.

[22] Churchill, *The Hinge of Fate,* p. 712.

[23] Hull, *The Memoirs of Cordell Hull,* p. 1369.

younger official, he too seemed to have difficulty in hearing what I said. No one can be so deaf as a Turk who does not wish to be persuaded."[24]

Menemencioğlu argued once again that Turkey was not sure as to what the Soviets would do after the war, and that the Allied bases could not be separated from the question of Turkey's entry into the war. Before making such a drastic move, Turkey must obtain concrete assurances from the Western Powers in order to prevent her falling into Soviet sphere of influence after the war.[25] Upon Menemencioğlu's return from Cairo on November 8, İnönü discussed the results of the Cairo Conference with the members of his cabinet as well as with the prominent leaders of the Republican People's Party.

The Allied leaders were to try again. Prime Minister Churchill and President Roosevelt both sent separate messages to İnönü inviting him to a summit meeting at Cairo. In his reply President İnönü insisted that "he would go to Cairo so long as he was not being invited merely to be told of decisions already reached at Tehran affecting Turkey, but was being asked to participate in 'a free discussion as between equals'." Roosevelt, Churchill, and Stalin had already agreed at Tehran to set the date of Turkey's entry into the war, February 15, 1944.[26] Acting on behalf of President Roosevelt, Secretary of State Cordell Hull assured İnönü that the Cairo Conference would be conducted in a spirit of free discussion as between equals.

At that point, İnönü decided to go to Cairo with Foreign Minister Menemencioğlu and the secretary general of the Ministry, Cevat Açıkalın. However, before his departure, İnönü reviewed with the members of the Council of Ministers the politico-military situation in the world. They considered the alternative courses of action that were open for Turkey in the light of present developments and possible future ones. İnönü was of the opinion that in order to meet the immediate pressure of the Allies Turkey had no

---

[24] Anthony Eden, Earl of Avon, *The Memoirs of Anthony Eden, Earl of Avon: The Reckoning* (Boston: Houghton Mifflin Co., 1965), p. 485.

[25] Ibid., p. 486.

[26] Hull, *The Memoirs of Cordell Hull,* p. 1365; Knatchbull-Hugessen, *Diplomat in Peace and War,* p. 197.

choice but to acquiesce to entering the war, provided that the Allies were ready, willing, and able to meet the security needs of Turkey.[27]

President İnönü and his staff left Ankara on December 3 on board the White Train. Extreme secrecy blanketed the whole trip to Adana where President İnönü saw two private planes waiting for him. One was sent by President Roosevelt, the other by Prime Minister Churchill. In one, Roosevelt's son-in-law, Major John Boettiger, was to accompany İnönü; in the other Churchill's son, Randolph Churchill, was waiting to take the Turkish president to Cairo.[28] Not to offend any of the rival leaders, İnönü boarded Roosevelt's private plane and Menemencioğlu boarded Churchill's private plane. They arrived in Cairo on December 4. For the next three days, President İnönü held almost continuous meetings with Roosevelt and Churchill, followed by meetings among Menemenci-oğlu, Eden, and Harry Hopkins. Throughout the summit conference İnönü stood fast on his argument that Turkey would enter the war on the condition that the Turkish forces would be equipped "beyond the possibility of disaster."[29]

The following sidelight of the summit meeting, though amusing at first glance, reflects once again the often-recurring attitude of the Turkish diplomats when they are confronted with unacceptable demands. According to Robert E. Sherwood, "some mad wag in Cairo circulated the report that all the Turks wore hearing devices so perfectly attuned to one another that they all went out of order at the same instant whenever mention was made of the possibility of Turkey's entering the war."[30] The Turkish diplomats, İsmet İnönü included, were in the habit of hearing what they wanted to hear and were always unresponsive to demands that were contrary to the vital national interests of Turkey. The uncompromising attitude of İnönü at the Cairo summit meeting was no exception. Sherwood maintains that Roosevelt had shown a considerable amount of sympathy for the Turkish point of view and states that

[27] See Knatchbull-Hugessen, *Diplomat in Peace and War,* p. 197; Erkin, *Türk-Sovyet İlişkileri ve Boğazlar Meselesi,* p. 218.

[28] Elliot Roosevelt, *As He Saw It* (New York: Duell, Sloan and Pearce, 1946), p. 201.

[29] Altemur Kılıç, *Turkey and the World,* p. 106; see also Metin Toker, "Türkiye Üzerinde 1945 Kabusu," no. 17 *Milliyet* 12 Şubat 1971, p. 5.

[30] Robert E. Sherwood, *Roosevelt and Hopkins* (New York: Harper and Brothers, 1948), p. 799.

on one occasion the President had declared "that it was quite understandable that these distinguished and amiable gentlemen should 'not want to be caught with their pants down'."[31]

Yet, at the end of the three days' intensive conversations İnönü agreed to preparations being made for air bases to be ready for the Allies by February 15, 1944. In the interval, the Allies were to continue to send supplies to Turkey, and British specialists in civilian clothes would come to Turkey where military talks would be held. On February 15, the Allies were to ask permission to send aircraft into these bases.[32] This was an unavoidable concession to the Allied leaders, but İnönü succeeded in postponing, at least for another two months, his final decision on Turkey's entry into the war. İnönü, apparently, was quite happy with the outcome of his encounter with Roosevelt and Churchill. This attitude may be deduced from Foreign Secretary Eden's account of İnönü's departure from Cairo. He writes:

> The Turkish party left Cairo at midday on December 7th. The Prime Minister and I went to see them off. On the airfield President Inonu embraced Mr. Churchill in farewell. This attention delighted the Prime Minister, who said as we drove back into Cairo: "Did you see, Ismet kissed me." My reply, perhaps rather ungracious, was that as this seemed to be the only gain from fifteen hours of hard argument, it was not much to be pleased with. Mr. Churchill said no more to me, but that night, when he went to bed he remarked to his daughter Sarah: "Do you know what happened to me today, the Turkish President kissed me. The truth is I'm irresistable. But don't tell Anthony; he's jealous.[33]

Upon his return to Ankara, İnönü convened the members of the Council of Ministers, his military advisers, and the prominent members of the Republican People's Party into a special meeting at his residence at Çankaya and informed them that he had agreed, in principle, to Turkey's entry into the war. Among his advisers, apparently only Foreign Minister Menemencioğlu and Marshal

---

[31] Ibid., p. 800.

[32] Eden, *Memoirs*, p. 497; Hull, *The Memoirs of Cordell Hull*, p. 1369. The communiqué issued at the end of the summit meeting stated that the three leaders examined the general political situation, "taking into account the joint and several interests of the three countries" and that the "closest unity" existed between them in their attitude to the world situation. See *Ayın Tarihi*, no. 121, Aralık 1943, p. 41; *U.S. Department of State Bulletin*, December 11, 1943, pp. 412–13.

[33] Eden, *Memoirs*, p. 497.

214 / The Warrior Diplomats

Fevzi Çakmak, Chief of the General Staff expressed their doubts as to the advisability of such a dramatic move at a time when Germany still possessed a formidable force of retaliation against Turkey. According to Menemencioğlu, von Papen had warned him that "compliance with the Allied requests for Turkey's entry into the war would inevitably lead to German reprisals" with the "complete destruction" of Istanbul and İzmir.[34] Marshal Çakmak, on the other hand, argued that the Turkish army was not in a position to undertake offensive operations against Germany with second-rate weapons given by the British which were actually captured German and Italian materials.[35] He therefore suggested that the final decision should be postponed until such time as the Allies were able to equip the Turkish army with a large quantity of modern weapons.

Then it was decided to ask for a joint staff meeting between the British and Turkish military leaders to review the military situation prior to the declaration of war upon Germany. On December 28, 1943, a British military delegation arriving in Ankara was asked by Marshal Çakmak to send more equipment to Turkey and twice the number of air squadrons than the British could afford to give. The British delegation headed by Air Marshal Linnell, in view of the intransigence of their Turkish counterparts, saw no reason to waste any more time. The British mission left Ankara on February 3, 1944, and shortly thereafter the Allied deliveries of armaments ceased.

The relations between Turkey and the Western Allies were somewhat strained. Then, İnönü approached the Soviet Union and proposed that an agreement between the two countries be signed for closer political cooperation, including security guarantees in the Balkans. The Soviets replied that the only way such an accord could be reached was for Turkey to enter the war against Germany.[36] In order to placate the Allies, İnönü ordered the closing of the Straits to the passage of the auxilary ships of the German navy, which had been a sore spot in the Turkish-Allied Powers relations

---

[34] von Papen, *Memoirs*, p. 516. At the time, von Papen and the German government were able to follow the negotiations between Turkey and Britain thanks to the activities of the German spy Cicero who was regularly stealing the official documents from the British Embassy and turning them over to von Papen. See Moyzisch, *Operation Cicero*, pp. 136–48.

[35] Kılıç, *Turkey and the World*, p. 107.

[36] Hull, *The Memoirs of Cordell Hull*, p. 1376.

for some time.[37] İnönü also decided to dismiss Menemencioğlu, who, in the past had opposed increased collaboration with the Allies and the entry of Turkey into the war on the side of the Western Powers. Menemencioğlu was known for his pro-German sympathies.[38] In accordance with the directive of National Chief İnönü, the government announced on June 15, 1944, that due to the fact that the Council of Ministers had disapproved the conduct of the foreign relations of Turkey by the Minister of Foreign Affairs, Menemencioğlu had asked to be relieved of his responsibilities.[39] In fact, by June 15, 1944, Menemencioğlu had outlived his usefulness. In this connection, Marshal Çakmak was known also for his pro-German views. After serving twenty-two years as Chief of the General Staff, he retired from active military service on January 12, 1944, ostensibly because of old age. Note that his retirement had come in the wake of the Cairo Summit Conference.

Soon after the dismissal of Menemencioğlu, on July 3, prime minister and Acting Minister of Foreign Affairs, Saracoğlu, informed the British and American ambassadors to Ankara that his government was prepared "immediately" to accede to their demand that Turkey should break off diplomatic relations with the Axis Powers but at the same time would like to receive British and American assurances that Turkey would be treated as a full ally and would receive assistance from the United States and Britain with respect to war materials and to the disposition of surplus Turkish exports and the provision of essential Turkish imports.[40] Although Saracoğlu had said that Turkey "was prepared immediately to accede" to the Allied request, it took a full month for the Turkish government to sever its relations with Germany. What is interesting at this juncture is that the day before such an important announcement was made, İnönü tried for the last time to act as mediator between Germany and the Western Allies.[41] The main reasons behind this last attempt

---

[37] For the details of this controversy see von Papen, *Memoirs,* pp. 526–27, and *Ayın Tarihi,* no. 127, Haziran 1943, pp. 6–7.

[38] See Aydemir, *İkinci Adam,* vol. 2, p. 251; Kılıç, *Turkey and the World,* pp. 103, 108. It is reported by von Papen that following his meeting with Foreign Secretary Eden in Cairo during November 4–6, 1943, Menemencioğlu had told him that the Allies were applying extreme pressure upon Turkey for her severing commercial relations with Germany. *Memoirs,* pp. 506–7.

[39] Nadir Nadi, *Perde Aralığından,* p. 176.

[40] Hull, *The Memoirs of Cordell Hull,* pp. 1372–73.

[41] von Papen, *Memoirs,* p. 527.

at mediation were twofold. In the first place, in the final stages of the Second World War, İnönü was extremely worried about the consequences of the pro-Soviet policies of the United States and Britain and about the consequences of a Soviet victory against Germany. He firmly believed that victorious Soviet Russia would establish its hegemony over Eastern Europe and the Balkans and pursue an expansionist course of action in the Middle East. Second, despite the officially cordial ties of friendship with the Western Powers, the Turks were never strongly anti-German; on the contrary, Germany enjoyed great popularity among the Turks.[42]

When he decided to break off relations with Germany on August 2, 1944, İnönü instructed Premier Saracoğlu to declare in the Grand National Assembly that such an action did not necessarily constitute declaration of war upon Germany and that the commencement of a state of war depended upon the reaction of the Third Reich.[43]

On February 20, 1945, the Turkish government was confronted with a demand by the three Allied Powers. The British ambassador, Sir Maurice Peterson, on that date had given a memorandum to Foreign Minister Hasan Saka explaining the fact that, in accordance with the Yalta Conference decision, only those states that had fought against the Axis Powers or those states which would declare war upon the enemy states by March 1, 1945, would be invited to attend the United Nations Conference on International Organization at San Francisco.

İnönü discussed this mater of utmost importance with his top advisers and decided to accede to the demand of the Allies. The Grand National Assembly was called into an extraordinary session on February 23 which unanimously approved the decision of the government to declare war upon the Axis Powers.[44]

Because of the existence of several great powers of roughly equal strength before and during the Second World War period President İnönü was able to maneuver himself out of trouble by dealing with the revisionist powers or the status quo powers or with both simultaneously, or by taking advantage of the geopolitical position of Turkey. But the defeat of the Axis Powers, together

---

[42]Roderic H. Davison, *Turkey*, p. 146.

[43] See Soysal, *Dış Politika ve Parlamento*, p. 108.

[44] Ibid., p. 110.

with the economic and military exhaustion of France and Britain, made it extremely difficult to face up to the rising red-hot sun of the hostile Soviet power without being too dependent on one single major power, i.e., the United States.

During the post-World War II period, President İnönü's options were reduced to two: One, he might take a resolute stand in the defense of the territorial integrity and independence of Turkey; or, two, he might warn the Western Powers, particularly the United States, that the Soviet Union constituted a threat to not only the Middle East but to the whole world, thus calling their attention to the necessity of building a collective defensive shield.

The National Chief was not at all surprised when on March 19, 1945, a few days after the declaration of war by Turkey upon the Axis Powers, the Soviet Union denounced the 1925 Treaty of Friendship and Neutrality and a little later demanded territorial concessions from Turkey. In fact, V. Molotov on June 7, 1945, pointedly told Ambassador Selim Sarper in Moscow that there were two conditions for the conclusion of a new treaty between the two countries: The restoration of the Kars-Ardahan region to the Soviets, and the granting of bases to the USSR on the Turkish Straits.[45] İnönü's answer to the territorial demands of the Soviets was firm. In his State of the Nation speech of November 1, 1945, İnönü declared: "We wish to make it unequivocally clear that we do not owe an inch of Turkish territory to anyone. We shall live and die as honorable people."[46]

In its note of August 7, 1946, listing a number of alleged violations of the provisions of the Montreux Convention by Turkey during the Second World War, the Soviet Union asserted that since that convention had not prevented the use of the Straits by enemy powers, it should be revised as proposed at the Potsdam Conference. The Soviet note demanded that the new regime of the Straits be established by the Black Sea powers and that Turkey and the Soviet Union should organize a joint means of defense as the powers most interested and capable of guaranteeing freedom to commercial navigation and the security of the Straits. This note was also transmitted to Britain and the United States. There followed a series of notes

---

[45] See Necmeddin Sadak, "Turkey Faces the Soviets," *Foreign Affairs,* April 1949, p. 459.

[46] Türk Devrim Tarihi Enstitüsü, *İnönü'nün Söylev ve Demeçleri* (Istanbul: Milli Egitim Basımevi, 1946), p. 396.

exchanged between the four powers. Turkey, the United States, and Britain expressed their agreement on the need for the revision of the Montreux Convention in an international conference, but rejected the Soviet demands for the establishment of a new regime for the Straits, consisting only of the Black Sea powers, and the establishment of Soviet bases on the Straits.[47]

Apparently, on the question of whether Turkey should or should not engage in direct pourparlers with the Soviet Union, there were two opposing views within the higher echelons of the Turkish government. Those who were worried about the prevailing tension between Turkey and the Soviet Union were in favor of the acceptance, in principle, of the Soviet suggestion of bilateral talks as a gesture of compromise.[48] The second group of officials, including the secretary general of the Ministry of Foreign Affairs, Erkin, Prime Minister Recep Peker, and President İnönü, were completely against any bilateral talks with the Soviets. It appears that Premier Peker suggested the sending of an extremely brief and curt reply to the Soviets, leaving no chance for such direct pourparlers. On the other hand, true to his penchant for meticulous attention to detail and diplomatic rules, İnönü instructed Secretary General Erkin to prepare a detailed note replying point by point to Soviet charges of misconduct during the recent war, examining each Soviet claim one at a time and explaining their unacceptability, and expressing Turkey's good will and spirit of conciliation by agreeing to participate in an international conference for the revision of the Montreux Convention. Following the preparation of the draft note, İnönü convened the Council of Ministers, and after lengthy discussions over the text he approved the contents of the note, which was to be sent to the Soviet Union on October 18, 1946.[49]

In his State of the Nation speech on November 1, 1946, İnönü gave a detailed account of the question of the Turkish Straits and the exchange of notes between Turkey and the USSR. He declared that inasmuch as the United Nations charter guarantees

---

[47] For the texts of these notes see U.S. Department of State, *The Problem of the Turkish Straits,* publication No. 2752, compiled by Harry N. Howard, pp. 47–68.

[48] The then secretary general of the Ministry of Foreign Affairs, Feridun Cemal Erkin, does not disclose the identity of the members of this group in his work. *Türk-Sovyet İlişkileri ve Boğazlar Meselesi,* p. 305.

[49] See Ibid., pp. 305–7.

the territorial integrity and sovereign rights, "no obstacle should exist to prevent the adjustment and improvement of the relations between ourselves and the Soviet Union."[50]

While showing no sign of retreat or giving in to Soviet demands, İnönü repeatedly expressed his desire to see closer military and economic cooperation established between Turkey and the United States. The Cold War brought about an identity of interest between the two powers. A gesture of friendship toward Turkey and a show of force in her support were evident in sending the remains of the formed Turkish ambassador to Washington, Mehmet Münir Ertegün, to Istanbul aboard the battleship *U.S.S. Missouri* on April 5, 1946. On November 23, 1946, another group of American naval vessels visited Istanbul, an indication that the United States was determined to assist Turkey in case she was attacked by the Soviet Union. Such naval demonstrations of friendship were shortly followed by the American military and economic assistance program under the Truman Doctrine of March 12, 1947.[51]

In September 1948, during the initial phase of the negotiations leading to the signing of the North Atlantic Treaty, İnönü instructed the Turkish ambassador to Washington, Feridun Cemal Erkin, to inform the United States government that Turkey would be pleased to receive an invitation to participate in the negotiations. However, Erkin's request and the ensuing official approaches of the Turkish government went unheeded by the United States. In answer to a personal message of İnönü, on April 13, 1949, President Truman stated that it was the United States' policy to continue to accord friendly and careful consideration to the security problem of Turkey. However, he did not think that it was feasible to include Turkey, at that time, in the North Atlantic alliance.[52]

Although the Marshall Plan aid was extended to Turkey and Turkey was admitted into the Council of Europe, İnönü's deter-

[50] *Resmi Gazete,* 2 Kasım 1946, no. 6448, p. 1.

[51] See Haluk Ülman, *İkinci Cihan Savaşının Başından Truman Doktrinine Kadar Türk-Amerikan Diplomatik Münasebetleri, 1939–1947* (Ankara: Ankara Üniversitesi Siyasal Bilgiler Fakültesi Yayınları no. 128–110, 1961).

[52] See Mehmet Gönlübol ve Haluk Ülman, "İkinci Dünya Savaşından Sonra Türk Dış Politikası: Genel Durum," *Olaylarla Türk Dış Politikası: 1919–1965* (Ankara: Dışişleri Bakanlığı Matbaası, 1968), p. 200.

mined efforts to secure the commitment of the United States within a formal alliance or through NATO were as yet thwarted.

It is noteworthy also that under the impact of the ideological polarization of the world into two opposing camps, İnönü — that master of European diplomacy — seemed to loose his flexible and cautious attitude in his diplomatic maneuvers. His foreign policy decisions seemed to reflect certain ideological coloring, his pronouncements echoed much of the Cold War phrases. He appeared to undergo certain difficulties in readjusting himself to the conditions created by bipolar concentration of power in the world. He seemed, too, to be vulnerable to political leverage by the leader of the West, the United States.

Under these circumstances, İnönü could not help seeking Turkey's national security and survival under the defensive shield of the Western democracies. But there was a price which the National Chief was required to pay for the admittance of Turkey into the Western democratic community of nations and their defensive system; it was the loosening and eventual opening up of the tight grip of his regime over public and political opponents. And İnönü, a realistic practitioner of power politics, was willing to pay the price, but only in installments. But then, liberalization of the internal regime was to work against İnönü and leave him no time to devise a new set of strategies to meet the requirements of internal and international politics. In the end, President İnönü left the task of firmly identifying Turkey with the West to his opponents, the leaders of the Democratic Party.

Principal Advisers of İnönü

During the presidency of İnönü, six men served as his prime ministers. Among these, Celal Bayar remained in office only about three months. This was a transition period and at the time İnönü was preoccupied with the problem of establishing himself as the undisputed leader. Bayar was succeeded by Refik Saydam who served only three years and five months. The next prime minister was Şükrü Saracoğlu who had the longest tenure in office, four years and one month. Then there was quick succession of prime ministers: Recep Peker, Hasan Saka, and Şemsettin Günaltay. Their appointments were largely influenced by the internal as well as external political developments.

During the same period only four Ministers of Foreign Affairs served the National Chief: Şükrü Saracoğlu, Numan Menemencioğlu, Hasan Saka, and Necmeddin Sadak. Saracoğlu and Saka later became prime ministers. Only Menemencioğlu was a career foreign service officer and only he was dismissed from his post. Again only Menemencioğlu and Sadak were the late entries into İnönü's team of foreign policy advisers.

However, İnönü was his own prime minister and foreign minister. He was in absolute control of the foreign relations of Turkey from 1938 to the middle of 1950. Other cabinet members, the Chiefs of the General Staff, prominent members of the Republican People's Party, and the staff of the Ministry of Foreign Affairs were, from time to time, called upon to express their views on foreign policy issues. Because of the heavy blanket of secrecy over matters of foreign relations, one can not accurately weigh the influence of the foreign policy advisers in the final decision-making process. Therefore one is bound to remain within the limits of the obvious!

Following the election of İsmet İnönü as President, Prime Minister Celal Bayar tendered his resignation. The same day, İnönü asked Bayar to form the new cabinet. There were, however, few important changes in the new Council of Ministers as desired by İnönü. The Minister of Interior, Şükrü Kaya, was replaced by Dr. Refik Saydam; Minister of Foreign Affairs, Dr. Tevfik Rüştü Aras, was removed and his place taken by the former Minister of Justice, Şükrü Saracoğlu; and Hilmi Uran was appointed Minister of Justice. It is reported that as far as İnönü was concerned these important changes were made necessary because of "the mismanagement of the domestic and external affairs of Turkey on the part of the responsible Ministers."[53] At the time, President İnönü might have wished to bring in his own team, but he acted prudently by not removing the entire cabinet which had been appointed by Atatürk. Such a drastic change in the composition of the Council of Ministers might have weakened his position in the country. However, a few months later, President İnönü indicated his desire

---

[53] See Aydemir, *İkinci Adam*, vol. 2, p. 27.

to reconstitute the Grand National Assembly and the government. In conformity with İnönü's directives, the Central Committee of the Republican People's Party decided to hold new elections and on January 25, 1939, Prime Minister Celal Bayar submitted his resignation to İnönü. For the next six years, Celal Bayar was thus removed from political limelight. The National Chief appointed Dr. Refik Saydam as prime minister. Dr. Saydam was a close associate of both Atatürk and İnönü. Later when Dr. Saydam had to make a choice between İnönü and Bayar, he sided with İnönü and did not assume a ministerial post in the first cabinet of Bayar. When İnönü became president, Dr. Saydam entered the cabinet of Bayar as the Minister of Interior.[54] During the critical years of the Second World War, Prime Minister Dr. Saydam maintained cordial and close relations with President İnönü who was actually in charge of foreign relations. Dr. Saydam died in office on July 8, 1942.

Şükrü Saracoğlu succeeded Dr. Saydam. Saracoğlu, at the time, was known for his pro-British and pro-French views. In his memoirs, the British ambassador to Ankara, Sir Hughe Knatchbull-Hugessen, describes his relations with Saracoğlu in these words:

Like his chief, the President, he was wholeheartedly with us and, if events had gone more propitiously, would have been more so still. There was a delightful informality about him and almost undiplomatic habit of saying exactly what he thought whenever possible. This informality very rapidly overcame the usual conventions. . . . We frequently dined tete-à-tete together at one of the three restaurants, Karpiç, the Pavilion or the Station Restaurant — opportunities for long, frank and exhaustive conversations. My large hip-flask, which holds rather more than a bottle of whiskey, accompanied me. Saracoğlu christened it my "Revolver." He had a keen sense of humor, a quality indeed which is frequent among his countrymen and in a form somewhat akin to its English counterpart, so seldom met with elsewhere.[55.]

After the fall of France, the Germans had tried to have Foreign Minister Saracoğlu replaced by someone with German sympathies. To this end, the Third Reich had disclosed certain secret documents that were found in the archives of the French Ministry of Foreign Affairs which allegedly referred to certain conversations between the French ambassador to Ankara, Massigli, and Saracoğlu concern-

---

[54] See Ibid., p. 223.

[55] Knatchbull-Hugessen, *Diplomat in Peace and War*, pp. 201–2.

ing the bombing of Baku oil fields of the Soviet Union by Allied planes flying over Turkey.[56] The German government also had claimed in July 1940 that Turkey was prepared to launch an offensive operation against the Soviet Union with Allied help.[57] These fabrications had been condemned by Prime Minister Saydam in a statement before the Grand National Assembly saying: "To those who, on the basis of such groundless documents, accuse Turkey of bad faith and thus try to implicate Turkish statesmen in such dishonorable conduct, there is only one response that can be made by us and that is our scornful disassociation with them." He went on to say that the appointment and dismissal and every other activity of Turkish statesmen was only subject to the approval of the Grand National Assembly and no one else.[58] Saracoğlu had received full support from Dr. Saydam as well as from President İnönü.

Saracoğlu was not only disliked by the Third Reich but by the Soviet leaders as well. The Kremlin leaders had ample opportunity to get to know him well during his long stay in Moscow, from September to October 1939, for talks aiming at the possible strengthening of the Turco-Soviet relations. Saracoğlu's pro-Western orientation was known to them. They most probably had also heard Saracoğlu's comment on the commencement of the Russo-German War. It is reported by Franz von Papen, the then German ambassador to Ankara, that upon hearing the news of the German invasion of the Soviet Union Saracoğlu had expressed his joy by saying *"ce n'est pas une guerre, c'est une croisade."*[59] Feridun Cemal Erkin relates one of the episodes concerning the Soviet tactics in trying to get rid of Saracoğlu. He maintains that in January 1946 Kremlin leaders began to apply direct pressure upon President İnönü to have Prime Minister Saracoğlu removed and have him replaced by another person who would be amenable to the wishes of the USSR. According to Erkin, during a reception by a foreign ambassador in

[56] See Franz von Papen, *Memoirs,* p. 463.

[57] See Philip P. Graves, *Britain and Turk* (London: Hutchinson, 1941), p. 244; Kılıç, *Turkey and the World,* p. 84.

[58] Quoted in Ahmet Şükrü Esmer and Oral Sander "İkinci Dünya Savaşında Türk Dış Politikası," *Olaylarla Türk Dış Politikası: 1919–1965* (Ankara: Dışişleri Bakanlığı Basımevi, 1968), p. 135; see also Ataöv, *Turkish Foreign Policy,* pp. 76–79.

[59] von Papen, *Memoirs,* p. 479.

honor of the acting minister of Foreign Affairs, Nurullah Sumer, the host had the audacity to approach Sumer and tell him that the prevailing distrust that the Kremlin leaders felt toward Premier Saracoğlu and his cabinet was the major reason why the Turco-Soviet relations had been deteriorating recently. Unfortunately, Erkin, then secretary general of the Ministry of Foreign Affairs, does not disclose either the name or the nationality of this foreign envoy. He says that having been told of such an undiplomatic and discourteous act, he himself called in the foreign diplomat to the Ministry and informed him in the strongest terms possible that "Turkey does not permit the foreign representatives to interfere in her domestic affairs and neither does she tolerate public statements by such envoys concerning their approval or disapproval of the conduct of the Turkish Government."[60] It is interesting to note, however, that a few months after this episode, on August 5, 1946, Premier Saracoğlu resigned on the grounds of "ill health."

Upon Saracoğlu's resignation, İnönü asked Hilmi Uran, the vice chairman of the Republican People's Party, to form the new cabinet. Uran declined the offer and instead recommended Recep Peker for the Prime Ministry. Recep Peker, as directed by İnönü, was to follow a much harder line vis-à-vis the Soviet Union. He was, however, known to be a defender of the one-party system and strong leadership. As prime minister he would manage the affairs of his cabinet as he saw fit. In internal matters he did not wish to be subservient to the will of President İnönü. His tendency to use strong man tactics in dealing with the opponents of the regime must have been considered useful by İnönü. But, the National Chief saw to it that Peker did not have sufficient power to challenge his leadership. Up to then it was customary to appoint the prime minister as deputy leader of the party; however, İnönü denied Recep Peker that position when he appointed him on August 12, 1946.[61]

During his term of office, Recep Peker tried to maintain strict control over the emerging opposition within the Republican People's Party and to muzzle the Democratic Party leadership as well as suppress the leftist underground activities.

---

[60] Erkin, *Türk-Sovyet İlişkileri ve Boğazlar Meselesi*, pp. 275–77.
[61] See Aydemir, *İkinci Adam*, vol. 2, p. 452.

About this time President İnönü was seeking economic and military assistance from the United States. Yet, the U.S. congressional leaders and American political commentators were strongly critical of the nature of the political regime in Turkey. In light of such strong criticism of his regime, İnönü had to revise his attitude toward his political opponents. As put aptly by Karpat, "The views expressed in the U.S. Congress, and the necessity of establishing closer relations with the West, may be assumed to have had some impact on political developments in Turkey.[62] Then, too, according to the opponents of the İnönü regime, the signing of the Charter of the United Nations by Turkey and her desire to join the Western community of nations had necessitated the easing of the political restrictions. The small opposition group in the Republican People's Party and the Democratic Party leadership were pressing for the establishment of a truly multiparty regime and the elimination of restrictions over political freedoms. Under such external and internal pressures, President İnönü began to exhibit a conciliatory attitude toward his critics and even went so far as to issue a declaration promising to establish a working relationship between the government and opposition parties.[63] On the other hand, İnönü's prime minister, Recep Peker, was hoping to continue the one-party dictatorship and to increase the pressure against the opposition. Thus, there appeared a clear-cut conflict of interests between President İnönü and Premier Peker. For a while Premier Peker had the backing of a strong majority in the People's Party and in the Grand National Assembly.[64] But one by one his supporters deserted him. Although Peker was a close associate of Atatürk and a warrior with exceptional qualities, he could not challenge the position of İnönü; he did not possess enough political power. He had to give in. It was announced on September 9, 1947, that due to "ill health" Recep Peker had asked President İnönü to relieve him of his responsibilities as prime minister.[65]

İnönü's decision to appoint Hasan Saka, the Minister of Foreign Affairs in both the Saracoğlu and Peker cabinets, as the next

---

[62] Karpat, *Turkey's Politics,* p. 189.

[63] See his 12 July 1947 Multi-Party Declaration in *Ulus,* 12 Temmuz 1947.

[64] Karpat, *Turkey's Politics,* p. 194.

[65] See Aydemir, *İkinci Adam,* vol. 2, p. 460.

prime minister on September 10, 1947, was a move designed to alleviate the internal and external pressures that were inflicted upon İnönü in the middle of 1947. It was a move also to prevent an open breach within the party between his own and Peker's supporters.

In spite of such a move, sixteen months later, on account of strong differences of opinion between President İnönü and the parliamentary group of the party on the one side and Prime Minister Hasan Saka on the other, Premier Saka felt obliged to resign in January 1949. İnönü once again asked Hilmi Uran to form the new cabinet. But again Uran declined the offer, suggesting that Şemsettin Günaltay be appointed prime minister. The latter was an eminent historian, a professor of history at the University of Ankara, and a prominent member of the liberal group in the party. Günaltay was also in favor of granting greater freedom in religious matters. The fact that İnönü's regime was moving toward a greater tolerance of the liberal demands of the opposition parties and the religious demands of the people, Günaltay's qualifications appealed to İnönü.

Şemsettin Günaltay was appointed prime minister on January 15, 1949, and served until May 22, 1950. Following the general elections on May 14, 1950, he transferred the government to Adnan Menderes whose Democratic Party had won a decisive victory.

President İnönü's first foreign minister was Şükrü Saracoğlu. When Saracoğlu became prime minister, Numan Menemencioğlu, then the secretary general of the Ministry of Foreign Affairs, took over his post as foreign minister. It is very likely that President İnönü's appointment of Menemencioğlu as Minister of Foreign Affairs was intended to prevent further deterioration of Turco-German relations and to maintain a balance of pro-Allied and pro-Axis sympathizers in the key positions of the Saracoğlu cabinet, which was formed at a time when the German power in Europe was at its peak and the German forces were stationed in Greece and Bulgaria, across the borders from Turkey. This assumption is based on the following facts: Menemencioğlu at the time was regarded by many as having pro-Axis feelings; since Menemencioğlu was not a deputy in the Grand National Assembly prior to his appointment, he was ineligible for a ministerial appointment. However, on August 10, 1942, he was elected deputy from Istanbul and four days later he assumed the post of foreign minister; he was dismissed from his post on June 15, 1944, just before the breaking of diplomatic relations between Turkey and the Axis Powers in August 1944.

With regard to Menemencioğlu's personal character and his qualifications as foreign minister, the then British Ambassador Sir Hughe writes that although they had a number of disagreements and differences of views and interests this fact had not lessened his respect for Menemencioğlu's outstanding talents and his admiration for the foreign minister's devoted service to his country. He adds: "I have always found him a warm personal friend and I consider him to be one of the cleverest men I have ever met. The combination of an unusually active mind, keen intellect and abnormally retentive memory with an upbringing in the tense diplomatic atmosphere of Turkey in the days of the Sublime Porte, the revolution and wars of the early years of the century could not fail to produce something exceptional. On this was grafted an education in a Jesuit College. I have never encountered anyone with a mind better mobilized for instant action in any circumstances. . . . Business with him was short and direct. His grasp of a subject quick as lightning. No time was wasted and there was seldom danger of misunderstanding."[66]

Following the dismissal of Menemencioğlu, Prime Minister Saracoğlu served as acting foreign minister until September 13, 1944, at which time Hasan Saka was appointed Minister of Foreign Affairs. Saka was retained as foreign minister in the cabinet of Recep Peker, and when Peker resigned, Hasan Saka succeeded him. The last foreign minister of President İnönü was Necmeddin Sadak, a prominent journalist, the editor and publisher of *Akşam* newspaper. Sadak served not only in the Hasan Saka cabinet but also in the cabinet of Premier Şemsettin Günaltay until succeeded by Fuad Köprülü on May 22, 1950.

---

[66] Knatchbull-Hugessen, *Diplomat in Peace and War*, p. 201.

Chapter Twelve

CELAL BAYAR:
"THE DEMOCRATIC CHIEF"

BAYAR'S SUMMIT DIPLOMACY

President Bayar was not a military man. Nevertheless, when confronted with difficult issues and circumstances, he exhibited the strong will power and self-assurance of a well-trained and disciplined career military officer. In fact, on account of his activities during the War of Independence as a guerrilla fighter, he often, in a boastful fashion, described himself as *Çeteci* (guerrilla). He viewed himself as a man who was to lead the nation in its battles against the old stagnant order. He was determined to open up new frontiers in the modernization process and transform Turkey in the image of the most advanced societies of the West. For the realization of that objective he saw himself as an indispensible leader with a unique and historic mission.

As Bayar saw it, the world in 1950 was in the midst of a deadly struggle between the free nations and the evil communist power, the Soviet Union. Since the end of the Second World War, all efforts of the free nations of the West for the establishment of a durable and just peace had been frustrated by the Soviets. The international communist conspiracy, as organized and directed by the Kremlin leaders and backed by Soviet military power, was attempting to destroy the free nations from within and was getting ready to launch a frontal assault through the gaps that existed along the security network of the Atlantic Pact. To meet the communist threats, according to Bayar, the free nations had to build a much stronger and uninterrupted defensive shield — a solid peace front — while strengthening their own individual societies economically as well as militarily.[1]

In the past, Atatürk had pursued the objective of avoiding military and economic alignment with and depending on a single major power. His foreign policy was free of ideological considerations. He had had a greater latitude of choice in terms of determining the nature and scope of Turkey's involvement in world affairs. However, since the end of the Second World War, the latitude of choice of İnönü and Bayar was greatly reduced, and in fact it was limited to the necessity of seeking military and economic alignment with one of the two world powers, the United States. As noted earlier, İnönü was unsuccessful in that objective. As soon as he took the office of the presidency, in order to protect Turkey's national security and to help close the gap in the southeastern flank of the Atlantic alliance, Bayar intensified Turkey's diplomatic efforts in seeking stronger military ties with the United States. He also sought further economic aid from the United States in order to implement his economic development schemes.

Bayar's diplomacy was marked by dynamism, resourcefulness, and assertiveness in its drive to realize foreign policy objectives. Bayar was willing and ready to take greater risks which at times appeared as adventurism and brinkmanship.[2] At times, when a wait-and-see attitude would have been perfectly understandable and may have been much more prudent, Bayar acted boldly and unhesitatingly, disregarding the threatening gestures of the Kremlin leaders. The summit diplomacy of President Bayar, including the intensive person-to-person contacts of Bayar and Prime Minister Menderes with the leaders of the Middle East as well as with the heads of government of the West, not only helped to close the gap

---

[1] On Bayar's perception of the state of affairs in the world in 1950, see his State of the Nation speech of November 1, 1950, *Resmi Gazete,* 2 Kasım 1950, no. 7646, pp. 4–6.

[2] For example, his decision to send troops to Korea was subjected to bitter criticism on the part of the opposition parties. But this criticism was not centered on the substance of that decision, but rather on the form in which it was taken, i.e., without obtaining authorization from the Grand National Assembly, see Soysal, *Dış Politika ve Parlamento,* pp. 196–99. İsmet İnönü identified the conduct of the Turkish government on the Cyprus problem in 1955 as "adventurism." Soysal, *Dış Politika ve Parlamento,* p. 240.

in the containment policy of the United States but also ushered Turkey into international politics as one of its active participants.

It was the domestic economic and political problems which eventually caused Bayar's downfall. Somehow he could not handle his internal opponents as successfully as his external adversaries. He may have been swayed by his victories at the polls which seemed to suggest that he could do anything he pleased in the domestic political arena. He was very much prone to rejoicing over his victories in domestic politics and his achievements in the international arena.

This chapter will be limited to a review of two highly important strategies of President Bayar: the strategy of alliance with the West; and the strategy of building a bridge between the West and the Middle East, which was called the Baghdad Pact.

In the face of continued Soviet threats, President Bayar renewed earlier efforts for the entry of Turkey into NATO. Turkish ambassadors in the twelve NATO countries were instructed to raise the question of Turkey's membership with the governments concerned and to try to have them withdraw their objections to Turkey's inclusion in the Atlantic Pact.

The invasion of South Korea provided an opportunity for Bayar to demonstrate his strong desire for solidarity with the West and Turkey's dedication to the principle of collective security of the Charter of the United Nations. It had been only a few weeks after he had assumed the presidency that Bayar decided to take an unprecedented and bold step; he sent a contingent of 5,000 Turkish troops to Korea. By this move, Bayar hoped to strengthen his position in demanding membership in NATO. The immediate dividend of such an investment was the association of Turkey with such phases of the military planning work of NATO as were concerned with the defense of the Mediterranean.[3] Upon being informed of this action, Bayar in private did not hide his deep regret and disillusionment. He viewed this decision as an inadequate response to Turkey's continued efforts to establish a strong line of defense with the Western powers. He instructed the Turkish ambassador to Washington, Feridun Cemal Erkin, to approach the United States government, inviting it to establish direct contractual ties

---

[3] On the North Atlantic Council's decision see, U.S. Department of State, *Bulletin,* vol. 23, no. 589, October 16, 1950, p. 632.

with Turkey. But Ambassador Erkin found the United States unwilling to take such a step.[4] Thereupon, Bayar substituted another formula which envisaged merely the adherence of the United States to the Treaty of Mutual Assistance signed in Ankara on October 19, 1939, between France, Great Britain, and Turkey.[5] Due to the fact that the scope of this new alliance limited the area of mutual assistance to an act of aggression against Turkey or to a state of war in the Mediterranean, it was, according to Bayar, in complete harmony with the United States foreign policy. The United States kept this proposal under consideration for a long time and then turned it down. As a third alternative, Bayar approached the United States in the Spring of 1951 for the formation of an Eastern Mediterranean Pact, based on the Atlantic Pact pattern, and including France, Great Britain, the United States, and Turkey.[6] The United States government, however, did not feel that the time was ripe for such a pact. On the other hand, in order to protect its interests in the Middle East, Great Britain showed willingness to admit Turkey into NATO, provided that she was ready to assume her appropriate role in the defense of the Middle East.[7] Bayar accepted such a condition with the understanding that his co-sponsorship of the proposal for the establishment of a Middle East Defense Organization would open the way for Turkey's membership in NATO.[8] The consistent efforts of Bayar finally produced the much sought after results. On September 20, 1951, the North Atlantic Council decided to recommend to the member governments the accession of Turkey and Greece to the North Atlantic Treaty Organization.[9]

---

[4] See U.S. Congress, *Congressional Record*, Senate 82nd Cong., 1st Sess. (Washington: Government Printing Office, 1951), p. 2760.

[5] "Turkey Invites U.S. to Join Treaty of Mutual Aid with Britain and France." *New York Times*, 2 March 1951, p. 1.

[6] See *New York Herald Tribune*, 29 April 1951, p. 2–5.

[7] See Statement of Foreign Secretary Herbert Morrison in the House of Commons, Great Britain, *Parliamentary Debates, Commons*, vol. 480 (1950–51), p. 1228.

[8] On the text of the Four-power (Britain, France, Turkey, and the United States) Proposals for a Middle East Command which was presented to Middle Eastern Powers on October 13, 1951, see U. S. Department of State, *Bulletin*, vol. 25, no. 643, October 22, 1951, pp. 647–48; see also Hurewitz, *Diplomacy in the Near and Middle East*, pp. 329–32.

[9] U.S. Department of State, *Bulletin*, vol. 25, no. 640, October 1, 1951, p. 523.

In his reply to President Truman's message of September 21 welcoming Turkey into NATO, after expressing his personal thanks as well as those of the Turkish government for the United States' efforts for the admission of Turkey to the Atlantic Pact, President Bayar said, "Turkey fully appreciates the great value of cooperation between our two friendly countries which are wholeheartedly devoted to the policy of world peace and prosperity. . . . It is an added pleasure for me to affirm that Turkey will never fail to carry out the obligations that will devolve upon her within the Atlantic Pact community which she is about to join. I assure you that the Turkish Government is equally looking forward to cooperation with our great friend the United States of America within this organization, toward the defense of the free world."[10]

President Bayar's success was twofold: He not only obtained a formal commitment from the United States to defend Turkey against the Soviet Union, but also secured formal acceptance of Turkey into what was then known as the Western-Christian-Democratic family of nations which hitherto had kept the door shut to the Moslem Turks.

Turkey's membership in NATO opened up the way for a greater number of person-to-person contacts between the Turkish and Western leaders. Bayar believed firmly in the necessity of such face-to-face discussions of common problems with the leaders of the Allied Powers. Consequently, during the ten-year period of Bayar's administration, the state visits of Turkish and Allied leaders reached unprecedented proportions. Global and regional political, economic, and military issues were directly handled at summit meetings.

Following the entry of Turkey into NATO, General Eisenhower, the supreme allied commander, came to Ankara on March 3, 1952, for two days of talks with President Bayar and other high governmental officials on the question of Turkey's military integration into the Western defense system.

---

[10] Ibid., no. 643, October 22, 1951, p. 650. On the occasion of Turkey's entry into NATO, the editor of *Zafer* newspaper observed: "There has been a great and honorable share of the blood of our Korean hero's in the signatories' ink used at Ottawa for the invitation extended to Turkey for her entry into the Atlantic community. . . . Today's Turkey is a source of power for peace, and not a liability." *Zafer,* 22 Eylül 1951, p. 1.

In order to strengthen Turkish-Greek friendship and use it as a lever for a new Balkan Pact, President Bayar invited the Greek deputy prime minister and Foreign Minister Venizelos to Ankara in January 1952. The Ankara talks culminated in a joint communiqué pledging the initiation of effective and close cooperation between the two countries. A few months later, King Paul and Queen Frederika of Greece came to Ankara on June 1, 1952, on a state visit. President Bayar and Foreign Minister Köprülü reciprocated by visiting Greece in November 1952. The high level talks not only brought Turkey and Greece closer to each other but also opened up the way for Yugoslavia's closer cooperation with the two powers. The preparatory talks between Turkey, Greece, and Yugoslavia led to the signing of a five-year Treaty of Friendship and Collaboration in Ankara on February 28, 1953.[11]

On June 18, 1953, Prime Minister Marshal Papagos and Foreign Minister Stefanopoulos of Greece once against visited Ankara for talks on closer integration of Yugoslavia with Turkey and Greece. Later President Tito paid an official visit to Turkey in April 1954. During this visit, high level talks between Bayar and Tito led to an agreement on the establishment of a new Balkan alliance between Turkey, Greece, and Yugoslavia. This was followed by an official visit of Premier Menderes to Belgrade in May 1954. Finally, on August 9, 1954, the foreign ministers of the three powers signed a formal twenty-year military pact at Bled, Yugoslavia.[12] This agreement was followed by the state visit of President Bayar to Yugoslavia in September 1954.

In keeping with his policy of establishing closer understanding and cooperation through summit meetings with the leaders of Western Allies, President Bayar sent Prime Minister Menderes and Foreign Minister Köprülü to allied capitals in 1952 and 1953. And upon the invitation of President Eisenhower, he visited Washington in January 1954. On his last day in Washington, Bayar addressed a joint session of the Congress. He said: "I assure you and the people of the United States that the memory of your noble deeds will live forever in the heart of every Turk." Bayar underlined

---

[11] *New York Times,* 29 February 1953, p. 1.

[12] See *Ayın Tarihi,* no. 249, Agustos 1954, pp. 85–88.

his approach to the problems confronted by the free world in these words: "Turkey is fighting to the best of her ability against the subversive efforts which try to paralyze the United Nations and destroy NATO. According to our way of thinking, unless the efforts we dedicate toward peace are sincerely reciprocated by deeds, our desire for peace will only be a mirage."[13] His state visit was followed in June 1954 by the visit of Premier Menderes and his delegation to Washington for talks on the possibility of increasing the economic and military assistance of the United States to Turkey.[14]

The following state visits were also part of Bayar's summit diplomacy. In March 1954 Chancellor Konrad Adenauer of West Germany visited Ankara for three days of talks. Prime Minister Joseph Laniel of France came to Ankara in September 1954 for four days of meetings. This was followed by the visit by Premier Pella of Italy in November 1954. In November 1957 President Gronchi of Italy paid a state visit to Turkey. In May 1958 President Bayar went to Bonne for a state visit, and in June 1959 Bayar returned the state visit of the Italian president. In December 1959 President Eisenhower visited Ankara.

Premier Menderes and foreign ministers also maintained intensive person-to-person contacts with their Western counterparts, either on a bilateral basis or in meetings of the UN organs and the NATO Council of Ministers, in order to discuss common political, economic, and military problems. It is noteworthy that during the 1950s there were no diplomatic contacts between the Turkish statesmen and the Soviet leaders.

The hopes of bringing Yugoslavia into the Western defensive system were shattered when, in the eyes of President Tito, the danger of Soviet aggression subsided. With Yugoslavia turning toward neutralism and the Cyprus issue dividing Greece and Turkey, the usefulness of the Balkan Pact became highly questionable. In fact, by 1955 the Balkan Pact was a dead letter.

The Cyprus problem between Turkey and Greece caused the breakdown of the cooperation between the Allies within the Balkan Pact and NATO. It further revived the deep-rooted animosity

---

13 U.S. Department of State, *Bulletin,* vol. 30, no. 764, February 15, 1954, pp. 247–49.

14 On text of joint communiqué see Ibid., no. 781, June 14, 1954, pp. 912–13.

between the two peoples. Here only the principal demands of Turkey over Cyprus and the final settlement need mentioning.[15]

When the incipient demands of the Greek-speaking Cypriots for self-determination were transformed by the Greek government into a union of the British island colony with Greece, Turkey first claimed that Cyprus should continue to be a British crown colony. If the status quo of the island were to change, however, Turkey later declared that because of Cyprus' proximity to Turkey and the presence of a large Turkish community on the island, Cyprus should be reunited with Turkey for security reasons. Rejecting the idea of the union of Cyprus with Greece, the Turkish government, in order to reach a compromise solution, changed its earlier position and called for the partitioning of the island between Greece and Turkey. When the British government came out with another compromise plan, the interim plan (Macmillan) for seven years, although insisting on the partition of the island, Bayar hastened to point out that the "idea of partition was not irreconcilable with the principle of partnership,"[16] as suggested under the interim plan. Despite the opposition of Greece, the plan was put into effect in Cyprus on October 1, 1955, and the Turkish government sent its representative to Cyprus. But the conflict between Greece on the one side and Turkey and Britain on the other persisted. Neither the Council of Ministers of NATO nor the General Assembly of the UN could find a satisfactory solution.

Meanwhile, bilateral contacts between Turkey and Greece were re-established by the beginning of 1959, first at the foreign ministers level, then at the heads of government level. Premier Menderes and Premier Karamanlis met in Zurich between February 5 and 11, 1959. During their talks Karamanlis seemed to have

---

[15] For an extensive treatment of the Cyprus problem see Fahir F. Armaoğlu, *Kıbrıs Meselesi, 1954–1959: Türk Hükümeti ve Kamu Oyunun Davranışları* (Ankara: Ankara Üniversitesi Siyasal Bilgiler Fakültesi Yayınları no. 156–138,1963); Turkish Information Office, *Turkish Views on Cyprus* (New York: 1956); Ahmet Şükrü Esmer, "Cyprus: Past and Present," *Turkish Yearbook of International Relations*, 3 (1962): pp. 35–46; A. Suat Bilge, "Le Conflit Cypriote," *Turkish Yearbook of International Relations*, 4 (1963): 23–36; Stanley Kyriakides, *Cyprus: Constitutionalism and Crisis Government* (Philadelphia: University of Pennsylvania Press, 1968); Mehmet Gönlübol, et. al., *Olaylarla Türk Dış Politikası: 1919–1965* (Ankara: Dışişleri Bakanlığı, 1968), pp. 287–337; Ferenc A. Váli, *Bridge Across the Bosporus: The Foreign Policy of Turkey*, pp. 219–71.

[16] Quoted in Kılıç, *Turkey and the World*, p. 173.

abandoned his demand for the annexation of Cyprus, and Menderes seemed willing to give up the idea of partitioning the island. It appears that Premier Menderes, in his negotiating strategy, succeeded in convincing his Greek counterpart that beyond accepting an independent state of Cyprus Turkey's position could not be compromised. Once that conclusion was reached and once the establishment of a new status quo was considered preferable over the continuation of the dispute, agreement between the negotiating parties was a natural outcome.

Thus, pragmatic considerations and reason prevailed over emotions. The Turkish and Greek statesmen showed courage and imaginativeness in trying to restore the friendship between their two countries. They decided to establish a new state in Cyprus, the Republic of Cyprus, in whose government the Greeks and Turks would have almost equal voice. They also promised to protect and preserve the new state by assuming equal obligations under treaties to be put into force between Turkey, Greece, Cyprus, and Britain. The decisions and principles worked out between the two heads of government were then brought to a conference of all concerned in London. On February 23, 1959, it was announced in London that the Greek and Turkish Cypriot leaders and the governments of Turkey, Greece, and Britain had agreed to the drafting of a new set of treaties as well as the Constitution of Cyprus on the basis of the agreements reached between the leaders of Turkey and Greece at Zurich.[17]

The drafting of treaties, as well as the Constitution, was completed later and signed on August 16, 1960. By that time, however, the Bayar administration had been overthrown. The fact that the union of Cyprus with Greece had been prevented and that the establishment of an independent state was provided for, with Turkey obtaining legal rights in the preservation of the new status quo in the island, the 1959 Zurich and London agreements would have to be considered an unqualified diplomatic victory for the Bayar administration.

President Bayar was firmly convinced that Turkey, as a member of the free world, and as a member of NATO, could no longer

---

[17] See *Conference on Cyprus: Documents Signed and Initialled at Lancaster House on February 19, 1959,* Cmnd. 679, 1959. On further developments on the Cyprus question see Chapter XIII.

remain aloof from the momentous developments in the Middle East. The defense of this region against possible Soviet attacks demanded the establishment of a regional alliance and the eventual linking of that alliance with NATO. By building a bridge between the Middle East and the West, Bayar was not only able to expand Turkey's participation in the affairs of the region, but also to help the West to maintain its dominant position in the Middle East.

On the eve of the adherence of Turkey to NATO, Bayar agreed to act as co-sponsor of the plan for the establishment of a Middle East Defense Organization, which was to help to maintain the network of British bases in the region and to keep the Arab countries within the Western sphere of influence. However, this move met with the rising tide of Arab nationalism in Egypt and Syria. Rebuffed by the revolutionary leadership of these countries,[18] Bayar, in line with the Northern Tier Alliance concept of John Foster Dulles, approached the conservative leadership of the other Middle Eastern powers. As a first step, a mutual assistance pact between Turkey and Pakistan was concluded on April 2, 1954. When King Hussein of Jordan visited Ankara in August 1954, Bayar emphasized the urgency of the establishment of defensive ties with Jordan. However, talks between Bayar and King Hussein remained inconclusive. Later, the prime minister of Iraq, Nuri al-Said, was invited to Ankara in October 1954. Talks between Premier al-Said and Premier Menderes prepared the ground for a Turkish-Iraqi pact. Premier Menderes and Foreign Minister Köprülü visited Baghdad in January 1955 for further talks on the pact between the two countries. On their way to Ankara, Menderes and Köprülü visited the capitals of Syria and Lebanon in order to urge these countries to join the prospective pact.

President Bayar also paid a state visit to Pakistan in February 1955 and held talks with the president of Pakistan on the question of regional security. On his way home, Bayar visited Baghdad where on February 24, 1955, heads of government of Turkey and Iraq signed the Pact of Mutual Cooperation (the Baghdad Pact).[19]

Bayar invited President Camille Chamoun of Lebanon to Ankara, and at the end of five days of talks, from April 1 to 6,

[18] See John C. Campbell, *Defense of the Middle East* (New York: Harper, 1958), pp. 39–48.

[19] Text of the Baghdad Pact in Hurewitz, *Diplomacy in the Near and Middle East*, pp. 390–91.

1955, it was announced that Lebanon and Turkey would establish close contacts and consult with each other on the question of the security of the region. This statement was interpreted in Syria and Egypt as a move which would ultimately lead to Lebanese accession to the Baghdad Pact. Thus these two powers applied strong pressure upon Lebanon not to fall into the Western trap. In the end, despite further friendly talks held between Bayar and Chamoun during Bayar's six-day state visit to Beirut, which began on June 16, 1955, Lebanon declined to join the Baghdad Pact.

Meanwhile, Bayar intensified his diplomatic efforts in order to include the United States and Britain and other conservative regimes of the Middle East into his defensive arrangement. On April 5, 1955, Great Britain acceded to the Baghdad Pact, followed by Pakistani accession on September 23. Three days later, Bayar left Ankara on a state visit to Tehran and there urged the Iranian ruler to join the pact. Iran joined the Baghdad Pact on November 3, 1955. On that day, Bayar was in Amman urging King Hussein to become a party to the pact. The Jordanian monarch declined the offer.

Despite willingness to participate in the Economic, Counter-Subversive Activities, and Military Committees and its financial contribution to the Baghdad Pact, the United States preferred to remain outside the pact, so as to avoid further antagonizing Egypt, Syria, and Israel.

As a result of the establishment of the Baghdad Pact organization, the Middle Eastern powers were divided into two opposing camps. The strongly anti-Western and revolutionary states of the region, namely Egypt and Syria, viewed the Baghdad Pact, which was composed essentially of conservative regimes such as Iraq, Iran, Pakistan, and Turkey as another instrument of imperialism of the West. Moreover, Turkey became the target of the anti-imperialist attacks emanating from Cairo. The relations between Turkey and Cairo and Damascus were strained to the breaking point.[20]

Although President Bayar was successful in building a bridge between at least some of the Middle Eastern powers and the West, this bridge proved, in the final analysis, to be unsafe and unreliable; one of its main supports, Iraq, was too weak to stand up against

---

[20] See Hisham B. Sharabi, *Government and Politics of the Middle East in the Twentieth Century* (Princeton, N.J.: D. Van Nostrand, 1956), pp. 69–70.

the tide of Arab nationalism and collapsed altogether in July 1958. Another development which contributed to the weakening of the Baghdad Pact was the joint Israeli-Anglo-French military action against Egypt in October 1956. In order to review the fast moving developments in Egypt, Bayar and Premier Menderes rushed to Tehran on November 7, 1956, and met with the heads of states and prime ministers of the other Baghdad Pact members. They could not help deploring the situation and condemned the aggression perpetrated against Egypt. They also called for the withdrawal of the invasion forces from Egyptian territory and invited Great Britain and France to respect the territorial integrity and political independence of Egypt. The Baghdad Pact members met once again in Baghdad on November 17, 1956, in order to bring their influence to bear on the powers involved in the Suez crisis for a speedy settlement of the immediate question of invasion. The prime ministers of the four regional powers of the Baghdad Pact met a third time in Ankara in January 1957 in the presence of President Bayar and the crown prince of Iraq. In a communiqué issued on January 21, 1957, at the end of the Ankara Conference, they noted with satisfaction the complete withdrawal of Anglo-French forces from Egypt in deference to the United Nations resolutions. They welcomed the resolution of the United Nations General Assembly calling upon Israel once again to withdraw behind the armistice line. They felt that the maintenance of peace in this area should be the continuing responsibility of the United Nations. The four powers came to the conclusion that subversive activities in their region continued unabated. They agreed that vigorous steps should be taken to meet the challenge of false and subversive propaganda. In this connection, they noted that President Eisenhower's plan for the Middle East recognized the threat posed by communist propaganda and subversion to the countries of the Middle East. Therefore, the Baghdad Pact members expressed their full support of the Eisenhower plan.[21]

Deeply concerned over communist penetration into Syria, Bayar let it be known that Turkey would not remain undisturbed by the Soviet armed buildup in that country. It was at this time that Turkish troops were gathered not far from the Syrian border,

---

[21] See U.S. Department of State, *Bulletin,* vol. 31, February 11, 1957, pp. 216–17.

which precipitated a number of minor border incidents between the two countries. Backed by the Soviet Union, Syria protested the Turkish troop movements. Apparently, President Bayar's intention was to dramatize the Soviet buildup in Syria before the free world and indicate to the United States that Turkey would fully support some kind of intervention or preventive action in Syria if the United States decided upon such a move. In response to Soviet charges against Turkey, the United States reiterated its support of Turkey. Thus an acute crisis was in the making. A communist-socialist-nationalist coalition's attempted overthrow of King Hussein's regime in Jordan in April 1957 had added further fuel to an already explosive situation in the Middle East.

At this time a Summit Conference was convened between President Bayar, King Faisal II, and King Hussein. The two Hashimite monarchs came to Istanbul on August 22, 1957, to confer with Bayar. Bayar then informed the president of Lebanon and the king of Saudi Arabia that Turkey did not have any aggressive designs on Syria but was seriously concerned over the possibility of Syria turning into a Soviet satellite. Thereupon, on October 20, King Saud made an offer of mediation which was accepted by Bayar but turned down by Syria. Instead Syria brought the matter to the Security Council of the United Nations, charging that Turkey was planning to invade Syria.[22]

After prolonged debate in the Security Council, no formal resolution was adopted and the tension began to dissipate by December 1957 on account of the cautious attitude displayed both by the United States and by the Soviet Union in order to avoid a head-on collision in the Middle East.

The Baghdad Pact was soon to be imperiled by a revolution in Iraq and by an equally grave governmental crisis in Lebanon. On the day the revolutionaries, led by Brigadier Abd al-Karim Kassem, struck against the monarchy in Iraq and executed King Faisal II, Crown Prince Abd al-illah, and Premier Nuri al-Said, the heads of state of Turkey, Iran, and Pakistan were holding a summit meeting, as decided upon much earlier, in Ankara. In an official communiqué issued on July 17, 1958, the three heads of state expressed their regret at the turn of events in Iraq and in an

---

[22] See Mehmet Gönlübol, et. al., *Olaylarla Türk Dış Politikası, 1919– 1956* (Ankara Dışişleri Bakanlığı Matbaası, 1968), pp. 253–63.

indirect reference to the assassination of the Iraqi leaders "condemned such manifestations of savagery which they said had been inspired by external enemies of Iraq."[23] However, for pragmatic reasons, that is, the need to salvage the Baghdad Pact, Bayar reversed his attitude toward the revolutionary regime in Iraq. On July 31, Turkey extended recognition to the new revolutionary regime of Brigadier Kassem.

Yet the strong current of revolutionism in the Middle East had by this time done irreparable damage to the fragile bridge called the Baghdad Pact. The prime ministers of the Baghdad Pact, attending the fifth meeting of the Ministerial Council between July 28 and 29, 1958, in London, nevertheless declared that the need for the pact was now more urgent than it had been. They were actually concerned about how to revive and revitalize the defensive arrangement of the West in the Middle East without the participation of Iraq. Iraq itself was not present at the London meeting and no definite statement had been made at Baghdad as to the attitude of the new revolutionary regime toward the pact. Iraq's participation in the pact was nominal until March 24, 1959, at which time its decision to withdraw did not come as a surprise to the other pact members. In August 1959, the secretariat of the Baghdad Pact was re-established in Ankara and the name of the pact was changed to the Central Treaty Organization.

At the Ankara Summit Conference in July 1958 between the presidents of Turkey and Pakistan and the Shah of Iran, the three heads of state, following their discussion of the Lebanese crisis, decided to send a message to President Eisenhower expressing their approval of the landing of the United States marines in Beirut. This message left no doubt as to the stand taken by Turkey, Iran, and Pakistan on the confrontation between the revolutionary and status quo forces in the Middle East.[24]

Such an unequivocal support of the United States led to the signing of Bilateral Agreements of Cooperation between the United States and Turkey, Iran, and Pakistan on March 15, 1959. Under these agreements the United States promised, in case of aggression against these three powers, to take such appropriate action — including the use of armed force — as might be mutually agreed

---

[23] Ibid., p. 264.

[24] See U.S. Department of State, *Bulletin,* vol. 34, August 4, 1958.

upon.[25] For the purpose of strengthening the Turkish economy, the United States jointly with the Organization for European Economic Cooperation and the International Monetary Fund had in August 1958 povided Turkey with the much desired $359 million loan. As a result of the Bilateral Agreement of Cooperation, Turkey opened her territory to the establishment of intermediate range ballistic missile bases. This agreement, according to President Bayar, gave Turkey the much sought-after specific United States commitment of defense, which, despite Turkey's membership in NATO and the Baghdad Pact, had hitherto been lacking. Through these agreements the United States became no less linked to Turkey, Iran, and Pakistan than if it had signed the original Baghdad Pact.

President Bayar's intensive diplomatic activities designed to protect Turkey's national security and to enhance her image and prestige in the international arena came to a sad and dramatic end. For the first time in her recent history, Turkey was to act as host to the foreign ministers of the NATO countries, the NATO Council of Ministers meeting, between May 2 and 4, 1960, in Istanbul. This meeting coincided with serious internal disturbances. Foreign dignitaries and Western newsmen witnessed student demonstrations and the enforcement of martial law regulations. Premier Menderes had to cancel his welcoming speech at the first ceremonial session of the Council of Ministers meeting in order to stay in Ankara to be in charge of the internal developments. The martial law atmosphere and student demonstrations did not help the image of Turkey as a member of the free world. In fact, the internal affairs of Turkey were quite embarrassing for the ostensibly democratic regime of President Bayar.

THE PRIME MINISTER AND
FOREIGN MINISTERS OF BAYAR

President Celal Bayar chose Adnan Menderes as his most trusted lieutenant and prime minister. Until he entered politics by joining the Liberal Republican Party in 1930, and later the Repub-

---

[25] For a critical analysis of this agreement see Hamza Eroğlu, "Türkiye — Amerika Birleşik Devletleri İkili İşbirliği Anlaşması." *Turkish Yearbook of International Relations* 1 (1960): 23–64.

lican People's Party, Menderes was a wealthy farmer in Aydın. In 1931, he was elected deputy and served as inspector of the Republican People's Party in western Anatolia. For fourteen years he remained an obscure backbencher in the Grand National Assembly, never achieving a committee chairmanship; he spent his spare time earning a law degree from the Ankara Law School. During all this time, he observed and learned how the government worked and how the politicians acted.

In 1945 Menderes abruptly ended his long obscurity and joined Celal Bayar, Fuad Köprülü, and Refik Koraltan in presenting a resolution to the Republican People's Party demanding that the party program be liberalized and that the government put into effect the democratic liberties promised under the Constitution. Soon the four rebels launched their own Democratic Party in 1946. The same year, Menderes engaged in an extensive campaign on behalf of the Democratic Party promising civil liberties, an end to economic restrictions, and free enterprise instead of the state-directed economy. Menderes was elected deputy in July 1946. In the next elections in 1950 he was re-elected.

Adnan Menderes shared President Bayar's vision of grandeur. He had supreme self-confidence and had predicated himself the mission defined by his leader. He aspired to the historical role of "Adnan the Builder."

At no time in the history of the republic was such mutual trust, close cooperation, and understanding established between a president and his prime minister as between Celal Bayar and Adnan Menderes. Bayar, the decision maker and supervisor, particularly in domestic affairs, preferred to remain behind the scene most of the time and let Menderes run the affairs of the government. Inspired and directed by his leader, Menderes became, for all practical purposes the single most important person in the country.

As far as was humanly possible, Menderes adamantly refused to delegate any authority whatever, often seeming to be everywhere at once, making every decision, including those most trivial. His energy and dynamism were seemingly inexhaustible. His workday was a twelve to eighteen-hour affair, punctuated by impulsive trips into the countryside to inspect one of his pet projects. He seemed to be on top of all areas of the administration, possessing an unusual memory for detail. As he entrenched himself in power, he appeared to be an astute politician. He excelled in political oratory. He treated the general public, the peasantry, as it would please them to be treated and thus gained tremendous popularity. He became a popular, persuasive leader. As a result of these qualities, coupled with his long tenure in office, more often than not, the Democratic Party administration came to be referred to as "the Menderes regime."

This popularity of Menderes must have served President Bayar's objectives well. He did not seem to mind Menderes' popularity nor his seemingly captivating personality. Apparently the two agreed as to the delineation of their respective duties and responsibilities, rights, and privileges. The dominating personality of President Bayar precluded any possibility of personal clashes.

Despite the similarity of objectives between the two, there were subtle differences in their personalities and in their social and political backgrounds. Bayar was always more reserved, dignified, and solemn than his Prime Minister; he was also more ambitious, harsh, vindictive, and courageous than Menderes. Bayar was a master of authoritarianism of Ottoman vintage. He was, no doubt, an experienced power politician. On the other hand, Menderes not only lacked these qualities but, in a sense, was the antithesis of Bayar.[26] Menderes was suave and outspoken, easily irritated, yet more timid and docile. These differences in their personalities came to the surface more distinctly under the strains and stresses of their trials at Yassıada. According to one observer, Menderes "soon changed from a confident, hard-driving Prime Minister into a sniveling, cowardly figure. . . . Through the early cases he had maintained the sharpness of mind which had kept him in office for ten years, but as the proceedings wore on he more and more often attempted to throw the guilt on his subordinates, and increasingly addressed the court in pleading, almost weeping tones."[27] In contrast to Menderes' poor and timid performance, Bayar throughout the proceedings maintained a dignified posture, challenging the

---

[26] Aydemir identifies the decade of Bayar-Menderes administration as the antithesis of the era of the War of Independence, the era of heroes. *Ikinci Adam,* vol. 2, p. 62.

[27] Weiker, *The Turkish Revolution,* p. 33. Aydemir argues that Menderes had had not one but a dual personality: a little Menderes and a great Menderes. In fact, these two personalities always clashed with each other, and on many instances, "little Menderes" tended to overwhelm his greatness. *Ikinci Adam,* vol. 2, p. 65.

authority of the court to try him and at times attempted to ridicule the prosecution. He did not yield under pressure. Often he flatly stated that he performed his powers and duties conscientiously and as he saw fit. He had no feeling of repentance. Thus, ultimately he gained a certain amount of admiration for his dignified conduct even among those who had caused his downfall. In the end, it was Menderes who was executed, not Bayar.

The first foreign minister of President Bayar was Mehmet Fuad Köprülü, a descendant of the famous Köprülü family of the Ottoman Empire, which provided the empire with a number of outstanding Grand Vezirs. Mehmet Fuad started his career as a high school teacher and later was appointed professor of history of Turkish literature. He held a number of chairs at the University of Istanbul and at the University of Ankara. In the 1940s he was a close associate of Celal Bayar and Adnan Menderes. He served as foreign minister of the Democratic Party administration until April 15, 1955. In July of that year he was appointed Minister of State and deputy prime minister and served until November 1955. The next month Köprülü reassumed the portfolio of minister of Foreign Affairs. However, six months later he resigned his post in protest of the policies and actions of Premier Menderes and a short time later resigned from the Democratic Party altogether.

Until the appointment of Fatin Rüştü Zorlu in November 1957, Ethem Menderes, no kin of Adnan Menderes, served as acting foreign minister. The last foreign minister of the Democratic Party administration was Fatin Rüştü Zorlu. He was a career foreign service officer prior to his entry into politics in the Democratic Party. Zorlu served as foreign minister until the coup d'état of May 27, 1960. Together with his fellow Democratic Party members, Zorlu was tried at Yassıada on numerous charges. At the end of the trials he was convicted on a number of counts. He was sentenced to death by the unanimous vote of the judges of the Yassıada Tribunal on September 15, 1961, and the next day he was executed.

BOLD BUT RIGID BAYAR

In contrast to the extremely cautious but flexible policy of his predecessors, President Bayar's responses to the world outside may be characterized as daring but inflexible. Furthermore, his foreign policy was greatly influenced by ideological considerations. He condemned the communist world and exhibited an unfriendly, if not hostile, attitude toward the Soviet Union. He rejected the policy of neutralism as being immoral. His speeches and statements were replete with such Cold War phrases as "the free world," "captive nations," "peace loving nations." He called for positive and concrete steps of good will and good neighborliness on the part of the Soviet Union before Turkey could normalize her relations with her northern neighbor. President Bayar did not consider Turkey's military and economic dependency on the United States as detrimental to her sovereignty and independence.

From Bayar's point of view, Turkey, as a member of NATO, could not remain inactive during the eventful years from 1955 to 1960, which witnessed the ebb and flow of the Arab-Israeli War, the internal communist forces, and the attempted penetration of the Middle East by the Soviet Union. As a Middle Eastern power, Turkey had to assume an active role in the affairs of the region. Indeed, Bayar's strategies and tactics entailed greater risks and dangers for Turkey. On the other hand, since his policy was inextricably interwoven with the foreign policies of the United States and of the West, the risks and dangers involved were the necessary consequences of his fundamental decision to stand and fall with the West against the Soviet bloc. The following may be singled out as the most important features of the foreign policy of the Bayar administration: (1) the abandonment of the policy of cautious neutralism vis-à-vis great power confrontations; (2) the establishment of a close alliance with a single major power, the United States, resulting in virtual dependency upon that power in terms of military power and economic development; (3) the viewing of the East-West power struggle through ideological lenses and explaining Soviet expansionist tendencies only through Marxist-Leninist ideology; and (4) the assuming of an active role in the alignment of the countries of the Middle East. Interestingly enough, such readjustments of foreign policy were considered by President Bayar as compatible with Atatürk's legacy: To pursue a policy of status quo and to show vigilance and determination against external threats and aggression, and to that end stand with the Western European powers. It may be said that, in the final analysis and despite the risks and dangers that were inherently involved in his summit diplomacy, President Bayar succeeded in protecting the vital national interests of Turkey at minimum cost.

Chapter Thirteen

PRESIDENTS GÜRSEL, SUNAY, AND KORUTÜRK: "THE GUARDIANS OF THE REGIME"

COLLECTIVE LEADERSHIP IN DECISION MAKING

A NEW PHENOMENON IN TURKISH POLITICS

As noted earlier, within the ranks of the Committee of National Unity there was no strong and decisive leader who could enlist the loyalty and unwaivering support of the military and civilian elites. The fact that no one could emerge as a strong man and that the prominent military and civilian personalities since 1961 had prudently avoided extreme measures of force in the ensuing power struggle, the practice of collective leadership initiated during the CNU administration continued to prevail. The collective leadership consisted of the president of the republic, the Chiefs of the General Staff, the commanding generals of the armed services, the other high-ranking generals, the prime minister, ministers, and influential leaders of the major political parties.

Since May 27, 1960, foreign and domestic policy decisions have more and more reflected the corporate needs, established traditions, and attitudes of the military and civilian institutions, such as the presidency, the officer corps of the armed forces, the career diplomats of the Ministry of Foreign Affairs, and the Grand National Assembly. It is noteworthy that the collective leadership was heavily weighed in favor of the military establishment. It was headed by presidents who were former high-ranking officers of the armed forces. On important occasions it met at the presidential palaces. And the deliberations of those military and civilian leaders in all likelihood may have been dominated by the presidents simply because of the fact that the office of the president is still the apex of state power, surrounded by a certain aura of sanctity and viewed with awe by both military and civilian leaders as well as by the general public. This no doubt is due to the traditional political culture which commands the highest respect and deference for the highest office in the land. Then, too, evidence indicates that the meetings of the National Security Council and the Supreme Military Council seemed to carry greater weight than the meetings of the Council of Ministers which, quite often, also included the military leaders.

THE ASCENDANCY OF THE MILITARY POINT OF VIEW

The political system of Turkey, in fact if not in law, was based on the principle of the leadership of warriors in civilian clothes who managed the affairs of the state in an authoritarian fashion. When the civilian intraelite political struggle for power seemed to threaten Turkey's vital national interests, warriors in military uniform did not hesitate to intervene in domestic politics, because they considered themselves as the guardians of the regime established by Atatürk.

During the 1960–1961 period, important domestic and foreign policy decisions were made by the Committee of National Unity itself or jointly by the CNU, the Chief of the General Staff, and the commanders of the land, air, and naval forces. From 1961 to 1971 military leaders preferred to remain behind the political scene. However, during the periods of internal disorder and unrest, such as in 1962 and 1963, and during the extremely critical months of the Cyprus conflict of 1963–1964, and 1967, the highest echelons of the military establishment were directly involved in the adoption of strategically important decisions. And since March 12, 1971, the high-ranking generals, for all practical purposes, have assumed political roles and have begun to exercise direct supervision over the conduct of the Council of Ministers.

Admittedly, the nature and extent of the ascendancy of the military over civilian institutions in general and the ascendancy

of the military point of view over the civilian point of view in particular are matters of conjecture. However, it is apparent that as
compared with the previous practice,[1] the military establishment,
particularly the senior members of the officer corps, since May 27,
1960, have begun to play a more active and direct role in domestic
and external affairs. The military slipped out of its purely instrumental role into one of formulating and executing substantive
domestic and foreign policies. In a broad sense, the military also
included those politicians who in the past had served as military
officers, and those "militarized civilian political leaders" whose
primary concerns were no different than those of the career military
men, namely, problems of national security.

In addition to the meetings held at the presidential palace in
Çankaya presided over by the presidents, there are three other
collective bodies with slightly different membership which are
involved in domestic and foreign policy decision making. These are
the National Security Council, the Council of Ministers, and the
Supreme Military Council.

Although attached to the prime ministry by law, the National
Security Council (NSC) is the most important military-civilian body
where national security decisions are made. It is presided over by
the president of the republic and chaired in his absence by the
prime minister. The statutory membership of the NSC, which
was created in 1962, includes the president, the prime minister,
minister of state, deputy prime minister, ministers of National
defense, interior, foreign affairs, finance, communications, and other
ministers as invited by the president. The Chief of the General
Staff and the chiefs of the armed services also take part in the
meetings of the NSC. The functions of the NSC include preparing
national security plans and programs and coordinating national
security activities. The day-to-day functioning of the council is
managed by the general secretariat headed by a secretary general,
who is usually a senior-ranking general.[2]

The Council of Ministers, usually chaired by the prime minister, is responsible to the Grand National Assembly for the general

---

[1] See Dankwart A. Rustow, "The Army and the Founding of the Turkish
Republic," *World Politics* 11 (1949): 513–22.

[2] See *T. C. Devlet Teşkilatı Rehberi* (Ankara: Türkiye ve Orta Doğu
Amme İdaresi Enstitüsü, 1968), pp. 124–25.

policy of the government and for insuring national security. On certain important occasions it is chaired by the president and attended by the Chief of the General Staff and chiefs of the armed services.

The Supreme Military Council, which is headed by the Chief of the General Staff and which includes the commanders of the army, navy, air force, and gendarmerie, in recent years has become a very important collective decision-making body. For example, critical decisions concerning internal security, the promulgation of martial law and its periodic extensions, or decisions about the deployment of Turkish troops are made in that council.

Since May 1960, the office of the Chief of the General Staff seems to have acquired paramount importance. Under the existing law, its primary responsibility is to prepare the armed forces for war and to direct and administer them. The Supreme Military Council and the office of the Legal Adviser serve as advisory bodies. It is by law attached to the prime ministry. As commander in chief of all armed forces, the Chief of the General Staff is appointed by the president, usually for a three-year period, upon the nomination of the Council of Ministers.[3] Since May 1960, the following generals served as Chief of the General Staff in succession: General Ragıp Gümüşpala, General Cevdet Sunay, General Cemal Tural, General Memduh Tağmaç, General Faruk Gürler, and General Semih Sancar, all former commanders of the land forces.

Again since May 1960, the following military and civilian leaders served as prime minister: General Cemal Gürsel, İsmet İnönü, S. H. Ürgüplü, S. Demirel, Nihat Erim, Ferit Melen, Naim Talu, and Bülent Ecevit. General Cemal Gürsel was not only the prime minister but also the head of state until his election to the presidency in October 1961. İsmet İnönü headed the first coalition cabinet in Turkey and because of the extraordinary political circumstances he was asked to head the second and the third coalition governments.

Suat H. Ürgüplü was an independent senator when he formed the fourth coalition cabinet. He had risen among the ranks of the Republican People's Party and had served in the Saracoğlu cabinet.

---

[3] The residence of the Chief of the General Staff, as well as the residences of the commanders of the land forces, the navy, and the air force are located at Çankaya near the presidential palace. These luxurious mansions were constructed in recent years.

In 1950 he had joined the Democratic Party. From 1952 to 1960, Ürgüplü had served as ambassador of Turkey in a number of Western capitals, and in 1961 he had been elected president of the Senate.

When Süleyman Demirel entered the political arena as a member of the Justice Party at the age of thirty-eight, he was an unknown political entity. However, within a very short period of time he achieved impressive success in politics. First he assumed the leadership of the Justice Party in 1964 following a bitter intra-party power struggle. Then he was appointed deputy premier in the coalition government of Ürgüplü. And finally, following the general elections of October 1965, Demirel at the age of forty-one became one of the youngest prime ministers of Turkey. After the general elections in 1969, Demirel was returned to power with a large majority and formed his own cabinet. When he was asked to step down by the military in March 1971, Demirel demonstrated his innate political qualities — wisdom, prudence, moderation, and pragmatism. He resigned. However, within a very short time he was able to transform his defeat into a political victory by effectively challenging the military in the political arena.

Nihat Erim, a distinguished professor of law and an experienced politician who had assumed a number of ministerial posts in the past as a member of the Republican People's Party, was the choice of the military leaders for prime minister to succeed Demirel. Erim was given the task of forming a nonpartisan government. As prime minister, Erim was unable to introduce far-reaching politico-socio-economic reforms because of the lack of support in the parliament for his programs. Erim resigned in December 1971, but was immediately reinstated by President Sunay. Erim could not stay in power very long because of the strong opposition in parliament to his policies and actions.

Erim was succeeded by Ferit Melen. A veteran political figure since 1950, Melen had entered into politics as a member of the Republican People's Party. He had served as cabinet minister during the 1960s. He had resigned from the Republican People's Party and had helped to form the National Reliance Party. He had been the Minister of Defense in the Erim cabinets. Melen's coalition government was composed of the Justice Party, the Republican People's Party, the National Reliance Party, and a number of independent ministers. Following the election of Admiral Korutürk as president, Premier Melen tendered his resignation in April 1973.

An independent senator, Naim Talu, was designated as the next premier. Talu had served as Minister of Commerce in the previous two governments, and prior to December 1971, he had been the president of the Central Bank of Turkey. As head of a coalition government, Talu was entrusted with the task of conducting the general elections. On account of the difficulties encountered in forming a new government, Talu remained in office as caretaker until January 25, 1974.

Bülent Ecevit, the leader of the Republican People's Party, headed the next coalition government. A controversial figure on the political scene since he had enunciated the left-of-center policy in the Republican People's Party, Bülent Ecevit was provided with the opportunity to demonstrate his statesmanship as well as his resourcefulness as a political leader. Ecevit was known during his school days at Robert College — a private American educational institution — as an introversive, shy, romantic person preoccupied with literature, especially poetry. Although he is reported to have said that political circumstances had been directly instrumental in his entry into politics and his rise to the leadership of the Republican People's Party, there can be no doubt that Ecevit possesses extra-ordinary intellectual capabilities in assessing the strengths and weaknesses of his would-be opponents and friends, in foreseeing the direction of the flow of political events, and in adopting the right strategies and tactics in the political arena.

Until he assumed the office of prime minister, Ecevit was an idealist, a political maverick in his own right, a dissident. His public pronouncements often left no doubt about the fact that he rejected some of the more salient features of the Turkish political culture, such as the inherent suspicion and distrust, the tendency toward authoritarianism, coercion, and elitism, and that he accepted the principle of theoretical perfection and envisaged the possibility of building a democratic regime based on the principle of consent of the governed and socio-economic as well as political equality. On account of his articulate idealism, Ecevit was able to attract a large number of followers among the members of his party, among the ranks of the intelligentsia and even among the general public as he gained greater recognition and power in the Republican People's

Party. He displayed impressive capabilities in articulating the politico-socio-economic expectations of his constituents and in formulating idealistic policies designed to meet their needs. He was also able to appeal to the emotional needs, patriotism, nationalism, and the hopes of his followers. He promised them a better and more prosperous future.

Ecevit's popularity in 1973 among the large segment of the intelligentsia, among the counterelite in particular, and among the working people rivaled that of his principal political opponent, Süleyman Demirel, whose power base was essentially the peasantry and the business circles. Ecevit was nicknamed by his followers as *Karaoğlan,* meaning the "Dark Complexioned Lad" — having similar qualities as the legendary folk hero Karaoğlan. His political slogan was *Ak Günler,* meaning "Bright and Prosperous Days to Come."

There is every indication, however, that as Ecevit assumed greater responsibilities in the government of his countrymen his idealism and romanticism have given way to pragmatism, realism, and moderation. His decision to share political power with the National Salvation Party leaders and his moderate policies and actions in the most recent Cyprus crisis support such an observation.

THE CAREER DIPLOMATS

The military-civilian collective leadership included also the top career foreign service officers of the Ministry of Foreign Affairs. Of the seven foreign ministers of the period since May 1960, five were career diplomats, the two exceptions being İhsan Sabri Çağlayangil, the foreign minister of the Justice Party, and Turan Güneş, the foreign minister of the Republican People's Party. This was in stark contrast to the previous practice. During the period from 1920 to 1960, of the eleven ministers of Foreign Affairs only two were career diplomats.

The appointment of Selim R. Sarper as the first minister of Foreign Affairs of General Cemal Gürsel implied that the Committee of National Unity was to rely on the expert counsel and experience of a well-known and highly respected professional diplomat who has had a distinguished diplomatic career. Sarper was succeeded by Feridun Cemal Erkin who had served as ambassador to such Western capitals as Rome, Washington, Paris, Madrid, and London. The appointment of Hasan F. E. Işık, the Turkish ambassador to Moscow, as the third career diplomat to be in charge of the Ministry of Foreign Affairs seems to have confirmed the intentions of the military-civilian collective leadership to rely on the special skills and knowledge of career foreign service officers.

Foreign Minister Işık was replaced by İhsan Sabri Çağlayangil who had had no diplomatic experience but who had served as governor of the Bursa province before he entered politics in 1961. Çağlayangil held the post of foreign minister until March 27, 1971, at which time he was succeeded by another career diplomat Osman E. Olcay. At the time of his appointment, Olcay was deputy secretary general of NATO. Olcay, however, served briefly in the first nonpartisan cabinet of Premier Erim. Ü. Haluk Bayülken, the permanent representative of Turkey in the United Nations, replaced Olcay in the second cabinet of Premier Erim. Bayülken held the post of foreign minister in the cabinet of Premier Talu who succeeded Premier Melen. Prime Minister Ecevit designated Turan Güneş as his foreign minister when he formed his government in January 1974.

Since May 1960, in addition to the inclusion of the ministers of Foreign Affairs into the foreign policy decision-making circles, the secretaries general, directors general of various departments, and other high-ranking career foreign service officers have exercised a considerable influence in the formulation and execution of foreign policy decisions. This observation is based on this writer's long-time association with a number of career officers and on interviews with others in the Ministry of Foreign Affairs. According to these career officers, before a foreign policy decision of major importance was made by the collective leadership, the issue on hand was thoroughly examined and alternatives were meticulously searched and reviewed within the Ministry. The top officials of the Ministry in turn relied on the expertise of the other career officers at lower levels both at home and abroad. Such a procedure, in the final analysis, provided the career officers with greater, and in a way, unprecedented, opportunity of shaping foreign policy decisions. Admittedly, the exact nature and scope of this influence on all issues of policy cannot easily be verified because of the blanket of secrecy that covers such matters.

The greater involvement of the professional diplomats in foreign policy decision making may be attributed to external as well as internal causes. The renewal of the intercommunal strife in Cyprus

in the 1960s, the public debate which was initiated by the counterelite during the middle of the 1960s over Turkey's politico-economic-
military commitments within the Western community of nations,
and the increase in East-West diplomatic, commercial, and cultural
contacts may be cited among the principal external causes. The
domestic political instabilities and the prevailing power vacuum
within the highest echelons of the government were, however, no
less important causes. The principle of diffusion of responsibility, a
sine qua non of collective leadership, facilitated the exercise of
greater power on the part of the career foreign service officers in
foreign policy decision making.

Moreover, during this period professional diplomats had begun
to specialize in political, economic, cultural, and military aspects of
international relations and had begun to claim that the complexities
of international affairs in the 1960s necessitated greater reliance on
their expert knowledge. Then, too, they considered themselves,
quite correctly, the most modern segment of the bureaucratic elite.
They were recruited by their peers and superiors who took great
pains in selecting the best that the best modern schools in Turkey
could produce. They were schooled to accept secular and rational
ideas. They belonged to the category of "modern individuals," the
elite class. In the Ministry of Foreign Affairs they had been subjected to a solid in-service training in the art of diplomacy: They
had been taught the formalistic and legalistic prescriptions of traditional Ottoman diplomacy as well as the prerequisites of modern,
democratic diplomacy. No wonder then that the career officers,
as the elite of the Turkish bureaucratic establishment, felt that the
task of promoting the national security and modernization objectives of their country was their own responsibility.

The biographical data of 474 foreign service officers justify
their claim to elite status and their demand for a leading role in
matters of foreign affairs.[4] A brief account of the place of birth and
educational background of the career officers is as follows.

BIRTHPLACE. Of the 474 career officers, 191 were born in
Istanbul, 52 in Ankara and 19 in İzmir. Twenty-four officers were

---

[4] This information is derived from *Dışişleri Bakanlığı 1967 Yıllığı* compiled by Hamid Aral. The yearbook is based on the official files of each of the
career officers. For an extensive treatment of the backgrounds of these professional diplomats as well as the organizational development of the Ministry of
Foreign Affairs see Metin Tamkoç, "Traditional Diplomacy of Modern Turkish
Diplomats," *Dış Politika — Foreign Policy* (December 1971), pp. 81–100.

born in foreign countries, some in cities formerly part of the Ottoman Empire. Birthplaces of two career officers are not known. The rest were born in various provincial cities in Anatolia.

HIGH SCHOOL EDUCATION. A preponderant majority of career officers, 265 to be exact, are graduates of private and public high schools located in Istanbul. A total of 84 officers are graduates from Ankara high schools and 10 career officers were graduated from İzmir high schools. On the other hand, only 56 officers are graduates of other provincial high schools. Forty-seven career officers have listed foreign high schools as their alma maters. Data on 12 career officers are not available.

UNIVERSITY EDUCATION. Two hundred eighty-nine career officers have graduated from the Faculty of Political Sciences in Ankara. Until 1937 this Faculty was located in Istanbul. The Faculty of Law of the University of Istanbul ranks as the second most important institution in the preparation of students for service in the Ministry of Foreign Affairs. The breakdown of the number of graduates of different faculties and schools is as follows: Faculty of Political Sciences, 289; Istanbul Law School, 52; Ankara Law School, 48; Istanbul School of Economics and Commerce, 12; Istanbul Faculty of Economics, 8; Faculty of Administrative Sciences of Middle East Technical University in Ankara, 6; Ankara School of Commerce and Economics, 2; Ankara War College, 2; Istanbul Faculty of Letters, 1. Five career officers have not listed their alma maters. Some of the career officers, in addition to their university education in Turkey, graduated from foreign universities. Fifty-five officers hold degrees from foreign colleges and universities.

There are six career diplomats holding Master of Arts degrees from foreign universities. Thirteen diplomats have been awarded LL.D. or doctorate degrees by foreign graduate schools and two diplomats possess Ph.D. degrees awarded by British universities.

FOREIGN LANGUAGES. Of the 474 career officers, 134 list French as their second language. Eighty-eight officers identify English as their foreign language. There are 172 career officers who claim to know two foreign languages, mainly French and either English, German, Spanish, or Italian. Seventy-four career officers list English, German, and French, or French, English, and Italian as their foreign languages. There are also those who list French, English, and Arabic; French, English, and Spanish; French, English, and Russian; French, English, and Bulgarian; or French, English, and Japanese as their foreign languages. There are six career diplomats who list four foreign languages. One diplomat lists six foreign languages. There is no information about four career officers.

WOMEN IN FOREIGN SERVICE. In 1968 there were eleven women career foreign service officers. Eight of these are graduates of the Faculty of Political Sciences, the other three are graduates of Ankara Law School, Istanbul Law School, and Bryn Mawr College in the United States.

It is noteworthy that of the 474 career foreign service officers, over 55 per cent were educated in Istanbul high schools, and almost 90 per cent were graduates of the universities in Ankara and Istanbul, the cultural, educational, and administrative centers of Turkey. The remaining 10 per cent hold degrees from foreign universities. Close to 5 per cent hold advanced degrees from foreign graduate schools. It is also significant that 40 per cent of the career officers were educated in French-speaking high schools, such as Saint Joseph, Saint Michel, Saint Benoit, and Galatasaray in Istanbul. Among these, 14 per cent were graduates of both Saint Joseph and the Faculty of Political Sciences, and 38 per cent were graduates of both Galatasaray and the Faculty of Political Sciences. A typical career foreign service officer, therefore, can be said to be a graduate of a French-speaking high school in Istanbul and a graduate of the Faculty of Political Sciences.

The foreign service officers constitute the backbone of the Ministry of Foreign Affairs. The Ministry approximates the most diffracted bureaucratic establishment in the Turkish administration. The Ministry is essentially immune to domestic political pressures. Its day-to-day functions do not affect the daily interests of the general public. The officials of the Ministry, therefore, are immune to the corruptive influences which normally plague other public service officers. Their clients are their own counterparts in foreign diplomatic establishments with whom they have many things in common.

THE GRAND NATIONAL ASSEMBLY

Once a passive observer of Turkish foreign affairs, the Grand National Assembly since 1961 has begun to take a brisk role in foreign relations activities. The assembly halls and committee rooms of the Grand National Assembly have come to witness lively, and at times bitter, debates and discussions on foreign policy issues which were once discussed and handled only at the summit of political power, the presidential palace. Prime ministers, foreign ministers, and defense ministers have appeared before the plenary sessions of the Grand National Assembly and its committees to explain the position of the government on specific issues, to answer questions, and to witness heated debates. The records of the Grand National Assembly indicate that during the last ten years Ministers of Foreign Affairs have addressed the plenary sessions of the two houses of the Grand National Assembly no fewer than forty times.

Prior to 1961, there was much theoretical confusion with respect to the proper role of the Grand National Assembly concerning the "conclusion" of treaties.[5] That confusion appears to have been eliminated under the provisions of the 1961 Constitution. Under the present arrangement, the Grand National Assembly enacts legislation authorizing ratification of treaties by the president. Moreover, the authority to declare war as well as to send troops to foreign countries and to allow the stationing of foreign troops in Turkey is specifically given to the Grand National Assembly. The 1961 Constitution did not institute any special method of supervision and control of the conduct of foreign relations of Turkey by the Grand National Assembly. The assembly utilizes the general methods of supervision and control of the activities of the executive branch of the government in foreign affairs. These general methods include general debates, parliamentary investigations, inquiries, and interpellations. Debates on the draft budget bills or draft bills concerning the approval of treaties are also among the important means of supervision and control of the conduct of the Council of Ministers.[6]

The İnönü administration (1961–1965) had to contend with an unruly legislature that had succumbed to partisan quarrels.

---

[5] On this question see Edip F. Çelik, *Milletlerarası Hukuk* (Istanbul: Istanbul Üniversitesi Hukuk Fakültesi Yayını, no. 205, 1965), pp. 122–23; Edip F. Çelik, "1961 Anayasasının Milletlerarası Andlaşmalarla İlgili Hükümleri," *Istanbul Hukuk Fakültesi Mecmuası* 28 (1962): 335–48; Seha L. Meray, "Türk Anaysa Sisteminde Andlaşmaların Görüşülmesi," *Siyasal Bilgiler Fakültesi Dergisi,* 19 (1964); A. Suat Bilge, "İcra Anlaşmaları," *Siyasal Bilgiler Fakültesi Dergisi,* 12 (1957).

[6] See Soysal, *Dış Politika ve Parlamento,* pp. 210–37.

General debates on the programs of the İnönü coalition cabinets as well as general debates on the draft budget bills often gave rise to bitter attacks on Premier İnönü and his Council of Ministers, mainly for partisan considerations. The opposition Justice Party and Turkish Labor Party deputies launched an intensive campaign of bitter criticism against the Council of Ministers for what they called "its inept handling of the Cyprus issue" and for "its failure to protect Turkey's interests in Cyprus." Since 1965, the Ürgüplü and Demirel governments also encountered heated debates in the Grand National Assembly on their handling of foreign relations in general, and on their policies concerning the Cyprus issue and bilateral relations between Turkey and the United States in particular.

The following general debates may be cited as illustrations. Meeting in joint session on March 16, 1964, the two houses of the Grand National Assembly — the National Assembly and the Senate of the Republic — after acrimonious debate approved the request of the authorization of Premier İnönü to land troops in Cyprus if and when the government deemed it necessary. On May 5 and 6, 1964, the National Assembly reviewed the policy of the government concerning Cyprus and the Turco-Greek relations. The National Assembly met once again on June 15, 1964, to consider the latest developments on the Cyprus problem. During the debate Premier İnönü asked for a vote of confidence before his expected departure for Washington for talks with President Lyndon B. Johnson. The National Assembly, by a vote of 200 to 192, with two abstentions, approved İnönü's policy on Cyprus and on Turco-American relations.[7] But during the general debate on September 7 and 8, 1964, all the opposition deputies who took the floor bitterly criticized Premier İnönü for his passive and inept handling of the vital interests of Turkey in Cyprus. Two days later, similar criticisms were echoed in the Senate when it also debated the Cyprus problem. On June 15, 1965, the National Assembly held a secret session to review the Cyprus policy of Premier Ürgüplü. Premier Demirel's foreign policy and his policy on the Cyprus problem were subjected to strong criticism by the opposition deputies in the National Assembly from December 27 to 29, 1965. A few days later the Senate also debated the conduct of the Council of Ministers in foreign affairs.

---

[7] *Cumhuriyet,* 16 Haziran 1964, p. 1.

For almost two years, no general debate took place in the Grand National Assembly on the Cyprus question, during which time the government was conducting bilateral and multilateral negotiations with Greece and NATO Allies in hopes of finding a satisfactory solution to the dispute between Turkey, Greece, and the Greek administration in Cyprus. Yet, debates on the draft budget bills provided occasion for the opposition deputies to register their criticisms of the handling of the Cyprus problem.

Upon the renewal of the intercommunal strife in Cyprus on November 15, 1967, the Grand National Assembly was kept fully informed by the government on the critical developments. The next day, the two houses of the Grand National Assembly were called into joint secret session. In this executive session, which lasted over eighteen hours, it was reported that Premier Demirel had asked the Grand National Assembly to authorize the government to deploy troops in Cyprus. The assembly expressed its approval by a vote of 432 to 1 with 2 abstentions.[8]

Not only on the Cyprus question but also on Turkish-American relations, the main opposition party, the Republican People's Party, and the Turkish Labor Party which, since its establishment in 1961, had taken a strong anti-American stand, bitterly attacking the Ürgüplü and Demirel governments in the parliament. During nearly every budget debate since 1965, they demanded more information on the American bases in Turkey and called for the transfer of such defense installations to Turkish jurisdiction. The Defense Cooperation Agreement of 1969 between Turkey and the United States was also made the target of their acrimonious attacks.

In recent years the number of official visits made by the members of the Grand National Assembly to foreign countries increased appreciably. This fact may also be considered as an indication of the greater involvement of the deputies and senators in the foreign relations of Turkey. In this connection the following visits of officials may be cited. In May 1963, a parliamentary delegation headed by Senator S. H. Ürgüplü, the president of the Senate, went to the Soviet Union for a two-week visit. Another parliamentary delegation headed by Fuat Sirmen, the president of the National Assembly, visited West Germany during October 1963. With a view to soliciting the support of the neutral and nonaligned

---

[8] See *Dışişleri Bakanlığı Belleteni,* no. 38, Kasım 1967, p. 24.

countries in the Cyprus debate in the General Assembly of the United Nations between December 1964 and February 1965, a number of parliamentary delegations visited Middle Eastern countries, North Africa, countries of French Africa, Central and South America and the Far East. During July and August 1966, another parliamentary group headed by F. Bozbeyli, the president of the National Assembly, paid a visit to the Soviet Union. During the Summer and Fall of 1967, a delegation headed by the president of the Senate, Atasagun, visited Czechoslovakia, Yugoslavia, and Great Britain. In order to participate in the deliberations of the General Assembly on the Cyprus question, a delegation headed by E. Akça, the chairman of the Committee on Foreign Relations of the National Assembly, went to New York in November 1967. Other parliamentary groups visited Bulgaria and Poland in June 1968, Albania in September 1968, Lebanon in December 1968, Pakistan in January 1969, Hungary in June 1969, and South Korea and Formosa in June and July 1969. Between 1964 and 1969, the members of the Grand National Assembly also hosted parliamentary delegations from France, West Germany, Romania, the Soviet Union, Italy, Bulgaria, Poland, South Korea, Albania, and Czechoslovakia.

The new role of the Grand National Assembly in foreign affairs may be attributed to three interrelated developments: First, the liberalization of the domestic political system; second, the relaxation of international tension and the increase in East-West diplomatic, commercial, and cultural contacts; and third, the renewal of the intercommunal strife in Cyprus.

THE CYPRUS CONFLICT AND THE DIPLOMACY OF THE COLLECTIVE LEADERSHIP

THE 1960 STATUS QUO

The final arrangements concerning the establishment of an independent Cyprus Republic were made during the period from April 1959 to July 1960. A delegation headed by General Cemal Madanoğlu, a prominent member of the Committee of National Unity, was sent to Cyprus by the CNU to attend the ceremonies marking the proclamation of the Republic of Cyprus on August 16, 1960.[9]

The Constitution of the Republic of Cyprus provided for a very complex legal system and structure concerning the equal participation of the Greek majority and Turkish minority in the management of the affairs of the people of Cyprus. It not only guaranteed the rights of the Cypriot Turks in the government and administration of Cyprus but also gave Turkey the right to protect the interests of the Cypriot Turks.

As far as Turkey was concerned, the settlement of the Cyprus problem opened the way for the restoration of friendly relations with Greece. Foreign Minister Selim Sarper, visiting Athens in October 1960, declared: "I am glad to say that there are no important problems between us that overshadow our friendship based on strong foundations and common ideals.[10] On the other hand, the Greeks, both in Cyprus and in Greece, seemed to have serious reservations about the nature and scope of the settlement. They maintained that settlement was brought about as a result of outside intervention, namely, intervention on the part of Turkey, and as such was contrary to the will of the majority of the people of the island. They argued that since the Constitution had placed the Turkish minority on the same political level with the Greek majority, the organic law was not only unrealistic but also undemocratic. More-

---

[9] Three treaties negotiated and signed between Greece, Turkey, Great Britain and the representatives of the Greek and Turkish communities came into force on that date. The Treaty Concerning the Establishment of the Republic of Cyprus provided for consultation and cooperation in the common defense of Cyprus. Under the provisions of the Treaty of Guarantee "either the union of Cyprus with any other power or partition of the island" was specifically prohibited. Article IV of the Treaty of Guarantee stated that "In the event of a breach of the provisions of the present Treaty, Greece, Turkey and the United Kingdom undertake to consult together with respect to the representations or measures necessary to ensure observance of those provisions. In so far as common or concerted action may not prove possible, each of the three guaranteeing Powers reserves the right to take action with the sole aim of re-establishing the state of affairs created by the present Treaty." The third treaty established an alliance between Turkey, Greece, and Cyprus. These three treaties were to be considered as integral parts of the Constitution of the Republic of Cyprus. See Great Britain, Colonial Office, *Cyprus: Documents Relating to Independence of Cyprus and the Establishment of British Sovereign Base Areas,* Cmnd. 1093, July 1960.

[10] Quoted in *The Turkish Yearbook of International Relations* (TYIR) 1 (1960): 205.

over, according to the Greeks, the extensive veto powers granted to
the leadership of the Turkish minority in governmental affairs was
bound to create an impasse in decision-making processes. The most
objectionable feature of the Constitution and the international
agreements, however, was the prohibition of the union of Cyprus
with Greece.[11]

Although a separate international entity was created, the
Republic of Cyprus was not based on a separate and distinct Cypriot
nation. It was no more than a protectorate of Greece and Turkey;
these two powers had, in fact, established condominium over
Cyprus. As one observer put it: "Externally, power lay with the
Turkish state and not with the Greek state; internally power lay
with the Greek community and not with the Turkish community.
The power of the Greek community was limited by the power of
the Turkish state, the power of the Turkish state was limited by
forces which were not native to the area itself."[12]

From the standpoint of the Greek leadership in Cyprus, the
extensive and disproportionate rights and privileges of the Turkish
minority could not be tolerated for long. The "imposed settlement"
had to be revised in conformity with the interests of the Greek
majority. The political developments since 1961 leave no doubt as
to the determination of the Greek leadership to bring about the
union of the island with Greece — which is called *Enosis* — even
at the risk of a military confrontation limited to the Cyprus region
and falling short of a war between Greece and Turkey.

The Turkish leadership both in Cyprus and in Turkey, on the
other hand, favored the continuation of the status quo of 1960;
to agree to reach a new arrangement in an already acceptable situation might jeopardize Turkey's interests in Cyprus.

The nature and scope of the Turkish reactions to Greek
actions were determined by the Turkish leaders on the basis of their
perceptions concerning: (1) the nature of the political atmosphere
in the international arena; (2) the possible unilateral or joint
responses of the United States and the Soviet Union to the moves
contemplated by Turkey; (3) the strengths and weaknesses of the

---

[11] See Stanley Kyriakides, *Cyprus: Constitutionalism and Crisis Government,* p. 122.

[12] Peter Calvocoressi, *International Politics Since 1945* (New York:
Frederick A. Praeger, 1968), p. 209.

political regime in Greece; and (4) the nature of the threats posed by the Cypriot Greek community to Turkey's interests in Cyprus.

From the standpoint of the perceptions of the Turkish governmental leaders, the political developments both in Cyprus and in its environment seemed to fall into two distinct phases, each of which required a different set of reactions. The first phase covered the period from 1961 to 1968. During this phase the Turkish reactions entailed diplomatic negotiations, diplomatic pressures, and limited use of force or limited police actions. In the second phase, which began in July 1974, the Turkish reactions involved limited military operations undertaken by the Turkish armed forces.

PHASE ONE: DIPLOMATIC PRESSURES AND LIMITED POLICE ACTIONS

Throughout 1961 and 1962, the Greek and Turkish leaders in Cyprus found themselves in opposite corners on questions concerning the interpretation and application of the Constitution. They could not agree as to the adoption of financial laws, the employment of civil servants, the municipal partition in the main cities, and the integration of the troops of the army. With a view to finding satisfactory solutions to such issues, President Gürsel invited President Makarios to Ankara for high level talks.[13] Apparently, such a Summit Conference between the Turkish leaders and President Makarios and his advisers was to no avail. Exactly a year later, in November 1963, President Makarios submitted to the Turkish Vice President Dr. F. Küçük and to Turkey, Greece, and Britain a number of proposals for amending the basic provisions of the Constitution in order to make it what he considered a workable document.[14] The Turkish leaders, both in Cyprus and in Turkey, considered these proposals as essentially designed to take away the rights of the Turkish community and to abrogate the bicommunal character of the Republic of Cyprus. In his note of December 6, 1963, Premier İnönü informed President Makarios that Turkey vehemently opposed such a move and demanded the implementation of the Cyprus Constitution.[15]

---

[13] See *The Turkish Yearbook of International Relations* 3 (1962): 165.

[14] See *TYIR* 4 (1963): 330. See also A. Suat Bilge, "Le Conflit Cypriote," pp. 32–34.

[15] See *TYIR* 4 (1963): 330.

Nevertheless, as a sign of good will Premier İnönü instructed his foreign minister to meet with the foreign ministers of Greece and Cyprus in Paris in order to search for a solution to the constitutional crisis in Cyprus. The tripartite negotiations ended on December 20, 1963, without any concrete result apparently because by that time President Makarios, in view of the cabinet crisis in Ankara,[16] had thought that the only way to revise the undesirable status quo in Cyprus was to resort to violence against the Cypriot Turks, and that he could compel the weak government of Turkey to choose a new agreement with him so as to put an end to terrorist activities in the island.

Upon the commencement of intercommunal strife in Cyprus, Premier İnönü first appealed to Great Britain and Greece for joint efforts in restoring peace in Cyprus. Then, on December 25, he declared that Turkey would use her right of intervention under Article IV of the Treaty of Guarantee. Simultaneously, he let Makarios know that the continuation of terrorist activities against the Cypriot Turks might lead to dangerous consequences and that he might be compelled to permit the Turkish military to take the situation in hand. To make İnönü's warning credible, the Turkish government ordered a single flight of five jet fighters over the terror-stricken city of Nicosia. President Makarios did not feel threatened by such a Turkish reaction. He seemed to think that the Turkish government could not carry out its threat of invasion of Cyprus because of the apparent asymmetry between such a drastic move and the issue under contention. He seemed to have noted, too, the high cost of such an invasion, not only to the Greeks but to the Turkish government as well. It appears that the Turkish leaders were also aware of the ominous consequences of the invasion of Cyprus. They therefore limited their reactions to a show of force such as naval maneuvers in the vicinity of Cyprus, troop mobilization and concentration along the southern shores of Turkey, and deployment of jet fighters over the Cyprus air space. However, in order to intimidate President Makarios, the Turkish leaders resorted to methods of psychological pressure. For example they asked special authorization from the Grand National Assembly for

---

[16] The second coalition cabinet of Premier İnönü had resigned on December 2, 1963. The third coalition government could be formed by İnönü only on December 24, three days after the commencement of civil strife in Cyprus.

the landing of troops in Cyprus. When that authorization was granted on March 16, 1964,[17] it was given wide publicity in the press and radio. At the same time in order to force Greece to stop her active support of the Makarios regime, the Turkish government announced that it abrogated the Convention of Establishment, Commerce, and Navigation signed between Turkey and Greece in 1930. Later the Turkish government began to expel Greek citizens residing in Istanbul; it suspended the Agreement on Mutual Exemption of Visas of 1955, and abrogated the Trade and Payment Agreement of 1953. However, it did not go so far as to break diplomatic relations with Greek government. When the situation seemed to deteriorate in Cyprus, the Turkish air force was ordered to make rocket and machine gun assaults on the Greek Cypriot positions on August 8 and 9, 1964. Describing such air operations as limited police action, the Turkish government hastened to warn the Greeks that if their offensive campaigns were to continue the Turkish air force would undertake much more extensive air strikes.[18]

Meanwhile, the Turkish government kept the door open for a negotiated settlement of the crisis. Its objective was to try to convince the Makarios regime and the Greek government that if they really tried to implement the Constitution of Cyprus and strove to obtain the trust and cooperation of the Turkish minority in the island, that would bring about an atmosphere of peace in the island. Although a conference was convened in London on January 15, 1964, it ended in failure because of the uncompromising stands taken by the Turkish, Greek, and Greek Cypriot negotiators. For the next three years no direct diplomatic negotiations could be arranged between the disputants. Following the military coup d'état in Greece on April 21, 1967, the military junta initiated steps for a Summit Conference between the prime ministers of Turkey and Greece. Their first meeting took place at Keşan in Turkey near the Greek border on September 9, 1967; the next day the talks were continued at Alexandroupolis. In the final communiqué issued on September 10, Premier S. Demirel and Premier Constantin Kollias expressed their belief that in view of the partnership of the

---

[17] *TYIR* 5 (1964): 225.

[18] In this connection George S. Harris maintains that such air operations were similar to the U.S. retaliation after the Tonkin Gulf incident in Viet Nam and were "designed to demonstrate that the United States had not deprived Turkey of its ability to take military action." *Troubled Alliance*, p. 118.

two countries in NATO it was essential to strengthen the bonds of cooperation and good neighborliness between the two countries. They also promised to take the necessary measures to facilitate those efforts designed to bring about a peaceful solution to the Cyprus conflict. They noted that they shared the view that all agreements between the two countries ought to be faithfully implemented.[19] As far as the Turkish government was concerned, this last point was an unqualified reiteration of the validity of the agreements concerning the status quo of Cyprus as well as the continued validity of the Constitution of Cyprus. It was hoped that further negotiations between Turkey, Greece, and Cyprus would lead to a mutually satisfactory settlement of the conflict.

Yet, only two months later, the cooperative and friendly spirit of the Summit Conference gave way to the fears of a direct military confrontation between Greece and Turkey on account of the renewal of intercommunal strife in Cyprus. On November 15, the military-civilian leadership of Turkey held an emergency meeting to review the critical situation in Cyprus. At the same time all armed forces were put on alert status. The next morning, still continuing its emergency meeting, the Council of Ministers issued a statement which declared that Turkey had decided to intervene in Cyprus militarily and that the Council of Ministers had called the parliament into an emergency session in order to obtain the necessary legislative authorization for that move. Meeting that afternoon, the Grand National Assembly deliberated the situation in Cyprus until the next morning and in the end approved the decision of the Council of Ministers. By this time, all commercial airports were closed to traffic and paratroopers were readied to embark on the transport planes. The troops along the border of Greece and along the southern shores of Turkey, as well as the naval and air force units, were placed in a state of readiness.[20]

On November 17, in its note to the Greek government the military-civilian leadership demanded the withdrawal of all the regular Greek troops that had been clandestinely sent to Cyprus and the removal of General George Grivas, the former guerrilla leader, from the island. Meeting on November 22, the Council of

---

[19] See *Dışişleri Bakanlığı Belleteni,* Eylül 1967, no. 30, pp. 40–41.

[20] See *Cumhuriyet,* 16–17 Kasım 1967; *Hürriyet,* 8–12, 15–17 Ocak 1968; *Dışişleri Bakanlığı Belleteni,* Kasım 1967, no. 38, pp. 22–52.

SATICI — Kaydi Kıbrıs çıkartmaları . . . Tanesi 25 kuruş . . . Denizi mavi, adası yeşil, renkli Kıbrıs çıkartmaları . . . Okul defterlerine, duvarlara, pencere camına ve de bilumum düz satıhlara hafifçe suda ıslatıp yapıştırdıktan sonra üstteki kâğıdı yavaşça çe kince Kıbrıs haritası defterinize veya pencerenize çıkıp evinizi şenlendirir ve de çocukları sevindirir . . . Haydi, Kıbrıs çıkartmaları.

VENDOR — Come and get it . . . Cyprus decals . . . 25 kuruş. . . . Its surrounding waters are blue, its island is green, colorful Cyprus decals . . . All you have to do is to soak these decals in water for a few seconds and then apply them face down on school notebooks, on walls, on windowpanes, and on all sorts of nonporous surfaces and when you pull the back cover slowly and carefully you will have the map of Cyprus on your school notebook or on your windowpane which will brighten your home and also will make your children happy . . . Come and get it, come and get it, Cyprus decals. . . . (Explanatory note: The words "decal" and "amphibious landing" are synonymous in Turkish. Cartoonist Ali Ulvi uses the word *Çıkartma* metaphorically. The man on the extreme left of the cartoon is meant to represent Prime Minister Süleyman Demirel. This cartoon appeared in *Cumhuriyet* newspaper during the very tense days of the Cyprus crisis on November 26, 1967, at which time the Turkish troops were readied for an amphibious landing on the island of Cyprus.)

Ministers and the military leaders reviewed the highly tense situation and considered the reply of the Greek government. At the end of the meeting they declared that as long as the threat to the security of the Cypriot Turks persisted, there would be no room for bilateral talks as requested by the Greek government. The same day a public demonstration in Istanbul, attended by some 100,000 people, which was given wide coverage in news bulletins, demanded the landing of troops in Cyprus and called for "war in the cause of peace." The statement of the Chief of the General Staff, General Cemal Tural, that the armed forces "had completed all preparations for a landing"[21] was a calculated warning. On November 23, it was announced that President Sunay had sent messages to the heads of government of the United States, the Soviet Union, Great Britain, France, and the Middle Eastern powers in which, it was said, he had reiterated the determination of Turkey to protect her legitimate rights, by force if necessary, and that Turkey would not assume any responsibility for the consequences of her actions.[22] This announcement was no doubt designed to reinforce the credibility of Turkey's threat of the invasion of Cyprus.

The general public was expecting an official announcement at any moment concerning the commencement of war with Greece. At the time, however, intense diplomatic negotiations were being conducted through the third-party mediators. Newspapers began to describe the situation as "one minute till twelve o'clock!" The clock never struck twelve, however; diplomatic negotiations had succeeded! Premier Demirel announced on November 30 that war had been averted. The Greek government had acceded to the demands of Turkey concerning the validity of the treaties of August 1960, the withdrawal of the regular Greek troops from Cyprus, the guaranteeing of the security of the Cypriot Turks, and the territorial integrity and independence of the Republic of Cyprus, that is, in brief, the restoration of the status quo of 1960 in the island.[23]

The November 1967 crisis, however, led to further division of Cyprus — to the physical isolation of the Turkish community. On December 29, the Turkish Cypriot leaders established what they called "The Provisional Turkish Administration" headed by Dr. F. Küçük, the vice president of the Republic of Cyprus, to be responsible for the affairs of the Cypriot Turks until such time as the full implementation of the Constitution of Cyprus.[24]

APPEALS TO FRIENDLY POWERS AND TO WORLD PUBLIC OPINION. In addition to their firm stand against the union of Cyprus

[21] *Cumhuriyet,* 23 Kasım 1967.
[22] Ibid., 24 Kasım 1967.
[23] See *Dışişleri Bakanlığı Belleteni,* Kasım 1967, no. 38, p. 52.
[24] For the details of this arrangement see Ibid., Aralık 1967, no. 39, pp. 78–79.

with Greece, the Turkish leaders engaged in an intensive campaign of propaganda designed to induce friendly foreign powers to adopt policies favorable to the Turkish point of view. For example, President Gürsel's message to heads of states of the Allied Powers stated in part: "I wish to bring to your attention these dastardly acts of massacre [of December 1963] undertaken against the Turks in Cyprus in this Twentieth Century when human rights and freedoms are enshrined in the most solemn universal documents and ask you most earnestly to do all in your power in order that this bloodshed be stopped forthwith. . . ."[25] On January 1, 1964, the Turkish government appealed to the Council of Europe to send a committee to Cyprus to study the recent events. A few days later, Premier İnönü sent messages to the heads of government of friendly powers in which he gave an account of the acts of terrorism in Cyprus and asked for their support in restoring peace and the rule of law in the island.[26] Similar appeals were made to the Council of Ministers of NATO, the Central Treaty Organization and to the Security Council of the United Nations.

On August 19, 1964, Premier İnönü sent messages to more than 100 foreign governments explaining Turkey's views on the latest developments in Cyprus and the legal grounds upon which air operations of the Turkish air force were based. Prior to and after every recourse to forceful measures, the Turkish government sent explanatory messages to friendly powers justifying such acts under the provisions of international agreements concerning Cyprus and under the principles of international law.

One such communication deserves particular mention. When the American ambassador was informed during the first days of June 1964 that Turkey was about to invade Cyprus, President Johnson chose to send a letter to Premier İnönü on June 5 which caused great consternation and resentment in Turkey toward the United States. President Johnson said in effect that since not all the avenues of consultation between the guarantors had been exhausted it could not be said that Turkey possessed the right of unilateral intervention; that the membership in NATO precluded the possibility of war between its members; that in the event of a

---

[25] For the text of this message see *Cyprus: Past/Present/Future* (Ankara: Ajans-Türk Matbaası, 1964), p. 5.

[26] Ibid., pp. 6–8.

Soviet retaliation against Turkey NATO Allies may not feel obliged to go to Turkey's assistance; and that arms supplied to Turkey by the United States could not be used in the invasion of Cyprus. President Johnson then added: "I must therefore inform you in the deepest friendship that unless I can have your assurance that you will not take such action without further and fullest consultation, I cannot accept your injunction to Ambassador Hare of secrecy and must immediately ask for emergency meeting of the NATO Council and of the United Nations Security Council." President Johnson then asked Premier İnönü to come to Washington for talks, requesting that he postpone all his decisions until that time.[27] The Council of Ministers, including the military leaders, met on June 10 to discuss the contents of the reply to be sent to President Johnson by Premier İnönü. İnönü's message made crystal clear the sense of disillusionment Turkey felt toward the United States' lack of understanding of and support for the rightful cause of the Turkish government. At the outset, İnönü informed Johnson that "we have, upon your request, postponed our decision to exercise our right of unilateral action in Cyprus conferred to us by the Treaty of Guarantee." Then, İnönü expressed his disappointment in these words: "The contents as well as the tone of your message has been most disappointing for your ally Turkey. It has also brought to light important differences of views on matters relating to the alliance ties between our countries." İnönü maintained that since the beginning of the Cyprus conflict Turkey had, on four occasions, felt the need to intervene in Cyprus and on each of these instances, she had informed the United States, who had each time asked her to postpone her action. İnönü refuted Johnson's claim that Turkey had not entered into consultation with the interested parties prior to deciding upon unilateral intervention. He went on to assure Johnson that in the event Turkey was compelled to dispatch troops to Cyprus, such an action would be undertaken in accordance with the objectives and provisions of international agreements. He argued that if war were to commence between Turkey and Greece, it could only come about as a result of an attack by Greece upon Turkey, in which case Greece would have to assume the responsibilities arising from such an attack. In reference to the consequences

---

[27] The text of President Johnson's letter is in *Middle East Journal,* 20 (Summer 1966): 386–88.

of an act of aggression against Turkey by the Soviet Union, Premier İnönü expressed the view that under such circumstances NATO members would be obliged to render assistance automatically. He maintained that in such an eventuality only the nature and amount of assistance would be left to the discretion of each NATO member. He argued that if the NATO countries were to engage in prolonged discussions as to who was at fault and as to whether the victim of aggression needed to be helped, such course of action would be contrary to the nature of the alliance and it would render NATO totally devoid of its original meaning. The only point on which İnönü could agree with President Johnson was the need to have face-to-face talks between the two leaders.[28]

With a view to gaining the support of the neutral and non-aligned nations, the Turkish leaders toward the end of 1964 broadened and intensified their propaganda campaigns. They decided to send good-will missions composed of senators and deputies of the Grand National Assembly, prominent intellectuals such as professors, writers, and newspapermen, to Afro-Asian-Latin American countries. These delegations were given the task of explaining Turkish views on the Cyprus conflict to their hosts and seeking their support in the General Assembly of the United Nations. This was an unprecedented move in the annals of recent Turkish foreign relations. Yet, it appears that such good-will missions have failed to bring about a favorable response in the neutral and nonaligned countries' official circles toward the Turkish viewpoint. On December 18, 1965, the UN General Assembly voted for a draft resolution by 57 votes for, 5 against, and 54 abstentions, urging all states to refrain from intervention in Cyprus.[29] That resolution in the final analysis amounted to disregarding the validity of international agreements and denying Turkey her right to protect her interests in Cyprus.

This was another source of bitter disappointment for Turkey. Foreign Minister Çağlayangil, in an attempt to soothe the public reaction against the General Assembly resolution, described it as "a still-born resolution devoid of all moral value, incapable of changing the course of Turkey's policy on Cyprus."[30] Nevertheless, anti-

---

[28] The Turkish text of these letters is in *Dışişleri Bakanlığı Belleteni*, Ocak 1966, no. 16, pp. 100–110.

[29] See *TYIR* 4 (1965): 264–65.

[30] Quoted in Ibid., p. 265.

United Nations feeling among the intellectual circles, as well as among the general public, reached its highest peak. The "biased" report of the UN mediator Plaza,[31] coupled with the incapability of the UN Peace-Keeping Force to protect the legitimate rights of the Cypriot Turks, led to the condemnation of the world organization. At the time, in order to express their indignation against the United Nations, Korean War veterans began a campaign of returning their UN service decorations to the secretary general. But, pragmatic considerations of the Turkish leaders prevailed over their emotional reactions, and they continued to cooperate with the United Nations in the restoration of peace and order in Cyprus.

EFFORTS OF MEDIATION. The Turkish leaders were amenable to the suggestion of their allies that the Cyprus conflict be resolved through peaceful procedures. Their only condition, however, was that the 1960 agreements be considered valid and provide the basis for such peaceful methods. Thus, following the failure of the London Conference, Premier İnönü accepted the joint U.S.-U.K. proposal of January 31, 1964, concerning the establishment of a peace-keeping force to be composed of troops from NATO countries. He also welcomed the mediation efforts of George W. Ball, the undersecretary of state, who was sent by President Johnson in February 1964. Despite their misgivings over the efficacy of the UN Security Council's intervention in the matter, the Turkish leaders accepted the resolution of March 4, 1964, which created the UN Peace-Keeping Force and which called for the appointment of a mediator by the secretary general.[32]

Then, Premier İnönü and Foreign Minister Erkin went to Washington for talks with President Johnson and Secretary of State Rusk. Continuing his high-level talks, İnönü met with the UN Secretary General U Thant in New York. He then flew to London and Paris for consultation with the British and French leaders. It appears that at the end of these talks, Premier İnönü reached the conclusion that the only way to protect his country's interests

---

[31] See the statement of the Turkish Ambassador at the United Nations Ibid., p. 260.

[32] See U.N. Security Council, The Cyprus Question, Resolution 186 (1964) [S/5575], March 4, 1964, in Security Council, Official Records, Nineteenth Year, Resolutions and Decisions (S.IN.F/19/Rev. 1), pp. 2–4.

in Cyprus was to apply pressure and limited military force against the Greek administration in Cyprus.[33]

Yet when the Turkish government used limited force, i.e., air strikes against the Greek positions in Cyprus in August 1964, the reaction of Turkey's allies and the Soviet Union was immediate and in a way threatening. The Security Council, meeting in an emergency session, called upon the parties to the dispute to undertake an immediate ceasefire. In his reply, Premier İnönü informed the Security Council that the Greek Cypriots were engaging in large-scale aggressions and declared that the UN Peace-Keeping Force had become "totally incapable of performing its functions." However, he said that in order to reconfirm Turkey's respect for the United Nations, his government had decided to stop the actions of the Turkish air force over Cyprus.[34] The secretary general of NATO asked Turkey to avoid a possible military confrontation with Greece. Soviet Premier N. S. Khrushchev called the air strikes "piracy" and "aggression" and demanded their immediate termination.[35] In his reply to Khrushchev, Premier İnönü called upon him to use his influence on the Greek leaders to keep faith in international law, in human rights, in moral principles, and to serve the cause of peace.[36]

Prior to the air attacks of August 8 and 9, 1964, upon the invitation of the UN mediator, Sakari Iuomioja, the representatives of Turkey, Greece, the United States, and Great Britain had been conducting exploratory talks in Geneva. The U.S. representative Dean Acheson's plan calling for "the union of Cyprus with Greece in exchange for cession of the tiny island of Castellarizon to Turkey, a Turkish military base in Cyprus, and compensation for those Turkish Cypriots who wished to emigrate to Turkey"[37] was accepted by Turkey as a basis for discussion.[38] However, this plan

---

[33] See İnönü's statement in the Grand National Assembly, T.B.M.M. Millet Meclisi, *Tutanak Dergisi*, 1964, Dönem 1, Cilt 32, pp. 274–80, 386–91; Cumhuriyet Senatosu, *Tutanak Dergisi*, 1964, Cilt 21, pp. 575–82; see also Metin Toker, "Bir Seyahatin Bilançosu," *Akis*, 3 Temmuz 1964.

[34] *TYIR*, 4 (1964): 226.

[35] Ibid.

[36] Ibid., p. 227.

[37] George S. Harris, *Troubled Alliance*, p. 117.

[38] Váli, *Bridge Across the Bosporus*, p. 256.

was rejected by Greece and the Geneva negotiation remained inconclusive. The UN mediator Galo Plaza's mission came to an abrupt end when the Turkish government found his report of March 26, 1965, totally unacceptable because of his questioning the validity of the international agreements of 1960.[39]

During the crisis of November and December 1967, the president of the United States dispatched Cyrus Vance as his special representative to Ankara on November 23 in order to avert a possible war between Turkey and Greece. Cyrus Vance was followed by the special representative of the UN secretary general, Jose Rolz-Bennet, and by NATO secretary general Manlio Brosio. For the next six days all attention was focused on the activities of these three mediators, especially those of Mr. Vance. Shuttling between Ankara, Athens, and Nicosia, they were able to prevent an imminent war. The Turkish Council of Ministers, presided over by President Sunay and attended by the Chief of the General Staff as well as by the service chiefs, remained in almost continuous session reviewing the latest diplomatic and military developments and considering proposals that were carried by Cyrus Vance between Ankara, Athens, and Nicosia. The compromise solution worked out by Mr. Vance was, however, considered by the Turkish leaders as provisional, designed to ameliorate the situation in the island. They maintained that that solution would not affect the final disposition of the Cyprus question and neither would it affect the validity of the existing international agreements concerning Cyprus.[40]

At this point some general observations seem to be in order. Since the beginning of the internal strife in Cyprus in December 1963, the Turkish leaders were subjected to pressure from both directions: The opposition parties, the military establishment, and the general public were demanding military intervention in Cyprus and definitive settlement of the Cyprus question; the United States and the Soviet Union were trying to prevent such an eventuality. The Turkish leaders were aware of the nature and scope of the internal and external constraints over their freedom of action. They knew that in spite of the military superiority of Turkey over Greece,

---

[39] Text of the Report in U.N. Security Council, *Report of the United Nations Mediator on Cyprus to the Secretary General,* S/6253, March 26, 1965.

[40] See Premier Demirel's note of December 3, to the U.N. Secretary General, *Dışişleri Bakanlığı Belleteni,* Aralık 1967, no. 39, p. 11.

a military victory over the Greeks was a virtual impossibility simply because the cost of such a military victory was too high.

Although at various times since 1954 the Turkish leaders have demanded the unification of Cyprus with Turkey, the partition of the island, or the establishment of a federal system of government in Cyprus, it may be said that such demands were made for the purpose of offsetting the excessive claims of the Greeks and/or placating the public opinion in Turkey. Ever since December 1963, their objective was the restoration of the status quo of 1960 in Cyprus and not the annexation of the island.

The diplomacy of the military-civilian leadership was marked by great reliance upon persuasive techniques which included: (1) laying strong emphasis on the principle of the sanctity of international agreements; (2) appealing to the principles of human rights, to reason, and to a sense of justice and fairness; (3) soliciting favorable response from world public opinion; and (4) expressing willingness to negotiate their differences of views with their opponents. Only when these techniques proved inadequate did the Turkish leaders resort to threats of force and limited use of physical force and then left the doors open for negotiations.

The Turkish leaders took judicious care to avoid pushing their opponents into a corner and thus making future accommodation of differences with Greece impossible. They also avoided placing Turkey in a position where she could not maneuver. While they continued to issue warnings, on only two occasions were air strikes actually carried out against the Cypriot Greek positions. These air operations were probably ordered to give credibility to their threats. It may, therefore, be said that the reactions of the Turkish leaders to the actions of the Greeks were proportionate to their limited objective, — restoring the status quo in Cyprus.

PHASE TWO: LIMITED USE OF MILITARY FORCE

As the second and most critical phase of the Cyprus conflict opened in July 1974, the Turkish leadership was to act much more quickly and decisively in order to prevent the fait accompli in Cyprus, that is, the union of Cyprus with Greece. Turkish leaders' assessment of the fundamental features of the foreign policy objectives and capabilities of the super powers, the foreign policy objectives and capabilities of Greece, and the capabilities of the global and regional security systems had led to the conclusion that Turkey could afford limited use of military force against her opponents.

As the Turkish leadership saw, détente had become an operational policy of the United States and the Soviet Union in the 1970s. The Arab-Israeli War of October 1973 had been the latest, and perhaps the most clear, demonstration of the new policy of "negotiation" rather than "confrontation" between the two super powers. From the start of the "October War," both sides had maintained constant contact. Instead of undertaking unilateral action, which no doubt would have aggravated the situation in the Middle East, both sides had strived and succeeded in achieving a ceasefire between the Arabs and Israelis and had arranged the disengagement of the opposing forces on the basis of reciprocal concessions from their respective clients. By the middle of 1974, the political climate in the world was much more relaxed than ever before.

At the begining of 1973, Greece had been under the iron grip of a military regime, and toward the end of the year it had come under the rule of yet another military junta. Colonel Georgios Papadopoulos, who had engineered the military coup d'état in 1967, had staged another coup on June 1, 1973, with a view to abolishing the monarchy and establishing a republic under his presidency. And yet a few months later, on November 25, Papadopoulos himself was overthrown in an army coup and was replaced by General Phaidon Gizikis. The domestic economic and political conditions in Greece further deteriorated under the Gizikis administration causing widespread violent demonstrations and riots. The Turkish leaders sensed that in order for the military junta to remain in power in Greece it had to accomplish a spectacular feat. The union of Cyprus with Greece would be just such a feat!

The situation in Cyprus was no better than the situation in Greece. The Greek community had been ripped apart for some time by the violent clashes between those supporting the cause of *Enosis* under the leadership of General George Grivas and those following the leadership of Archbishop Makarios. The latter, "while occasionally offering lip service to the sentiment for Enosis . . . invariably preferred in practice to be the biggest fish in the small pond of an independent Cyprus."[41] Although Makarios had been elected president for a third five-year term in February 1973 by the Greek community he was not sure that he could serve for that long in the face of violent opposition against his administration. A number of attempts had been made by the supporters of Grivas to assassinate Makarios.

Since November 1967 the Turkish Cypriot leadership had been excluded from the administration of the island. The talks between the Turkish and Greek leaders had been going on intermittently since 1968 but without any concrete result. These talks, by the middle of July 1974, were at an impasse.

From the standpoint of the Greek military junta, the chain of events in the Cyprus adventure had all the elements of a Greek tragedy. Originally conceived as a one-act play confined to a single setting, Cyprus, and involving the ouster of a petty tyrant, Archbishop Makarios, the drama was soon enlarged to include other major powers and reached its climax in the ignominious fall of the instigators of the plot and the widespread death and destruction on the tiny island that even the most peripatetic *deus ex machina* could not prevent. Here is a synopsis of the plot as it actually took place.

On July 15, the Greek National Guard and the battalion of regular Greek soldiers based in Cyprus, on orders from the military junta in Athens, marched on the presidential palace to get Makarios out. They were unable to get their would-be victim. Makarios escaped with his life and went into exile. Nicholas G. Sampson, a former guerrilla gunman and an unrelenting supporter of *Enosis*, was quickly installed as president. Appearing before the UN Security Council in New York, Makarios charged that "the Greek junta has extended its dictatorship to Cyprus"[42] and appealed to the United Nations to reinstate his government.

Hearing of the coup in Cyprus, Turkish Premier Bülent Ecevit rushed to London for consultations with the British leaders, urging them to take joint action against the Sampson administration. The U.S. Undersecretary of State Joseph J. Sisco joined the talks and recommended moderation in reacting to the developments in

---

[41] Robert W. Komer, "Partitioning Cyprus," *The Washington Post,* August 14, 1974, p. C 6.

[42] *Newsweek,* July 29, 1974, p. 44.

Cyprus. Premier Ecevit called for the removal of Sampson, the withdrawal of the 650 Greek officers commanding the Cypriot National Guard, and the guaranteed independence of Cyprus as his minimum conditions. The intense diplomatic negotiations in London, at the UN Security Council, and in Ankara and Athens between July 15 and July 20 sought to help to restore the status quo ante and to avert war between NATO partners Greece and Turkey.

When the diplomatic negotiations appeared to have failed in satisfying Turkey's demands, the Turkish government ordered her troops to land on Cyprus. On July 20, a task force of 6,000 men landed on the northern coast, seized a wide beachhead in Kyrenia, and pushed inland toward Nicosia. The Turkish government maintained that this move was consistent with the Treaty of Guarantee of 1960. Apparently, the initial actions of the Turkish forces were limited to the objective of compelling the Greek leadership to recognize the urgent need to help restore the status quo and at the same time to protect the Turkish community against the Cypriot National Guard.[43] Once the invasion was an accomplished fact, the Turkish government accepted the ceasefire resolution of the UN Security Council on July 20.

In the aftermath of the Turkish move, the head of the rebel government, Sampson, resigned and was replaced by Glafkos Clerides, an ally of Makarios. This was followed by the fall of the military junta in Greece. The former prime minister of Greece, Constantine Karamanlis, returned from his self exile in Paris and was sworn in as the head of a new civilian government. In a warmly worded message of congratulations to Karamanlis, Premier Ecevit urged that the two allies in NATO bury the bitter memories of the past and help to restore close cooperation and friendly relations between the two countries.[44]

Responding to the calls of the United States and Britain, the Turkish and Greek as well as the British foreign ministers met in Geneva on July 25, and after five days of heated negotiations reached a ceasefire agreement which also called for further talks

---

[43] See the text of the Turkish communiqué, *New York Times,* 21 July 1974, p. 20.

[44] Ibid., 25 July 1974, p. 13.

to begin on August 8, for securing the restoration of peace in the region and re-establishing the constitutional government in Cyprus.[45]

The second round of talks in Geneva collapsed on August 14 over the issue of separate enclaves for Turkish Cypriots. The next day, the second phase of the Turkish military operations was commenced. By the end of August 16, the Turkish forces had sliced off the northeastern third of Cyprus for an autonomous Turkish region. The aim of this second military move was to obtain militarily what the Turkish foreign minister had been unable to get at the conference table in Geneva.

In Athens, Premier Karamanlis declared that an "armed confrontation" by Greece was "impossible due to distance as well as the known accomplished fact"[46] — an apparent reference to the conceded military superiority of the Turkish position, both in Cyprus and on the mainland. Thus, a Greco-Turkish war was averted. However, when the Turkish government called for the resumption of talks at Geneva, Premier Karamanlis fired back by saying: "It would be naive for anyone to believe that Greece would be prepared to take part in negotiations under the pressure of accomplished facts."[47] He also announced the withdrawal of the Greek forces from NATO command. And Karamanlis turned down an invitation from newly-installed President Gerald R. Ford to discuss the situation in Washington.

The prevailing détente between the two super powers, the relaxed political atmosphere in the world, the internal political crises in Greece and within the Greek community in Cyprus, plus the pro-*Enosis* coup in Cyprus, which immediately received worldwide condemnation, provided the collective leadership of Turkey with an unprecedented opportunity to act decisively so as to create a much desired balance of power situation in Cyprus between the Turkish minority and the Greek majority. The limited use of military force was designed to achieve a better bargaining position for Turkey, as well as to protect the Cypriot Turkish minority. It became clear that the Turkish leaders were unwilling to resort to extensive and

---

[45] The text of Declaration on Cyprus by Britain, Greece, and Turkey, Ibid., 31 July 1974, p. 3.

[46] *New York Times,* 16 August 1974, p. 1.

[47] Ibid., 17 August 1974, p. 1.

decisive military campaign of conquest. Following the initial landing of troops on Cyprus, they had hoped that such a show of force
would speed up serious diplomatic negotiations with Greece over
the underlying issues in the Cyprus conflict. They were aware of
the fact that the fundamental issues were political and could only
be settled on the basis of mutual concessions, and that further esca-
lation of fighting would outweigh the prospective profits. This is
probably why in the second phase of the military operations the
Turkish troops were ordered to take over the control of certain
areas which might be used in future diplomatic bargaining.

Although the Turkish leaders seemed to have "decided to
move first and talk later,"[48] their actions were again proportionate
to their limited objective of guaranteeing the legitimate rights of the
Turkish minority in an independent Cyprus Republic. It appears
that they also knew *where and when to stop the use of limited
military force.*

THE IMPACT OF THE CYPRUS CONFLICT ON THE FOREIGN POLICY ORIENTATION OF TURKEY

A number of foreign affairs specialists have argued that the
1961–1968 phase of the Cyprus conflict has brought about a change
in the foreign policy orientation of Turkey. They have pointed out
the following as clear indications of Turkey's new orientation:
Normalization of cultural, economic, and diplomatic relations with
the communist bloc countries; greater sympathy for and moral
support of the struggle of independence of ex-colonial countries;
greater understanding of the policies of the neutral and nonaligned
nations and greater cooperation with the Arab-Afro-Asian countries;
and wide differences of views with NATO allies on a number of
economic, political, and military issues.[49] There were those who

---

48 This is the observation of the former U.S. ambassador to Turkey,
Robert W. Komer, in his article "Partitioning Cyprus." On the other hand,
Premier Ecevit is quoted as saying: "The Turkish Government did not resort
to armed action before all other means were tried, but to no avail." See Ümit
Haluk Bayülken, "The Cyprus Question and the United Nations," *Cyprus,*
special issue, *Dış Politika — Foreign Policy* (1974), p. 120.

49 See Mehmet Gönlübol, Haluk Ülman, "İkinci Dünya Savaşından Sonra
Türk Dış Politikası," *Olaylarla Türk Dış Politikası, 1919–1965* (Ankara:
Dışişleri Bakanlığı Matbaası, 1968), pp. 287–88.

even suggested that Turkey in the 1960s turned her back on the West and began to pursue a neutral foreign policy.[50] Ahmet Şükrü Esmer, a leading foreign affairs specialist, expressed the view that "the first awakening began with the commencement of the Cyprus conflict." And he attributed such an awakening to one incident. Esmer said: "President Johnson's letter, written in bad taste and form to Prime Minister İnönü and his threatening Turkey with the possibility of Soviet retaliation has compelled Turkey to revise her foreign policy orientation."[51] Among others, political commentator Nadir Nadi concurred in this view.[52] Similarly, Ferenc A. Váli argued that after President Johnson's undiplomatic and unwise letter to İnönü, the Turkish leaders began "the search for a new orientation."[53]

In these assertions one can detect: A certain tendency to view such a complex issue as the Cyprus conflict as if it had occurred in a vacuum; a certain tendency to overestimate the importance of the Cyprus question in the actual list of national priorities of Turkey; and a tendency to belittle the capabilities of the Turkish warrior diplomats to protect and promote the vital national interests of their country. The nature and extent of the impact of the Cyprus conflict on the foreign policy orientation of Turkey can best be assessed and understood if that conflict is viewed within its proper contexts, that is, the international and domestic political systems and structures and the forces at work in those arenas and if the pragmatism of the Turkish warrior diplomats is kept in mind.

It is important to remember that the Cyprus conflict erupted at a time when the international system and structure was undergoing dramatic changes. These changes were due to the emergence of parity in nuclear weapons and their delivery systems between the United States and the Soviet Union, to the revolution in ideologies, and to the resurgence of nationalism throughout the world.

During the 1960s, feeling less menaced and threatened by the Soviet Union, the leaders of Greece and President Makarios of Cyprus felt free to concentrate on their own immediate parochial interests. They thought that the political conditions in the region

[50] See A. Haluk Ülman and R. H. Dekmejian, "Changing Patterns in Turkish Foreign Policy, 1959–1967," *Orbis*, 11 (Fall 1967): 780–81.

[51] *Ulus*, 27 Temmuz 1967.

[52] *Cumhuriyet*, 11 Şubat 1969.

[53] Váli, *Bridge Across the Bosporus*, p. 131.

were propitious for revising "the undesirable status quo" in Cyprus. Similarly, since the fear of Soviet aggression seemed to have receded considerably, the focus of attention of the Turkish leaders as well as the intelligentsia was diverted to the developments in Cyprus. Acts of violence perpetrated against the Cypriot Turks caused great resentment bordering hostility against the Greeks. The Turkish leaders also felt free to apply pressure on the Greeks so as to prevent the union of the island with Greece and to restore law and order in Cyprus.

But once the conflict seemed to reach dangerous proportions, the United States, the NATO allies, and the Soviet Union moved in swiftly to prevent a catalytic war between Greece and Turkey. The developments in the Cyprus conflict in the 1960s were, to a great extent, regulated and controlled by the two super powers. The international system and structure have had a direct impact on the actions and reactions of the parties directly involved.

Admittedly, in the 1960s, the Cyprus conflict helped to open the debate in Turkey over the issues of foreign policy and their domestic consequences. Inasmuch as the allies of Turkey in NATO had declined to support the legitimate interests and rights of Turkey in Cyprus, the opposition parties and press, quite understandably, began to debate the advantages and disadvantages of close ties with the West. They, in fact, identified the United States as the friend of the Cypriot Greeks.[54] The Turkish public began to weigh "a nation's friendship and animosity towards Turkey by its stand over the Cyprus question."[55] Thus, by the middle of 1965, the Cyprus question had become a national issue with definite emotional overtones.

The newly-formed leftist groups and the Turkish Labor Party capitalized on the rising anti-American sentiments of the intelligentsia for their own political ends, accusing the government of timidity in its dealing with the United States on this national issue.

---

[54] For example see "Durum: Türk-Amerikan Münasebetlerinde Dönüm Noktası," *Milliyet,* 10 Haziran 1964; Metin Toker, "Aptal Dostu Olmaktansa . . ." *Akis,* 12 Haziran 1964, p. 7; Çetin Altan, "Paşa ve Durmuş Ağa," *Milliyet,* 28 Agustos 1964. In this connection George S. Harris writes: "It was commonly assumed by Turks at large that the United States was at heart in the Greek camp; some of the more extreme critics even affected to believe that Washington would stop at nothing in opposing Turkish desires." *Troubled Alliance,* p. 120.

[55] Metin Toker, *Milliyet,* 11 Aralık 1967.

They initiated an intensive propaganda campaign aimed at discrediting further the United States in the public eye by charging that the American bases in Turkey had in effect resurrected the capitulatory privileges that had been granted to foreign powers by the Ottoman Empire.[56] They went so far as to suggest that it was imperative for Turkey to wage "a second war of independence" against the United States in order to restore her sovereignty and independence.[57]

A number of university professors and foreign affairs specialists also voiced strong opposition against the presence of American military installations and personnel in Turkey at a time when they said "external threats against Turkey had begun to wane." They demanded a thorough reappraisal of Turkey's foreign policy commitments and called for the withdrawal from NATO advocating instead a neutral policy for Turkey.[58]

Freed from the anxieties of external dangers and encouraged by the liberalized internal political system, the intelligentsia by the middle of the 1960s had developed greater awareness of the socio-economic ills in the society which to a great extent was due to their greater familiarity with foreign literature on social welfare, social justice, and social democracy. They also had begun to observe a close link between the need of rapid socio-economic development and Turkey's foreign policy commitments. In their estimation, the Cyprus conflict had shown the extent of the "subservience of the governing elite" to the dictates of the United States. Such an undesirable consequence of the close ties with the West had to be remedied if the sovereignty, honor, and prestige of Turkey were to be restored.

---

[56] On anti-American literature see Ali Halil, *Atatürkcü Dış Politika ve NATO ve Türkiye* (Istanbul: Gerçek Yayınevi, 1968); Doğan Avcıoğlu, *Türkiyenin Düzeni* (Ankara: Bilgi Yayınevi, 1969); Avcıoğlu's articles in *Yön* magazine; the daily columns of İlhan Selçuk in *Cumhuriyet*, and Çetin Altan in *Milliyet* and *Akşam* newspapers.

[57] Mehmet Ali Aybar, the leader of the Turkish Labor Party, declared: "The second war of independence has started. The enemy is the United States. It will go out the way it came in. The passive resistance movement will be intensified. We will surround every American on duty in Turkey with a circle of hatred and vengeance. This circle will be closed in like a circle of fire around a scorpion." *Akşam*, 13 Kasım 1967.

[58] See A. Haluk Ülman, "Türkiye ve NATO," *Cumhuriyet*, 21–24 Mayıs 1968; Türkkaya Ataöv, "Türkiyenin Bağımsızlığı" *Cumhuriyet*, 29 Eylül 1967; Ülman and Dekmejian, "Changing Patterns in Turkish Foreign Policy."

As a result of anti-American sentiments expressed by the opposition parties, opposition press, and the counterelite, the streets of Ankara, Istanbul, and İzmir reverberated to shouts of "Yankee Go Home!" "Imperialist America!" and the like. The anti-American student demonstrations became more vituperative and violent which led to serious clashes with the police and security forces.

The coalition governments, as well as the Justice Party government, veered away from resorting to extreme measures against their critics and the students demonstrating in the streets in order not to repeat the mistakes committed by the Democratic Party administration. Then, too, they were somewhat restrained by the liberal atmosphere generated under the provisions of the 1961 Constitution.

Therefore, it may be suggested that in the 1960s the easing of international tension plus the internal political developments as well as the flow of events in the Cyprus conflict have helped to accelerate the ongoing re-evaluation of Turkey's foreign relations and her foreign commitments. However, it must be remembered that long before the eruption of the Cyprus crisis of 1963–1964, the Turkish leaders had already decided to improve Turkey's relations with the communist world, to support the anticolonial stand of the new nations, and to achieve better understanding and cooperation with the neutral and nonaligned countries.[59]

Although the Cyprus conflict cannot be said to have caused a change in the foreign policy orientation of Turkey, it nevertheless helped to reveal the fact that the close ties between Turkey and the West were based on complementary interests rather than on identical interests. It seems that the Turkish leaders have always distinguished between "alliance" relationship based on complementary interests and "community" relationship based on friendship and identity of interests. In their view, an "alliance" is a coalition of unequal states which for a certain period of time join their resources to defend themselves against a common danger. An alliance is

---

[59] See the statement of General Gürsel on the foreign policy of his administration in *Cumhuriyet*, 6 July 1960. And see also the program of the first cabinet of the new regime which was made public on July 11, 1960. The full text of the program is in Öztürk, *Türkiye Cumhuriyeti Hükümetleri ve Programları*, pp. 467–73.

usually dominated by one or two powerful members of the coalition and is based on the principle of self-help. As such, an alliance cannot outlive the dangers which cause its formation. Whereas, in spite of the disparity of power among the members of a community, all members tend to share common ideals and goals and together all strive to realize their common ideals. According to Turkish leaders, in a community based on friendship, mutual understanding, and respect, those who possess greater power do not tend to seek self-aggrandizement but instead assume greater responsibilities commensurate with their actual power status in order to achieve the common objectives of their community.

When Turkey joined the Atlantic Pact, the Turkish leaders were aware of the disparity in the level of economic development and national power among the members of the Western community of nations. Indeed, the disparity in national power and the scope of national interests between the United States and Turkey was a source of embarrassment for the Turkish leaders. However, they were inclined to think that once Turkey became a member of the Western community she would be treated as an equal member sharing common ideals and that the identity of interests would prevent the possibility of the creation of a superior-inferior relationship between Turkey and the United States, the leader of the community.

Evidence indicates that the troubles in the Turkish-Western or Turkish-American relations lie not so much in the fact that on a number of politico-economic-military issues there were wide differences of views, but on the perceptions concerning the nature of the association of Turkey with the West. The differences of views on Turkey's status within the Atlantic community seem to have surfaced during the Cyprus crises of 1963 and 1967. As perceived by the Turkish leaders, the West in general and the United States in particular disowned their responsibilities in solving the conflict on an equitable basis and disregarded the legitimate treaty rights of Turkey and the fundamental principles of international law which constituted the foundation of the Atlantic community. Moreover, the stand taken by the United States and the other Western powers meant that the West continued to consider Turkey as an occasional ally and not as a genuine member of their community.

In spite of their feelings that they had been betrayed by their associates, the Turkish leaders overcame their emotions. Unlike the

United States, they had never renounced power politics as the amoral, opportunistic pursuit of national interests by all expedient means. Turkey's national interests called for the continuation of her close ties with the United States and with the Atlantic alliance.

In order to adapt the defense cooperation within the framework of NATO to the requirements of the day, and to counteract charges that Turkey had become subservient to the will of the United States under the bilateral agreements of the 1950s, the Turkish leaders concluded a new Defense Cooperation Agreement with the United States in July 1969. This agreement reiterated the principles of the sovereignty of Turkey and was based on the concept of equal partnership between the two countries.[60]

Instead of pulling Turkey out of the Atlantic Pact, the Turkish leaders were determined to establish meaningful and enduring ties of partnership with the West. This was based on their belief that Turkey was spiritually an integral part of Europe and could not afford to stay out of it. Accordingly, they signed an agreement with the European Common Market in 1970, providing for the association of Turkey with the European Economic Community.[61] That agreement was another milestone in Turkey's drive for integration with the West, not only military, but also economic and political.

It is noteworthy that the present coalition government of Premier Ecevit chose to continue the policy of close cooperation and alliance with the West. In a recent article, Turan Güneş, the foreign minister of Premier Ecevit, identified NATO as a "genuinely effective defense organization" which, he said, rendered invaluable service not only to the cause of peace but also to the protection of the independence and freedom of its members. Güneş emphasized the need to preserve NATO until such time as "a more satisfactory world order" could be established.[62]

---

[60] For a detailed examination of this agreement see George S. Harris, *Troubled Alliance,* pp. 160–65.

[61] See Sam Cohen, "Peace at home, peace in the world," *The Guardian,* November 3, 1973.

[62] Turan Güneş, "Changing World Conditions, NATO and Turkey," *Dış Politika — Foreign Policy,* March 1974, p. 62. It is noteworthy that Foreign Minister Güneş echoed the views of his predecessor Ü. Haluk Bayülken. For Foreign Minister Bayülken's views see his speech before the National Assembly on February 21, 1973, excerpts of which are printed in *Dış Politika — Foreign Policy,* March 1973, pp. 67–82.

In spite of the many differences between Turkey and her Western Allies, especially with the United States, on economic, political, and military issues, and in spite of the easing of tension between the Atlantic alliance and the communist powers, it should be noted that the Turkish leaders have so far been reluctant to deviate from the traditional policy of economic, political, and military integration with the West. During the most recent Cyprus crisis of July–August 1974, the collective leadership of Turkey has attempted once again to find a peaceful solution to the crisis within the Atlantic alliance, and in a spirit of cooperation has maintained close communications with its NATO partners. The recognition of the legitimate rights and interests of Turkey in Cyprus by her NATO partners, and the even-handed policy of the United States vis-à-vis Greece and Turkey have had a great effect in restoring Turkey's faith in the Atlantic Pact. This action and reaction, in turn, has gone a long way in promoting the image of the United States as the defender of law and order in the world.

In response to the assertion mentioned above that Turkey's close alliance with the West has resulted in her subservience to the will of the United States, it may be said that it was highly improbable in the 1960s and it is extremely unlikely in the 1970s that those warrior diplomats who had fought hard in the past to create a sovereign state should be willing to trade the independence of their country for military protection. Instead, they have always exhibited an acute sensitivity over Turkey's inherent rights and have always dealt with the NATO partners as their equals.

Since 1963 the diplomatic and commercial relations between Turkey and her northern neighbor have been on the upsurge. For the first time in twenty-five years, a Turkish parliamentary delegation, headed by the president of the Senate, S. H. Ürgüplü, visited the Soviet Union in May and June 1963. At the invitation of the Soviet government, Foreign Minister Erkin visited Moscow between October 30 and November 6, 1964. Erkin's visit was followed up in January 1965 by a ten-day visit to Turkey by a Soviet parliamentary delegation headed by N. Podgorny. In May 1965 Soviet Foreign Minister A. Gromyko held talks in Ankara. Then, Premier S. H. Ürgüplü went to the Soviet Union for an eight-day visit in August 1965. For the first time in Turco-Soviet relations, Soviet Premier A. N. Kosygin and his delegation paid a seven-day official visit to Turkey in December 1966. Following his

visit to Romania in September 1967, Premier Demirel and his
delegation visited the Soviet Union for ten days between September
19 and 29, 1967. Again for the first time in Turco-Soviet relations,
President Sunay went to Moscow on a state visit in November 1969,
and President N. Podgorny returned Sunay's visit in April 1972.

As a result of these exchanges of visits, a number of cultural
exchanges and commercial agreements were signed between the
two countries. The Soviet Union promised to supply Turkey with
credits for a steel mill, an oil refinery, and other industrial establishments. In addition to the rapprochement between Turkey and
the Soviet Union as well as with the eastern European countries,
the Turkish government extended diplomatic recognition to the
government of the People's Republic of China in August 1971 and
severed its diplomatic ties with the nationalist government in
Formosa.[63]

The point needs to be stressed, however, that the normalization of diplomatic and commercial relations with the communist
powers occurred in the wake of the pattern already established
by Turkey's allies. Then, too, although the Turkish leaders are
interested in détente and have shown willingness to contribute
toward the further relaxation of tension in southeastern Europe
and the Middle East, they are much more sensitive than their allies
on the question of the security of these regions. For example, the
Turkish diplomats are more reserved in the negotiations that take
place in the European Security Conference about a mutual and
balanced force reduction than their NATO colleagues. The Turkish
diplomats fear that "such a reduction of forces in Central Europe
may lead to a redeployment of Soviet troops" along Turkey's
northeastern borders.[64] And that, of course, is a matter of great
concern to Turkey's leaders.

During the 1960s and the 1970s, the Turkish leaders also
sought better understanding and cooperation with all other nations
without regard to the nature of their internal regimes.

All of the foregoing adjustments in foreign policy were con-
sonant with the basic orientation of Turkey's foreign relations as

---

[63] See Fahir H. Armaoğlu, "Turkey and the People's Republic of China,"
Dış Politika — Foreign Policy, September 1971, pp. 109–27.

[64] Cohen, "Peace at home, peace in the world"; see also Ali Karaosmanoğlu, "Paradoxes in the Three Conferences on Détente," *Dış Politika — Foreign
Policy*, March 1974, pp. 99.

outlined by Atatürk, i.e., political-economic-military integration with the West. These adjustments were the necessary consequences of accurate reassessment of Turkey's vital national interests in light of the political, economic, ideological, and military changes in the world.

IV

Conclusions

"He who desires peace should pre-pare for war."

VEGETIUS

"One does not burn one's blanket to get rid of a flea."

TURKISH PROVERB

Chapter Fourteen

AN AGGREGATE VIEW OF THE
PRINCIPAL FOREIGN POLICY
DECISION MAKERS

The foregoing study suggests that throughout the last fifty years, with the exception of the Chiefs of the General Staff and the commanders of the land forces, air force and the navy, only a handful of individuals were intimately involved in the foreign policy decision making and in the management of the foreign relations of Turkey. These included six presidents, fifteen prime ministers and sixteen ministers of foreign affairs.

With the exception of Presidents Sunay and Korutürk, prior to their presidency, Atatürk, İnönü, Bayar, and Gürsel also served as prime minister. President İnönü is the only person who had also held the post of foreign minister.

All of the presidents sprang from middle-class families. All, except Bayar, were educated in the military high schools and graduated from the War College and later from the Military Staff Academy in Istanbul. All of them experienced the agonies of the decline and fall of the Ottoman Empire and the occupation of their motherland. All of them as ardent nationalists took active roles in the War of Independence. As the creator and builder of the new Turkish state, it was Atatürk who charted the course of the Turkish ship of state; all the other presidents served as the guardians at the helm and seekers of the destinations set by Atatürk.

The presidents, in arriving at foreign policy decisions, made a practice of taking a small group of advisers into their confidence.

296 / *The Warrior Diplomats*

These advisers included the prime ministers, foreign ministers, top military leaders and close associates, and influential leaders of political parties.

Besides Atatürk, İnönü, Bayar, and Gürsel, fifteen individuals served as prime ministers. All told, these nineteen prime ministers headed forty-one governments. Among them İnönü served ten times; Adnan Menderes headed five cabinets; Fevzi Çakmak, Celal Bayar, Refik Saydam, Şükrü Saracoğlu, Hasan Saka, Cemal Gürsel, Süleyman Demirel, and Nihat Erim succeeded themselves in office once. Ali Fethi Okyar assumed the office twice, while Mustafa Kemal, Rauf Orbay, Recep Peker, Şemsettin Günaltay, S. Hayri Ürgüplü, Ferit Melen, Naim Talu, and Bülent Ecevit, the incumbent, served only once as prime minister.

Prior to 1961, the prime ministers served as long as they were willing and able to carry out the directives of the presidents. In the history of the republic, only one prime minister — İsmet İnönü — received a vote of no confidence, that being in February 1965, in the National Assembly, thereby causing his resignation. İsmet İnönü was the first foreign minister who was elevated to the position of prime minister, the first prime minister who was elected president, the first president who was voted out of office, the first president who later assumed the office of prime minister, the first prime minister who headed the first coalition government, the first prime minister who had to resign because of the fact that he had received a vote of no confidence in the National Assembly, the first leader of the Republican People's Party who, after serving thirty-four years, was defeated by his own protégé in the election of the leadership of the party, the first former president who resigned his seat in the National Assembly and entered the Senate of the Republic as senator in accordance with the provisions of the 1961 Constitution. Thus, it may be said that İsmet İnönü was able to achieve an impressive record and succeeded in creating a legend of his own.

With the exception of Rauf Orbay, Adnan Menderes, and Suat Hayri Ürgüplü, all prime ministers came from middle-class families. Eight of them had had training in military high schools and seven of them graduated from the War College in Istanbul. Only Celal Bayar had had no formal university education. Among the rest, three were graduated from law schools and three from schools of political science, one from a technical university, one from a school of economics, and one from a private American college. In terms of their initial careers, of these nineteen prime ministers, nine had been military officers, four civil servants, three university lecturers or professors, two bank employees, one a farmer, and one an engineer.

Of the sixteen foreign ministers (those who later became prime ministers, such as İnönü, Saracoğlu, Saka, and those who served only as acting foreign ministers being excluded) nine were career foreign service officers, two journalists, two professors, two civil servants, and one a physician. Dr. Tevfik Rüştü Aras, a gynecologist, served the longest period — from March 4, 1925, to December 11, 1938.

All the presidents so far have acted as authoritarian leaders and concentrated political power in their hands as circumstances permitted. They have initiated reforms or accelerated their implementation from the top down, superstructural changes being given the utmost priority. They viewed foreign and domestic policies as inseparable aspects of the same issue — the modernization of Turkey, free from foreign intervention and domination. For them external events and foreign policy questions have had greater urgency over the questions of domestic policy.

Until 1961 the presidents have looked upon the task of foreign policy decision making as their own prerogative and privilege, even to the extent of excluding the members of the Grand National Assembly. All important foreign policy decisions up to 1961 were made at the presidential palace in Çankaya. The members of the Grand National Assembly, the intelligentsia, and the general public until the 1960s had never challenged the basic principles of foreign policy or Turkey's international commitments.[1] All agreed that foreign policy of Turkey was "national foreign policy."

However, the traumatic political crises of the 1960s were instrumental in widening the foreign policy decision-making circle

---

[1] It appears that this practice was even continued during the 1960s. We note for example, the government of Nihat Erim did not disclose the nature and scope of the negotiations preceding the decision to recognize the government of the People's Republic of China on August 5, 1971, and the reasons behind the decision to sever diplomatic relations with the government of Nationalist China. The Erim Government also declined to comply with the request of the major opposition Justice Party that such an issue of major importance be discussed and reviewed in an executive session of the Grand National Assembly. See Fahir H. Armaoğlu, "Turkey and the People's Republic of China," p. 120.

and in initiating steps toward greater public debate of the issues of foreign policy. As noted earlier, in the 1960s the responsibility of decision making shifted toward collective military-civilian leadership. Thus, the top military leaders began to assume a much greater and more active role; the career diplomats were given additional responsibilities and the members of the Grand National Assembly were consulted on major issues of foreign relations. Some of the important factors which necessitated the division of responsibility within a wider circle of foreign policy leadership include: The adoption of an ultrademocratic Constitution; the internal political instabilities and governmental crises; strong criticisms directed against the coalition cabinets by the opposition parties in general and by the Turkish Labor Party in particular; the absence of decisive leadership at the presidential level; the relaxation of the international tension and the friendly gestures by the Soviet Union; last but not least the Cyprus crises of 1963–64 and 1967.

In spite of the changes in the composition of the foreign policy decision makers, it may be said that the substance of Turkey's foreign relations has remained almost unchanged. The Turkish warrior diplomats knew all along that the conduct of foreign relations is a continuing process of making deliberate choices in the light of the politico-economic-military conditions in the world and that foreign policy strategies always carry the proviso "until further notice." Consequently, they have always reviewed and revised their strategies to meet the requirements of the day. In this sense, it may be said that they have regularly changed their responses to the world outside the boundaries of Turkey. However, such changes in strategies and tactics did not amount to a dramatic change in Turkey's foreign policy orientation.

The fundamental objective of the Turkish warrior diplomats was, and still is, to bring Turkey to the level of contemporary civilization and to make her an equal partner of the Western community of nations, and to protect the territorial integrity and political independence of Turkey against any aggression.

Chapter Fifteen

THE MEANING OF "PEACE AT HOME AND PEACE IN THE WORLD"

As one enters the building of the Ministry of Foreign Affairs, one's gaze is met by the words *Yurtta Sulh Cihanda Sulh,* (Peace at Home and Peace in the World) in large bronze block letters on the wall. Next to them is a huge map of Turkey, and in front is a gigantic bronze bust of Atatürk. This simple slogan, which appeals to one of the basic emotions of man — the hope for peace — has been repeated in the State of the Nation speeches of the presidents since 1938, in the programs of the governments, in the public utterances of high governmental officials, on banners stretched across the streets on national holidays, and even in the preamble to the 1961 Constitution. It is generally maintained by the specialists in Turkish affairs as well as by the present leaders of Turkey that this slogan constitutes the keystone of Turkey's foreign policy. These words are attributed to Atatürk who, in his State of the Nation speech of November 1, 1928, had said: "It is quite natural and therefore simple to explain the fact that a country which is in the midst of fundamental reforms and development should sincerely desire peace and tranquility both at home and in the world." But, Atatürk qualified his desire for peace by saying: "In the formulation of our foreign policy we pay particular attention to the safety and security of our country and to our capability to protect the rights of the citizenry against any aggression."[1] This meant that while Turkey's

---

[1] *Atatürk'ün Söylev ve Demeçleri* (Ankara: Türk Tarih Kurumu Basımevi, 1961), p. 356.

wish was to live in peace with all nations and maintain friendly relations with great and small powers alike, she was nevertheless prepared to prevent the infringement of her territorial sovereignty and political independence and she would not hesitate to take up arms against would-be aggressors.

Since this study is based on the proposition that foreign and domestic policies of Turkey were closely linked with the personal idiosyncracies, perceptions, images, and attitudes of the warrior diplomats, which were conditioned by their values, convictions, and previous experiences, the slogan "Peace at Home and Peace in the World" should be interpreted within the context of the fundamental values and convictions of the Turkish warrior diplomats. Their values and convictions may be summarized as follows: The international system, despite the general lip service to the concept of community relationship based on friendship, is basically anarchic, because it rests on unequal distribution of power; power politics is still the controlling dynamics of the international society; power is still the overriding consideration of nations; under such circumstances only those who possess power can claim humane, just, and generous treatment; moreover, to claim rights in the abstract, without regard to power is idle and foolish; the history of the relations of nations indicates clearly that territorial sovereignty and political independence is not freely given but is taken by force; national boundaries which cannot be defended by the bayonet cannot be protected by humanitarian principles; however, the objectives of nations must be proportionate to the means that are available for their realization; no right ought to be claimed beyond what force can possibly hold; one has to give up something to get something in return, unless one is prepared to seize it with arms; peace and war are the by-products of the interplay of national interests; the choice of war or peace is based on considerations of their operational expediency and utility; the condition of peace, internal and external peace, is most conducive to the realization of the domestic goal of modernization; however, if one desires peace, one must be prepared for war; there is not much hope of success in peaceful procedures in the settlement of disputes until one proves one's strength on the battlefield in the contest of wills; one must distinguish between friends and allies; friendships, if reciprocated, may endure, whereas alliances are bound to disappear when the common danger vanishes; one must avoid confronting the wrong enemy at the wrong time; one has to take advantage of the apparent weakness of the will of the opponent; one has to exploit the clashes of interests between one's opponents; one has to ascertain as accurately as possible who can oppose one's objectives and who may assist the realization of one's goals; alliances should not be based on ideological considerations; when negotiating with an opponent one must sense the accurate timing of necessary concessions, one must usually make concessions at the final hours of negotiations; international agreements, in order to be durable, must satisfy both parties; if the actual situation of international anarchy is to be prevented from turning into war of all against all, then, nations must be willing to submit themselves to a regularized structuring of their overall responses within the framework of a global security organization, based on the principles of sovereign equality of all nations and the principles of international law; within an organized society of nations the principle of sanctity of international agreements must be upheld by particularly strong powers; it is foolhardy, however, to expect the transformation of the international society into international community based on mutual understanding, trust, and love by way of creating an "ideal" international organization.[2]

Although the Turkish leaders were committed to the ideal condition of peace, as realistic practitioners of international and domestic power politics, they could not rest the destiny of their nation on such an abstract term and ideal condition as peace. In brief, peace was contingent upon the preparedness for war in external affairs and willingness to be prepared to resort to force against those who opposed Turkey's twin goals of national security and modernization.[3]

---

[2] Such values and convictions of the Turkish leaders may be found in their writings. A few of their works may be cited: Atatürk, *Speech,* and *Atatürk'ün Söylev ve Demeçleri;* İsmet İnönü, *İsmet Paşanın Siyasi ve İçtimai Nutukları* (Ankara: Başvekalet Matbassı, 1933); State of the Nation speeches of Presidents İnönü and Bayar in *Resmi Gazete* (1939–1959); "programs of cabinets" submitted to the Grand National Assembly for its approval, Kazım Öztürk, *Türkiye Cumhuriyeti Hükümetleri ve Programları* (Istanbul: Baha Matbaası, 1968); statements and speeches of Presidents Gürsel and Sunay may be found in *Dışişleri Bakanlığı Belleteni* (1964–).

[3] Note that since 1920 the Turkish governments instituted martial law in politically and strategically important regions of the country on numerous occasions, such as in 1920 to 1923, 1925–1927, 1939–1945, 1955–1956, 1960–1961, 1963, 1971–1973. Martial law empowered the governments to suppress the recalcitrant and reactionary elements and thus curtail opposition to reforms and to suppress the terrorist activities of the left-wing extremists. Internally, Turkey has had peace only when reactionary and subversive elements were suppressed. This was, of course, "peace" based on force and fiat.

The Turkish warrior diplomats conducted their relations with the external world in accordance with these convictions. Like their forefathers, they were trained in the rigorous school of experience which on the subject of politics had taught them the rules of survival. They had developed a sense of history and deep insight into the nature of man and his domestic and international society. Their policies and strategies were the result of the realistic and accurate assessment of the prevailing international system and structure, their actual functioning. Their policies and strategies were the result of the realistic appraisal of Turkey's power and the capabilities and goals of those states which opposed Turkey. At no time, however, even during the most propitious moments of the Second World War or at the height of the Cyprus dispute of the 1950s and the 1960s, did the warrior diplomats engage in foreign adventures. They knew very well that their foreign policy options were limited by Turkey's own capabilities and the power of the Soviet Union. Thus, they had always tried to strike a balance between Turkey's actual and potential power and her foreign and domestic goals.

Ever since the War of Independence, the leaders of Turkey were obsessed with the concept of internal and external sovereignty. At no time were they willing to make concessions detrimental to Turkish sovereignty. The warrior diplomats allocated large portions of both human and material resources to the national military establishment which, in the final analysis, has had negative consequences in terms of Turkey's rapid economic development.[4] As mentioned before, their decision to seek close alliance ties with the West was fundamentally based on their concern of maintaining the independence of Turkey and making her a truly modern nation.

Other than their full commitment to the civilized way of life, the warrior diplomats were not rigidly bound to any foreign ideology. Their foreign policy was not contaminated by democracy, fascism, national socialism, Marxism-Leninism, by abstract ideas about perpetual alliance and friendship, or by such elusive concepts as world community, internationalism, and peace. The either/or

---

[4] In 1974 there were 453,000 men under arms. The Turkish armed forces were the fourth largest force in NATO alliance. Again in 1974 defense budget of Turkey amounted to $995 million, which was 3.7 per cent of the gross national product. See The International Institute for Strategic Studies, *The Military Balance 1974–1975* (London: IISS, 1974), pp. 26 and 78. On Turkey's contribution to NATO see Ibid.

proposition never seemed to have dominated their thinking. By and large, they operated in between the white and black poles, in the gray area. They pursued a moderate course of action and avoided extreme alternatives.

On the question of how to hold the line of defense against revisionist powers, the warrior diplomats employed flexible strategies in accordance with the requirements of the changing circumstances. Their objectives were well defined and their strategies were clearly in accord with the needs and necessities of the time. They knew what they were doing on the chessboard of international politics.

During the period roughly from 1923 to 1945, the Turkish diplomacy was directed toward establishing friendly relations with all nations and cultivating new bases of friendship with old enemies. By exploiting the clashes of interests between opposing alliances thus attempting to isolate one or more opponents, the warrior diplomats managed to maintain belligerent neutrality in the Second World War. They made it clear that Turkey was not neutral but only outside the war and that she intended to stay that way unless she was attacked by one of the belligerents, namely, either the Soviet Union or the Axis Powers.

Due to the emergence of rigid power blocs during the Cold War period, the Turkish diplomacy seems to have lost much of its flexibility, reducing its contacts with the Communist bloc to a minimum, and has followed the pattern set by the major powers of the West. However, since the emergence of polycentrism and since the beginning of the relaxation of international tension, the Turkish diplomacy has regained its flexibility.

The foregoing study, which is based on the diplomatic correspondence and other papers located in the United States National Archives, the British Public Records Office, and the official documents of the Turkish government, as well as on the memoirs of foreign and Turkish statesmen and journalists, or the works of the students and scholars of Turkish affairs, suggests the following characteristics of the strategies, tactics, and style of the diplomacy of the warrior diplomats.

In terms of the settlement of disputes with foreign powers, the diplomacy of the warrior diplomats was marked by great reliance upon political and legal procedures of pacific settlement. It resorted to bilateral and multilateral diplomatic negotiations, fact finding, inquiry by international bodies, mediation, conciliation, and adjudication by the world court. Only when these methods proved inadequate did the warrior diplomats issue warnings and threaten their opponents, and in extremely exceptional circumstances resort to the actual use of force. The Turkish diplomats took judicious care to avoid placing their country or their opponents in a position where they could not manuever.

The warrior diplomats in the process of diplomatic bargaining exhibited an impressive amount of patience, sticking doggedly to negotiation positions and proposals in order to exploit the impatience of their opponents. They spent considerable time in long explanations of the various interpretations that might be attributed to political and legal terms, thus entering into long discussions over the questions of semantics. Their fastidious attention to terminology and words with flexible meanings, and their meticulous rendering of exact translations of draft agreements often frustrated the other negotiating parties.

When it was not in their interest to conclude agreements, the warrior diplomats haggled over minor details, introduced new and unexpected topics, and evaded crucial points. They turned deaf ears to unacceptable proposals, and at times simply failed to hear what was being said by their counterparts at the conference table.

Without prior approval from Ankara, the Turkish negotiators never committed themselves to new proposals because they were required to receive new instructions when new proposals were put before them by foreign diplomats or statesmen. Then they took abundant time to express their views. They were never willing to give in when threatened at the conference table, but simply withdrew to study the matter under consideration.

In a nutshell, the warrior diplomats were masterful diplomatic bargainers because they were patient and persistent in their positions and because they displayed deep insight into the intricacies of diplomacy and they were aware of the strengths and weaknesses of their opponents. They were also capable of making accurate and realistic assessment of the forces at work, and balancing their objectives and their means.

The diplomatic style of the warrior diplomats was marked by subtlety, courteousness in manner and tone, and strict adherence to the requirements of diplomatic practice and etiquette. Their diplomacy may be said to have contained the best features of the traditional Eastern and Western techniques and procedures for conducting foreign relations. As such it represented a synthesis of the Eastern and Western diplomacies.

It is small wonder then that the Turkish warrior diplomats have, for the last fifty years, been successful not only in protecting the territorial integrity and political independence of Turkey but also in accomplishing exemplary progress on the road to modernization.

Appendix
THE FOREIGN POLICY
DECISION MAKERS

Presidents	Prime Ministers	Foreign Ministers
	Mustafa Kemal Atatürk 5/3/20–1/24/21	Bekir Sami Kunduk 5/3/20–5/8/21
	Fevzi Çakmak 1/24/21–5/16/21	Fevzi Çakmak (Acting) 5/8/21–5/17/21
	Fevzi Çakmak 5/16/21–7/12/22	Yusuf Kemal Tengirşenk 5/17/21–10/27/22
	H. Rauf Orbay 7/12/22–8/13/23	İsmet İnönü 10/27/22–11/21/24
	Ali Fethi Okyar 8/13/23–10/29/23	
Mustafa Kemal Atatürk 10/29/23–11/10/38	İsmet İnönü 10/29/23–11/1/37	Şükrü Kaya 11/22/24–3/4/25
	Celal Bayar 11/1/37–11/11/38	Tevfik Rüştü Aras 3/4/25–12/11/38
İsmet İnönü 11/11/38–5/22/50	Celal Bayar 11/11/38–1/25/39	Şükrü Saracoğlu 12/11/38–8/14/42
	Refik Saydam 1/25/39–7/8/42	
	Şükrü Saracoğlu 7/9/42–8/12/46	Numan Menemencioğlu 8/14/42–6/15/44
		Şükrü Saracoğlu (Acting) 6/15/44–9/13/44
	Recep Peker 8/12/46–9/9/47	Hasan Saka 9/13/44–9/10/47

THE FOREIGN POLICY DECISION MAKERS
(Continued)

Presidents	Prime Ministers	Foreign Ministers
	Hasan Saka 9/10/47–1/14/49	Necmeddin Sadak 9/10/47–5/22/50
	Şemsettin Günaltay 1/15/49–5/22/50	
Celal Bayar 5/22/50–5/27/60	Adnan Menderes 5/22/50–5/27/60	M. Fuad Köprülü 5/22/50–4/15/55
		Adnan Menderes (Acting) 4/15/55–7/29/55
		Fatin Rüştü Zorlu (Acting) 7/29/55–12/9/55
		M. Fuad Köprülü 12/9/55–6/20/56
		Ethem Menderes (Acting) 6/20/56–11/27/56
		Fatin Rüştü Zorlu 11/27/57–5/27/60
Cemal Gürsel (Head of State) 5/27/60–10/26/61	Cemal Gürsel 5/27/60–10/26/61	Selim R. Sarper 5/30/60–3/15/62
Cemal Gürsel 10/26/61–3/28/66	İsmet İnönü 11/20/61–2/20/65	
		Feridun Cemal Erkin 3/24/62–2/24/65
	Suat Hayri Ürgüplü 2/20/65–10/27/65	Hasan F. E. Işık 2/24/65–10/27/65
Cevdet Sunay 3/28/66–3/28/73	Süleyman S. Demirel 10/27/65–3/27/71	İhsan Sabri Çaglayangil 10/27/65–3/27/71
	Nihat Erim 3/27/71–4/17/72	Osman Olcay 3/27/71–12/11/71
Fahri Korutürk 4/6/73–	Ferit Melen 4/17/72–4/15/73	Ü. Haluk Bayülken 12/11/71–1/25/74
	Naim Talu 4/15/73–1/25/74	
	Bülent Ecevit 1/25/74–	Turan Güneş 1/25/74–

The Biographical Sketches of the Foreign Policy Elite

Aras, Dr. Tevfik Rüştü

He was born in Çanakkale on February 11, 1883. His father was Hasan Rüştü Bey. He completed elementary school in İzmir, secondary school in Scopia, and graduated from *Numune-i Terakki* High School in Istanbul on August 19, 1900. He obtained his M.D. degree from the French Faculty of Medicine in Beirut. He specialized in gynecology in Paris.

Dr. Tevfik Rüştü Bey started his career as a gynecologist at Gureba Hospital in İzmir on May 2, 1908, and served there until October 31, 1909. While he was in İzmir he served also as editor in chief of the *İttihad* newspaper. On February 2, 1909, he was appointed Inspector of Health at Salonica and maintained this position until September 30, 1911. While in Salonica he served as member of the Committee of Union and Progress. In 1911, he was appointed member of the Board of Medicine in Istanbul. On September 1, 1912, he was appointed director of the Red Crescent Hospital in Scopia and on January 1, 1913, he was transferred to Red Crescent Hospital in Çanakkale as its director. In March 1913, he was appointed inspector general of Health at Istanbul. And on June 29, 1918, he was appointed member of the High Council of Health and served until June 30, 1920.

Dr. Tevfik Rüştü Bey joined the Grand National Assembly in Ankara as deputy of Menteşe in July 1920. He was appointed as presiding judge of the Court of Independence of the Çankırı and Kastamonu regions on September 9, 1920. He headed the Turkish political mission sent to Moscow between 1921 and 1923. On his return from Moscow, he was elected deputy from İzmir in August 1923 and served until 1939 in the Grand National Assembly. During this period, he served as chairman of the Turkish delegation in the Greco-Turkish Commission of Exchange of Population, 1923–24.

Dr. Tevfik Rüştü Bey was appointed Minister of Foreign Affairs on March 4, 1925, and held this portfolio until December 11, 1938, in İsmet Pasha's various cabinets and also in Celal Bayar's cabinet. He was appointed ambassador to London on January 26,

1939, and served until February 28, 1942, at which time he was succeeded by Rauf Orbay. During the next eight years, he withdrew from public life and, following the victory of the Democratic Party at the polls, was nominated by the Menderes government and appointed by the United Nations as Turkish representative of the U.N. Commission on Palestine in 1950 where he served until 1952. In that year, he was appointed chairman of the Board of Directors of the *İş Bankası* and in 1960 he resigned.

Dr. Tevfik Rüştü Aras spoke fluent French and some German, Russian, and English. He died on January 6, 1972, in Istanbul.

Dr. Aras' speeches delivered on important occasions during his term of office are published in 1935 under the title *Lozan'ın İzlerinde on Yıl: Tevfik Rüştü Aras'ın Nutukları*. A French translation of the same is also available. Dr. Aras has written a large number of articles since the 1930s. These are compiled by Dr. Aras himself into two books entitled *Görüşlerim*. The first volume was published in 1945 and the second in 1968. Unfortunately, these works do not contain inside information about the conduct of the foreign relations of Turkey during 1920s and 1930s. They deal instead with the broad issues of Turkey's foreign policy and Aras' own views on the major issues of international politics.[1]

ATATÜRK, MUSTAFA KEMAL

He was born in Salonica in 1881. His father, Ali Rıza Efendi, at the time of the birth of Mustafa Kemal, was a clerk in the Ottoman Debt Commission. Later Ali Rıza Efendi was engaged, not too successfully, in the lumber business. He died when Mustafa Kemal was nine years old, leaving his family very nearly impoverished. Mustafa Kemal's mother, Zübeyde Hanım, was a devoutly religious person. She had decided that her son should pursue a religious education. She had tried to exercise a domineering influence over her brilliant but rebellious son and her daughter, Makbule. But Mustafa Kemal had other plans for his education and future.

---

[1] Biographical data are compiled from the questionnaire completed by Dr. Tevfik Rüştü Aras and sent to this writer. On his personality see "Dispatch," November 22, 1927, Ambassador Grew to Department of State, U.S. National Archives, Turkey, File No. 867.031/2; see also Aral, *Dışişleri Bakanlığı 1967 Yıllığı*, pp. 149–52.

Following the death of his father, the family went to live with Mustafa's maternal uncle, a farmer. When he was twelve, he entered the military secondary school of Salonica as he had planned. It was his mathematics teacher who gave him the name *Kemal* meaning "perfection" because of his extraordinary mind. In 1895 he entered the Military High School at Manastır. While on vacation in Salonica he studied French and became a good friend of a Macedonian Turkish youth Ali Fethi. They were reading revolutionary literature of French authors and discussing the dismal conditions of the empire under the rule of Abdülhamit, the despot. Following his graduation from high school with high honors, Mustafa Kemal enrolled in the War College in Istanbul on March 13, 1899, where he started to take an active interest in the secret opposition movements calling for the deposition of Sultan Abdülhamit. The revolutionary young cadets of the War College, Mustafa Kemal included, founded the *Vatan* (Fatherland) Society and published a secret leaflet explaining their views on the need for revolution against the regime. Here in the War College, Mustafa Kemal established close friendship with his classmate Ali Fuat. Ali Fuat introduced him to his father, İsmail Fazıl Pasha, and his family. Ali Fuat's home was opened to Mustafa Kemal as if it was his own. This upper-class family with cosmopolitan outlook "made Mustafa's own background seem humble and drab."[2] Mustafa Kemal graduated in 1902 as lieutenant, and entered the Staff Academy. He graduated from the Staff Academy with high honors as staff captain on January 11, 1905.

Mustafa Kemal's first field assignment was the Fifth Army at Damascus where he founded the *Vatan ve Hürriyet* (Fatherland and Freedom) Society in October 1906. In June 1907 he was promoted to adjutant major. Mustafa Kemal wished to be transferred to Salonica which at that time was the center of revolutionary agitation. Eventually he was transferred to the Third Army at Salonica. However, once in Salonica, he only took part from a distance in the activities of the Committee of Union and Progress, a conspiratorial party, headed by men like Enver, Cemal, and Talat, who were determined to force Sultan Abdülhamit to restore the 1876 Constitution and who were to play leading roles in the affairs of the empire from 1908 to 1918. They were successful in forcing

---

[2] Lord Kinross, *Ataturk,* p. 21.

Abdülhamit to proclaim the restoration of the Constitution of 1876 following their initial coup d'état. As divisional Chief of Staff of the forces in Salonica, Mustafa Kemal participated in the suppression of the counter revolution of April 1909 in Istanbul. On September 6, 1909, he was appointed commander of the Third Army training course and later commander of the 38th Infantry Regiment. He served as Chief of Staff in suppressing the revolt in Albania in 1910. And the same year he was sent to France as a member of a military mission to observe military maneuvers.

In October 1911 he went to Tripoli to help to organize local resistance against Italian invasion. He was promoted to major on November 27, 1911, and the news of the First Balkan War prompted him to return and to participate in the defense of Edirne. He was appointed director of operations for the relief of Edirne. Then, with the help of his friend Ali Fethi Bey, Minister at Sofia, he was appointed military attaché in Sofia. The two friends had ample opportunity in Sofia to review the conditions in which the empire had found itself following the disastrous Balkan Wars.

On March 14, 1914, Mustafa Kemal was promoted to lieutenant colonel. Following the entry of the empire into the First World War, which he vehemently opposed, as commander he established the headquarters of the Nineteenth Division at Maidos, on the Gallipoli peninsula in February 1915. On June 1, 1915, he was promoted to colonel and on August 8, 1915, he was appointed commander of the Second Army Corps. His defense of Gallipoli against Allied invasion fleet saved the Ottoman Empire from an early collapse and its capital from the imminent danger of occupation. In January 1916 he was transferred to Edirne and later to the Caucasus front. Mustafa Kemal was promoted to brigadier general on April 1, 1916, at the age of thirty-five. In the Caucasus front he captured Bitlis and Muş from the Russians. He was appointed commander of the Seventh Army in Syria on July 5, 1917. In October of the same year he returned to Istanbul. He was appointed *aide de camp* to Crown Prince Vahdettin to accompany him on his trip of inspection in Germany from December 15 to January 5, 1918. It was this crown prince who, as Sultan Vahdettin, was to be overthrown by Mustafa Kemal in 1922.

Upon his return from Germany he was reappointed as commander of the Seventh Army in Syria on August 7, 1918, at a time when the empire was totally exhausted by the force of relentless

Allied advances. The day after the signing of the Armistice of Mudros, Mustafa Kemal took command of the army corps at Adana and then transferred his duties to his old friend Ali Fuat and returned to Istanbul on November 13, 1918, the day that the Allied fleet had anchored in the waters of Bosporus.

For five months Mustafa Kemal remained without military command; however, during those months he maintained close contact with his intimate friends Ali Fethi, H. Rauf, Kazım Karabekir, Refet, and İsmet, discussing with them the possibilities of bringing together the sporadic resistance movements against the Allied occupation forces into a viable nationalist movement of liberation. When he was appointed inspector general of the Ninth (later Third) Army on April 30, 1919, he began to see much more clearly the rising of the people under his leadership.

From the day of Mustafa Kemal's landing at Samsun on May 19, 1919, his biography and the history of the Turkish Revolution and the Republic of Turkey up to World War II were inseparably woven together. During the latter part of the 1920s and thereafter, no one in Turkey could match his popularity and his reputation of invincibility. When he died in Istanbul on November 10, 1938, in the palace of the former sultans, the whole nation mourned its loss, for he was considered the liberator and the renovator of Turkey. A temporary tomb was erected at the Ethnographic Museum in Ankara and on November 10, 1953, fifteen years after his death, his remains were solemnly transferred to a gigantic mausoleum erected in his honor in Ankara, the construction of which had been proceeding all that time. Atatürk had married and was later divorced; he had an adopted daughter.[3]

BAYAR, CELAL

Celal Bayar, who early in his life was known as Mahmut Celal, was born in Umurbey, a village of Bursa, on May 15, 1883.

---

[3] On the life and work of Atatürk see The Turkish National Commission for UNESCO, *Atatürk* (Ankara: Ankara University Press, 1963). This is the translation by Andrew J. Mango of the article prepared by U. Igdemir, E. Z. Karal, S. Omurtak, E. Sökmen, I. Sungu, F. R. Unat, and Hasan-Ali Yücel which originally appeared in *İslam Ansiklopedisi* in 1946; see also the work of Lord Kinross, *Ataturk;* Hikmet Bayur, *Atatürk: Hayatı ve Eseri* (Ankara: Aydın Kitapevi, 1962) ; and Aydemir, *Tek Adam.*

His parents immigrated to Turkey from Plevne in Bulgaria. His father, Abdullah Fehmi Efendi, was the principal of the Umurbey secondary school and *Müftü* (learned man in Moslem law). Mahmut Celal completed his elementary and secondary schooling at home. He then attended *College Français de l'Assumption* high school in Bursa, but did not go to the university. His first employpent was at *Ziraat Bankası* (Agricultural Bank) and later he served as manager of the *Deutsch Orientbank's* Bursa branch in 1907. He was appointed secretary of the Bursa and İzmir branches of the Committee of Union and Progress. In 1919 Mahmut Celal organized guerrilla forces against the Greek invasion of the İzmir region. He represented the Saruhan Sancak (Manisa) in the Ottoman Parliament from January 12 to March 16, 1920.

Mahmut Celal joined the Nationalist Movement in Ankara and served as deputy from Manisa in the Grand National Assembly from 1920 to 1923. During this time he was elected Minister of Economy on February 27, 1921, and served until January 14, 1922. During the absence of the Minister of Foreign Affairs, Yusuf Kemal Bey, he served briefly as Acting Minister of Foreign Affairs between February 9, 1922, and April 3, 1922. He was sent to the Lausanne Conference as a member of the Turkish delegation from November 1922, to July 24, 1923. In August 1923 he was elected deputy of the Republican People's Party from İzmir. On March 6, 1924, Mahmut Celal Bey was appointed Minister of Exchange of Population, Construction, and Resettlement. He was asked by Atatürk to take charge of the founding and management of Turkey's first major bank, the *İş Bankası*. Thus, Mahmut Celal Bey resigned from his post in the Council of Ministers on July 7, 1924, and on August 26, 1924, he established this *İş Bankası* and served as its director general until November 10, 1932, at which time he was appointed Minister of Economy in İsmet Pasha's cabinet. Celal Bayar served in that capacity until November 1, 1937. On that date Atatürk appointed him prime minister to succeed İsmet İnönü. Upon the death of Atatürk and the election of İsmet İnönü as president of the republic on November 11, 1938, Celal Bayar tendered his resignation but he was reappointed the same day as İsmet İnönü's first prime minister.

Celal Bayar served until January 25, 1939; he remained as deputy of the Republican People's Party until September 27,

1945. He resigned from the party on that date and on December 3, 1945, he resigned from his seat in the Grand National Assembly.

Then, together with three of his close friends, Celal Bayar established the Democratic Party on January 7, 1946. In the general elections of July 21, 1946, he was elected deputy from Istanbul. And following the general elections of May 14, 1950, on May 22 he was elected president of the republic by an overwhelming majority in the Grand National Assembly. Four years later Bayar was re-elected president. On November 1, 1957, the Grand National Assembly re-elected President Bayar to a third four-year term.[4]

President Bayar and his Democratic Party administration were overthrown by the Committee of National Unity following the May 27, 1960 coup d'état. He was sent to Yassıada where he was detained and tried by a military court. He was indicted in seven different cases for violation of numerous laws, including the Constitution. He was given a death sentence by the court on September 15, 1961. However, on the same day, his death sentence was commuted to life imprisonment by the Committee of National Unity. On July 8, 1966, Bayar was released from prison by the executive order of President Cevdet Sunay.

Bayar has a daughter and speaks French and English. At present he is writing his memoirs. He has published eight volumes under the title *Ben de Yazdım* (And So I Wrote). His other published work is entitled *Başvekilim Adnan Menderes* (My Prime Minister Adnan Menderes).

BAYÜLKEN, ÜMİT HALÛK

He was born in Istanbul in 1921. Following his high school education in Haydarpaşa Lycée in Istanbul, Bayülken was graduated from the School of Political Sciences in 1943. He entered the foreign service in January 1944. The next year he began his military service and upon his discharge in 1947 he returned to the Ministry of Foreign Affairs. The same year he was sent to Bonn as vice consul. Following a short assignment in the Ministry of Foreign Affairs, Bayülken was appointed member of the Permanent Delegation of Turkey to the United Nations. From 1953 to 1960

---

[4] See *Türk Ansiklopedisi,* Cilt 5, pp. 428–38.

Bayülken served in New York, and in 1960 he was recalled home and was appointed the chairman of the Policy Planning Group of the Ministry of Foreign Affairs. Three years later he was designated as assistant to the secretary general. In 1964 Bayülken was promoted to the rank of ambassador and became the secretary general of the Ministry. Two years later he was appointed ambassador to London, and in 1969 he became the permanent representative of Turkey at the United Nations. Bayülken was asked to join the Council of Ministers of Premier Erim as foreign minister on December 11, 1971. When Premier Erim resigned on April 17, 1972, Bayülken was retained as foreign minister by Prime Minister Ferit Melen. Premier Talu, who succeeded Melen, asked Bayülken again to serve as foreign minister in his coalition government. Bayülken thus served in three succeeding cabinets of Erim, Melen, and Talu, from December 11, 1971 to January 25, 1974.[5] Bayülken is married. He speaks fluent English and French.

BELE, REFET

He was born in Istanbul in 1881. His father was Mehmet Servet, a clerk in commercial courts. Mehmet Servet was born in Tirnova (Bulgaria). A graduate of the War College and later the Staff Academy, Refet Bele was commissioned as staff captain and served in the Balkan Wars and the First World War. He was an associate of Mustafa Kemal in the Third Army in Salonica in 1907 and accompanied Mustafa Kemal to Samsun where, as colonel, he was to be in charge of the Third Army Corps at Samsun. Later he resigned his commission. He was one of the four leaders who signed the Amasya Circular in June 1919. He also participated in the Sivas Congress. Then he was assigned the command of the Southern flank of the Western front commanded by Ali Fuat Pasha. He was appointed deputy from İzmir, Minister of Interior on September 6, 1920, and served until April 21, 1921. He conducted informal negotiations with the British officers concerning a possible meeting between Mustafa Kemal and General Harington, in June 1921. He was then appointed Minister of National Defense in August 1921, but resigned in January 1922, objecting ostensibly

---

[5] See Aral, *Dışişleri Bakanlığı 1967 Yıllığı*, pp. 411–12; *Cumhuriyet,* 11 Aralık 1971; Directorate General of Information, Ministry of Tourism and Information, *Biographies of the Members of the Cabinet,* Ankara, n.d.

to the separation of his functions from those of the Chief of the General Staff, but actually to Mustafa Kemal's tendency to concentrate all powers in his hands. Due to his extraordinary services during the battle of İnönü and Sakarya, he was promoted to the rank of brigadier general. Following the conclusion of the Armistice of Mudanya, he was appointed the representative of the Ankara government in Istanbul on October 19, 1922. When the sultanate was abolished on November 1, 1922, Refet Pasha took over the administration of Istanbul and Thrace in the name of the Grand National Assembly on November 4, 1922.

Refet Pasha, together with Rauf Bey, Kazım Karabekir Pasha, and Ali Fuat Pasha, opposed the abolishment of the sultanate and later the abolishment of the caliphate and then joined the Progressive Party.

Refet Pasha, prior to his joining the Progressive Party, was appointed Minister of Exchange of Population and Settlement on July 7, 1924, but had to resign his post on November 22, 1924. Like his friends in the Progressive Party, he was also accused of taking part in an abortive plot against the life of Mustafa Kemal and was arrested in June 1926 and tried at İzmir. However, he was acquitted by the Independence Tribunal.

A dynamic and active leader of the Nationalist Movement, Refet Pasha attempted to secure a much more important role in the movement by outdoing and outwitting Mustafa Kemal. Yet like the other four leaders, he was bound to remain in the background following the assumption of total power by Mustafa Kemal since 1923.[6]

---

[6] Halide Edib describes him in these words: "His face was as thin and strong as his slim, wiry and rather elegant military figure. . . . Energy of an unusual quality sparkled from his face, his eyes, his movements; and head, hair, and hands all talked together with dramatic gestures. His clothes were faultlessly cut, his spurs and buttons flashed, his boots were of the shiniest patent leather, his whole attire just glowed with fastidiousness." *The Turkish Ordeal,* p. 132; see also Aydemir, *Tek Adam,* vol. 3, p. 45; Peyami Safa, *Refet Paşa* (Istanbul: Orhaniye Matbassı, n.d.). According to S. I. Aralov, "Refet Pasha was elegant, refined and European in outlook but he could not be trusted. Together with Rauf Bey and Karabekir Pasha he was plotting to overthrow Mustafa Kemal. He was insidiously against the War of Independence. He has had ties with the religio-feudal elements and with the representatives of the bourgeoisie compradore. He was hostile toward Soviet Russia because of its support of the new regime in Turkey." *Bir Sovyet Diplomatının Türkiye Hatıraları,* pp. 125–26.

CEBESOY, ALİ FUAT

Although Ali Fuat Pasha was a member of an aristocratic and cosmopolitan family of Istanbul, the son of İsmail Fazıl Pasha, he came to assume a prominent role in the National Struggle. According to Aydemir, if fate and history had not brought forth Mustafa Kemal it is most likely that Ali Fuat would have held up the banner of rebellion and assumed the leadership of the Nationalist Movement. For Aydemir reports that it was Ali Fuat who on behalf of Mustafa Kemal first rebelled against the government of Istanbul.[7] On the other hand Ali Fuat Pasha's misfortune and certain unavoidable circumstances had, from the time of his dismissal as commander of the Western front, been instrumental in his loss of a leading role in the National Struggle. However, he had never lost his deep feelings of attachment to Mustafa Kemal, whom he considered as his leader. Though brokenhearted in later years, Ali Fuat remained loyal and dedicated to his friend, comrade-in-arms, and chief.

Ali Fuat Cebesoy was born in Istanbul on Sepember 24, 1882. He attended the grammar school in Erzincan and graduated in 1893. He enrolled in the French Lycée of St. Joseph in Istanbul and graduated in 1898. Then he was admitted to War College in Istanbul in 1898 and completed his studies there in 1902. He graduated from the Staff Academy in 1905 as staff captain and was assigned to the Third Cavalry Division in Salonica. Then he was sent to Rome as military attaché in 1908. During the War of Tripoli he was charged with a special mission in the Balkans in repressing a rebellion in Albania. He was promoted to major in 1911. He was the Chief of Staff of the army corps that marched against Montenegro. In 1912 he was promoted to lieutenant colonel and two years later he was given the rank of colonel. In 1915, he was appointed commander of the Twentieth Army Corps in Palestine and commanded the defense of Jerusalem. He was promoted to brigadier general in 1917. He remained in the Palestine and Syrian front until the Armistice of Mudros. After the armistice Ali Fuat Pasha took over the command of the army corps in Adana from Mustafa Kemal. While at Adana he took a leave of absence and upon returning to Istanbul got in touch with Mustafa Kemal

---

[7] Aydemir, *Tek Adam,* vol. 3, p. 43.

to discuss with him the possibilities of resistance to Allied invasions and occupations. They decided to move the Twentieth Army Corps commanded by Ali Fuat Pasha from Adana to Ankara. Upon his return to Adana, he executed this decision.

Ali Fuat Pasha met with Mustafa Kemal, Rauf Bey, and Colonel Refet in Amasya and the four friends issued the first circular of the Nationalist Movement on June 22, 1919. Ali Fuat Pasha was appointed by the Sivas Congress' Representative Committee as the commander of the Western front.

Ali Fuat Pasha was appointed the first ambassador of the government of the Grand National Assembly and was sent to Moscow on November 21, 1920. He signed the treaty of friendship with Soviet Russia on March 16, 1921, and served as ambassador to Moscow until May 10, 1922.

Following his quasi-exile in Moscow, Ali Fuat Pasha was elected vice president of the Grand National Assembly in 1922. Opposing the tendency of personal rule of Mustafa Kemal, Ali Fuat Pasha, together with H. Rauf Bey, Refet Pasha, Kazım Karabekir Pasha and others, formed the "Second Group" in the Grand National Assembly. He was, at the time, both deputy from Ankara and inspector of the Second Army. However, under the order of Mustafa Kemal he was relieved from his military position early in November 1924, which precipitated another disagreement between the two old friends. Earlier Ali Fuat Pasha had found himself in disagreement with Mustafa Kemal on the question of the abolishing of the caliphate.

In view of these disagreements and clashes of views, Ali Fuat Pasha and Rauf Bey, Kazım Karabekir Pasha, Refet (Bele) Pasha, and their followers established an opposition party — the Progressive Party — on November 17, 1924.

An important crisis came to its boiling point when Ali Fuat Pasha and his friends in the Progressive Party and others who had no intimate relations with Ali Fuat Pasha and his close friends were accused of plotting against the life of Mustafa Kemal. They were arrested and tried in İzmir between June 15 and July 13, 1926, but were acquitted. Ali Fuat Pasha withdrew from public life from 1926 to 1933. Yet, upon the request of Mustafa Kemal he re-entered politics in 1933 and was elected deputy of the Republican People's Party. He was appointed Minister of Public Works on April 3, 1939, in Dr. Refik Saydam's cabinet and served until

July 8, 1942 . He was reappointed to the same portfolio in Şükrü
Saracoğlu's cabinet from July 9, 1942, to March 8, 1943. He was
appointed Minister of Communications on March 15, 1943, and
served until August 12, 1946. On November 1, 1947, he was
elected president of the Grand National Assembly.

Ali Fuat Pasha maintained his seat in the Grand National
Assembly as deputy from Konya until the general elections on
May 14, 1950; on that date he was re-elected as an independent
deputy from Eskişehir and in the 1957 general elections he was
re-elected as an independent deputy from Istanbul. He retired
from public life in 1960 and died on January 10, 1968. Ali Fuat
Pasha spoke fluent French and some German. He published the
following works: *Milli Mücadele Hatıraları* (Memoirs of the
National Struggle) (Istanbul: Vatan Neşriyatı, 1953); *Moskova
Hatıraları* (Memoirs of Moscow) (Istanbul: Vatan Neşriyatı,
1955); *Siyasi Hatıraları: 2 Cilt* (Political Memoirs, 2 vols.) (Istanbul: Vatan Neşriyatı, 1957-1960). It is interesting to note also
that Ali Fuat Pasha remained a confirmed bachelor all his life.[8]

ÇAĞLAYANGİL, İHSAN SABRİ

He was born in Istanbul in 1908, the son of M. Sabri. He
completed his elementary schooling in Bilecik in 1919, the secondary
schooling at Istanbul Lisesi in 1923. Çağlayangil was graduated
from Ankara Erkek Lycée in 1926 and then attended Istanbul Law
School where he graduated in 1930. His first job was in the
General Directorate of Public Security of the Ministry of Interior.
He was made chief of police in the Malatya province in 1935.
He was appointed director of the First and later the Fourth Department of the General Directorate of Public Security in 1937. He
served as instructor in the Police Institute in Ankara. Çağlayangil
was promoted to deputy director general of the General Directorate
of Public Security in Ankara. He was appointed governor of the
Yozgat-later-Antalya-province in 1948. Then he served as governor
in the following provinces: Çanakkale in 1953; Sivas in 1954;
Bursa from 1954 to 1960. Çağlayangil entered politics in 1961 as
a candidate of the Justice Party and in the 1965 general elections

---

[8] Most of the information on Ali Fuat Pasha's biography is based on a
questionnaire submitted by this writer and completed by him in July 1967.

he was elected senator from Bursa. He was appointed Minister of Labor on February 22, 1965, and on October 27, 1965, he was appointed Minister of Foreign Affairs. He is married and has one daughter. He speaks fluent French, English, and Russian.[9]

ÇAKMAK, FEVZİ

Born in Istanbul on January 12, 1876, he was the son of Çakmakoğlu Ali Sırrı, an artillery colonel. He attended the Rumeli Kavagı elementary school and then the Soğukkuyu secondary school. He was graduated from the *Kuleli* military high school in Istanbul. He then went to the War College in Istanbul and following his graduation as lieutenant in 1895 he entered the Staff Academy and was graduated as staff captain in 1898. His first appointment was at the Fourth Section of the office of the General Staff. Upon his extraordinary service in the European territories of the Ottoman Empire, he was promoted to colonel in 1907. He was then appointed commander of the Thirty-Fifth Division and governor of Taşlica sancak on the Austria-Hungarian border. In 1910 he was appointed Chief of Staff of the Western Corps. He then served as commander of the operational section of the Vardar Army in 1912. After the Balkan Wars he was appointed division commander and a few months later commander of the Fifth Corps in Ankara. In March 1914, he was promoted to brigadier general and during the First World War participated in the Gallipoli campaign and for a month he served as acting group commander of Anafarta in December 1915. In September 1916, he was appointed commander of the Fifth Corps and then transferred to the Caucasian front as commander of the Second Army in July 1917. He assumed the command of the Seventh Army in the Syrian front and in July 1918 he was promoted to major general. During the latter part of 1918 he was appointed Chief of the General Staff and in May 1919 he resigned his post. Then in early 1920 he served as Minister of War of the Ottoman government.

Despite his original misgivings about the success of the Nationalist Movement, on April 8, 1920, Fevzi Çakmak joined the nationalists in Ankara. He was elected Minister of National Defense

---

[9] Aral, *Dışişleri Bakanlığı 1967 Yıllığı,* p. 163; *Kim Kimdir Ansiklopedisi,* p. 185.

in the first Council of Ministers of the Ankara regime on May 3, 1920. Then on January 24, 1921, he was elected by the members of the Council of Ministers, in fact by Mustafa Kemal, as the first prime minister of the government of the Grand National Assembly. He also maintained his post as Minister of National Defense. He served as prime minister until succeeded by Rauf Bey on July 12, 1922. From May 8 to May 17, 1921, he served as acting Minister of Foreign Affairs. He was promoted on April 3, 1921, to lieutenant general. When he stepped down as prime minister, he was appointed Chief of the General Staff on July 12, 1922, and served in that capacity until January 12, 1944. He was promoted to the rank of marshal by the Grand National Assembly in recognition of his services during the War of Independence. Since then he was known as Mareşal Çakmak, the only marshal in the Turkish army since Atatürk's death. Marshal Çakmak retired from active military service on January 12, 1944.

Marshal Çakmak entered the burgeoning political scene in the post-World War II period and was elected deputy from Istanbul as an independent on the Democratic Party ticket in 1946. Then together with other disenchanted deputies and leaders of the Democratic Party, he established the Nation Party on July 20, 1948. He died in Istanbul on April 10, 1950, at the age of seventy-four. It is reported that he knew French and English.[10]

DEMİREL, SÜLEYMAN SAMİ

He was born in İslamköy, a village of the Isparta province. His father, Hacı Yahya Efendi, and his mother still live in that village. Demirel completed his elementary schooling in İslamkoy in 1936, then attended secondary and high schools in Afyonkarahisar and was graduated in 1942. He took the entrance examination and was admitted to the Civil Engineering Faculty of the Istanbul Technical University. He graduated in February 1949. His first job was at the General Directorate of Electrical Studies in Ankara as a design engineer. He held that position until September 1952. In the meantime, he was sent to the United States as a trainee and

---

[10] *Türk Ansiklopedisi,* Cilt 11 (Ankara: Milli Egitim Basımevi, 1963), pp. 334–35; *Cumhuriyet,* 11 April 1950.

between 1949 and 1950 he worked in the Bureau of Reclamation of the U.S. government. Demirel was appointed director of Dams Division of the General Directorate of State Hydraulics Administration in Ankara in September 1952. Two years later he was awarded an Eisenhower Exchange Fellowship to study in the federal, state, and private agencies in the United States. Upon his return to Ankara, Demirel was appointed director general of the State Hydraulics Administration in September 1955. Early in 1960, he entered the Reserve Officers School to begin his military service. From July 13, 1960, to December 31, 1961, he served in the Research and Development Department of the Ministry of National Defense. Following his discharge from the army, Demirel was appointed as a part-time instructor of civil engineering in the Engineering Faculty of the Middle East Technical University in Ankara on February 23, 1961, and served in that capacity until 1964. As a contractor, Demirel built the water supply system of the Middle East Technical University. He also served as consultant to the Morrison-Knudsen Company in Ankara between 1962 and 1964. Meanwhile Demirel had entered into politics by joining the Justice Party in 1962. He was elected member of the Executive Committee of the Justice Party in October 1962, and in November 1964 he was elected leader of the party. At the time when he was appointed deputy prime minister in the coalition cabinet of Premier Ürgüplü on February 20, 1965, Demirel was not a deputy in the Grand National Assembly. In the October 1965 elections, he was elected deputy from Isparta, and was appointed prime minister on October 27, 1965.

Following the general elections held on October 12, 1969, Demirel was returned to power with a large majority and formed his new cabinet which, on November 12, 1969, received a vote of confidence in the National Assembly by a vote of 263 to 165. However, on March 12, 1971, he was asked to resign by the high-ranking generals of the armed forces.

Demirel is married but has no children. He speaks fluent English.[11]

---

[11] See the biography prepared by the Justice Party. See also *Dışişleri Bakanlığı Belleteni* Ekim 1965, no. 13, p. 67; Turkish Embassy, Washington, *Turkish Digest* March 1969, vol. 5, no. 3, December 1969, vol. 5, no. 12.

ECEVİT, BÜLENT

Bülent Ecevit was born in Istanbul on May 25, 1925. His father was Professor Fahri Ecevit, a former member of parliament. Ecevit attended Robert College, a private American institution in Istanbul. He was graduated with a B.A. degree in literature in 1944. The same year he was employed as an English translator at the General Directorate of Press and Tourism. From 1944 to 1946, Ecevit took courses in English literature at the Faculty of Linguistics, History, and Geography in Ankara.

In 1946 Ecevit was appointed assistant press attaché in London. While there he took courses in Sanscrit and history of art at the London University. Upon his return to Ankara in 1950, Ecevit was employed at *Ulus* newspaper. After completing his military service in 1952, Ecevit returned to *Ulus* and worked as translator, art critic, and later as political columnist. He went to the United States in 1954, and worked for a short while for the *Winston-Salem Journal*. After his return home, Ecevit was awarded a Rockefeller Foundation Scholarship and in 1957 he went back to the United States. He took course work at Harvard University.

In 1957 Ecevit ran on the Republican People's Party ticket and he was elected deputy from Ankara. He participated in the deliberations of the Constituent Assembly which drafted the 1961 Constitution. In the 1961 general elections, Ecevit was re-elected. He won re-election in 1965, in 1969, and in 1973.

Ecevit served between 1961 and 1965 as Minister of Labor in İnönü's coalition governments. Having been designated as the next secretary general of the Republican People's Party by İnönü, Ecevit was elected to that post at the end of the 18th Congress of the party in October 1966. Ecevit maintained his position in the party as the secretary general until April 17, 1972, at which time he resigned because of the strong differences of opinion with İsmet İnönü, the leader of the Republican People's Party, on the question of the party's participation in the coalition government of Premier Melen. However, the re-election of Ecevit as secretary general at the 5th Extraordinary Congress of the Republican People's Party on the following day led to the resignation of İsmet İnönü from the leadership of the party. The Congress which met again on May 14, 1972, elected Bülent Ecevit as the leader of the party. On January 25, 1974, Ecevit was able to form the 9th coalition government of Turkey and he became prime minister.

Ecevit, who started his career as a writer in the field of literature, continued his work later as a journalist. While he was still a student at Robert College, he translated into Turkish two books in verse by the famous Indian poet Rabindranat Tagore. Of these, the first one was published in 1941, and the second in 1943. Ecevit's poems, translations in verse and articles on art have appeared in different magazines and journals. Ecevit also translated in verse a work by T. S. Eliot under the title "Cocktail Party" which was published in 1963. He was one of the founders of the *Forum* magazine to which he contributed political articles. Among his political works are *Left of the Center, This Order Should be Changed,* and *Atatürk and Reforms,* all published in Turkish between 1966 and 1970.

Bülent Ecevit is married but has no children. He speaks fluent English.[12]

ERİM, NİHAT

He was born in Kandıra (Kocaeli) in 1912. He was graduated from the elementary, secondary, and high school divisions of Galatasaray Lycée. He attended the law school of the University of Istanbul and was graduated in 1936. He received his doctorate from the University of Paris Law School in 1939. His doctoral dissertation was entitled *Le Positivisme juridique et le droit international.* He also received a certificate from the *Institute des Hautes Études Internationales* in Paris. He joined the staff of the Ankara Law School in 1939 as associate professor. His associate professorship thesis was entitled "The Future of the League of Nations." He was promoted to professor in 1942. The qualifying work for his professorship was a book entitled *A Course in Public Law.* While he was a professor of public law, he also served as the legal adviser of the Ministry of Foreign Affairs. In 1945 he was appointed a member of the Turkish delegation attending the

---

[12] See *Yankı,* 10 Şubat 1974; Directorate General of Information, Ministry of Tourism and Information, *Biographies of the Members of the Cabinet,* Ankara, n.d.

United Nations Conference on International Organization in San Francisco. The same year he was elected deputy from Kocaeli on the Republican People's Party ticket. Erim received his first ministerial appointment in the Hasan Saka cabinet on June 8, 1948, as Minister of Public Works. Upon the resignation of Premier Saka, Erim was appointed deputy prime minister and Minister of State in the Ş. Günaltay cabinet on January 15, 1949. He served until May 22, 1950, when the Democratic Party government of Menderes replaced the Republican People's Party government of Günaltay. From 1947 to 1955 Erim served as editor in chief of *Ulus, Yeni Ulus,* and *Halkcı* newspapers, the organs of the Republican People's Party. After the 1950 general elections, Nihat Erim returned to his teaching position at the Ankara Law School. However, in 1953 he resigned his post. From 1956 to 1962 Erim served as a member of the European Human Rights Commission. Professor Erim was the head of the Turkish delegation responsible for drafting the Constitution of the Republic of Cyprus.

Professor Erim was a member of the Constituent Assembly that convened in January 1961. He was once again elected deputy from Kocaeli in the October 1961 general elections. After the resignation of the Justice Party government, Erim was chosen as premier-designate by President Sunay, following consultations with the high-ranking generals of the armed forces on March 19, 1971. The cabinet formed by Erim was approved by President Sunay on March 27, 1971, and a few days later received the vote of confidence of the National Assembly. Following the resignation of a number of ministers in his cabinet, Premier Erim submitted his resignation to the president on December 11, 1971, but he was asked to form another cabinet. This he also did, but because of the difficulties encountered in the enactment of the necessary reform bills, Premier Erim once again resigned on April 17, 1972, giving "extreme fatigue" as the reason for his resignation.[13] Nihat Erim

---

[13] Premier Erim later explained the reasons for his resignation in these words: "The reform bills, being delayed in the Parliament, worsening relations between political parties, a split in one of the main parties (RPP) becoming quite open and a bitter discussion between the RPP and the Martial Law Commanders, undermining the Government's Parliamentary support." "The Turkish Experience in the Light of Recent Developments," *The Middle East Journal* 26 (Summer 1972): 251.

is married and has two children. He speaks fluent French and English.[14]

ERKİN, FERİDUN CEMAL

He was born in Istanbul in 1899. His father was Mehmet Cemal Bey. He was graduated from Galatasaray Lycée in 1920, and from Paris Faculty of Law in 1925. Between 1925 and 1926, Erkin served as a clerk in the Turkish delegation to the Mixed Commission of Exchange of Population. He joined the foreign service in 1928 and was assigned to the Turkish Embassy in London as first secretary. In 1929 Erkin was appointed secretary of the office of political counselor, and in 1932 was appointed chief of the Third Section of the First Department in the Ministry. In 1934 Erkin was transferred to Berlin as counselor. The next year, he was appointed consul general in Beirut. In 1937 he was designated as director general of the Department of Economic and Commercial Affairs in the Ministry. The following year he was sent to Berlin as consul general. In 1939 Erkin returned to the ministry as director general of the First Department. In 1942 he was made first deputy secretary general and in 1945 he was promoted to the rank of ambassador and was appointed secretary general of the Ministry. Erkin served as ambassador to Rome from 1947 to 1948, to Washington from 1948 to 1955, and to Madrid from 1955 to 1957. Erkin was assigned to Paris in April 1957 and then to London in August 1960. On March 24, 1962, he was appointed Minister of Foreign Affairs and served in that post until February 24, 1965. In the October 1965 elections Erkin, as a candidate of the Republican People's Party, was elected deputy from Ordu. Later he resigned from the party. Erkin is a widower. He speaks fluent French and English. Recently he has published a book simultaneously in Turkish and in French. The Turkish edition is entitled, *Türk-Sovyet İlişkileri ve Bogazlar Meselesi.*[15]

---

[14] Premier Erim's biography is based on a questionnaire sent by this writer and completed by Erim in 1968. Data since 1968 are gathered from newspapers.

[15] Aral, *Dışişleri Bakanlığı 1967 Yıllığı*, pp. 161–62.

GÜNALTAY, ŞEMSETTİN

He was born in Kemaliye (Egin) in 1883. His father, İbrahim Efendi, was a religious man. Günaltay completed his elementary and secondary schooling in *Ravaza-i Terakki* and then went to Istanbul and was graduated from Vefa High School. First he pursued a religious education, then he enrolled in the Teacher's College in Istanbul, graduating in 1905. Günaltay continued his higher education at the Faculty of Natural Sciences, University of Lausanne. Upon returning to Turkey, he taught at various high schools in Cyprus, in the Mitylene island, and in İzmir. He was at the time a member of the Committee of Union and Progress. After the Balkan Wars, he went to Istanbul and was appointed teacher of biology at Vefa High School. In Istanbul, Günaltay became associated with Ziya Gökalp who urged him to study Turkish history. Some time later he was appointed instructor of Turkish and Islamic history at the Faculty of Letters of the University of Istanbul. He also served as instructor of history, religion, and Islamic philosophy at the Süleymaniye School of Theology. In 1915 he was appointed director of the faculty of divinity and professor of Islamic religion. The same year he entered politics and was elected deputy from Ertuğrul Sancak and served until 1920. He was appointed member of the Istanbul Municipal Council and, after 1922, was elected first deputy mayor of Istanbul. In 1923, he was elected deputy from Sivas and joined the Grand National Assembly. In 1927, he was elected deputy from Erzincan on the Republican People's Party ticket and served until the 1954 elections. He joined the Turkish Historical Society in 1930, and while maintaining his deputyship in the Grand National Assembly he taught Turkish history at the University of Ankara. He was elected president of the Turkish Historical Society. Günaltay was appointed prime minister and served until the appointment of Adnan Menderes following the general elections of May 14, 1950. During the 1954 and 1957 general elections he was a candidate of the Republican People's Party and was defeated both times. Günaltay joined the Constituent Assembly on January 6, 1961. He was elected senator from Istanbul on October 15, 1961, but four days later he died in Istanbul. Günaltay was married and knew excellent Persian, Arabic, and French. He published a large number of works on religion and on ancient and recent Turkish history.[16]

GÜNEŞ, TURAN

He was born in Kandıra, Kocaeli province on April 25, 1921. Güneş was graduated from *13cü İlk Okul,* Beyoğlu in 1933, and then attended the junior and senior divisions of Galatasaray Lycée. He was graduated from Galatasaray in 1941. Güneş enrolled in the Faculty of Law of the University of Istanbul and was graduated in 1945. Güneş had chosen the academic career, and with that objective in mind he went to Paris to work toward his doctorate degree. He was awarded an LL.D. degree by the Faculté de Droit. His doctoral dissertation was entitled *Le gouvernement representatif et les partis politiques.* Güneş returned to Istanbul and entered the academic career at his alma mater as assistant of constitutional law. In 1954, he was appointed associate professor following the acceptance of his associate professorship thesis. The English translation of the title of his thesis is "The Contemporary Meaning and Functioning of Parliamentary Regime."

Güneş' political career began when he joined the Democratic Party in 1954, and in that year he was elected deputy from Kocaeli. Then Güneş joined the ranks of the founders of the Freedom Party in 1957. When the Freedom Party merged with the Republican People's Party in 1958, Güneş became a member of the latter. He took part in the deliberations of the Constituent Assembly in 1961 and then returned to his academic career this time at the Faculty of Political Sciences in Ankara. In 1965 Güneş was promoted to professor of public law at Ankara University. The English translation of the title of his professorship work is "The Regulatory Acts of the Administration in the Turkish Positive Law."

Güneş was elected the Republican People's Party deputy from Kocaeli in the 1973 election while serving as deputy secretary general of the party. Güneş was appointed Minister of Foreign Affairs on January 25, 1974. He is married and has two children. He speaks French and Italian.[17]

---

[16] See Gövsa, *Türk Meşhurları Ansiklopedisi,* pp. 155–56; Aydemir, *İkinci Adam,* vol. 2, pp. 471–72; *Cumhuriyet,* 20 Ekim 1961, p. 1.

[17] Based on a questionnaire completed by Güneş in 1968; see also *Yankı,* 4–10, Şubat 1974, p. 6.

GÜRSEL, CEMAL

He was born in Erzurum in 1895. His father was Abidin Bey. Gürsel completed his elementary schooling in Ordu, then graduated from the Erzincan *Askeri Rüştiyesi*. Following his graduation from the *Kuleli Askeri Lisesi* in Istanbul, Gürsel attended the War College in Istanbul. Due to the First World War, his graduation from the military Staff Academy was delayed until 1929. He served as lieutenant in the 15th Artillery Division at Çanakkale in 1915, participated in the Gallipoli campaign and was promoted to first lieutenant in 1917. During the Palestine campaign in 1918, he was taken prisoner by the British and sent to Egypt as a prisoner of war. After the war he was released and joined the nationalist forces in Ankara in 1921. Gürsel served in the 1st Division and participated in the War of Independence until 1922. From that date until 1958 he was promoted regularly and served as commander of company, battalion, regiment, division, corps. From 1954 to 1956 he was commander of the Second Military Zone based in İzmir. In 1957, a full general, he was appointed commander of the land forces, a post which he held until May 3, 1960. On that day, on account of his strong letter of criticism of the conduct of the Bayar administration against its opponents and the students, General Gürsel was relieved of his duties and retired from the army. A few days before the coup d'état of May 27, 1960, General Gürsel must have joined the conspiratorial group of officers who had formed the Committee of National Unity to overthrow the government, for on May 27, he became the chairman of the CNU and assumed as well the positions of the head of state and commander in chief of the armed forces. From May 30, 1960, to October 26, 1961, Gürsel also served as prime minister. On October 26, 1961, General Gürsel was elected the president of the republic. President Gürsel became seriously ill in February 1966, and on the basis of a medical report of the Board of Health, on March 28, 1966, he was declared by the Grand National Assembly no longer capable of exercising the duties of his office. He died in Ankara on September 14, 1966; he is survived by his wife and his son.[18]

---

[18] *Kim Kimdir Ansiklopedisi*, pp. 330–31; *Dışişleri Bakanlığı Belleteni*, Eylül 1966, p. 26; Mustafa Atalay, *Cemal Gürsel'in Hayatı* (Istanbul: Nurgök Basımevi, 1960).

Işık, Hasan Fikret Esat

He was born in Istanbul on October 21, 1916, the son of Esat Pasha, a physician. He was graduated from Galatasaray Lycée in 1937, and the Faculty of Law, University of Ankara in 1940. Işık entered the foreign service in September 1940, and was assigned to the Department of Protocol as third secretary. He served as vice consul in Paris from 1945 to 1949. Işık was promoted to first secretary and assigned to the Department of Commerce of the Ministry. Later he served as permanent delegate in the European office of the United Nations in Geneva between 1952 and 1954. He was promoted to director general of the Department of Commerce and Commercial Agreements in the Ministry and remained in that post until 1957. He served as assistant secretary general in charge of Economic Affairs from 1957 to 1962. His first ambassadorial appointment was in Brussels where he served until 1962. Then he was appointed ambassador to Moscow in October 1964 and served until February 1965. On February 24, 1965, Işık was appointed Minister of Foreign Affairs and served until October 27, 1965, when he was reappointed ambassador to Moscow. Işık is married and has one child. He speaks fluent French and English.[19]

İnönü, İsmet

He succeeded Mustafa Kemal Atatürk as president. Under President Atatürk he served as Chief of the General Staff, Minister of Foreign Affairs, and prime minister. His biography is also inseparably woven together with the history of the Republic of Turkey from 1923 to the present. He is simply known as the *Pasha* or İsmet Pasha.

İsmet İnönü was born in İzmir on September 24, 1884. His father was Kurumoğlu Hacı Reşit Bey who at the time of his death had been the chief of the judicial division of the Ministry of War. İsmet attended the elementary school at Sivas and then the military secondary school in the same city and was graduated in 1895. He then went to Halıcıoğlu Artillery School in Istanbul and was graduated in 1900. Following his training in the Artillery College

---

[19] Aral, *Dışişleri Bakanlığı 1967 Yıllığı,* pp. 162–63; *Dışişleri Bakanlığı Belleteni,* Şubat 1965, pp. 77–78.

in Istanbul he attended the Staff Academy in Istanbul, and was graduated as staff captain on September 26, 1906.

He joined his first field unit in Edirne on October 2, 1906. Then he went to Yemen as Chief of Staff to put down the rebellion of İmam Yahya betwen 1910 and 1913. He was promoted to major on April 12, 1912, and on April 16, 1913, he was assigned to the First Section of the Çatalca Army Headquarters. He was then transferred to the Third Section of the office of the Chief of the General Staff on December 15, 1913. He was later assigned to the Fifth Army's office of the Chief of Staff on August 2, 1914. He was promoted to lieutenant colonel on November 29, 1914, and a few days later was assigned to the General Headquarters of the commander in chief. He was appointed to the Second Army at Diyarbakır as Chief of Staff on October 2, 1915, and promoted to colonel on December 14, 1915. He was appointed commander of the Twentieth Corps in Palestine on May 1, 1917. On October 24, 1918, he was appointed undersecretary of the Ministry of War and served in that position until November 22, 1918; he also served in various posts in the Ministry between November 22, 1918, and March 19, 1920.

İsmet joined the nationalists in Ankara on April 9, 1920. He was appointed Chief of the General Staff in the provisional Executive Committee of the Grand National Assembly on April 25, 1920. He was elected Chief of the General Staff in the first Council of Ministers of the Grand National Assembly on May 3, 1920. Maintaining the same post, he was appointed commander of the northern section of the Western front in Anatolia on November 10, 1920. He was promoted to brigadier general on the occasion of his first victory at İnönü on January 10, 1921, from which in 1934 his surname was to be taken. He resigned his post as Chief of the General Staff and was appointed commander of the Western front in May 1921. He was promoted to lieutenant general on August 31, 1922, for his extraordinary services during the victory campaign of 1922. On August 30, 1926, he was promoted to general of the army and on June 30, 1927, he retired from active military service.

As chief delegate of the Ankara government, İsmet negotiated the Armistice of Mudanya between October 3 and 11, 1922, and signed the final document on October 11, 1922. He was appointed chief delegate of the Ankara government at the Lausanne Peace

Conference which lasted from November 1922 to July 1923. He signed the peace treaty of Lausanne.

He was appointed Minister of Foreign Affairs in the cabinet of Rauf Bey on October 27, 1922, prior to his departure for the Lausanne Conference. Following the resignation of Rauf Bey as prime minister, İsmet Pasha was again appointed Minister of Foreign Affairs in the cabinet of Ali Fethi Bey on August 14, 1923 and served until the resignation of Ali Fethi Bey on October 24, 1923.

İsmet Pasha was appointed prime minister of the first cabinet of the Republican regime on October 29, 1923, and as such he maintained the portfolio of the Ministry of Foreign Affairs. He resigned on March 6, 1924, but the same day was reappointed as prime minister. In this second cabinet he assumed, in addition to the post of Minister of Foreign Affairs, the post of Minister of National Defense. After the elections of August 1923 he became a deputy from Malatya and held on to this deputyship until 1972. He resigned from the prime ministry on November 22, 1924, and was succeeded by Ali Fethi Bey. But upon Ali Fethi Bey's resignation he was again appointed prime minister on March 4, 1925, and from that day to November 1, 1937, he was appointed prime minister four times. He was succeeded by M. Celal Bayar on November 1, 1937.

Upon the death of Mustafa Kemal Atatürk, İsmet İnönü was unanimously elected by the Grand National Assembly as the second president of the Republic of Turkey on November 11, 1938. Following the general elections in 1943 and 1946 he was again elected to second and third terms as president of the republic. He was, however, succeeded by M. Celal Bayar as president following the general elections of May 14, 1950, during which the Republican People's Party, of which İsmet İnönü was the leader since the death of Atatürk in 1938, underwent a decisive defeat.

However, İsmet İnönü returned to the Grand National Assembly as the main opposition leader on May 22, 1950, and served as such until May 27, 1960. İsmet İnönü, as the leader of the Republican People's Party was elected a member of the Constituent Assembly and began to take part in its deliberations from January 6, 1961, until October 14, 1961. In the general elections of October 1961, İnönü was elected deputy from Malatya and then on October 20, 1961, he was appointed prime minister and formed the first coalition government. Due to the difficulties in maintaining a stable government composed of the representatives of the Republican People's Party and its main opposition, the Justice Party, İnönü resigned and on June 27, 1962, formed the second coalition government and then the third coalition government on December 25, 1963, which lasted until February 20, 1965. He was succeeded by Prime Minister Suat Hayri Ürgüplü as the leader of the fourth coalition government. Until May 1972 İsmet İnönü served as the leader of the main opposition party in the Grand National Assembly. At the Vth extraordinary Congress of the Republican People's Party in May 1972, İnönü lost his leadership of the party which he had held for thirty-four years.

İsmet İnönü, the former four-star general, former Minister of Foreign Affairs, former prime minister, former president of the republic, and former leader of the Republican People's Party was the eldest statesman in Turkey when he died in Ankara on December 25, 1973. İnönü is survived by his wife Mevhibe İnönü, his daughter Özden Toker, and two sons. One son, Ömer İnönü, is a businessman, and the other, Erdal İnönü, professor of theoretical physics. İsmet İnönü spoke French, German, and English.[20]

KARABEKİR, KAZIM

He was born in Istanbul in 1882. His father was Mehmet Emin Pasha from a well-known family in Karaman. Like Mustafa Kemal and Ali Fuat, he graduated from the War College and from the Staff Academy as captain in 1905. He rendered brilliant service during the Balkan Wars and the First World War. During the armistice period, he remained in close touch with Mustafa Kemal and urged him to take the initiative in organizing a movement of national survival. He himself as commander of the Fifteenth Army Corps at Erzurum helped to organize the first nationalist Congress

---

[20] On İnönü's military career see supplement to *Ulus* newspaper, "İnönü'nün Hatıraları," starting from February 11, 1968; on his political career see Hamid Aral, *Dışişler Bakanlığı 1967 Yıllığı*, pp. 146–48; see also "Dispatch of November 22, 1927," Ambassador Joseph C. Grew to the Department of State, U.S. National Archives, Turkey, File No. 867.031/2; Şevket Süreyya Aydemir, *İkinci Adam*, 3 vols. (Istanbul: Remzi Kitapevi, 1966–1968).

in that city on July 23, 1920. And when Mustafa Kemal was dismissed from his position as inspector general of the Ninth Army on July 8, 1920, Kazım Karabekir Pasha disregarded the orders of Istanbul government to arrest Mustafa Kemal and take over his position; instead he assured his friend that he and his troops would remain loyal to Mustafa Kemal and execute only his orders.[21]

Kazım Karabekir Pasha, under Mustafa Kemal's orders, attacked Armenia and captured Sarıkamış, on September 30, 1920, and drove the Armenian forces out of Kars on October 30, 1920, compelling the Armenians to sue for peace, which was signed at Gümrü on December 3, 1920. This was the first international treaty between the Ankara government and a foreign power and was signed by Kazım Karabekir Pasha. He also helped to conclude the Treaty of Kars with the Soviet Republics of Armenia, Georgia, and Azerbaijan on October 13, 1921.

Karabekir Pasha became the leader of the opposition Progressive Party on November 17, 1924. He was accused of taking part in the plot against the life of Mustafa Kemal and arrested, released, and again arrested and tried in İzmir in June 1926. He was acquitted and then retired from political life, never being able to reconcile his differences with Mustafa Kemal. He returned to public life after the death of Atatürk in 1938 and was elected Republican People's Party deputy from Istanbul in 1939. On August 5, 1946, he was elected president of the Grand National Assembly and served as deputy from Istanbul until his death on January 26, 1948.

Kazım Karabekir Pasha was married and was survived by two daughters. He published a number of works on the Nationalist Movement and the War of Independence. His works include: *Erzincan ve Erzurum'un Kurtuluşu* (Liberation of Erzincan and Erzurum) (Istanbul: Ebuzziya Basımevi, 1939); *Ülkümüz Kuvvetli Bir Türkiyedir* (Our Aim is to Build a Strong Turkey) (Istanbul: İktisadi Yürüyüş Basımevi, 1947); *İstiklâl Harbimizin Esasları* (The Essential Principles and Objectives of Our War of National Liberation) (Istanbul: Sinan Matbassı, 1951).[22]

[21] Lord Kinross, *Ataturk,* p. 207.

[22] See Lord Kinross, *Ataturk;* Aydemir, *Tek Adam,* vol. 3, p. 43; Elaine D. Smith, *Turkey: Origins of the Kemalist Movement and the Government of the Grand National Assembly* (Washington: Public Affairs Press, 1959), p. 170.

KAYA, ŞÜKRÜ

He was born in İstanköy in 1882. His father was Ahmed Rüştü Bey. He graduated from Galatasaray Lycée, he then attended the law school of Istanbul and studied law at the University of Paris. He served as secretary in the commercial division of the Ministry of Foreign Affairs, Ottoman government between February 16, 1912, and July 14, 1913. He was appointed Justice of the Peace at Edirne on July 6, 1913, and served until October 12, 1913. Şükrü Kaya Bey was then promoted to Judge of the First Instance, at Edirne, but three days later on October 13, 1913 he was appointed provincial inspector; on November 20, 1914, he was appointed director of Settlement of Refugees and Tribes. He was promoted to director general of Settlement of Refugees and Tribes on March 2, 1916. He was promoted to provincial inspector first class on December 22, 1916, and resigned from this post on January 4, 1918. He went to İzmir and began service as a teacher at Buca High School on October 9, 1918, but on January 7, 1919, he was arrested by the British authorities. He was sent to Malta as a prisoner, but later managed to escape. He was appointed the mayor of İzmir following the withdrawal of the Greek forces. In August 1923, he was elected deputy from Mugla and served in the Grand National Assembly until November 11, 1938. He was appointed Minister of Agriculture on August 20, 1924 and served until his appointment as Minister of Foreign Affairs in Ali Fethi Bey's cabinet on November 22, 1924. Following the resignation of Ali Fethi Bey's cabinet, he lost his post as Minister of Foreign Affairs on March 3, 1925. Later, however, he was appointed Minister of Interior on November 1, 1927, in İsmet Pasha's cabinet and served until November 11, 1938. During his long term in office as Minister of Interior, Şükrü Kaya Bey served twenty-seven times as acting Minister of Foreign Affairs. He was also elected as secretary general of the Republican People's Party. He retired from politics in November 1938, and died on January 15, 1959. His knowledge of foreign languages included French and English.[23]

---

[23] Aral, *Dışişleri Bakanlığı 1967 Yıllığı*, p. 149; see also "dispatch" on his biography by Admiral Mark L. Bristol to Department of State, December 6, 1924, U.S. National Archives, Turkey, File No. 867.002/79.

KORUTÜRK, FAHRİ

The sixth president of the republic, Fahri Korutürk, was born in Istanbul in 1903. His father, Osman Sabit, was a civil servant in the Ministry of War. After completing his studies in the Imperial School of Naval Sciences, Korutürk was graduated from the Naval War College in 1923. He served as a teacher in various naval institutions as well as in the navy. He attended the Staff Academy and became a staff officer in 1934. The following year he took up his first foreign assignment in Rome as military attaché. In 1936 Korutürk, as a naval expert, participated in the Montreux Conference concerning the regime of the Turkish Straits. Then, Korutürk was promoted to the rank of lieutenant commander and sent to Berlin in 1937. He served as military attaché in Stockholm and then transferred to Berlin again in 1942. He was then promoted to the rank of commander.

Korutürk served as commander of the Naval War Academy during 1945 and 1946, as fleet commander upon his promotion to vice admiral in 1953, as chief of Intelligence in the office of the Chief of the General Staff in 1954, and as fleet commander between 1955 and 1956. During the next two years Korutürk served as commander of the Marmara and the Straits region. In 1957 Korutürk was promoted to admiral and appointed as the commander of naval forces.

Upon his retirement from active military service following the May 27, 1960 coup d'état, Admiral Korutürk was appointed ambassador to Moscow by the Head of State General Cemal Gürsel. When he was designated ambassador to Madrid in 1964, Admiral Korutürk declined the offer. He retired from diplomatic service in 1965.

Korutürk's political career began when he was appointed senator on June 10, 1968, by President Sunay. In the Senate, he served as the chairman of the Presidential Quota which consisted of fifteen presidential appointees. Admiral Korutürk was elected president of the republic on April 6, 1973, at the age of seventy. President Korutürk is married and he has three children. He speaks German, Italian, and English.[24]

---

[24] See *Cumhuriyet,* 7 Nisan 1973, p. 1; *Devir,* no. 24, 16 Nisan 1973, pp. 12–13.

KÖPRÜLÜ, MEHMET FUAD

He was a descendent of the famous Köprülü family of the Ottoman Empire, which provided the Ottoman sultans with a number of Grand Vezirs. Mehmet Fuad was born in Istanbul on December 4, 1888. His father, İsmail Fazıl Bey, was chief secretary of the Beyoglu, Second Criminal Court. He graduated from Ayasofya Merkez Rüştiyesi and then from Mercan İdadisi (high school) in Istanbul. Mehmet Fuad attended the Istanbul Law School between 1908 and 1910, but did not graduate. He started his career as a teacher of literature at Mercan High School and then taught at Kabataş, Istanbul, and Galatasaray High Schools between 1910 and 1913. He was appointed instructor and later professor of history of Turkish literature at the University of Istanbul in 1913. Ten years later he was appointed director of the Faculty of Letters of the University of Istanbul. Between 1923 and 1929 he also served as professor of diplomatic history and Turkish history at the School of Political Science in Istanbul. In 1924 he was also serving as professor of history of Islamic religion at the Faculty of Divinity. Mehmet Fuad was appointed Dean of the Faculty of Letters of the University of Istanbul in 1934. A year before, he was promoted to the highest rank attainable by a professor, namely, Ordinarius Professor.

Like all the leading intellectuals in the one-party period, he entered politics and was elected deputy from Kars in 1935. For the next ten years he served as the Republican People's Party deputy in the Grand National Assembly.

Köprülü was expelled from the party on September 21, 1945, and with three other friends founded the Democratic Party. He was elected Democratic Party deputy from Istanbul in the 1946 elections and until 1957, he represented Istanbul in the Grand National Assembly. In the first cabinet of Menderes, he was appointed Minister of Foreign Affairs on May 22, 1950, and served until April 15, 1955. On July 29, 1955, Köprülü was appointed Minister of State and deputy prime minister and served in that capacity until November 30, 1955. In the fourth cabinet of Menderes, Köprülü assumed the portfolio of Minister of Foreign Affairs on December 9, 1955. However six months later on June 20, 1956, Köprülü resigned his post. Due to his disagreements with the policies and actions of Menderes, Köprülü resigned from the Democratic Party on September 7, 1957 and went into opposition, as did many of the prominent personalities of the Democratic Party. Despite his opposition to the Menderes regime, following the coup d'état of May 27, 1960, Professor Köprülü was arrested and sent to Yassıada for trial. However, Köprülü was acquitted and in September 1961 was released from Yassıada. The same year he re-entered politics by founding the Free Democratic Party with a number of his associates, apparently for the purpose of wooing the remaining Democratic Party sympathizers after that party was abolished by the order of the Committee of National Unity on September 29, 1960. But the activities of the Free Democratic Party were to no avail.

Professor M. Fuad Köprülü was married and had one daughter. He died in Istanbul on June 28, 1966. Köprülü had published several works on the history and literature of Turkey including *Milli Tetebbular* (1915), *Türkiye Mecmuası* (1925), *Hukuk ve İktisat Mecuması* (1931–1939), *Ülkü Mecmuası* (1941–1942), *Türk Edebiyatı Ansiklopedisi* (1936). He was awarded a number of honorary degrees including one by Heidelberg University, 1927, one by the University of Athens, 1937, and by the Sorbonne University, 1939. Professor Köprülü spoke Persian, French, German, and English.[25]

KUNDUK, BEKİR SAMİ

He was born in the Caucassus region in 1861. It is difficult to pinpoint accurately the exact place and date of the birth of Bekir Sami Bey. One writer maintains that he was of Caucasian origin and was born in 1862,[26] whereas another says that he was born in 1871.[27] Other sources, such as *Who's Who* and encyclopedias, state that he was born in Sivas in 1862. In view of the fact that he assumed a position in the Ministry of Foreign Affairs in 1883 it is more likely that the earlier date is correct. His father, Musa Kundakov, a tsarist and later Ottoman general, in 1865 led a large group of Ossetion and Chechen refugees from the Caucassus region to the Tokat area in north central Anatolia. Following his

[25] See Aral, *Dışişleri Bakanlığı 1967 Yıllığı*, pp. 156–57.
[26] Dankwart A. Rustow, "The Army and the Founding of the Turkish Republic," p. 526.
[27] Aral, *Dışişleri Bakanlığı 1967 Yıllığı*, p. 1217.

private tutoring at home, Bekir Sami Bey attended Galatasaray Lycée in Istanbul and then studied at the Faculty of Political Science in Paris.

Bekir Sami Bey joined the Ministry of Foreign Affairs in 1883. He was appointed third secretary of the Ottoman Embassy in St. Petersburg in 1887 and returned to Istanbul in 1889 to the Division of Translation of the Ottoman government. He was appointed consul general at Mesina in September 1896. Then he served as consul general at Kermanshah (1897–1899), at Sina (1899–1901), at Batum (1901–1902), and at Malta (1903–1904). He was appointed chief secretary of the Tripoli province in December 1904. He served as governor of *Sanack* of Cebel-i Garb (1907), and of Amasya (1908). He was then promoted to governor of the following provinces: Van (1909); Trabzon (1910–1911); Bursa (1913); Beirut (1913–1915); and Aleppo (June 18, 1915–September 21, 1915). While governor of Aleppo he was dismissed by the Ottoman government.

After the Armistice of Mudros, Bekir Sami Bey was elected a member of the Representative Committee by the Erzurum Congress and also by the Sivas Congress. He participated in the last Ottoman Parliament as deputy from Amasya from January 12, 1920, until the formal occupation of Istanbul at which time he returned to Ankara. He was elected a member of the Provisional Executive Council of the Grand National Assembly on April 25, 1920. He was elected the first Minister of Foreign Affairs in the first Council of Ministers of the Grand National Assembly on May 3, 1920, and served in that position until May 8, 1921, at which time he was asked to resign because of his fundamental disagreements with Mustafa Kemal on foreign and domestic policies. In August 1923, he was re-elected deputy from Tokat. He joined the leading ranks of the opposition Progressive Party. His political life came to an end when he failed to get re-elected deputy in the 1927 general elections. He died in Istanbul in 1932.[28]

MELEN, FERİT

He was born in Van in 1906. He graduated from the Faculty of Political Sciences in 1931. He entered the civil service and in

---

[28] Ibid.

1933 became a member of the Board of Inspectors of the Ministry of Finance. While in this position, he was sent to France for a year for internship in the French Ministry of Finance. In 1943, Melen was appointed director general of the Indirect Taxation Department of the Ministry of Finance and a year later he became director general of Revenues.

It was in 1950 that Melen entered politics and was elected deputy from Van on the Republican People's Party ticket. After four years in the National Assembly, he lost in the general elections and returned to work as a financial adviser until 1957, at which time he was re-elected deputy from Van again on the Republican People's Party ticket. Melen joined the Constituent Assembly as Republican People's Party representative in 1961. Although he was not a deputy in 1962, he nevertheless was appointed Minister of Finance in the second coalition cabinet of Premier İnönü and held the same post in İnönü's third coalition cabinet until February 20, 1965. In 1964 Melen was elected senator from Van. Opposing the Republican People's Party's left-of-center platform, Melen resigned from the party and with forty-eight other deputies and senators who had also resigned from the party, he helped to establish a new party called the Reliance Party. Melen was elected the vice president of the Reliance Party. He was appointed Minister of National Defense in the first cabinet of Nihat Erim on March 27, 1971, and he held the same post in the second cabinet of Premier Erim. Ferit Melen succeeded Erim as Premier on May 22, 1972. He is married and has two children. He speaks French.[29]

MENDERES, ADNAN

He was born in 1899 in Aydın. His father, İbrahim Etem, had immigrated to Aydın from Greece. In Aydın, İbrahim Etem Bey had married the daughter of a wealthy landowner, Hacı Ali Pasha of Tire.[30] Adnan was orphaned soon after birth, thereby falling heir to 30,000 acres of cotton and wheat land watered by

---

[29] See The State Information Organization of Turkey, *Turkish Digest,* vol. 1, no. 2, June 1972, p. 2; *Cumhuriyet,* 26 Mart 1971, p. 7.

[30] Şevket Süreyya Aydemir maintains that Menderes' grandfather had migrated to Eskişehir from Crimea and that he was a Crimean Tartar. "Menderes'in Dramı," *Cumhuriyet,* 18 Şubat 1969, p. 4.

the Menderes River. It was affection for his birthplace that led him to choose Menderes as his surname in 1934.

He completed his elementary schooling in Aydın and was then sent to live with his grandmother in İzmir where he entered the American International College, a Congregational mission school, at thirteen. Menderes was transferred to İttihat ve Terakki High School in İzmir. Much later, while he was a deputy in the Grand National Assembly, he completed the Ankara Law School by taking the end-of-year examinations.

Following his graduation from high school, he went to Istanbul and joined the Reserve Officers School. Adnan saw no combat in World War I, but made up for that after the war by joining the guerrilla forces fighting against the Greek invasion of western Anatolia. After the war, Adnan returned to farming. In 1930, he entered politics by joining the Liberal Republican Party headed by Ali Fethi Okyar. Upon the closing of the party, he joined the Republican People's Party at the suggestion of Celal Bayar who had come to Aydın with a delegation to reorganize the Republican People's Party in that province. In 1931, he was elected deputy to the Grand National Assembly at Atatürk's personal order. He served as inspector of the Republican People's Party in western Anatolia.

In 1945, Menderes joined Celal Bayar and two other deputies in presenting a resolution demanding that the government put into effect the democratic liberties promised under the Constitution. Soon the four rebels launched their own Democratic Party. In 1946 he was elected deputy from Aydın. In the next elections in 1950, he was elected deputy from Istanbul. Then on May 22, 1950, he was appointed the first prime minister of the Democratic Party administration. On March 9, 1951, he reshuffled his cabinet. Following the general elections of May 1954, he was reappointed as prime minister. Upon the resignation of a number of cabinet ministers, Menderes formed a new cabinet on December 9, 1955. He was reappointed prime minister on November 1, 1957, following the victory of the Democratic Party in the general elections of October 27.

On February 17, 1959, Adnan Menderes miraculously survived an airplane crash outside of London which killed fifteen other members of the Turkish delegation going to London to sign the Cyprus agreement. Many superstitious people in Turkey attributed his escape from certain death to his superhuman qualities. This incident made a deep impression among the more conserative people, reconfirming their absolute devotion to Adnan Menderes. "A few months before the revolution, when he visited the town of Tarsus, a follower was all prepared, like Abraham in the Old Testament, to sacrifice his own son for Menderes' glory."[31]

When the Committee of National Unity seized power on May 27, 1960, Menderes, together with all the Democratic Party leaders and deputies, were arrested and detained at War College and were then sent to Yassıada for trial. At the Yassıada trials, Menderes was convicted in ten different cases. The tenth case involved the violation of constitutional guarantees of property rights, judicial autonomy, freedom of association, free elections, etc.

At the end of his trials, Menderes was sentenced to death eight times in eight different cases on September 15, 1961. Apparently, because of his unprecedented popularity with the majority of the population, the Committee of National Unity, fearful of his possible return to power in a general election, decided not to commute the death sentence passed on him at the Yassıada trials.[32] He was executed on September 17, after recovering from what was said to have been an overdose of sleeping pills. Menderes is survived by his wife and two sons. He spoke fluent English and French and some Greek.[33]

MENDERES, ETHEM

He was born in İzmir in 1899. He completed his elementary, secondary, and high school education in İzmir and Aydın. He received his LL.B. degree from the Faculty of Law of the University of Ankara. Menderes began his career as an administrator serving as a member of the Executive Council of the Aydın province from May 1933 to October 1938. In November 1938 he was elected mayor of the city of Aydın and served until February 1945.

[31] Kemal H. Karpat, "Economics, Social Change and Politics in Turkey," *Turkish Yearbook of International Relations,* 1 (1960): 6.

[32] See Weiker, *The Turkish Revolution, 1960–1961,* p. 12; Robinson, *The First Turkish Republic,* p. 270.

[33] *Türk ve Dünya Meşhurları Ansiklopedisi,* pp. 292–93; Mustafa Atalay, *Adnan Menderes ve Hayatı* (Ankara: Sevinç Matbaası, 1959); Şevket Süreyya Aydemir, "Menderes'in Dramı," *Cumhuriyet,* 16 Şubat 1969.

He joined the emerging Democratic Party in Aydın and in the 1950 elections he was elected deputy of the Democratic Party from Aydın. He entered the cabinet following the 1954 general elections as Minister of National Defense on May 17, 1954, and served until November 30, 1955. In the meantime, he was also appointed as Minister of State on September 15, 1955. In the fourth cabinet of Premier Menderes he was the Minister of Interior and held that position until December 12, 1956. On October 12, 1956, he was appointed also Minister of Public Works. He held that portfolio until he was appointed Minister of National Defense on January 19, 1958. At the time of the military coup d'état Ethem Menderes was in charge of the Ministry of National Defense. After the coup he was arrested and sent to Yassıada for trial. He was sentenced to life imprisonment. Ethem Menderes was released from prison in 1966.[34]

Menemencíoğlu, Numan

Numan Menemencioğlu was the first career diplomat to be appointed as the Minister of Foreign Affairs. He was born in Baghdad in 1891. His father was Menemenlizade Ahmet Rifat Bey, who at one time served as Minister of Finance and senator in the Ottoman Parliament. Following the completion of his elementary and secondary schooling in Salonica, Numan attended the French high school "For Lycée" in Istanbul. He received his LL.B. degree at the law school of the University of Lausanne and then he joined the foreign service of the Ottoman Empire. He was sent to Vienna as third secretary of the Ottoman Embassy in 1914, and was promoted to the rank of second secretary in 1917. He was then assigned to Bern. There appears to be no information in published materials on him for the period from 1917 to 1923. Apparently he was in Europe. In January 1923 while in Bern he was confirmed as the second secretary of the Turkish legation by the government of the Grand National Assembly. On June 16, 1923, Menemencioğlu was transferred to the Turkish Mission in Budapest as first secretary. During 1926 and 1927, he served as Charge d'Affaires in Hungary. He was appointed consul general on June 14, 1927, in Beirut.

---

[34] See Afşin Oktay, ed. *Who's Who in Turkey* (Ankara: Kültür Matbaası, 1958), p. 118; Aral, *Dışişleri Bakanlığı 1967 Yıllığı,* p. 158.

Returning to Ankara he was appointed director general of the First Department of the Ministry of Foreign Affairs on June 1, 1928. The following June he was promoted to the rank of minister and was appointed as the undersecretary of the Ministry. On June 11, 1933, he was promoted to the rank of ambassador and appointed as the secretary general of the Ministry. He was elected deputy from Gaziantep and joined the Grand National Assembly on April 5, 1937, but he simultaneously served as the political undersecretary of the Ministry of Foreign Affairs. However, when the political undersecretaryships in Ministries were abolished, he was once again appointed secretary general of the Ministry of Foreign Affairs on December 2, 1937. He was appointed foreign minister on August 14, 1942, and served until June 15, 1944.

Following his resignation Menemencioğlu was appointed ambassador to Paris on November 30, 1944, and served until November 2, 1956, at which time he retired from foreign service. He re-entered into political life and was elected deputy from Istanbul in 1957, on the Democratic Party ticket. Menemencioğlu died in Ankara on February 15, 1958. He was married and spoke fluent French and German.[35]

OKYAR, ALİ FETHİ

He was born in Pirlepe in 1880, the son of İsmail Bey. After completing his secondary education at Manastır military secondary and high schools, he attended the War College in Istanbul and graduated in 1903 from the Staff Academy in Istanbul. He was appointed as staff captain in the Third Army and also served as military attaché in Paris in 1908. He served as Chief of Staff of the Ottoman forces in the Tripoli campaign. He retired from military service as lieutenant colonel and was appointed minister to Sofia. He was instrumental in the appointment of Mustafa Kemal as military attaché to Sofia.

Ali Fethi was interested in a political rather than in a military career. He was elected a member of the Central Committee of the Association of Union and Progress during the Young Turk Revolution of 1908 and later secretary general. He was elected deputy

---

[35] See Aral, *Dışişleri Bakanlığı 1967 Yıllığı,* pp. 153–54; *Cumhuriyet,* 16 Şubat 1958, p. 1.

from Istanbul in the Chamber of Deputies in 1913. He was appointed Minister of Interior in İzzet Pasha's cabinet on October 14, 1918, and served until November 11, 1918, when İzzet Pasha was replaced by Tevfik Pasha as Grand Vezir. Then, he began publishing a daily newspaper *Mimber,* opposing the policies of the government. Mustafa Kemal contributed articles to *Mimber* criticizing the decision of the sultan to dissolve the parliament on November 21, 1918. When Damat Ferit was installed as Grand Vezir on March 7, 1919, Ali Fethi was arrested and later deported to the island of Malta by the British authorities and was held prisoner for two years. Upon his release from Malta he joined the ranks of nationalists in Ankara. As deputy from Istanbul, he was elected Minister of Interior by the Grand National Assembly. In the Spring and Summer of 1922, Mustafa Kemal sent Ali Fethi on a peace mission to Rome, Paris, and London. In London Lord Curzon did not wish to receive him as the representative of the Ankara government, and he telegraphed Mustafa Kemal saying that the only hope of achieving the national objective was to continue the military operations.

Ali Fethi was elected deputy from Istanbul on the People's Party ticket in August 1923. Upon Rauf Bey's resignation, he was elected prime minister by the Grand National Assembly on August 14, 1923. He also maintained the portfolio of the Minister of Interior. But a few months later, upon the request of Mustafa Kemal, Ali Fethi Bey resigned from the prime ministry on October 24, 1923, so as to precipitate an artificial cabinet crisis and open up the way for the establishment of the Republic. Following the resignation of Premier İsmet Pasha, Ali Fethi Bey was reappointed as prime minister with the portfolio of the Ministry of National Defense on November 22, 1924.

During the early months of 1925, a reactionary Kurdish revolt had occurred in eastern Anatolia and the cabinet of Ali Fethi Bey was censured by the Grand National Assembly on the grounds that it had not taken strong measures against the rebels. This development led to Ali Fethi Bey's resignation on March 3, 1925. He was then appointed ambassador to Paris on March 27, 1925. However, he was summoned by Mustafa Kemal on August 9, 1930, from his quasi-exile as ambassador to France to become the leader of an opposition Liberal Republican Party established on August 12, 1930. However, when it appeared that a large number of reactionary elements were flocking to the Liberal Republican Party standard, the cabinet of İsmet Pasha then suppressed the party on November 17, 1930.

Ali Fethi Bey, was later appointed ambassador to London on March 31, 1934. He served there until January 4, 1939. He re-entered politics and was elected deputy of the Republican People's Party from Bolu in early 1939, and on May 26, 1939, he was appointed Minister of Interior in Dr. Refik Saydam's cabinet. He remained in that post until March 12, 1941, and died in Istanbul on May 7, 1943, at the age of sixty-three. Ali Fethi Bey spoke excellent French, German, and English. He was survived by a son who is a professor of economics, Dr. Osman Okyar, and a daughter.[36]

OLCAY, OSMAN E.

He was born in Istanbul in 1924. Following his graduation from the French language Saint Joseph Lycée at Kadıköy he enrolled in the School of Political Sciences at Ankara. Olcay was graduated in 1944, and joined the Ministry of Foreign Affairs in January 1945. He served for two years in the military as a reserve officer and returned to the Ministry in March 1947. His first foreign assignment was in London, where he served in the chancery of the Turkish consulate and was later promoted to vice consul. In 1951 he was promoted to second secretary of the Turkish Embassy in London. Then he returned to the Ministry in 1952 and served in various departments of the Ministry. Olcay was posted to the permanent delegation of Turkey to NATO in 1954 as first secretary of the legation, and in 1956 he was promoted to first secretary of the embassy. Returning home Olcay was appointed deputy director general of the NATO department in the Ministry of Foreign Affairs and the following year he was promoted to the position of the director general of the NATO department. In 1964 he was appointed ambassador to Finland and in 1966 ambassador to India. While he was in India in January 1969, Olcay was asked to join the NATO Secretariat as deputy secretary general of NATO. Osman E. Olcay was appointed Minister of Foreign Affairs in the first

---

[36] See İbrahim A. Gövsa, *Türk Meşhurları Ansiklopedisi* (Istanbul: Yedigün Neşriyatı, 1946), p. 291; *Cumhuriyet,* 9 Mayıs 1943, p. 1.

cabinet of Premier Nihat Erim on March 27, 1971, and served until December 11, 1971. Then, he was appointed chief of the Permanent Delegation of Turkey in the United Nations. Olcay is married but has no children. He speaks fluent French and English.[37]

ORBAY, HÜSEYİN RAUF

Born in Istanbul in 1881, he was the son of Vice Admiral Mahmut Muzaffer who was later appointed senator by the sultan. Rauf Bey, as he was known throughout the War of Independence period, attended elementary and secondary schools at Tripoli, then went to the naval high school in Istanbul. He received his commission in the navy following his graduation from the Naval College in 1905. He won fame as the captain of the cruiser *Hamidiye* during the Balkan Wars of 1912–1913. He headed the Ottoman delegation negotiating the exchange of prisoners of war with the Russians in Copenhagen in 1917. He was also appointed a member of the Ottoman delegation at the Brest-Litovsk Peace Conference in March 1918. He resigned as Chief of the Naval Staff on June 5, 1918, and later, on October 14, he was appointed Minister of Marine in İzzet Pasha's cabinet. He was head of the Ottoman delegation at the armistice talks in Mudros. He signed the armistice agreement of October 30, 1918. Later on February 27, 1919, he resigned from active military service.

He was a friend of Mustafa Kemal since 1909 and during the armistice days he met quite often with Mustafa Kemal to discuss the affairs of the state in secret. He joined the ranks of Mustafa Kemal in Amasya in June 1919 and attended the historic meetings of the Erzurum and Sivas Congresses and was elected a member of the Representative Committee. Thus, he took an active part in the formative period of the Nationalist Movement and worked in close cooperation with Mustafa Kemal both in Sivas and in Ankara.

Rauf Bey was elected deputy from Sivas and joined the last Ottoman Parliament as a leading member of the Association for the Defense of Rights of Anatolia and Rumelia on January 12, 1920. He was instrumental in the adoption of the National Pact by the Chamber of Deputies of the Ottoman Parliament on January 28, 1920. However, he was arrested in the Chamber of Deputies

---

[37] See Aral, *Dışişleri Bakanlığı 1967 Yıllığı*, pp. 582–83; *NATO Newsletter*, January 1969; *Cumhuriyet*, 26 Mart 1971, p. 7.

together with other nationalist deputies by the British occupation authorities and deported to Malta on March 16, 1920, where he was held in confinement until October 25, 1921. Upon his release he returned to Ankara and was elected by the Grand National Assembly as minister of Public Works on November 17, 1921, and served until January 14, 1922. Then, on March 1, 1922, he was elected vice president of the Grand National Assembly. He was elected by the Grand National Assembly as prime minister on July 12, 1922.[38] He served as acting Minister of Foreign Affairs from November 6, 1922, to July 30, 1923, i.e., during the Lausanne Conference. He was elected deputy from Istanbul as a member of the People's Party in August 1923 and resigned from the prime ministry on August 13, 1923, and also from the (Republican) People's Party on November 9, 1924.

Together with Ali Fuat Pasha, Kazım Karabekir Pasha, Refet Pasha, Rüştü Pasha, Dr. A. Adnan Bey, Rauf Bey established the Progressive Party on November 17, 1924. However, this party was closed by the government on June 3, 1925. He was accused of and tried in the Independence Tribunal and sentenced *in absentia* to ten years' banishment in 1926 for plotting against Mustafa Kemal's life. However, he had left Turkey into self exile in 1925 only to return on July 5, 1935. He re-entered politics and was elected deputy from Kastamonu in October 1939. He then accepted an appointment as ambassador to London on March 23, 1942, and served until March 9, 1944. Upon his return to Turkey, he retired from political life, and died in Istanbul on July 16, 1964.[39]

PEKER, RECEP

He was born in Istanbul in 1888. His father was Mustafa Şahabeddin. He attended the Kocamustafapaşa Military School

---

[38] The U.S. delegate at Ankara, Robert W. Imbrie, in his dispatch on July 16, 1922, describes Rauf Bey in these words: "He was educated in England, has travelled in America, speaks English fluently, believed friendly to Russia but not to Bolshevik principles, very friendly disposed toward the U.S., a man of charming personality and unusual ability." U.S. National Archives, Turkey, File No. 867.002/63. On the other hand the first Soviet Ambassador to Ankara, S. I. Aralov, identifies Rauf Bey as "an enemy of Soviet Russia. A man who has instigated the burning of the Soviet embassy building in Ankara." *Bir Sovyet Diplomatının Türkiye Hatıraları* (trans.) Hasan Ali Eliz (Istanbul: Burçak Yayınevi, 1967), p. 126.

[39] See "Rauf Orbay'ın Hatıraları" *Yakın Tarihimiz,* vols. 1–4; see also Aydemir, *Tek Adam,* vol. 3, p. 42.

and was graduated from Kuleli Military High School in Istanbul. Peker was graduated from the War College in 1907. He entered the military career as lieutenant and served at Edirne, Kırklareli; he participated in the Yemen campaign in 1910, in the Italo-Turkish War of 1911, the Balkan Wars, and the First World War. After the war he entered the Military Staff Academy in 1919. He was promoted to major in 1920. In February 1920 he joined the Nationalist Movement in Ankara and was elected secretary general of the Grand National Assembly. Major Recep served also as the chief of the Bureau of Intelligence of the General Staff until August 1920. He was elected deputy from Kütahya on August 11, 1923, and from that day until the general elections of May 1950, he remained a member of the Grand National Assembly. When the (Republican) People's Party was founded in October 1923, he was appointed its first secretary general. Meanwhile he also served as the editor in chief of *Hakimiyet-i Milliye* newspaper, the organ of the party. Recep Peker was appointed Minister of Finance on May 21, 1924 and served in that capacity until November 22, 1924, at which time he was appointed Minister of Interior and Minister of Exchange of Population and Construction and Settlement in Ali Fethi Okyar's cabinet. In the next cabinet of İsmet İnönü, he was appointed Minister of National Defense on March 4, 1925, and served until November 1, 1927. Peker served as Minister of Public Works between October 15, 1928 and September 27, 1930. He was appointed secretary general of the Republican People's Party on March 9, 1931 and served in that capacity until June 25, 1936. From 1935 to 1942, Recep Peker was also an instructor of the history of the Turkish Revolution at Ankara University and published a book concerning the National Struggle entitled *İnkilap Tarihi Dersleri Notları*. He came to be regarded as one of Turkey's foremost orators. He entered the Saracoğlu cabinet as Minister of Interior on August 17, 1942. On August 12, 1946, Recep Peker was appointed prime minister and served until September 9, 1947. Recep Peker died in Istanbul on April 2, 1950. He was married and is survived by three sons.[40]

---

[40] See İbrahim A. Gövsa, *Türk Meşhurları Ansiklopedisi* (Istanbul: Yedigün Neşriyatı, 1946), p. 308; *Ulus,* 3 Nisan 1950, p. 5. On his personality see "Dispatch," October 19, 1928, Ambassador Grew to Department of State, U.S. National Archives, Turkey, File No. 807–002/99.

SADAK, NECMEDDİN

He was born in Isparta in 1890. His father was Şehabeddin Sadık Bey. Necmeddin completed his elementary and secondary schooling in İzmir. Then he attended Galatasaray Lycée in Istanbul. After graduating from high school in 1910, Necmeddin Sadak went to France to begin his university education and there he attended the Faculty of Letters of the University of Lyon. He finished his studies in 1914. He started his career as translator in the Ministry of Education in Istanbul and was later promoted to the post of examiner of compiled and translated works. In 1916 he was appointed assistant instructor of sociology in the Istanbul University. In 1920 he was promoted to professor of sociology. In the meantime, he had begun to publish the daily newspaper *Akşam* in 1918. He was the publisher and editor in chief of this newspaper throughout his life with the exception of the period when he served as Minister of Foreign Affairs. Necmeddin Sadak entered into active politics in 1927 when he was elected deputy from Sivas. From 1927 to 1950 he was a member of the Grand National Assembly. Probably because of his astute analyses and comments in his newspaper editorials, he was appointed as Minister of Foreign Affairs on September 10, 1947, and served until May 22, 1950, after which Sadak returned to journalism in *Akşam* newspaper. He died on September 21, 1953, in New York. Sadak was married and spoke fluent French, and he knew some German and English.[41]

SAKA, HASAN

He was born in Trabzon in 1886. His father was Sakaoğlu Hafiz Yusuf Efendi. Saka completed his elementary, secondary, and high school education in Trabzon. He then came to Istanbul and enrolled in 1905 in the School of Political Science. Following his graduation in 1908, he went to Paris and studied in *École Science Politique* and was graduated in 1912. Upon his return from Paris, Hasan Saka was appointed as instructor of Economics and Finance in his alma mater between 1915 and 1916. In 1919 he was appointed director of the Board of Inspectors of the Ministry of Food. The same year Saka was elected deputy from Trabzon

---

[41] Aral, *Dışişleri Bakanlığı 1967 Yıllığı*, pp. 155–56; *Türk ve Dünya Meşhurları Ansiklopedisi*, p. 265; *Akşam*, 22 Eylül 1953, p. 1.

and joined the Ottoman Parliament. Following the occupation of Istanbul, he went to Ankara and joined the Grand National Assembly. He served as deputy from Trabzon in the Grand National Assembly from 1920 to 1950. He was elected Minister of Finance on May 19, 1921, and served until April 24, 1922. Then Hasan Saka was appointed Minister of Economy on May 11, 1922, and served in that post until July 22, 1922. He was appointed member of the Turkish delegation that was sent to the Lausanne Conference in November 1922. Upon his return from Lausanne, he joined the Ali Fethi Okyar cabinet as Minister of Economy on August 14, 1923. He was reappointed to that post on October 29, 1923, and served in İsmet İnönü's cabinet until March 6, 1924. From March 6, to November 22, 1924, Hasan Saka served as Minister of Commerce. On March 4, 1925, he was appointed once again as Minister of Finance and resigned on July 13, 1926. While maintaining his deputyship in the Grand National Assembly, Hasan Saka taught economics and finance courses in the Ankara Law School and in the School of Political Science from 1925 to 1942. On September 13, 1944, he was appointed Minister of Foreign Affairs in the Saracoğlu cabinet. He served as the chairman of the Turkish delegation attending the United Nations Conference on International Organization in San Francisco. Upon Saracoğlu's resignation, he was reappointed as Minister of Foreign Affairs in the Recep Peker cabinet. And following the resignation of Premier Peker he was asked to form the new cabinet on September 10, 1947. Hasan Saka resigned on June 8, 1948, but the same day he was reappointed as prime minister. He resigned once again on January 14, 1949, on account of strong differences of opinion between himself and the Parliamentary Group of the Republican People's Party and President İnönü. He retired from political life following his defeat in the general elections of May 14, 1950. Hasan Saka died on July 29, 1960. He was married and had two children. He spoke fluent French.[42]

SARACOĞLU, ŞÜKRÜ

He was born in Ödemiş on January 1, 1887, of Mehmet Tevfik, a saddler. He completed his elementary and secondary

[42] See Çankaya, *Mülkiye Tarihi ve Mülkiyeliler,* pp. 623–24; Aral, *Dışişleri Bakanlığı 1967 Yıllığı,* p. 155.

education in Ödemiş and then attended high school in İzmir graduating in 1906. Then he attended the School of Political Science in Istanbul, graduating in 1909. Much later he went to Geneva and enrolled at the *École des Sciences Politiques et des Economiques* of the University of Geneva and was graduated in 1919. His career began, however, in 1909 when he was appointed civil servant in the provincial administration in İzmir; at the same time he taught mathematics at İzmir High School. Later he was appointed principal of the School of Commerce of Union and Progress. Upon his return to Turkey from Geneva, Saracoğlu participated in the War of Independence. He briefly served as deputy from İzmir in the Ottoman parliament in 1920. After the war, he was elected deputy from İzmir and joined the Grand National Assembly in 1923. From 1923 to 1950 he was a member of the Grand National Assembly and a prominent member of the Republican People's Party. He entered the cabinet of Ali Fethi Okyar as Minister of Education in November 1924. When Prime Minister Okyar resigned in March 1925, Saracoğlu was appointed chairman of the Turkish delegation in the Greco-Turkish Commission of Exchange of Population in 1925. He did not have a ministerial post until November 1, 1927, at which time, İsmet İnönü appointed him as Minister of Finance. He resigned on December 25, 1930, because of ill health. He was then sent to the United States in 1931 to study some economic matters. On May 25, 1933, he was appointed Minister of Justice. When the last İnönü cabinet resigned, he was once again retained as Minister of Justice by Prime Minister Celal Bayar. In the second cabinet of Celal Bayar, Saracoğlu was appointed Minister of Foreign Affairs on November 11, 1938. Upon Celal Bayar's resignation, Saracoğlu entered the cabinet of Dr. Saydam again as Minister of Foreign Affairs and he maintained his position until he was appointed prime minister on July 9, 1942, upon the death of Dr. Saydam. For almost a month, until the appointment of Numan Menemencioğlu, Premier Saracoğlu also held the portfolio of the Ministry of Foreign Affairs. And upon Menemencioğlu's resignation on June 15, 1944, Saracoğlu served as acting minister of Foreign Affairs until September 13, at which time Hasan Saka was appointed to that post. After the general elections in July 1946, Prime Minister Saracoğlu resigned on August 5, 1946, it is said, "on account of his ill health." His long and invaluable service to his country was rewarded by his election to the presidency of the Grand National Assembly on November 1, 1948. He was re-elected to the same post the following year and served until May 14, 1950. In the general elections held on that day, he was not elected as a candidate of the Republican People's Party because of the landslide victory of the opposition Democratic Party. Şükrü Saracoğlu died in Istanbul on December 27, 1953. He had excellent knowledge of the French and German languages. He was married and is survived by two sons and a daughter.[43]

SARPER, SELİM RAUF

He was born in Istanbul in 1899. His father was Esat Rauf Bey. He completed his elementary schooling in Sivas, secondary schooling at Robert College in Istanbul, and attended high school in Magdeburg, Germany, graduating in 1917. While a foreign service officer, Sarper took the required examinations and obtained an LL.B. degree from the Ankara Faculty of Law in 1935. Sarper's first job was with the French Railroad Company in Adana where he worked as a translator in 1923. In 1925 he served as clerk of the Court of Independence of Eastern Provinces. He joined the foreign service in 1927. The next year he was sent to Odessa as vice consul. He was then transferred to the Moscow Embassy as third secretary. In 1930 he was promoted to second secretary. Returning to Ankara in 1931, he was appointed to the executive office of the Minister of Foreign Affairs as second secretary. Sarper was transferred to Alexandroupolis in 1933 and to Odessa in 1935 and then to Berlin as consul. In 1938 he returned to Ankara and was appointed section chief in the second department of the Ministry. Sarper left the Ministry and was appointed secretary general of the Directorate of Press and Broadcasting in June 1940 where he served until he was appointed ambassador to Moscow in 1944. Two years later Sarper was appointed ambassador to Rome. In 1947, Sarper was designated ambassador and permanent representative of Turkey at the United Nations in New York. For ten years he remained in that post. Then he was transferred to the NATO headquarters in Paris as Turkey's permanent representative. After

[43] Mücellitoğlu Ali Çankaya, *Mülkiye Tarihi ve Mülkiyeliler,* 2 vols. (Ankara: Örnek Matbaası, 1954), vol. 2, pp. 644–46.

serving two years in Paris, Sarper was appointed secretary general of the Ministry of Foreign Affairs. On May 30, 1960, he was appointed by General Gürsel as Minister of Foreign Affairs, a post which he held until his resignation on March 15, 1962. Meanwhile he was elected member of the Constituent Assembly, serving in that body from January 6, 1961 to October 15, 1961. As a candidate of the Republican People's Party, he was elected deputy from Istanbul on October 15, 1961, and served for four years. In the 1965 general election he was defeated in his bid for re-election. But after the general elections, he was appointed as senator by President Gürsel. Sarper is married and has two daughters. He speaks fluent French, English, and German.[44]

SAYDAM, DR. REFİK

He was born in Istanbul on September 8, 1881. His father, Ahmet Efendi, from Çankırı province, was an oil merchant in Istanbul. He completed his elementary schooling in Fatih, Istanbul, and his secondary schooling at Fatih Military School. Then he graduated from the Çengelköy Military Medical High School. He received his M.D. degree from the Military Medical School on October 22, 1905. He served as military medical officer at Gülhane Hospital in Istanbul in 1907 and in the 3rd Army in 1908. Then he went to Germany and attended the Berlin Military Medical Academy in 1910. He served in the army during the Balkan Wars. He was appointed deputy inspector general of Health during the First World War. He joined the ranks of Atatürk in May 1919 and accompanied Atatürk to Samsun. Dr. Saydam was elected deputy from Beyazıt in the First Grand National Assembly, 1920–1923, and from 1923 to 1942 he represented Istanbul in the Grand National Assembly. He was, from its inception, a member of the Republican People's Party. He assumed his first ministerial post on March 10, 1921, as Minister of Health and served until December 24, 1921. Again he was appointed to that post on October 29, 1923, and served until November 22, 1924. He was reappointed as Minister of Health on March 4, 1925 in the cabinet of Premier İnönü and served in that capacity until November 1, 1937. Dr. Saydam did not assume a ministerial post in the first cabinet of

---

[44] See Aral, *Dışişleri Bakanlığı 1967 Yıllığı,* pp. 159–60.

Premier Celal Bayar who succeeded İnönü on November 1, 1937. But when İsmet İnönü succeeded Atatürk as the president of the Republic, and reappointed C. Bayar as his prime minister, Dr. Saydam entered Bayar's cabinet as Minister of Interior on November 11, 1938. Upon the resignation of Premier Bayar, President İnönü on January 25, 1939, appointed Dr. Saydam as his next prime minister. Following the general elections of April 1939, Dr. Saydam reconstituted his cabinet on April 3, 1939. Dr. Refik Saydam died in Istanbul on July 8, 1942. He spoke both French and German. He was a confirmed bachelor.[45]

SUNAY, CEVDET

He was born in Trabzon in 1900. He was graduated from the *Kuleli Askeri Lisesi* (military high school) in Istanbul in 1917. He was then graduated from the War College and Military Staff Academy in 1930. Following the completion of his studies in the military high school, he was commissioned as third lieutenant and sent to the Palestine front in September 1917. Sunay was wounded and captured as a prisoner of war by the British in 1918. Upon his release he joined the nationalist forces and participated in the War of Independence and served in the Gaziantep front in 1920. Later he served in the Western front as lieutenant in the 41st Artillery Regiment in 1921. After the war he continued his studies in the War College and was later admitted to the Military Staff Academy in 1927. Sunay was appointed commander of the Third Battery, 4th Artillery Division in Edremit in 1930. He was promoted to major and assigned to Operations Section, IVth Corps, in 1934; he was appointed Chief of Staff of the 1st Cavalry Division in Karaköse; he was appointed commander of the 3rd Battalion, 5th Artillery Regiment in 1938; he was assigned to Operations Section, IVth Corps in 1939; he was promoted to lieutenant colonel in 1940; he was assigned to the military Staff Academy as assistant instructor of tactics in 1942; he was appointed commander of the 72nd Artillery Regiment in 1943; he was promoted to colonel and assigned to the military Staff Academy as an instructor of tactics in 1943; in 1947 he was appointed commander of armored artillery

---

[45] See *Siyasi İlimer Mecmuası,* Agustos 1943; *Türk Ve Dünya Meşhurları Ansiklopedisi,* p. 272; *Cumhuriyet,* 9 Temmuz 1942, p. 2.

regiment; he was appointed commander of armored brigade in 1948. Sunay was promoted to brigadier general in 1949 and the following year he was appointed director of operations, of the office of the General Staff. Two years later Sunay was promoted to the rank of major general and appointed commander of the 33rd Division. In May 1955 he was appointed commander of the IXth Corps in Erzurum. In August 1955 he was promoted to lieutenant general and in September 1957 he was assigned to the Operations Division of the office of the General Staff. In August 1958 he was appointed Deputy Chief of the General Staff. In August 1959, he was promoted to general of the army. Following the May 27, 1960 coup, General Sunay was made the chief of the land forces and in August of that year he was appointed Chief of the General Staff and served in that capacity until he was elected president of the republic. President Sunay is married and has a son, a medical doctor.[46]

TALU, NAİM

Talu was born in Istanbul in 1919. He completed his elementary and secondary education in the same city and was graduated from the Kabataş Lycée. He enrolled in the Faculty of Economics of the University of Istanbul. Upon his graduation Talu served in the army. After his military service he was employed briefly at Sümerbank, a state enterprise, and then joined the staff of the Central Bank of Turkey in 1946. In his banking profession, Talu was promoted regularly and in 1966 he was appointed the acting director general of the bank. The next year Talu was appointed president of the Central Bank.

Talu's political career began when on December 11, 1971, Premier Erim appointed him as Minister of Commerce, a post which he held again in the Ferit Melen cabinet until April 15, 1973. He succeeded Melen and formed his own coalition government. Talu remained in office as prime minister until he was succeeded by Bülent Ecevit on January 25, 1974. Talu is married and has two children. He speaks English.[47]

---

[46] See *Dışişleri Bakanlığı, Belleteni,* Mart 1966, no. 18, pp. 96–97.
[47] See The State Information Organization, *Fact-File on Turkey,* May, 1972; *Cumhuriyet,* 16 Nisan 1973.

TENGİRŞENK, YUSUF KEMAL

He was born in Boyabat in 1878. His father was a judge, Hasan Raci Efendi. He completed his elementary schooling in Boyabat in *Subyan Mektebi,* his secondary schooling in Boyabat and Taşköprü secondary schools. Then he attended *Numune-i Terakki* and *Fatih Askeri Rüştiyesi* schools in Istanbul, graduating in 1892. He enrolled in *Kuleli* and later military medical schools hoping to become a medical doctor. But due to illness he could not continue his medical training. Then, he began to study law at Istanbul Law School and received his law degree in 1904. Some years later while he was in Paris he attended the Faculty of Law of Paris and received a doctorate degree in political and social sciences in 1913.

He started his career as teacher first at Piripaşa Jewish School in 1901 and then switched to journalism and contributed articles to *Sabah* newspaper between 1902 and 1908. Following his graduation from law school, he was employed there as instructor of criminal law and private international law. He was elected deputy from Kastamonu in 1908 and entered the parliament. The same year, he resigned his seat in the parliament. He was appointed as educational inspector in Paris in September 1909 and served until August 31, 1914. Upon his return to Istanbul he was appointed deputy inspector general of the Ministry of Justice in September 1914, and on June 1, 1915, he was promoted to inspector general of the Ministry of Justice. On November 23, 1915, he was appointed undersecretary of the same Ministry and served until the end of the First World War. During this time he also taught economics courses at Istanbul Law School and international law at the War College. He was elected deputy from Kastamonu in the last Ottoman Parliament in November 1919 and following the formal occupation of Istanbul he joined the nationalists in Ankara. He served as deputy of Kastamonu in the Grand National Assembly from 1920 to 1923. Yusuf Kemal Bey was elected Minister of Economy on May 3, 1920, and served until January 30, 1921, at which time he was chosen as Minister of Justice. Then, on May 16, 1921, he was elected Minister of Foreign Affairs to succeed Fevzi Pasha, acting Minister of Foreign Affairs. Yusuf Kemal Bey served in that post until October 26, 1922. He was elected deputy from Sinop in August 1923; however, he resigned on

January 11, 1924, to assume the post of representative of the Turkish Republic in London. He resigned on May 16, 1924, and returned to Ankara, where he was appointed professor of economics at the Ankara Law School. He maintained his professorship from 1925 to 1941. During the interval he was appointed Minister of Justice from September 27, 1930, to May 25, 1933. He was a deputy first from Sinop and later from Istanbul until 1950. He was elected a member of the Constituent Assembly on January 6, 1961, and served until October 15, 1961. He published a book containing his recollections in 1967, entitled *Vatan Hizmetinde*. He spoke fluent, French, German, and English.[48] He died in Istanbul on April 16, 1969.

ÜRGÜPLÜ, SUAT HAYRİ

He was born in Damascus on August 13, 1903. His father was Şey-ül İslam M. Hayri Bey. Ürgüplü was graduated from Galatasaray Lycée in 1922 and received his LL.B. degree from Istanbul Law School in 1926. He served as translator in the Greco-Turkish Court of Arbitration and later served as secretary to the Turkish-Romanian Court of Arbitration between 1925 and 1929. He was appointed judge of the First Commercial Court in Istanbul in 1929. He served as legal adviser to the Bank of Securities from 1932 to 1952. In 1939 he entered politics and was elected Republican People's Party deputy from Kayseri, and until 1952 he was a member of the Grand National Assembly. Ürgüplü was appointed minister of Customs and Monopolies on March 8, 1943, and served until February 19, 1946. Prior to the 1950 general elections he joined the Democratic Party and was elected deputy from Kayseri. In 1952 he was appointed ambassador to Bonn and resigned his seat in the Grand National Assembly. In September 1955 Ürgüplü was appointed ambassador to London. From 1957 to 1960 he served as ambassador to Washington and then as ambassador to Madrid. He retired from diplomatic service on August 4, 1960. On October 15, 1961, Ürgüplü was elected deputy from Kayseri as an independent on the Justice Party ticket. On October 26, 1961,

---

[48] Aral, *Dışişleri Bakanlığı 1967 Yıllığı*, p. 145; *Kim Kimdir Ansiklopedisi* [Encyclopedia of Who's Who] (Istanbul: Nebioğlu, 1961–1962), p. 606; see also U.S. National Archives, Turkey, File No. 867.002/63 and File No. 867.00/1421.

he was elected president of the Senate of the Republic and served until October 1963. He served as prime minister of the fourth coalition cabinet from February 20, 1965, to October 27, 1965. Ürgüplü is married and has one son. He speaks fluent French and English.[49]

ZORLU, FATİN RÜŞTÜ

He was born in Istanbul on April 20, 1910. Graduating from Galatasaray Lycée in Istanbul in 1926, Zorlu obtained his B.A. degree from the Faculty of Political Science in Paris in 1930 and his LL.B. degree from the Faculty of Law of the University of Geneva in 1932. He joined the Ministry of Foreign Affairs in 1932 and two years later he was sent to Geneva as the secretary of the Turkish delegation attending the Disarmament Conference. In 1936 he also served as the secretary of the Turkish delegation attending the Montreux Conference on the Turkish Straits. The following year he was assigned to the Turkish Mission at the League of Nations. Zorlu then was transferred to the Turkish Embassy in Paris as first secretary in 1939. Three years later he was promoted to counselor of the embassy in Moscow. In 1943 he was assigned to Beirut as vice consul. Three years later, Zorlu returned to the Ministry of Foreign Affairs and was appointed the director general of the Department of Commerce. From 1947 to 1949 Fatin Rüştü Zorlu served as the chairman of the Turkish delegation at the European Economic Council. During this time, he also served as chairman of the Turkish delegation at the Havana Conference in 1947. He was promoted to assistant to the secretary general in charge of the economic affairs in 1948. Zorlu was appointed secretary general of the International Cooperation Administration in 1950. The same year he was elected deputy of the Democratic Party from Çanakkale and entered politics. Zorlu was appointed deputy prime minister and Minister of State on May 17, 1954, and served until July 29, 1955, at which time he was appointed Acting Minister of Foreign Affairs. On November 29, 1955, he was forced by the Democratic Party deputies in the Grand National Assembly to resign from his cabinet post. However, two

---

[49] *Dışişleri Bakanlığı Belleteni,* Şubat 1965, no. 13, p. 77.

years later, on July 28, 1957, he was again appointed as Minister of State and on November 27, 1957, he assumed the post of Minister of Foreign Affairs.

Fatin Rüştü Zorlu served as foreign minister until the coup d'état of May 27, 1960. On that day, he was arrested and sent to Yassıada for trial. Zorlu was found guilty on many counts and was sentenced to death by unanimous vote of the Yassıada tribunal on September 15, 1961. The next day he was executed. Zorlu was married to the daughter of ex-Minister of Foreign Affairs Dr. Tevfik Rüştü Aras. He spoke fluent French and English.[50]

---

[50] See *Hariciye Vekaleti Yıllığı, 1959,* p. 180; *Who's Who in Turkey, 1960,* pp. 191–92; *Current Biography Yearbook, 1958* (New York: The H. W. Wilson Co., 1958), pp. 496–98; Aral, *Dışişleri Bakanlığı 1967 Yıllığı,* p. 159.

SELECTED BIBLIOGRAPHY

DOCUMENTS AND OFFICIAL PUBLICATIONS

France. Ministère des affaires étrangères. Documents diplomatiques. *Conference de Lausanne sur les affaires du prochenorient, 1922–1923.* Recuel des actes de la conference. Ier serie, tome 4. Paris.

Great Britain. *British and Foreign State Papers.* Vols. 143, 144, 145, 279. London: H.M.S.O.

————. Colonial Office. *Cyprus: Documents Relating to Independence of Cyprus and the Establishment of British Sovereign Base Areas.* Cmnd. 1903. London: H.M.S.O. 1960.

————. Colonial Office. *Conference on Cyprus: Documents Signed and Initialled at Lancaster House on February 19, 1959.* Cmnd. 679. London: H.M.S.O. 1960.

————. Foreign Office. *Treaty Series. No. 16 (1923) Treaty of Peace with Turkey and other Instruments Signed at Lausanne on July 24, 1923.* Cmnd. 1929. London: H.M.S.O. 1923.

————. Foreign Office. *Convention Regarding the Regime of the Straits, with Correspondence Relating thereto.* Montreux, July 20, 1936. London: H.M.S.O. 1936.

————. Public Records Office. Files of the Foreign Office. 1918–1923.

T. C. Başbakanlık (The Republic of Turkey. Prime Ministry) *Resmi Gazete.* [The Official Gazette], 1920–1970. Ankara.

————. Dahiliye Vekaleti (The Republic of Turkey. Ministry of Interior) *Ayın Tarihi* [The History of the Month]. 1933–1950. Ankara.

————. Dışişleri Bakanlığı (The Republic of Turkey. Ministry of Foreign Affairs) *Dışişleri Bakanlığı Belleteni* [The Bulletin of the Ministry of Foreign Affairs] 1964–1971. Ankara.

————Dışişleri Bakanlığı (The Republic of Turkey. Ministry of Foreign Affairs) *Ceremonial and Protocol Practice Followed in Ankara.* 1968. Ankara.

————. Ministère des affaires étangères. *Le livre rouge. La question de Mossoul (Octobre 1918–Mars 1925)*. n.p., n.d.

————. Ministère des affaires étrangères. *La question de Mossoul, à la 35me session du conseil de la societé des nations*. Lausanne: Imprimerie de la societé suisse de publicité, 1925.

————. State Information Organization. *Turkish Digest*, vol. 1, 1972. Ankara.

————. Türk Devrim Tarihi Enstitüsü [The Institute of the Turkish Revolution]. *İnönü'nün Söylev ve Demeçleri* [The Speeches and Statements of İnönü]. Istanbul: Milli Egitim Basımevi, 1946.

————. Türk İnkilap Tarihi Enstitüsü [The Institute of the Turkish Revolution] *Atatürk'ün Söylev ve Demeçleri* [The Speeches and Statements of Atatürk]. Ankara: Türk Tarih Kurumu Basımevi, 1961.

————. Türkiye Büyük Millet Meclisi [The Grand National Assembly of Turkey]. *Zabıt Ceridesi* "Tutanak Dergisi" [The Records of the Grand National Assembly], 1920–1970. Ankara: T.B.M.M. Matbaası.

————. Türkiye ve Orta Doğu Amme İdaresi Enstitüsü [The Institute of Public Administration of Turkey and the Middle East]. *T. C. Devlet Teşkilatı Rehberi* [The Governmental Organization Manual of the Republic of Turkey]. Ankara: T.O.A.I.E., 1968.

U. S. Congress. 66th Cong., 2nd Sess. Senate. Document no. 266. *A Report of the American Military Mission to Armenia* by Maj. Gen. James G. Harbord, 1920.

————. Department of State. *The Bulletin of the Department of State*. Vols. for the years 1945–1971. Washington D.C.

————. Department of State. *Papers Relating to the Foreign Relations of the United States*. Vol. 2 (1923) Washington: Government Printing Office, 1938; and vol. 2 (1926) published in 1941.

————. Department of State. *The Problem of the Turkish Straits*. Publication no. 2752 (comp.) Harry N. Howard. Washington: Government Printing Offiice, 1947.

————. National Archives. Turkey, Files from 1918 to 1930.

U.S.S.R. Ministry of Foreign Affairs. *Documents and Materials Relating to the Eve of the Second World War*. Moscow: Foreign Languages Publishing House, 1948.

MEMOIRS

Aralov, S. I. *Bir Sovyet Diplomatının Türkiye Hatıraları* [The Memoirs of Turkey of a Soviet Diplomat]. Translated by Hasan Âli Ediz. Istanbul: Burçak Yayınevi, 1967.

Byrnes, James F. *Speaking Frankly*. New York: Harper and Brothers, 1947.

Child, Richard W. *A Diplomat Looks at Europe*. New York: Duffield, 1925.

Churchill, Winston S. *The Gathering Storm*. Boston: Houghton Mifflin, 1948.

————. *The Grand Alliance*. Boston: Houghton Mifflin, 1950.

————. *The Hinge of Fate*. Boston: Houghton Mifflin, 1950.

————. *Closing the Ring*. Boston: Houghton Mifflin, 1951.

————. *Triumph and Tragedy*. Boston: Houghton Mifflin, 1953.

Eden, Anthony (Earl of Avon) The Memoirs of, *Facing the Dictators*. Boston: Houghton Mifflin, 1962.

Grew, Joseph C. *Turbulent Era: A Diplomatic Record of Forty Years, 1904–1945*. Boston: Houghton Mifflin, 1952.

Hull, Cordell. *The Memoirs of Cordell Hull*. New York: Macmillan, 1948.

Kılıç, Ali. *Kılıç Ali Hatıralarını Anlatıyor* [Kılıç Ali Relates his Memoirs] Istanbul: Sel Yayınları, 1955.

Knatchbull-Hugessen, Sir Hughe. *Diplomat in Peace and War*. London: John Murray, 1949.

Papen, Franz von. *Memoirs*. New York: E. P. Dutton, 1953.

Rawlinson, A. *Adventures in the Near East, 1918–1922*. London: Andrew Melrose, 1923.

Roosevelt, Eliot. *As He Saw It*. New York: Duell, Sloan & Pearce, 1946.

Truman, Harry S. *Memoirs*. 2 vols. London: Hodder and Stoughton, 1955.

Yalman, Ahmet Emin. *Turkey in My Time*. Norman Okla.: University of Oklahoma Press, 1956.

BOOKS

Ağaoğlu, Samet. *Kuvayı Milliye Ruhu* [The Spirit of the National Struggle]. Istanbul: Nebioğlu Yayınevı, 1945.

Akkerman, Naki Cevat. *Demokrasi ve Türkiyede Siyasi Partiler Hakkında Kısa Notlar* [Brief notes on Democracy and the Political Parties in Turkey]. Ankara: Ulus Basımevi, 1950.

Akşin, Abdülahat. *Atatürk'ün Dış Politika İlkeleri ve Diplomasisi* 2 cilt. [Atatürk's Foreign Policy Principles and his Diplomacy, 2 vols.] Istanbul: İnkilap ve Aka Kitapevleri, 1962–1964.

Aral, Hamid, Comp. *Dışişleri Vekaleti Yıllığı, 1953* [The 1953 Yearbook of the Ministry of Foreign Affairs]. Ankara: Güzel Istanbul Matbaası, 1954.

————. *Hariciye Vekaleti Yıllığı, 1959* [The 1959 Yearbook of the Ministry of Foreign Affairs]. Ankara: n.p., n.d.

————. *Dışişleri Bakanlığı Yıllığı, 1964–1965* [The 1964–1965 Yearbook of the Ministry of Foreign Affairs]. Ankara: n.p., n.d.

————. *Dışişleri Bakanlığı 1967 Yıllığı* [The 1967 Yearbook of the Ministry of Foreign Affairs]. Ankara: Ankara Basım ve Ciltevi 1968.

Aras, Tevfik Rüştü. *Görüşlerim* [My Views]. Istanbul: Semih Lütfü Basımevi, vol. 1, 1945.

Armaoğlu, Fahir F. *Kıbrıs Meselesi, 1954–1959: Türk Hükümeti ve Kamu Oyunun Davranışları* [The Cyprus Question, 1954–1959: The Reactions of the Turkish Government and the General Public] Ankara: Siyasal Bilgiler Fakültesi Yayınları no. 156–138, 1963.

Aşkun, Vehbi Cem. *Sivas Kongresi* [The Sivas Congress]. Istanbul: İnkilâp Kitapevi, 1963.

Atalay, Mustafa. *Cemal Gürsel'in Hayatı* [The Life of Cemal Gürsel]. Istanbul: Nurgök Basımevi, 1960.

_____. *Adnan Menderes ve Hayatı* [The Life Story of Adnan Menderes]. Ankara: Sevinç Matbaası, 1959.

Ataöv, Türkkaya. *Turkish Foreign Policy, 1939–1945.* Ankara: Faculty of Political Sciences, 1965.

_____. *Amerika NATO ve. Türkiye* [The United States, NATO and Turkey]. Ankara: Siyasal Bilgiler Fakültesi, 1969.

Atatürk, Mustafa Kemal. *A Speech Delivered by Ghazi Mustapha Kemal, President of the Turkish Republic.* Leipzig: K. F. Koehler, 1929.

_____. *A Speech Delivered by Mustafa Kemal Atatürk, 1927.* Istanbul: Ministry of Education Printing Plant, 1963.

Aydemir, Şevket Süreyya. *Tek Adam: Mustafa Kemal* [The One Man: Mustafa Kemal]. 3 vols. Istanbul: Remzi Kitapevi, 1963–1965.

_____. *İkinci Adam: İsmet İnönü* [The Second Man: İsmet İnönü] 3 vols. Istanbul: Remzi Kitapevi, 1966–1968.

Avcıoğlu, Doğan. *Türkiyenin Düzeni: Dün-Bugün-Yarın* [The Socio-Economic-Political Order of Turkey: Yesterday-Today-Tomorrow] Ankara: Bilgi Yayınevi, 1969.

Balta, Tahsin Bekir. *Türkiyede Yürütme Kudreti* [The Executive Power in Turkey] Ankara: Ajans-Türk Matbaası, 1960.

Başgil, Ali Fuat. *Le Révolution militaire de 1960 en Turquie, ses origines.* Geneva: Perret-Gentil, 1963.

Bayur, Himet. *Son Yirmibeş Yıllık Tarihimize Bakışlar* [A Review of the Last Twenty-Five Years of our History]. Istanbul: Devlet Basımevi, 1938.

_____. *Türk İnkilap Tarihi,* 2 Cilt [The History of the Turkish Revolution 2 vols.] Istanbul: Maarif Matbaası, 1940–1943.

_____. *Türkiye Devletinin Harici Siyaseti* [The Foreign Policy of the Republic of Turkey]. Istanbul: A. Sait Matbaası, 1942.

_____. *Atatürk: Hayatı ve Eseri* [Atatürk: His Life and his Work]. Ankara: Aydın Kitapevi, 1962.

Bıyıklıoğlu, Tevfik. *Atatürk Anadoluda, 1919–1921* [Atatürk in Anatolia, 1919–1921]. Ankara: Türk Tarih Kurumu Basımevi, 1959.

Berkes, Niyazi. *The Development of Secularism in Turkey.* Montreal: McGill University Press, 1964.

Cebesoy, Ali Fuat. *Moskova Hatıraları* [Memoirs of Moscow]. Istanbul: Vatan Neşriyatı, 1955.

Çelik, Edip F. *Milletlerarası Hukuk* [International Law]. Istanbul: Hukuk Fakültesi Yayını, no. 205, 1965.

_____. *100 Soruda Türkiye'nin Dış Politika Tarihi* [The History of the Foreign Policy of Turkey in 100 Questions]. Istanbul: Gerçek Yayınevi, 1969.

Çankaya, Mücellitoglu Ali. *Mülkiye Tarihi ve Mülkiyeliler* [The History of the School of Political Science and its Alumni]. Ankara: Örnek Matbaası, 1954.

Dahl, Robert A. *Democracy in the United States: Promise and Performance,* 2nd ed. Chicago: Rand McNally, 1972.

Davison, Roderic H. *Reform in the Ottoman Empire, 1856–1876.* Princeton, N.J.: Princeton University Press, 1963.

———. *Turkey.* Englewood Cliffs, N.J.: Prentice-Hall, 1968.

Degras, Jane, ed. *Soviet Documents on Foreign Policy,* vol. 1. London: Oxford University Press, 1951.

Dodd, C. H. *Politics and Government in Turkey.* Berkeley: University of California Press, 1969.

Dursunoğlu, Cevat. *Erzurum Kongresi Sırasında Atatürk'ün Düşünceleri* [Atatürk's views during the Erzurum Congress]. Ankara: Türk Tarih Kurumu Basımevi, 1967.

———. *Milli Mücadelede Erzurum* [Erzurum during the National Struggle]. Ankara: Ziraat Bankası Matbaası, 1946.

(Adıvar), Halide Edib. *The Turkish Ordeal.* New York: Century, 1928.

Erkin, Feridun Cemal. *Türk-Sovyet İlişkileri ve Boğazlar Meselesi* [The Turco-Soviet Relations and the Question of the Turkish Straits]. Ankara: Başnur Matbaası, 1968.

Eroğlu, Hamza. *Türk Devrimi Tarihi* [The History of the Turkish Revolution] Ankara: Kardeş Matbaası, 1967.

Esen, Bülent Nuri. *Türk Anayasa Hukuku.* Birinci Fasikul [The Turkish Constitutional Law] Fascicle I. Ankara: Ayyıldız Matbaası, 1968.

Evans, Laurence. *United States Policy and the Partition of Turkey.* Baltimore: Johns Hopkins Press, 1965.

Fenik, Mümtaz Faik. *1939 Harbi: Türkiye-İngiltere İttifakı* [The Second World War: The Anglo-Turkish Alliance]. Ankara: Zerbomat Basımevi, 1941.

Fisher, Sidney N. *The Middle East: A History.* New York: Alfred A. Knopf, 1960.

Frey, Frederick W. *The Turkish Political Elite.* Cambridge, Mass.: The M.I.T. Press, 1965.

Gönlübol, Mehmet ve Cem Sar. *Atatürk ve Türkiyenin Dış Politikası, 1919–1938* [Atatürk and Turkey's Foreign Policy, 1919–1938]. Istanbul: Milli Egitim Basımevi, 1963.

Gönlübol, Mehmet ve Türkkaya Ataöv. *Turkey in the United Nations.* Ankara: Institute of International Relations, Ankara University, 1960.

Gövsa, İbrahim A. *Türk Meşhurları Ansiklopedisi* [The Encyclopedia of Turkish Notables]. Istanbul: Yedigün Neşriyatı, 1946.

Gözübüyük, Şeref ve Suna Kili. *Türk Anayasa Metinleri* [Texts of Turkish Constitutions]. Ankara: Ankara Üniversitesi Siyasal Bilgiler Fakültesi Yayınları, no. 75–57, 1957.

Halil, Ali. *Atatürkcü Dış Politika ve NATO ve Türkiye* [Atatürkist Foreign Policy and NATO and Turkey]. Istanbul: Gerçek Yayınevi, 1968.

Harington, Sir Charles. *Tim Harington Looks Back.* London: John Murray, 1940.

Harris, George S. *The Origins of Communism in Turkey.* Stanford, Calif.: Hoover Institution, 1967.

———. *Troubled Alliance: Turkish American Problems in Historical Perspective.* Washington, D.C.: American Enterprise Institute for Public Policy Research, 1972.

Howard, Harry N. *The Partition of Turkey*. Norman, Okla.: University of Oklahoma Press, 1931.

Hurewitz, J. C. *Diplomacy in the Near and Middle East,* 2 vols. Princeton, N.J.: D. Van Nostrand, 1956.

Institute of International Relations. Faculty of Political Science. University of Ankara. *Turkey and The United Nations.* New York: Manhattan Publishing Co., 1961.

İpekci, Abdi ve Ömer Sami Coşar. *İhtilalin İçyüzü* [The Inside Story of the 1960 Revolution]. Istanbul: Uygun Yayınevi, 1965.

Kandemir, Feridun. *Siyasi Dargınlıklar* [Political Frictions]. Istanbul: Ekicigil Matbaası, 1955.

Karaosmanoğlu, Yakup Kadri. *Zoraki Diplomat* [Reluctant Diplomat]. Istanbul: İnkilap Kitapevi, 1955.

Karpat, Kemal H. *Turkey's Politics: The Transition to a Multi-Party System.* Princeton, N.J.: Princeton University Press, 1959.

_____, ed. *Political and Social Thought in the Contemporary Middle East.* New York: Frederick A. Praeger, 1968.

Kılıç Altemur. *Turkey and the World.* Washington, D.C.: Public Affairs Press, 1959.

Kim Kimdir Ansiklopedisi [Encyclopedia of Who's Who]. Istanbul: Nebioglu, 1961–1962.

Kyriakides, Stanley. *Cyprus: Constitutionalism and Crisis Government.* Philadelphia: University of Pennsylvania Press, 1968.

Lerner, Daniel. *The Passing of Traditional Society: Modernization in the Middle East.* New York: The Free Press, 1964.

Lewis, Bernard. *The Emergence of Modern Turkey,* 2nd ed. London: Oxford University Press, 1968.

Lewis Geoffrey. *Modern Turkey,* 3rd ed. New York: Praeger Publishers, 1974.

Lord Kinross. *Ataturk: A Biography of Mustafa Kemal, Father of Modern Turkey.* New York: William Morrow and Co., 1965.

Mears, E. G. *Turkey.* New York: Macmillan, 1924.

Moyzisch, L. C. *Operation Cicero.* New York: Bantom, 1952.

(Abalıoğlu), Nadir Nadi. *Perde Aralığından* [A Peek From Behind the Curtain] Istanbul: Cumhuriyet Yayınları 1964.

Oktay, Afşin, ed. *Who's Who in Turkey.* Ankara: Kültür Matbaası, 1958.

Olaylarla Türk Dış Politikası, 1919–1965 [The Foreign Policy of Turkey through Events, 1919–1965]. Compiled by M. Gönlübol, C. Sar, A. Ş. Esmer, O. Sander, H. Ülman, A. S. Bilge, D. Sezer. Ankara: Dışişleri Bakanlığı Matbaası, 1968.

Öztürk, Kazım. *Türkiye Cumhuriyeti Hükümetleri ve Programları* [The Governments of Turkey and Their Platforms]. Istanbul: Baha Matbaası, 1968.

Özbudun, Ergun. *The Role of the Military in Recent Turkish Politics.* Cambridge, Mass.: Harvard University, Center for International Affairs, 1966.

_____. *Batı Demokrasilerinde ve Türkiye'de Parti Disiplini.* [Party Discipline in Western Democracies and in Turkey]. Ankara: Ankara Universitesi Hukuk Fakültesi Yayınları, no. 235, 1968.

Price, G. Ward. *Extra-Special Correspondent.* London: George G. Harrap, 1957.

Riggs, Fred W. *Administration in Developing Countries: The Theory of Prismatic Society.* Boston: Houghton Mifflin, 1964.

Robinson, Richard D. *The First Turkish Republic: A Case Study in National Development.* Cambridge, Mass.: Harvard University Press, 1963.

Safa, Peyami. *Refet Paşa.* Istanbul: Orhaniye Matbaası, n.d.

Selek, Sabahattin. *Anadolu İhtilali* [The Anatolian Revolution]. Istanbul: Istanbul Matbaası, 1963-1965.

Sforza, Count Carlo. *Makers of Modern Europe: Portraits and Personal Impressions and Recollections.* Indianapolis: Bobbs Merrill, 1928.

_____. *Diplomatic Europe Since the Treaty of Versailles.* New Haven, Conn.: Yale University Press, 1928.

Sharabi, Hisham B. *Government and Politics of the Middle East in the Twentieth Century.* Princeton, N.J.: D. Van Nostrand, 1956.

Sherrill, C. H. *A Year's Embassy to Mustafa Kemal.* New York: Methuen and Co., 1934.

Sherwood, Robert E. *Roosevelt and Hopkins.* New York: Harper and Brothers, 1948.

Smith, Elaine D. *Turkey: Origins of the Kemalist Movement and the Government of the Grand National Assembly.* Washington, D. C.: Public Affairs Press, 1959.

Söylemezoğlu, Galip Kemali. *Hariciye Hizmetinde 30 Sene* [Thirty Years in the Service of Foreign Ministry]. Istanbul: Maarif Basımevi, 1955.

Soysal, Mümtaz. *Dış Politika ve Parlamento* [Parliament and Foreign Policy]. Ankara: Ankara Üniversitesi Siyasal Bilgiler Fakültesi Yayınları no 183-165, 1964.

Tamkoç, Metin. *A Bibliography on the Foreign Relations of the Republic of Turkey, 1919-1967, and Brief Biographies of Turkish Statesmen.* Ankara: M.E.T.U. Faculty of Administrative Sciences, No. 11, 1968.

Toynbee, Arnold J. *The Western Question in Greece and Turkey.* London: Constable and Co., 1922.

Tunaya, Tarık Zafer. *Türkiye'de Siyasi Partiler, 1859-1952* [Political Parties in Turkey, 1859-1952]. Istanbul: Dogan Kardeş, 1952.

Türkgeldi, Ali. *Moudros ve Mudanya Mütarekelerinin Tarihi* [The History of the Armistices of Moudros and Mudania]. Ankara: Güney Matbaacılık, 1948.

Ülman, A. Haluk. *İkinci Cihan Savaşının Başından Truman Doktrinine Kadar Türk-Amerikan Diplomatik Münasebetleri, 1939-1947* [The Turkish–American Diplomatic Relations from the Beginning of the Second World War to the Truman Doctrine, 1939-1947]. Ankara: Siyasal Bilgiler Fakültesi Yayınları no. 128-110, 1961.

Váli, Ferenc A. *Bridge Across the Bosporus: The Foreign Policy of Turkey.* Baltimore: The Johns Hopkins Press, 1972.

Webster, Donald E. *The Turkey of Ataturk.* Menasha, Wisc.: George Banta, 1939.

370 / The Warrior Diplomats

Weiker, Walter F. *The Turkish Revolution, 1960–1961.* Washington, D.C.:
The Brookings Institution, 1963.
Zeine, Zeine N. *The Struggle for Arab Independence.* Beirut: Khayat's, 1960.

DISSERTATIONS

Ataöv, Türkkaya. "Turkey and the World: 1939–1959." New York, Syra-
cuse University, 1960.
Conker, M. C. "Le Bosphore et le Dardanelles. Les Conventions des Détroits
de Lausanne, 1923, et Montreux, 1936." Lausanne. Faculté de Droit de
l'Université de Lausanne, 1938.
Eralp, Orhan. "Turkey and State Succession." London. University of Lon-
don, 1939.
Hün, Haluk. "Projet de la Fédération Gréco-Turquie." Paris. Faculté de
Droit et des Sciences Economiques, 1959.
Karal, H. İbrahim. "Turkish Relations with Soviet Russia During the Na-
tional Liberation War of Turkey, 1918–1922." (Los Angeles, University of
California, 1967.
Tamkoç, Metin. "Allied Occupations of the Ottoman Empire Following the
Armistice of Mudros of October 30, 1918." Washington, D.C., George-
town University, 1960.

ARTICLES

Açıkalın, Cevat. "Turkey's International Relations." *International Affairs*
October 1947.
Altan, Çetin. "Paşa ve Durmuş Ağa" [Pasha and Durmuş Agha]. *Milliyet*
28 Agustos 1964.
Armaoğlu, Fahir H. "Turkey and the People's Republic of China." *Dış
Politika — Foreign Policy.* September 1971.
Ataöv, Türkkaya. Türkiye'nin Bagımsızlığı" [The Independence of Turkey]
Cumhuriyet. 29 Eylül 1967.
Aydemir, Şevket Süreyya. "Menderes'in Dramı" [The Drama of Menderes].
Cumhuriyet. 19 Şubat 1969.
Bayur, Hikmet. "Birinci Genel Savaştan Sonra Yapılan Barış Antlaşmaları-
mız [Our Peace Agreements Concluded after the End of the First World
War] *Belleten* 30, no. 117, part II (Ocak 1966) p. 149.
Bayülken, Ü. Haluk. "The Cyprus Question and the United Nations." *Dış
Politika — Foreign Policy: Cyprus,* 1974.
Bilge, A. Suat. "İcra Anlaşmaları" [Executive Agreements]. *Siyasal Bilgiler
Fakültesi Dergisi* 12 (1957).
_____. "Le Conflit Cypriote." *The Turkish Yearbook of International
Relations* 4 (1963).
Brown, Constantin. "The Tragicomic Exit of the Ottoman Dynasty." *Asia*
24 (June 1924).

Çelik, Edip F. "1961 Anayasasının Milletlerarası Andlaşmalarla İligili Hüküm-leri" [The Provisions of the 1961 Constitution Concerning International Agreements]. *Istanbul Hakuk Fakültesi Mecmuası* 28 (1962).

Davison, Roderic H. "Turkish Diplomacy from Mudros to Lausanne." *The Diplomats: 1919–1939.* ed. Gordon A. Craig and Felix Gilbert. Princeton, N.J.: Princeton University Press, 1953.

Erim, Nihat. "The Development of the Anglo-Turkish Alliance." *Asiatic Review* October 1946.

————. "Milletlerarası Daimi Adalet Divanı ve Türkiye: Musul Meselesi" [The Permanent Court of International Justice and Turkey: The Mosul Question]. *Ankara Üniversitesi Hukuk Fakültesi Dergisi.* 3 (1946).

————. "The Turkish Experience in the Light of Recent Developments." *The Middle East Journal.* Summer 1972.

Esmer, Ahmet Şükrü. "Cyprus: Past and Present." *The Turkish Yearbook of International Relations* 3 (1962).

Gerede, Hüsrev. "Hatıralar" [Recollections]. *Yakın Tarihimiz* 1, no. 6 (5 Nisan 1962): 163.

Gidel, Gilbert. 'L'avis consultatif de la cour permanente de justice." *L'Europe nouvelle* 28, no. 2–4 (1946): 328–43.

Harris, George S. "The Role of the Military in Turkish Politics." *The Middle East Journal.* Spring 1965.

Meray, Seha L. "Türk Anayasa Sisteminde Andlaşmaların Görüşülmesi" [Debates on International Agreements in the Turkish Constitutional System]. *Siyasal Bilgiler Fakültesi Dergisi.* 19 (1964).

Orbay, Rauf. *"Rauf Orbay'ın Hatıraları"* [Memoirs of Rauf Orbay] *Yakın Tarihimiz.* 4 vols. 1962–63.

Rustow, Dankwart A. "The Army and the Founding of the Turkish Republic." *World Politics* 11 (1949).

————. "Turkey: The Modernity of Tradition." *Political Culture and Political Development.* ed. L. W. Pye and S. Verba, Princeton, N.J.: Princeton University Press, 1969.

————. "Ataturk As Founder of a State." *Prof. Dr. Yavuz Abadan'a Armağan.* Ankara: Ankara Üniversitesi Siyasal Bilgiler Fakültesi Yayınları no. 280, 1969.

Sadak, Necmeddin. "Turkey Faces the Soviets." *Foreign Affairs.* April 1949.

Savcı, Bahri. "Modernleşmede Devlet Başkanımızın Rolu" [The Role of our Head of State in the Process of Modernization] *Prof. Dr. Yavuz Abadan'a Armağan.* Ankara: Siyasal Bilgiler Fakültesi Yayınları no. 280, 1969.

Sherwood, W. B. "The Rise of the Justice Party in Turkey." *World Politics* 20 (October 1967): 54–65.

Shutleworth, D. I. "Turkey, From the Armistice to the Peace." *Journal of the Central Asian Society* 11 (1924): 61–62.

Simpson, Dwight J. "Development As a Process — the Menderes Phase in Turkey." *The Middle East Journal,* Spring 1965.

Tamkoç, Metin. "The Question of the Recognition of the Republic of Turkey by the United States." *The Turkish Yearbook of International Relations* 1 (1960).

_____. "Turkey's Quest for Security Through Defensive Alliances. *The Turkish Yearbook of International Relations* 2 (1961).

_____. "Traditional Diplomacy of Modern Turkish Diplomats." *Dış Politika — Foreign Policy,* December 1971.

_____. "Stable Instability of the Turkish Polity." *The Middle East Journal,* Summer 1973.

_____. "The Warrior Diplomat: İsmet İnönü." *Dış Politika — Foreign Policy,* December 1973.

Tengirşenk, Yusuf Kemal. "Milli Mücadelede Ruslarla İlk Temaslarımız." [Our Early Contacts with the Russians During the National Struggle]. *Yakın Tarihimiz* 4, no. 43 (20 Aralık 1962): 97.

Tevetoğlu, Fethi. "Atatürk'ün Kapattırdığı Kızıl Teşekkül: Yeşilordu." [The Green Army: The Organization Closed by the Order of Atatürk]. *Türk Kültürü* 5, no. 49 (Kasım 1966): 62.

Toker, Metin. "Aptal Dostu Olmaktansa . . ." [Instead of Having a Stupid Friend . . .]. *Akis* 12 Haziran 1964.

Ülman, A. Haluk. "Türkiye ve NATO." [Turkey and NATO]. *Cumhuriyet.* 21–24 Mayıs 1968.

Ülman, A. Haluk and R. H. Dekmejian. "Changing Patterns in Turkish Foreign Policy, 1959–1967." *Orbis* 11 (Fall 1967).

Weiker, Walter F. "Associates of Kemal Atatürk 1932–1938." *Belleten* 34 (1970).

Westerman, William L. "The Abolishing of the Ottoman Phantom Caliphate." *Asia* 24 (May 1924).

INDEX

Abalıoğlu, Yunus Nadi. *See* Yunus
  Nadi Bey
Abd al-Illah, 240
Abdülmecid, 90, 92
Abdullah Azmi Efendi, 8
Acheson, Dean, 275
Açıkalın, Cevat, 210, 211
Adana summit conference, 208–210
Adenauer, Konrad, 234
Adıvar, Dr. Adnan
  on American war vessels in Turkish
    waters, 181
  brief biography of, 12 n. 3
  co-founder of Progressive Party, 26
  leading advocate of Westernism,
    12–13
  as Minister of Public Health, 87
  prominent figure of Nationalist
    Movement, 8
  relieved of official duties, 185
Adıvar, Halide Edib
  on Bekir Sami Bey's dismissal, 190
  brief biography of, 12 n. 3
  leading advocate of Westernism,
    12, 190
  leading female nationalist, 8
  relieved of official position, 185
Afghanistan, Friendship Treaty with,
  184
Ağralı, Fuat, 8
Ahmet Rüstem Paşa, 81
Akça, E., 262

Albania, 262
Alexander (king of Yugoslavia), 200
Alexander, Sir Harold, 209
Alexandretta. *See* Hatay
Alexandroupolis summit conference
  (1967), 267
Ali Fethi. *See* Okyar, Ali Fethi
Ali Fuat Pasha. *See* Cebesoy, Ali Fuat
Ali, Kılıç, 8
Ali Rıza Pasha, 82
Alliance, Treaty of (Turkey, Greece,
  Cyprus), 263 n. 9
Allied Powers. *See* NATO
Allied Powers of World War I, 137,
  152
Amasya
  Circular of, 77
  Protocol of, 83
American bases in Turkey, 242, 261,
  285
Amman, 238
Anatolia, 1, 69, 76, 83, 134, 137, 177,
  257
Anatolian
  Agency, 156
  peasant, 102
  revolution, 77
  Turks, 8
Anglo-French rivalry over Turkey,
  159–60
Anglo–Turkish military commission,
  210

Tamkoç, Metin.
    The warrior diplomats : guardians
of the national security and
modernization of Turkey / Metin
Tamkoç. -- Salt Lake City :
University of Utah Press, c1976.
    xix, 394 p. : ill. ; 24 cm.
    Bibliography: p. [363]-372.
    Includes index.
    ISBN 0-87480-115-X

    1. Turkey. Ordu--Political
activity. 2. Statesmen--Turkey--
Biography. 3. Turkey--Politics and
government--1918-1960. 4. Turkey--
Politics and government--1960-
    I.Title.   (Cont. on next card)